AF371380

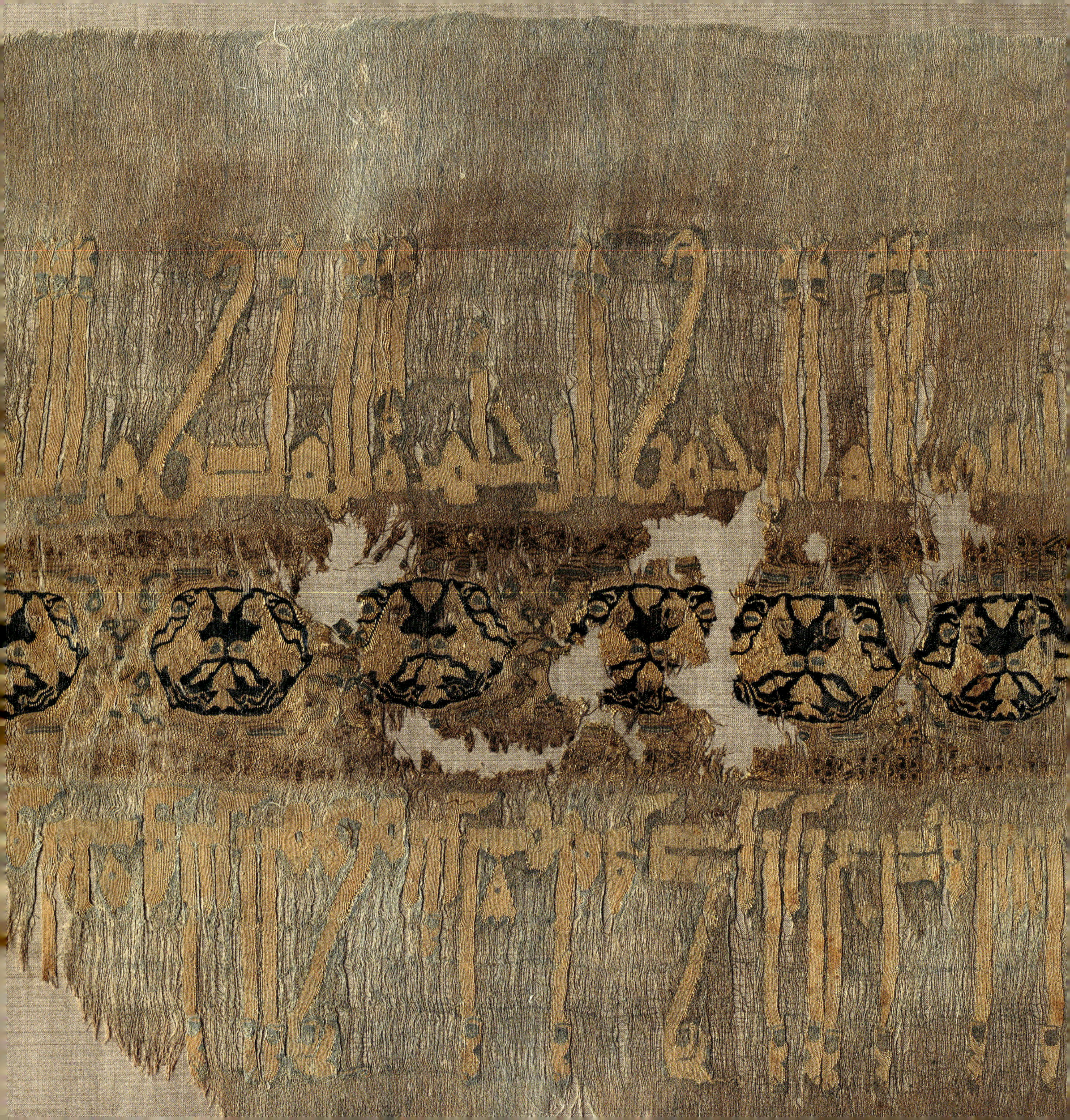

Social Fabrics:
Inscribed Textiles from Medieval Egyptian Tombs

EDITED BY MARY MCWILLIAMS AND JOCHEN SOKOLY

With contributions by Robin Hanson, Mary McWilliams, Meredith Montague, Nasser Rabbat, Jochen Sokoly, David Stern, Katherine M. Taronas, Julie H. Wertz, Elizabeth Dospěl Williams, and Meredyth Lynn Winter

Harvard Art Museums
Cambridge, Mass.

Distributed by Yale University Press
New Haven and London

CONTENTS

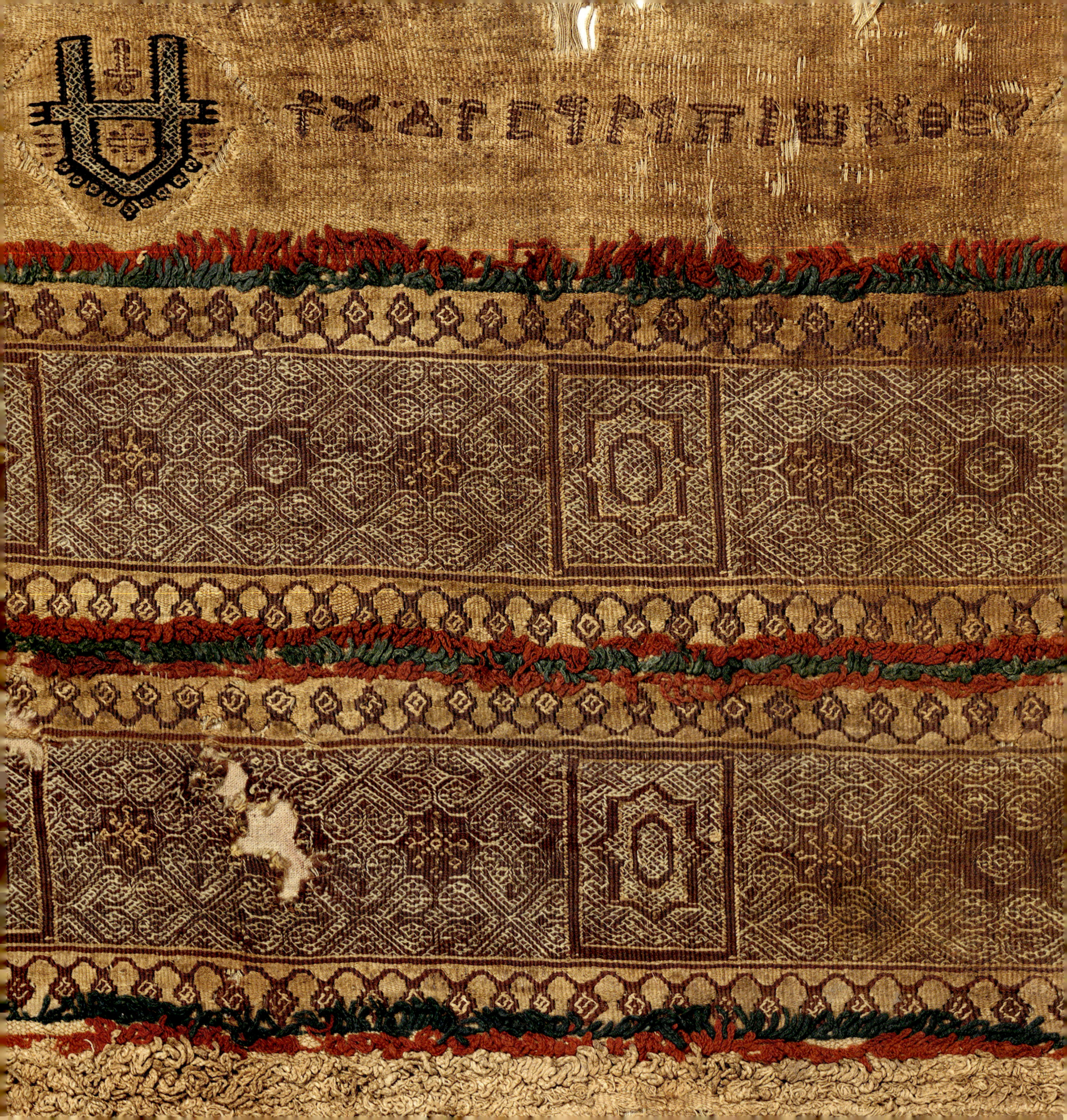

FOREWORD

Social connections sustain us as human beings, creating bonds rooted in mutual support, shared history, and common purpose. Sadly, our capacity for building and nurturing these connections has been sorely taxed over the last year. As I write this in December 2020, the COVID-19 pandemic is still burning worldwide; its effects on our ability to come together in laughter and joy, grief and pain, have been hard felt. And yet the human desire to seek out one another has refused to let up: socially distanced birthdays with drive-by parades, outdoor dining while enduring winterlike temperatures, and even traditional Thanksgiving meals shared via Zoom are just some of the ways we have sought comfort and closeness despite the public health crisis we face.

It is easy to think that we are somehow outsmarting our circumstances, leaning on technology and modern conveniences to deal with disconnection and dislocation more creatively than past generations ever could. However, the objects highlighted in *Social Fabrics* reveal humanity's long history of searching for like-minded communities and fostering complex systems of procurement, manufacture, communication, and demarcation to preserve and deepen such relationships. Our problems may be specific to our time, but our impulses are thoroughly unoriginal.

True that Zoom is a long way from the medieval Egyptian textile industry; but both examples demonstrate how individuals have exploited contemporary means to further social ends. The story that unfolds over these pages shows how the interplay of politics, economics, and geography led to the production of objects seemingly invested with great power and prestige — in turn embraced by a populace eager to announce and display their affiliations and loyalties. Of course, this also reminds us of inequities past and present: the riches flowing from Egypt's highly successful textile industry were anything but equally experienced, much as our numerous disparities — economic, racial, and regional, among others — have produced very different experiences of the current pandemic.

The closer we look, the more we understand how connection is just the other side of division. Indeed, some of the adaptations and developments in tiraz textiles that you will read about here came about expressly because one group rejected or was excluded (whether by design or by implication) from the symbols and meanings conveyed by these fabrics. As a result, those communities introduced new techniques, new words, new manners of display to draw from established tradition while moving in a direction better suited to different beliefs and practices. From one form of division sprang a new form of connection.

Social Fabrics, as both an exhibition and a catalogue, has likewise given us the rewarding opportunity to forge new connections. The project is enormously dependent on the loans we have secured from seven generous institutions. We are grateful for the cooperation of our colleagues at these museums and research institutes, whose names are recognized on the following pages. In addition, the project would not have been possible without support from the Andrew W. Mellon Publication Funds, including the Henry P. McIlhenny Fund; the Islamic and Later Indian Art Scholarship Support Fund; the Eric Schroeder Fund; and the M. Victor Leventritt Lecture Series Endowment Fund.

I am deeply grateful to Mary McWilliams and Jochen Sokoly for assembling this foundational yet accessible introduction to the history, purpose, meaning, and materiality of tiraz and the interwoven communities of the medieval Islamic world. What at first glance may seem to be small fragments far removed from the issues of our day are in fact revealed to be precursors and close companions to the ways we still order society and organize our social relations.

Martha Tedeschi
Elizabeth and John Moors Cabot Director
Harvard Art Museums

ACKNOWLEDGMENTS

The myriad interactions between individuals and institutions that bring forth exhibitions and publications have never seemed more significant. As we draft this expression of gratitude to the many colleagues and collaborators who have contributed to our project, nations around the globe are straining to contain a pandemic, and the countless connections and transactions that weave together the very fabric of society are on hold or attenuated as a result of quarantine or social distancing.

With ten catalogue contributors and seven lenders to the exhibition, our debt of gratitude is both deep and wide. To provide historical context and explicate works of art from different eras and confessional communities, we were most fortunate to have the collaboration of Nasser Rabbat of the Massachusetts Institute of Technology, Elizabeth Dospěl Williams of the Dumbarton Oaks Research Library and Collection, and David Stern of Harvard University. For technical and chemical analyses, we are indebted to Julie Wertz of the Harvard Art Museums, Robin Hanson of the Cleveland Museum of Art, and Meredith Montague of the Museum of Fine Arts, Boston. For innumerable contributions to the entire project, we are grateful beyond words to two highly talented doctoral candidates at Harvard, Katherine Taronas and Meredyth Lynn Winter.

At Harvard, we wish to thank András Riedlmayer of the Fine Arts Library, Scott Walker of the Harvard Map Collection, and Peter Der Manuelian of the Harvard Museum of the Ancient Near East (previously the Semitic Museum). Special thanks to Professors Gülru Necipoğlu and David Roxburgh for enabling Jochen Sokoly to spend time at the university as an Aga Khan Fellow in 2020. We also thank Sean Roberts, former program director of art history at Virginia Commonwealth University, School of the Arts in Qatar, and the Faculty Research Grants program at VCU for supporting Sokoly's research and travel to Harvard on several occasions.

This project could not have succeeded without the continuing support of Martha Tedeschi, the Elizabeth and John Moors Cabot Director of the Harvard Art Museums, and Susanne Ebbinghaus, the George M.A. Hanfmann Curator of Ancient Art and Head of the Division of Asian and Mediterranean Art. Our work has depended heavily on the expertise, professionalism, and goodwill of colleagues at the museums, including Jennifer Aubin, Jane Braun, Anne Driesse, Francine Flynn, Katya Kallsen, Mary Kocol, Daron Manoogian, Molly Ryan, and Megan Schwenke. For the catalogue, special recognition is due to Micah Buis, Sarah Kuschner, Cheryl Pappas, Zak Jensen, Becky Hunt, and Adam Sherkanowski; and for installation design, Elie Glyn. Throughout the project, Jennifer Atkinson, Mary Lister, and their colleagues in Collections Management coordinated and executed innumerable tasks and transits. Amy Brauer, Monique Goodin, Shiva Mihan, and Rachel Parikh provided rock-solid curatorial and administrative support within the Division of Asian and Mediterranean Art. And Matthew Rogan, curatorial assistant for special exhibitions and publications, once again proved himself indispensable.

To our colleagues beyond Cambridge, we extend sincere thanks for providing advice, information, and images, and for devoting valuable time granting access to collections and archives. At the Museum of Fine Arts, Boston, we were assisted by the resourceful librarians at the William Morris Hunt Memorial Library and by Richard Newman in the analytical lab; our understanding and appreciation of these textiles were immeasurably advanced by multiple sessions in the textile conservation lab with Pamela Parmal and Meredith Montague. At the Cleveland Museum of Art, we wish to thank Sonya Rhie Mace and Peter Buettner. We are grateful to Amy Dunn, James Hanks, Katherine Kasdorf, and Marisa Szpytman of the Detroit Institute of Arts; Gudrun Bühl and Joni Joseph, formerly of Dumbarton Oaks, and Alyson Williams of the Dumbarton Oaks Research Library; Navina Haidar, Eva Labson, Eva DeAngelis-Glasser, Sarah Szeliga, and Angela Salisbury of the Metropolitan Museum of Art, New York; and Sumru Krody, Ana Kiss, and their colleagues at the Textile Museum in Washington, D.C. From the University of Pennsylvania's Kislak Center for Special Collections, Rare Books, and Manuscripts, we thank Arthur Kiron, Sarah Reidell, and Abigail Lang. The welcome support of Ann Goodman and Vahid Kooros made possible the radiocarbon testing and dye analysis. Finally, we are deeply grateful to

Louise Mackie, Milton Sonday, and the late Nanette Kelekian for generously sharing lifetimes of knowledge and expertise.

Colleagues abroad who have provided valuable help in the course of our research include Francesca Leoni of the Ashmolean Museum, Oxford University; Mina Moraitou of the Benaki Museum, Athens; and Roland-Pierre Gayraud of France's National Center for Scientific Research (CNRS).

To a degree we could not have imagined at the outset of this project, we look forward to welcoming the public to our exhibition.

Mary McWilliams and Jochen Sokoly
December 2020

DATES, TRANSCRIPTIONS, AND TRANSLITERATION

Year 1 in the Islamic (Hijri) calendar corresponds to 622 of the Common Era (CE). Throughout the catalogue, years are CE unless otherwise indicated. When Hijri (H) and CE dates are both provided, the H dates are placed first, followed by a forward slash and the CE dates: H/CE.

In the catalogue entries, Arabic, Coptic, and Greek texts are transcribed in their proper scripts. Brackets and ellipses indicate missing text, and parentheses indicate speculative readings when letters or words are missing. Ellipses within parentheses indicate indecipherable text. Dates are rendered in the verbal sequence of the original text. In the translations, periods (full stops) are used for clarity and to indicate a complete text. The Islamic names of God (e.g., the Merciful, the Compassionate) are capitalized. In this volume, Jochen Sokoly is responsible for Arabic transcriptions and translations.

Foreign words and proper nouns that have entered the English language or have a generally recognized English form are anglicized. Place names follow English usage and reflect current national borders. False English plurals for Arabic words are used. Place names and names of historical personages with no English equivalent are transliterated. Diacritical marks are omitted, with the exception of the letters 'ayn (') and hamza ('). Following common usage, the term "tiraz" is used both as an adjective (tiraz inscription or tiraz workshop) and as a noun; as the latter, the singular and plural are identical.

TABULAR DATA IN CATALOGUE ENTRIES

Measurements are given in centimeters as warp × weft, or when warp direction cannot be determined, as length × width, according to the orientation of the pattern. Overall dimensions are provided for objects that consist of two or more fragments.

The technical description of weave structures in the catalogue entries and glossary follows a modified version of that proposed by Irene Emery (*The Primary Structures of Fabrics*, 1966) and Louisa Bellinger (*Catalogue of Dated Tiraz Fabrics*, 1952). To avoid speculating on dye or bleach processes, we use the terms "ecru" or "off-white" to designate darker or lighter shades of linen and cotton. For brevity, "polychrome" is used in place of a list of individual colors. When an individual color has been analyzed, reference is made to the table of results on p. 58. In this volume, Mary McWilliams is responsible for tabular data.

Provenance is included only where information beyond that contained in the object's credit line is available.

CONTRIBUTORS

ROBIN HANSON
Associate Conservator of Textiles
Cleveland Museum of Art

MARY MCWILLIAMS
Norma Jean Calderwood Curator of Islamic and Later
Indian Art
Harvard Art Museums

MEREDITH MONTAGUE
Head of Textile Conservation
Museum of Fine Arts, Boston

NASSER RABBAT
Aga Khan Professor and Director of the Aga Khan Program
for Islamic Architecture
Massachusetts Institute of Technology

JOCHEN SOKOLY
Associate Professor of Art History of the Islamic World
Virginia Commonwealth University, School of the Arts in
Qatar

DAVID STERN
Harry Starr Professor of Classical and Modern Jewish and
Hebrew Literature
Harvard University

KATHERINE M. TARONAS
Ph.D. Candidate, History of Art and Architecture
Harvard University

JULIE H. WERTZ
Beal Family Postgraduate Fellow in Conservation Science
Straus Center for Conservation and Technical Studies,
Harvard Art Museums

ELIZABETH DOSPĔL WILLIAMS
Associate Curator, Byzantine Collection
Dumbarton Oaks Research Library and Collection

MEREDYTH LYNN WINTER
Visiting Fellow
Center for Middle Eastern Studies, Harvard University

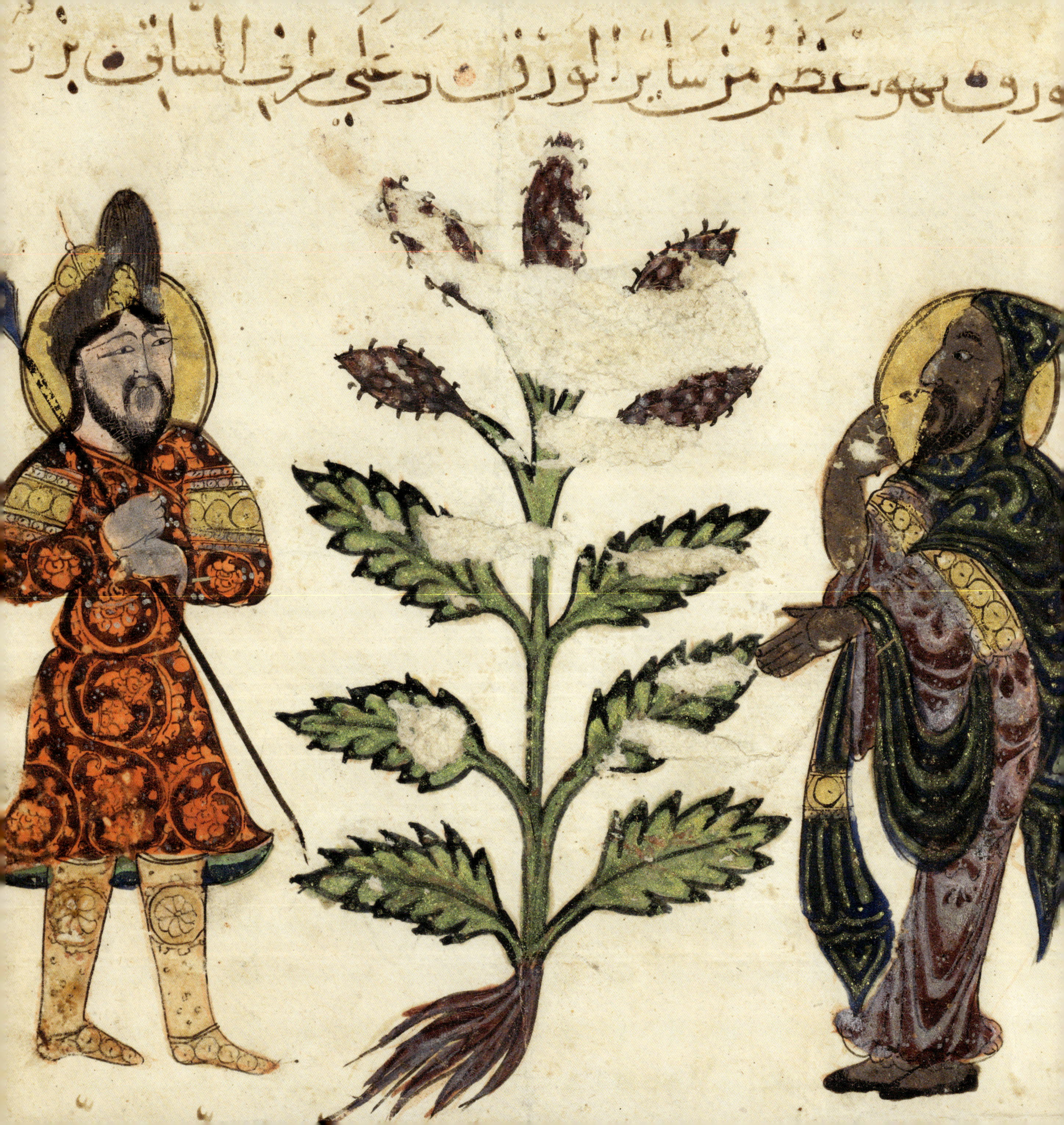

ورق وهو أعظم من سائر الورق دعي على رأس الساق بزر

MARY MCWILLIAMS AND JOCHEN SOKOLY

Threads with Meaning: A Short Introduction

From the swaddling clothes of infancy to the burial shrouds at the end of life, woven fabrics touch nearly every aspect of human existence. Inevitably, then, we attach meaning to the creation and use of textiles — one of the most ancient, pervasive, and intimate art forms. Across cultures, the various materials and processes of fabricating and ornamenting textiles have inspired countless metaphors for human experience and thought. Woven fabrics have functioned for millennia as necessities and luxuries, most obviously as garments, shelter, and furnishings, but also as a medium of exchange and a form of wealth, the production of which sustains livelihoods and offers an early pattern of industrial organization. Thoroughly integrated into human affairs, textiles serve as important socioeconomic indicators. Their manufacture, appearance, and consumption provide vital clues to understanding societies and the place of the individual therein.

On the campuses of the universities where we work, on the east coasts of North America and the Arabian Peninsula, respectively, it could be said that dress is dictated first and foremost by social mores and trends in fashion. Yet we also observe students and colleagues consciously acting on economic, environmental, and ethical concerns in the styling, manufacture, and sourcing of their garments. Of course, the most easily decoded expressions of personal interest or political belief are verbal messages inscribed on clothing or banners. The message-textiles of our own experience, however, offer only a superficial parallel to those that form the core of the exhibition *Social Fabrics: Inscribed Textiles from Medieval Egyptian Tombs*. The latitude given to dress as a form of personal expression in the twenty-first century would have been inconceivable to a medieval Egyptian. Conversely, the extraordinary artistry invested in medieval textiles and their value as an economic asset for both individuals and the state are virtually unimaginable to those of us living in consumer-driven economies.

Social Fabrics examines a transformative period in Egyptian history through products of its dynamic and sophisticated textile industry. The title is intended as more than a play on words: the fabrics in question served as a visual form of social communication in a society that was ethnically, linguistically, and religiously diverse. Produced in the centuries following the Arab Muslim conquest of Egypt in 641, these fabrics reveal the varied and interlacing strands of Egyptian society through inscriptions, ornament, and weave structures. In this volume's opening essay, Nasser Rabbat introduces and illuminates the medieval era, when Egypt was ruled first by the Rashidun caliphs (641–61) in the Arabian Peninsula, and then by a sequence of hereditary caliphates: the Umayyads (661–750) in Syria, the Abbasids (750–969) in Iraq, and finally the Fatimids (969–1171), who relocated their imperial capital to Egypt (see the maps on pp. 8–9). Rabbat charts the development of the cities of al-Fustat and Cairo and delineates the creation as well as the destruction of architectural complexes, tying the changing urban landscape to the profound cultural and political transformations that also shaped textiles.

Ancient textiles survived in remarkable numbers due to Egypt's dry climate and low water table. In the late nineteenth and early twentieth centuries, thousands of textiles in an array of patterns and colors were excavated from Egyptian burial grounds and rubbish heaps dating to the late antique and medieval eras (c. 3rd–13th century). In some instances, the excavations were carried out according to the scholarly standards of the day, but much of the digging was the work of the antiquities trade, whose primary goal was to bring vendible objects to an international market. As is obvious at a glance, these fabrics have not survived in pristine condition; they bear discolorations and losses from long centuries of intimate contact with human bodies in graves. Equally destructive was their contact with excavators, who often removed the damaged portions of garments and shrouds, preserving only the decorated parts.

The essay by Mary McWilliams explores the enthusiasm among early collectors for these fragile, fragmentary, and in some ways esoteric artifacts. Focusing on the major collectors behind five of the museums lending textiles to the exhibition, she examines the historical circumstances and individual motivations that helped make North America one of the major repositories for tiraz textiles in the first half of the twentieth century.

Inscribed with Arabic texts, the core fabrics in this exhibition fall into the category of tiraz textiles, narrowly or broadly defined. Most were created from around 800 to 1150, when government control over the content of inscriptions was most rigorously enforced. The majority were produced in Egyptian workshops, while others arrived from Iran, Iraq, and Yemen. In Islamic lands during the medieval era, textiles enhanced with Arabic inscriptions — woven, embroidered, or painted — were highly prized. They expressed the immense prestige accorded to the Arabic language within Islamic cultures and

connected all who produced, owned, or viewed them in a web of communication based on the written word.

A narrow definition of tiraz textiles reserves the term for inscribed textiles that reflect a privileged network headed by the caliph, the temporal and spiritual ruler of the Islamic empire. Such fabrics were distributed as part of annual salary disbursements to officials and administrators or as gifts to favored courtiers or foreign dignitaries. They are identifiable by protocollary inscriptions that employ strictly regulated formulae: usually opening with an invocation to God, the texts incorporate the name and titles of the ruling caliph, often followed by a chain of delegation mentioning the administrator(s) who requisitioned and carried out the textile order, and occasionally the place and date of manufacture. One of the most revealing historical mentions of tiraz textiles is offered by Ibn Khaldun (d. 1406) in his *Muqaddima* (Introduction):

> One of the splendors of power and sovereignty . . . was to inscribe their names . . . in the borders of garments designed for their wear, made of silk or brocade. . . . Thus, the royal robes are bordered with a tiraz. It is an emblem of dignity reserved for the sovereign, for those whom he wishes to honor by authorizing them to make use of it, and for those whom he invests with one of the responsible posts of government.[1]

So defined, tiraz textiles clearly projected their owners' position at the top of the power structure. For this exhibition, however, we have adopted a more liberal definition of tiraz to include textiles that other scholars have sometimes designated as "tiraz-style." The fabrics in the latter category emulate the appearance of the officially inscribed textiles and are in fact conceptually unthinkable without them. The impetus for merging the two categories grew out of Jochen Sokoly's examination of almost two thousand inscribed textiles. His study yielded numerous examples of textiles closely related in terms of the style and quality of their epigraphy, ornament, and weave structure, but differing in the naming of members of the ruling elite and the occasional use of gold thread. Some textiles that lack the chain of delegation nevertheless state that they were produced in tiraz workshops (see cats. 34–35).

A more inclusive definition of tiraz offers multiple advantages for this project. With less reliance on the content of the

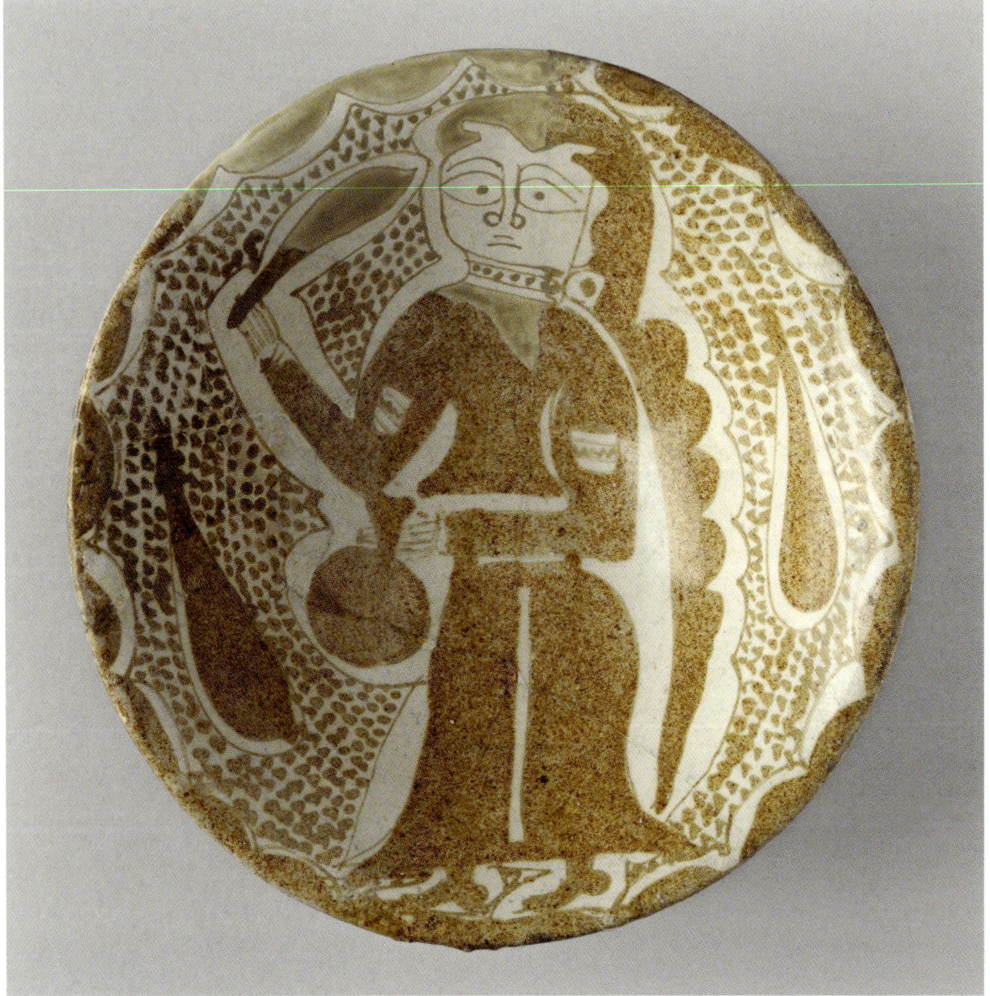

Fig. 1 Bowl with standing figure holding a bottle, Iraq, Basra, 10th century. Earthenware, luster-painted over opaque white glaze, 4.1 × 13.7 cm. Harvard Art Museums/Arthur M. Sackler Museum, The Norma Jean Calderwood Collection of Islamic Art, 2002.50.70.

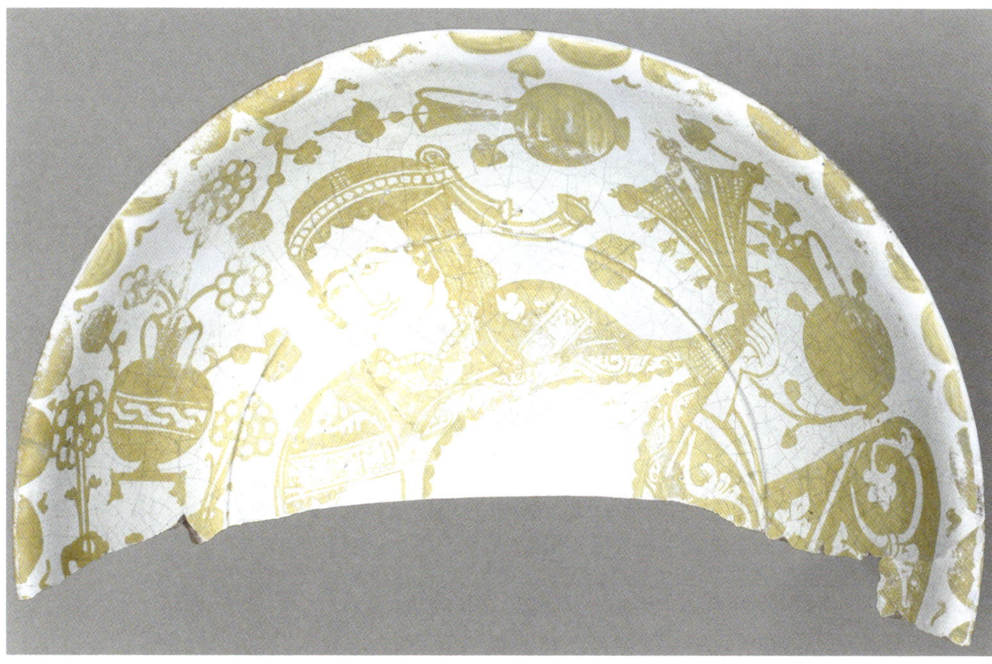

Fig. 2 Fragment of a bowl with a lute player, Egypt, late 10th–early 11th century. Earthenware, luster-painted over opaque white glaze, diameter: 38 cm. Benaki Museum, Athens, ΓΕ 11121.

Fig. 3 Drawing of two warriors, Egypt, 11th century. Ink on paper, 14 × 14 cm. Museum of Islamic Art, Cairo, 13703.

text, we can identify tiraz in a range of pictorial representations of figures wearing garments ornamented with what are undoubtedly inscription bands, although the writing is often rendered schematically. Tenth-century ceramics from the Abbasid era preserve many such representations, as seen in two Iraqi bowls in the Harvard Art Museums: one with a seated male figure in patterned trousers (cat. 7), the other portraying a standing female dressed in a long garment with tiraz bands decorating both upper arm sleeves (Fig. 1). More detailed renditions may be found in ceramics made in Fatimid Egypt, such as a fragmentary bowl in the Benaki Museum in Athens with a curly-haired lutenist wearing tiraz bands on which Arabic letters are discernible (Fig. 2). Similarly, in a rare Fatimid ink drawing in the Museum of Islamic Art in Cairo, two warriors sport tiraz bands (Fig. 3). Here the artist celebrates both Arabic script and the textile medium in the boldly lettered armbands and accompanying floriated inscription, the elaborate patterns of the garments, and the interlace pattern enclosing the entire work. The continued resonance of tiraz textiles in the Abbasid realm is manifested in the illustrations accompanying a famous manuscript of the *Maqamat* (Assemblies) by al-Hariri, made in Baghdad in 1237 and now in the Bibliothèque nationale in Paris (Fig. 4). In these lively scenes, the artist has positioned figures and furnishings to maximally display the golden inscription bands.

Using the tiraz rubric in a more inclusive manner allows room for the appearance and concept of tiraz to encompass the purely epigraphic Abbasid embroideries and the multicolored Fatimid tapestries enhanced with figural and vegetal patterns (see, for example, cats. 1, 18). In his essay in this volume, Sokoly analyzes the political and religious content of Abbasid and Fatimid era tiraz inscriptions, revealing the ambitions of individuals, groups, and dynasties that ruled Egypt. Careful and subtle reading of texts uncovers tensions between the disintegrating Abbasid central government and the governors of Egypt and offers for the Fatimid period a poignant interpretation of the burial context in which the vast majority of tiraz textiles were preserved. Sokoly provides a more detailed picture of the dynamic relationships between Egypt's Arab Muslim ruling elite and Christian communities and addresses the phenomenon of language shift in medieval Egypt.

The essay by Elizabeth Dospěl Williams further expands the definition of tiraz — albeit with qualifications — to incorporate the practice of inscribing textiles in Coptic and Hebrew within Christian and Jewish communities. Williams analyzes the changing degrees of integration and regulation of the Christian population of Egypt, the presence of Arabic-language tiraz in Coptic paintings and burials, and the practice of gifting Coptic-inscribed textiles. The essays by Sokoly and Williams demonstrate that although the inscribed textiles are rich in content, a broader textual, visual, and

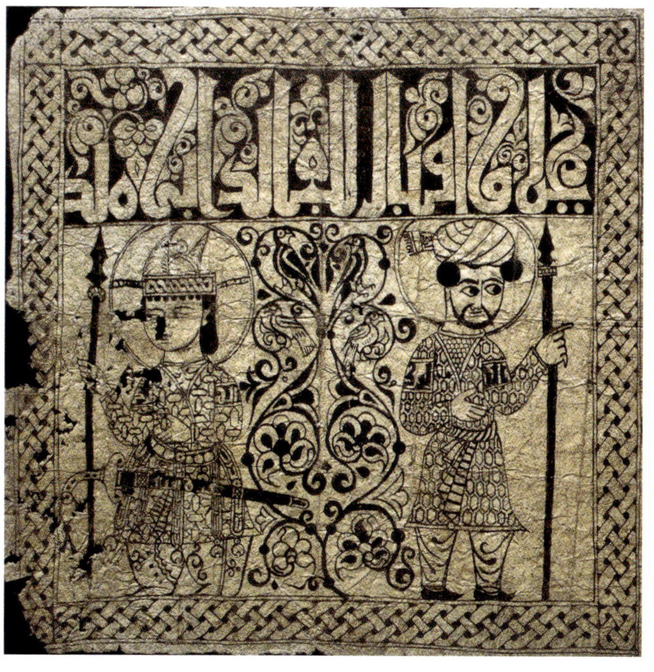

archaeological record is needed to grasp the fraught position of non-Muslim (dhimmi) communities in medieval Egypt.

To explore the evolution of textile practices and the reinvention of late antique ornament in the Islamic era, the exhibition includes a small number of Egyptian textiles created during the Byzantine era (c. 400–641; see the map on p. 8). For much of the medieval period, indigenous artisans formed the backbone of the Egyptian textile industry. The final essay in the catalogue contributes to the material understanding of late antique and medieval Egyptian textiles through technical analysis. Authors Julie Wertz, Meredyth Lynn Winter, Robin Hanson, and Meredith Montague address weaving and patterning techniques, the relationship between radiocarbon dating and dye analyses, and the composition and use of gold threads. Adaptable and resilient in the face of a changing world, Egyptian weavers maintained certain workshop practices even as they assimilated the technique and aesthetic of embroidery, made brilliant use of silk as a patterning element, and created some of the most virtuoso tapestries in history. Terms used throughout the volume to describe materials and processes are defined in an illustrated glossary at the back.

Fragmentary and decontextualized as they may be, the varied textiles brought together for this exhibition are rich with meaning. Their inscriptions, patterns, and manufacturing techniques tell of a wide range of human aspiration, intention, experience, and learning. Some of the texts convey membership in the upper echelons of power, while others only imitate the exercise of privilege. If the Fatimid tiraz prominently declare tenets of Isma'ili Shi'ism, the Coptic blessings on shawls seek to maintain Christian identity. All reflect a broader culture in which literacy was highly valued, if not widespread. All are vital social fabrics.

1   Cited in Serjeant 1972, 7–8.

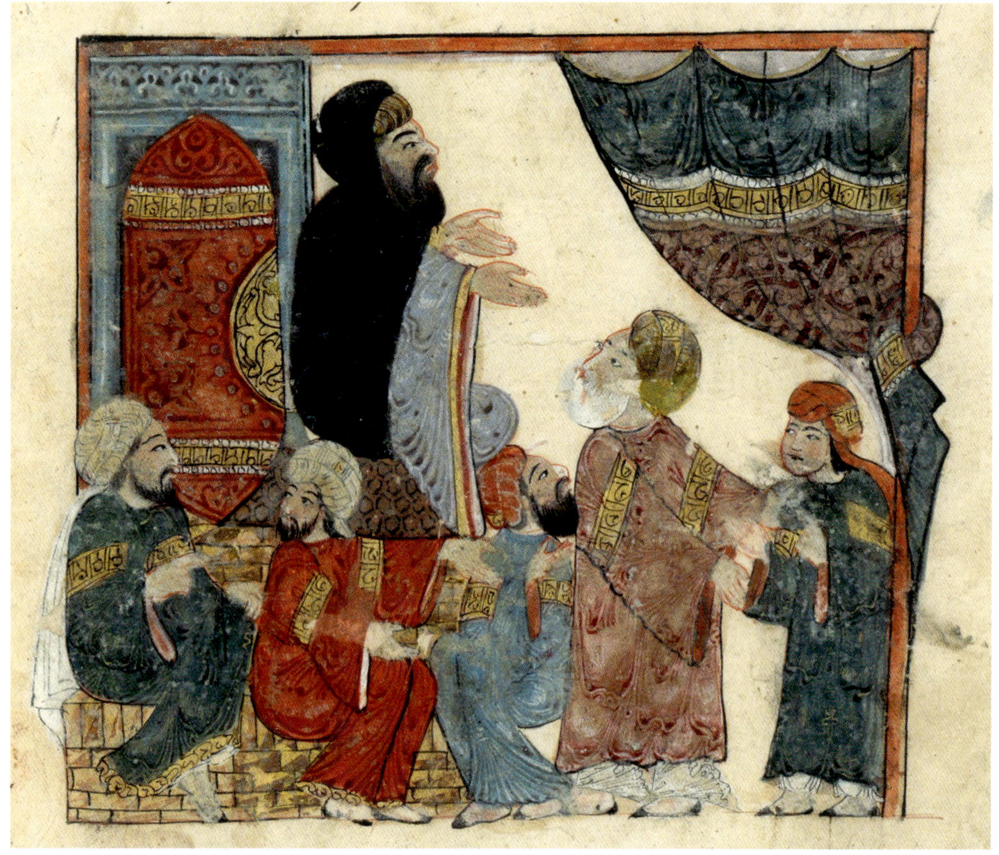

Fig. 4 *Abu Harith Witnesses Abu Zayd and His Son Fighting in Front of a Judge*, illustration from a manuscript of the *Maqamat* (Assemblies) by al-Hariri, Iraq, Baghdad, 1237. Color and gold on paper, 37 × 28 cm. Bibliothèque nationale de France, Paris, MS ARABE 5847, fol 114v.

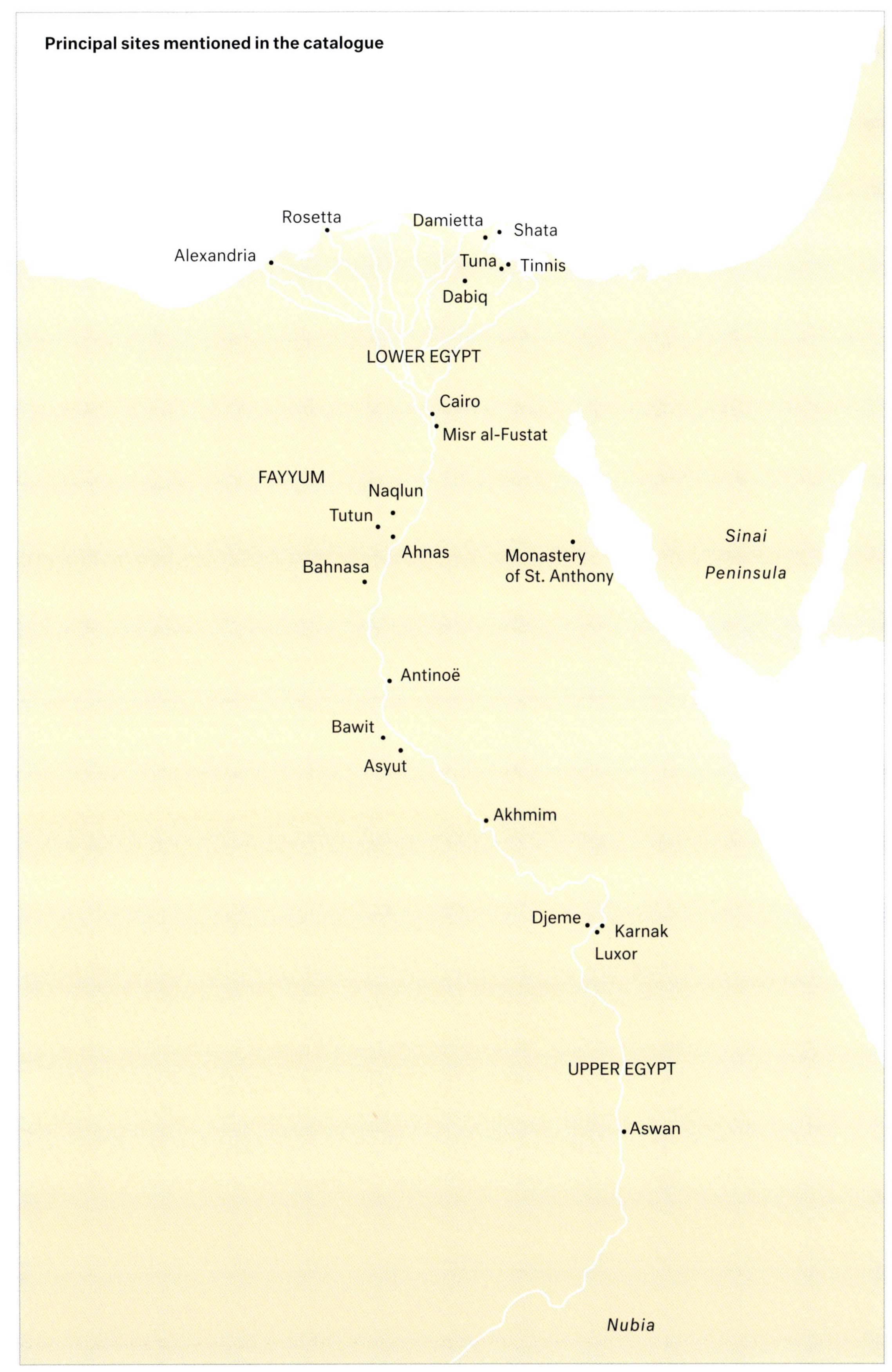

Rosetta
Damietta
Shata
Alexandria
Tuna
Tinnis
Dabiq
LOWER EGYPT
Cairo
Misr al-Fustat
FAYYUM
Naqlun
Tutun
Ahnas
Bahnasa
Monastery
of St. Anthony
Sinai
Peninsula
Antinoë
Bawit
Asyut
Akhmim
Djeme
Karnak
Luxor
UPPER EGYPT
Aswan
Nubia

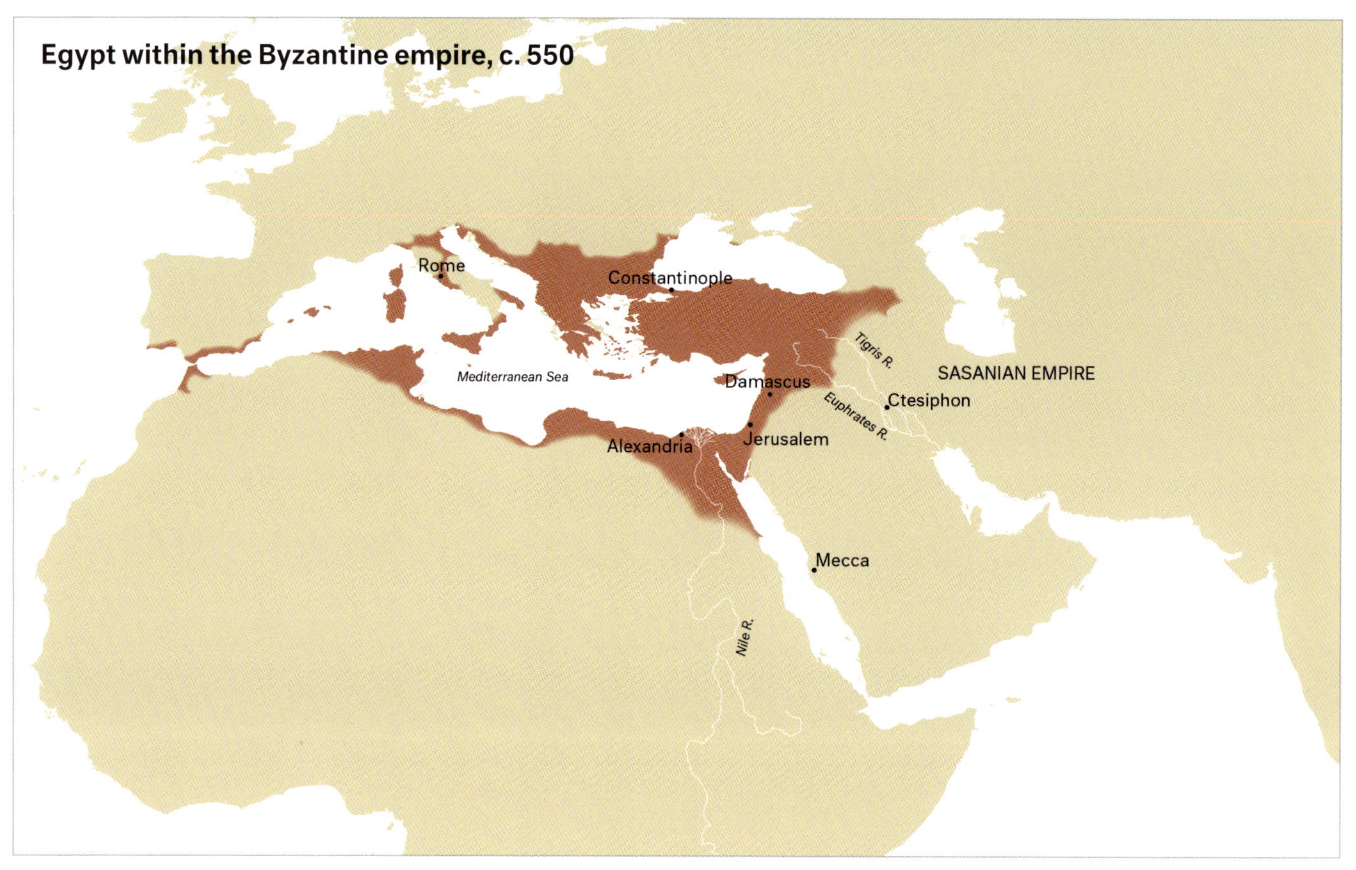

Egypt within the Byzantine empire, c. 550

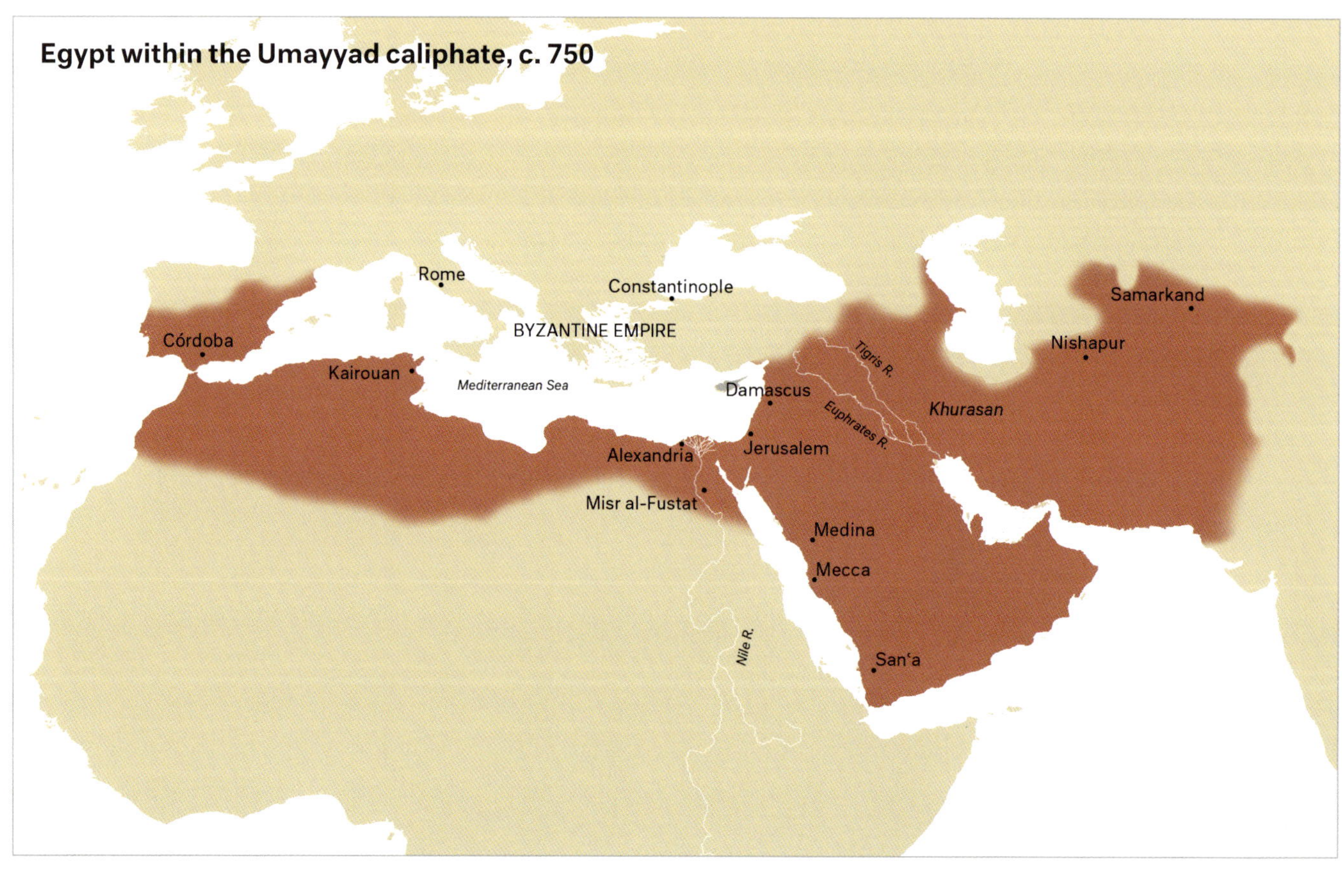

Egypt within the Umayyad caliphate, c. 750

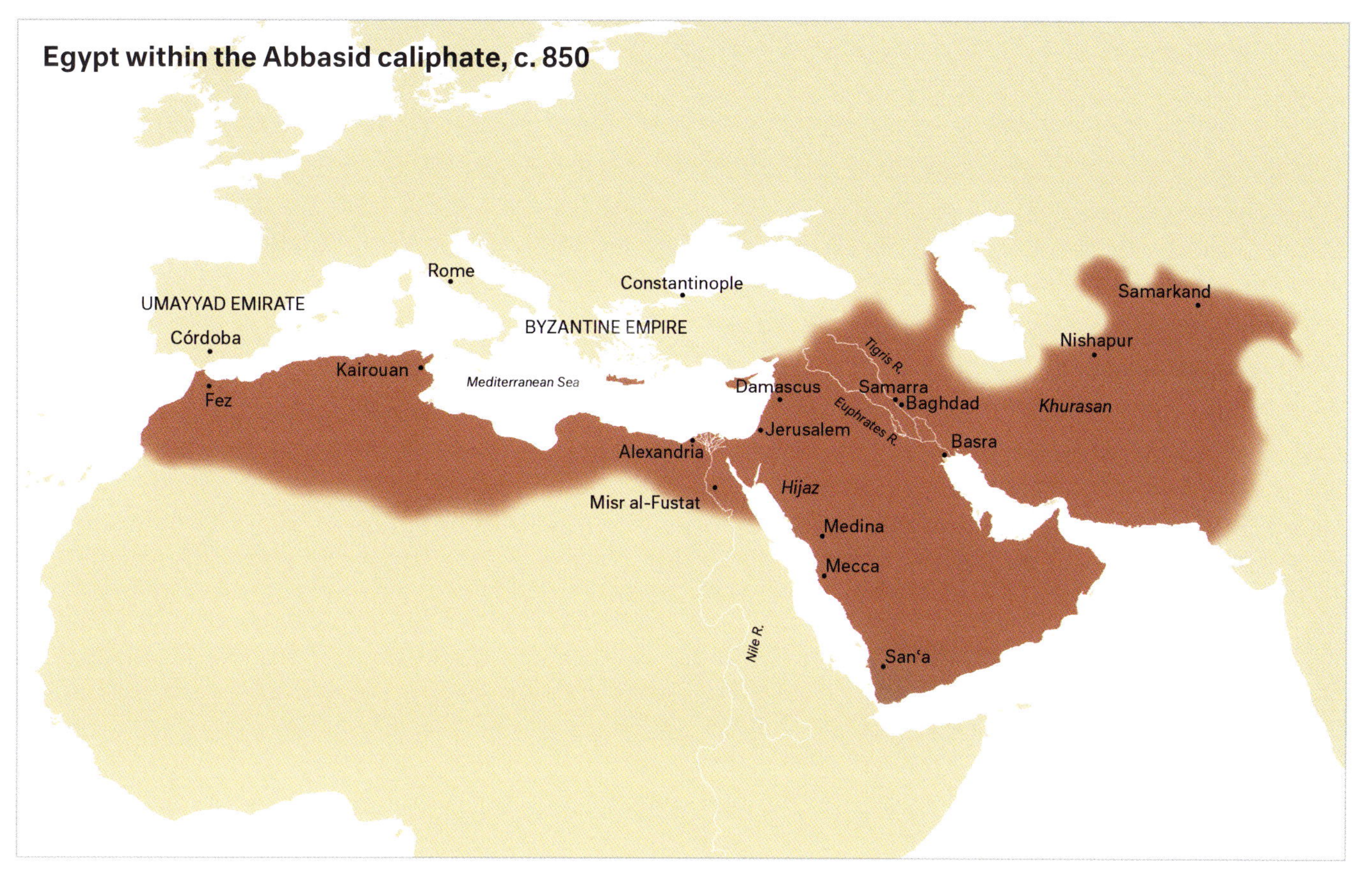

Egypt within the Abbasid caliphate, c. 850
UMAYYAD EMIRATE
Rome
Constantinople
Samarkand
Córdoba
BYZANTINE EMPIRE
Nishapur
Kairouan
Mediterranean Sea
Tigris R.
Fez
Damascus
Samarra
Baghdad
Khurasan
Euphrates R.
Alexandria
Jerusalem
Basra
Misr al-Fustat
Hijaz
Medina
Mecca
Nile R.
San'a

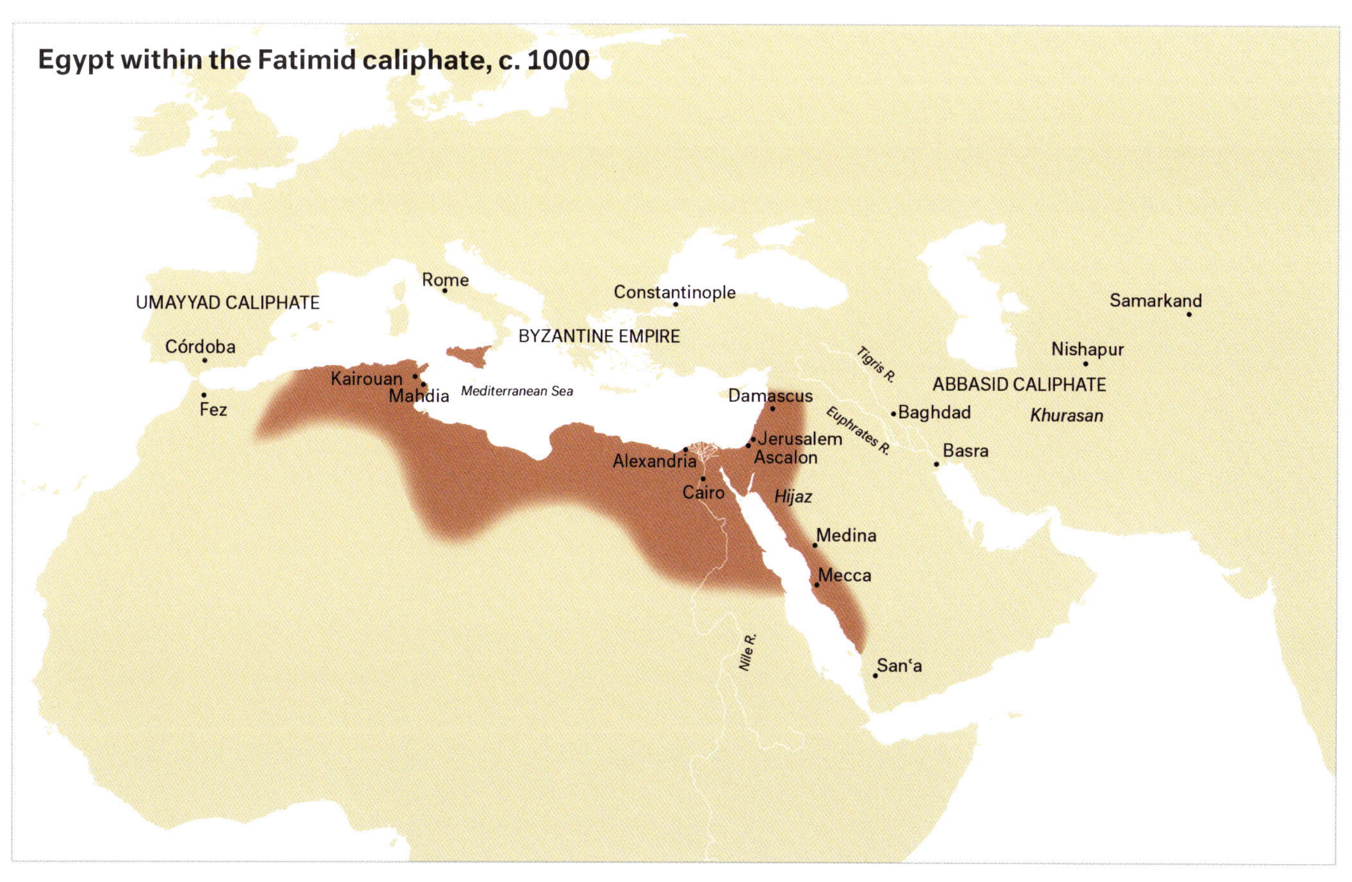

Egypt within the Fatimid caliphate, c. 1000
UMAYYAD CALIPHATE
Rome
Constantinople
Samarkand
Córdoba
BYZANTINE EMPIRE
Nishapur
Kairouan
Mediterranean Sea
Tigris R.
ABBASID CALIPHATE
Fez
Mahdia
Damascus
Baghdad
Euphrates R.
Khurasan
Alexandria
Jerusalem
Basra
Ascalon
Cairo
Hijaz
Medina
Mecca
Nile R.
San'a

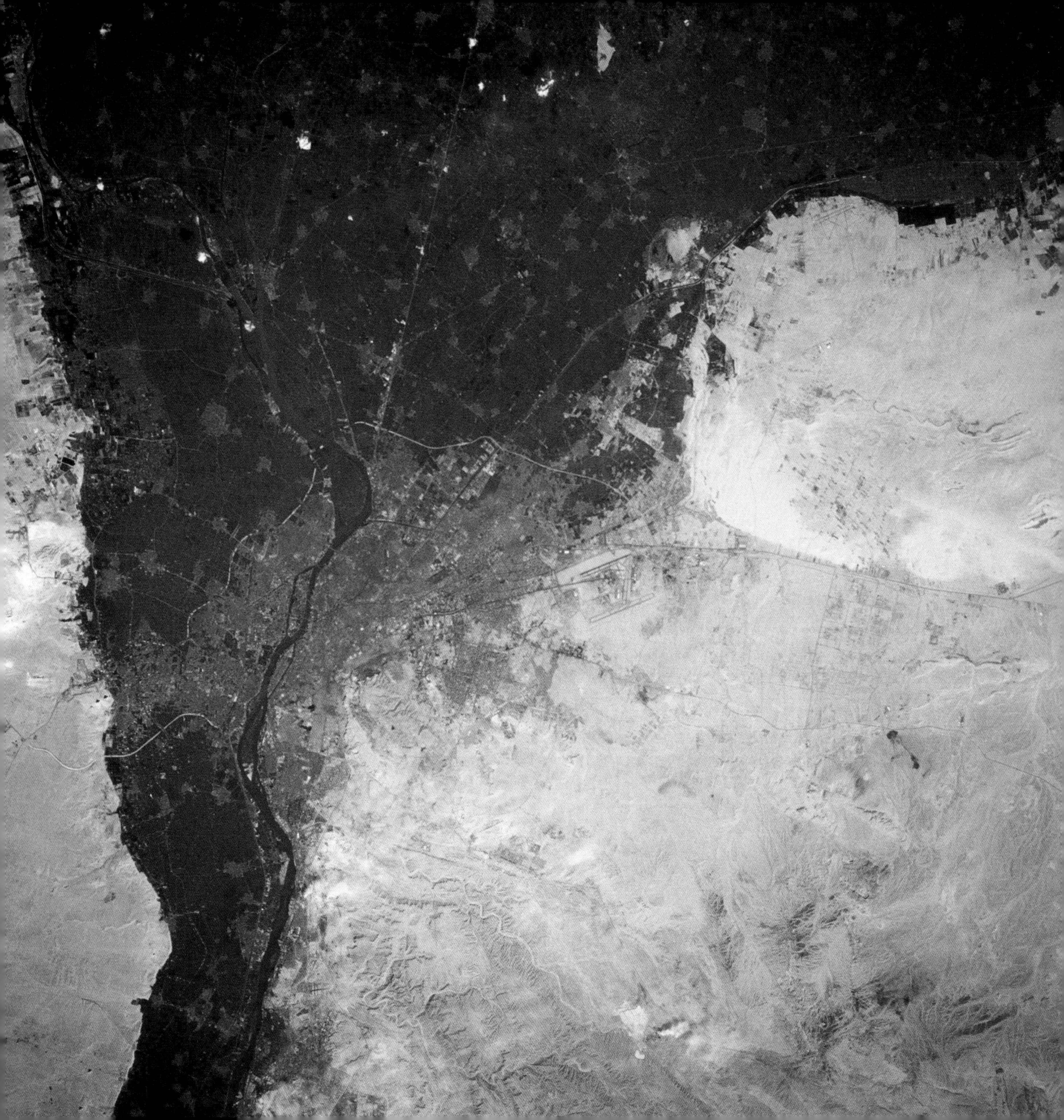

Under the Sign of Mars: A Brief Historical Overview of Egypt, 641–1171

Egypt was probably the first country to form a sense of itself as a nation, long before the advent of nationalism as we know it.[1] It is believed that as early as pharaonic times, Egyptians conceived of their homeland as one with a distinct character, a single source of wealth (the Nile), and fixed natural boundaries formed by deserts to the east and west, obstructive cataracts in the Nile to the south, and the Mediterranean Sea to the north. So solid was this notion that it outlasted all larger imperial formations that absorbed Egypt as a province, from the Persian empire in the sixth century BCE to the Arab conquest of the seventh century CE, and lived on in various religious, cultural, social, and artistic expressions if not in political fact.[2] The Egyptian sense of self was of course dampened after the Arab conquest by the universalist message of Islam and by the introduction of Arabic as the lingua franca of the southern and eastern Mediterranean, but it never died out. It stayed near the surface throughout centuries of Islamic rule, bursting into view on several occasions in response to historical and geopolitical developments. Chief among them was the emergence of the Fatimid dynasty (969–1171), which created in Egypt a counter-caliphate independent of Abbasid Baghdad, and later the founding of the Mamluk military empire (1250–1517), with its center firmly entrenched in Cairo. The Mamluk sultanate waged jihad against the Crusaders and Mongols and succeeded in establishing itself as the premier Islamic empire of its time.

In the early Islamic period, Egypt was one of the richest provinces of the caliphate, contributing massively in taxes and grains to the coffers of the Umayyads in Syria (r. 661–750) and the Abbasids in Iraq (750–1258). Watered by the mighty Nile, with a well-organized agrarian system that had been honed over millennia by a centralized government, the country was described with the aphorism *Arduha Dhahab* (Its Land Is Gold) — apocryphally attributed to its Muslim conqueror in 640, ʿAmr ibn al-ʿAs (r. 640–648).[3] Indeed, the inhabited part of the country was essentially a continuous, albeit narrow, strip of verdant agricultural land, crisscrossed by irrigation canals and dikes and running along the two banks of the Nile, from Aswan in the south to where the river bifurcates into the two branches of Rosetta (Rashid) and Damietta (Dumyat), framing an exceedingly fertile delta between. From ancient times, these two slightly different ecological zones — the linear riverine strip surrounded by desert on both sides and the lush delta bordering the Mediterranean — were distinguished as Upper Egypt (south) and Lower Egypt (north). Villages and small rural towns dotted the river banks and the delta's green tapestry, among them only a few larger cities; meanwhile the pre-Islamic, Hellenistic capital Alexandria, perched on the Mediterranean away from the Nile, turned its back to the land whence came its wealth.[4]

The Arab Muslim conquerors were enchanted by Alexandria's opulence, but they opted to settle outside the city and away from the coast for security reasons. They founded a new *misr* (usually translated as garrison town but more akin to a colony, plural *amsar*) in 642 at the strategic head of the Nile delta, almost twelve miles south of where the river splits. Located on the east bank of the Nile, the encampment was flanked by the spurs of the al-Muqattam Hills to the east and the ancient canal (*al-khalij*), which purportedly connected the Nile to the Red Sea in pharaonic times, to the west. It controlled both the riverine and land passages from Lower to Upper Egypt and the highway that led north to Syria. In pharaonic times, the site linked the old capital Memphis, a few miles to the south on the west bank of the Nile, just beyond the Giza pyramids, and the religious city of An, or Heliopolis, situated farther inland and slightly northeast. But when the Arab Muslim conquerors arrived, the site was sparsely inhabited and guarded by the Roman fortress of Babylon, which was named Qasr al-Shamʿ (Palace of Candle) by the Arabs and still stands in part today.

Cairo and the apex of the Nile delta, as seen from the space shuttle *Columbia* (STS-62), March 4–18, 1994. NASA Image and Video Library, STS062-108-058.

The new *misr* was established next to the river (which receded east by more than 150 meters in consequent centuries) around the old fortress. It reportedly grew around the tent of ʿAmr ibn al-ʿAs, the amir (general) of the army and one of the shrewdest companions of the Prophet Muhammad, who had kept his shelter standing when he left for a year to besiege Alexandria because he found a dove had built a nest in the folds of the tent. Following a pattern established by the Arab Muslim armies in Iraq and elsewhere, ʿAmr parceled the encampment into *khitat* (lots, singular *khitta*) among the various tribes that constituted his army and plotted a congregational mosque in the center, next to what would become his own *dar al-imara* (palace of government).[5] Each tribe granted a *khitta* was responsible for its construction. The settlement was called al-Fustat, a name that according to most Arabic sources refers to the amir's tent (*fustat*) but is more likely derived from the Roman military term *fossatum*, or defensive trench (Fig. 1). Within fifty years, what started as a camp around a central mosque evolved into the capital city of Egypt and the gate of the Islamic empire to (North) Africa.

For the next three centuries, al-Fustat grew by annexing its northern satellites and erasing their names. Following a revolt against the Umayyads in 750, the Abbasids chased the last Umayyad caliph, Marwan II (r. 744–750), and killed him as he attempted to flee across the Nile. They founded a new encampment, al-ʿAskar (the Troops, so named because it housed the Abbasid army), to the northeast of al-Fustat, in an area of the original camp of ʿAmr left as open space. This became the center of power in Egypt for a little more than a century, with its own congregational mosque, a *dar al-imara*,

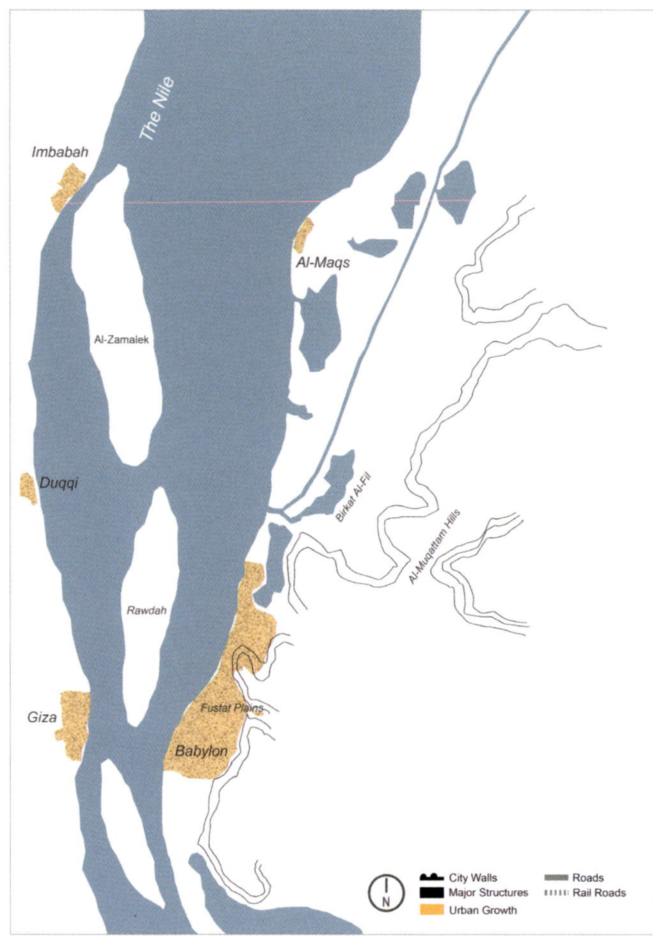

and markets. When Ahmad ibn Tulun (r. 868–884), the ambitious amir sent by the Abbasids to govern the country, eventually proclaimed himself an independent ruler, he constructed a new settlement between 876 and 879 to the northwest of al-ʿAskar, on the slopes of Mount Yashkur, west of the al-Muqattam Hills. He erected a sumptuous palatial center that later became the subject of legend and, next to it, a congregational mosque bearing his name. The mosque, which still stands today in almost its original form, is considered one of the most serene mosques in the Islamic world (Fig. 2). Ibn Tulun divided the land surrounding his complex into wards to be built by his generals for the lodging of their troops, after the model of Samarra, then the Abbasid capital in Iraq where he had served the caliph. The entire settlement became known as al-Qattaʾiʿ (the Allotments). It was eventually destroyed (except for the mosque and fragments of the aqueduct that brought water to the palatial complex) by another invading Abbasid army sent from Iraq in 905 to punish the descendants of Ibn Tulun, who had built a dynasty

Fig. 1 Map of al-Fustat on the Nile, 8th century.

Fig. 2 Mosque of Ibn Tulun, Cairo, built 879.

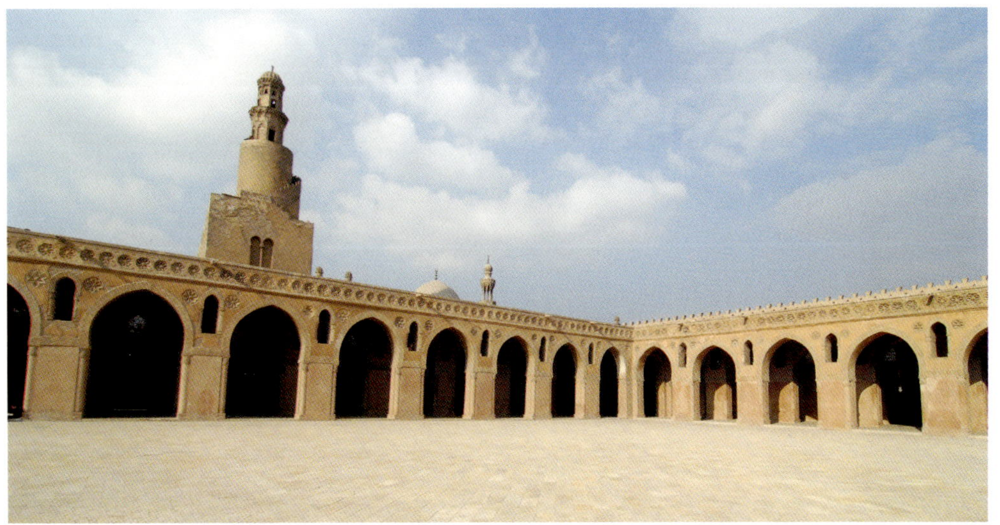

of their own in Egypt in a brazen challenge to Baghdad's authority. Along with what remained of the older al-ʿAskar, the site became part of the *kharab* (ruined area) delimiting the northern border of the continuously expanding al-Fustat, which had become a major trade emporium thanks to its location between Africa and the Mediterranean and its port on the navigable Nile. Not one of these successively built towns had been fortified.[6]

Although most histories of Egypt rightly focus on its capital city as both the site of major domestic and transnational events and the theater upon which they have been enacted, the affairs of the rest of the country in the early Islamic period deserve a few words. Contrary to popular belief, Egypt did not submit so easily to Islamic dominion. Over the first few centuries post-conquest, many Copts (Christian Egyptians) converted to Islam for a variety of reasons and mingled with the new Arab Muslim settlers, primarily in the capital and big cities (see the essays by Jochen Sokoly and Elizabeth Dospěl Williams in this volume). A majority, however, tenaciously held onto their religion despite the financial burden imposed on them in the form of a jizya (poll tax). Recent scholarship estimates that Islam did not achieve majority adherents in Egypt until after the end of the Fatimid caliphate in the twelfth century or perhaps even later, although some argue that it was actually reached in the ninth century.[7] Moreover, the mostly Christian countryside revolted dozens of times against the central rule in al-Fustat in the first three centuries of Islamic dominance.[8] The revolts were brutally put down, as the authority was loath to allow any disruption in the delivery of taxes and goods, especially in a country that heavily depended on highly structured agricultural production. The same severity was later meted out against the occasional Bedouin uprisings, which not only threatened agricultural communities but could also interrupt the trade routes along the Nile and across the Sahara Desert.[9]

The year 969 marked a turning point in the history of Egypt. The Fatimids, after three failed attempts in previous decades, managed to finally conquer the country. Named after Fatima, the youngest and favorite daughter of the Prophet Muhammad and the wife of his cousin ʿAli ibn Abi Talib (d. 661), who was the fourth Rashidi or "Rightly Guided" caliph and the first imam (leader) of the Shiʿites, the Fatimid caliphate was the first and only caliphate in Islamic history to profess Ismaʿilism (a more esoteric form of Shiʿism than the now dominant Twelver Shiʿism) as its creed. Aside from the short reign of ʿAli between 656 and 661 and the even more tragic attempt to reclaim the caliphate by his son al-Husayn (d. 680), the Fatimids were the only descendants of the Prophet to rule an Islamic empire before the claimants of the modern age.[10] Their dramatic rise in 909 in Ifriqiya (in modern Tunisia) and their conquest of all of North Africa and Sicily, followed by Egypt, the Hijaz, and Syria, formed a viable counter-caliphal project led by a divinely consecrated imam. It actually represented a potential watershed in Islamic history, which could have led to the "Ismailification" of the Islamic world and its unification under a dynasty of the family of the Prophet. But the plan failed: the Fatimid caliphate was overthrown in the late twelfth century by Salah al-Din (Saladin). Its great capital, founded by the commander of the Fatimid invading army, Jawhar al-Siqilli, and called al-Qahira (the Victorious, because it was founded under the sign of Mars, *al-Qahir* in Arabic), lived on to become one of the most famous, if not *the* most famous, Islamic capitals (Fig. 3).

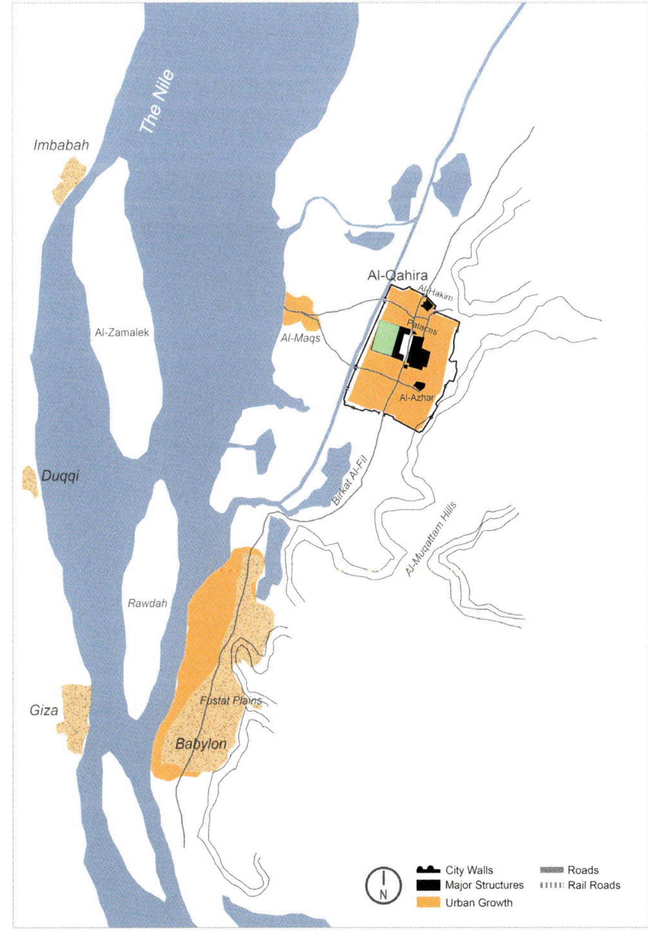

Fig. 3 Map of Cairo, al-Fustat, and the land between them, 10th century.

Cairo (the Italian distortion of al-Qahira) was a born metropolis. While the city evolved with its ruling dynasties, from the beginning it was meant to be more than a political center of Egypt, and its role as such never waned until the arrival of the Ottomans in 1517. It was first established as an encampment (*manakh*) for the estimated thirty thousand Fatimid Maghribi Berber soldiers and their families and as a fortress and stronghold (*hisnun wa ma'qalun*) three miles to the north of al-Fustat, from which it was separated by lowlands that flooded each year.[11] A parcel of land about 1 by 0.8 miles surrounded by walls made of unbaked brick (*libn*), the encampment quickly evolved into the new capital of the Fatimid caliphate after the arrival of Caliph al-Mu'izz li-Din Allah (r. 953–975) from Tunisia in 972. The new royal city was exclusively reserved for the caliph; his family; a large, mixed retinue of military and civilian functionaries; and the various divisions of his army. Jawhar had begun to build a palatial enclosure, named the Great Palace (also known as the Eastern Palace), in the center of the encampment before al-Mu'izz's arrival. This was followed a decade later by the Small Palace (Western Palace), built by al-'Aziz (r. 975–996), son of al-Mu'izz, and separated from the Great Palace by a large open square used for processions and parades, named quite literally

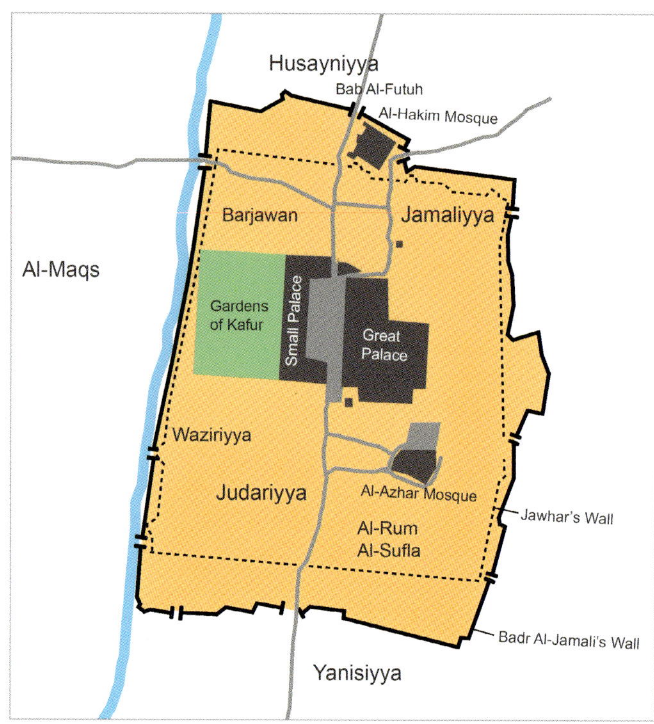

Bayn al-Qasrayn (Between the Two Palaces).[12] Following the traditional layout of the *amsar*, Jawhar divvied the rest of the city into *khitat* on which the various tribal and ethnic groups that made up the Fatimid army could build their homes, as they were forbidden to live in al-Fustat. A main commercial artery traversed the city from south to north and was open to traffic in the daytime.[13] Jawhar built a *musalla al-'id*, or open space for the two holiday prayers, just outside the walls to the north.[14] He also began the construction of a Friday mosque, al-Azhar (971–72), outside the palace in the southeastern sector, which in time became the single most prominent center of learning in the (Sunni) Islamic world.[15] Twenty years later, al-'Aziz began building another Friday mosque outside the north wall of the royal city, which was completed by his son al-Hakim and thus became known as al-Hakim Mosque (990–1010). Other mosques and mausolea followed in and around the royal enclosure, but al-Azhar remained the dynastic mosque of the Fatimids until the fall of the caliphate (Fig. 4).

In the two centuries of Fatimid rule, Cairo and al-Fustat grew side by side as separate entities: the former as the exclusive domain of the caliph and the political center of the caliphate, and the latter as the unwalled economic powerhouse of the country, where the common people lived. Elaborate ceremonials governed Cairo's configuration and layout and punctuated its days.[16] The location of every royal

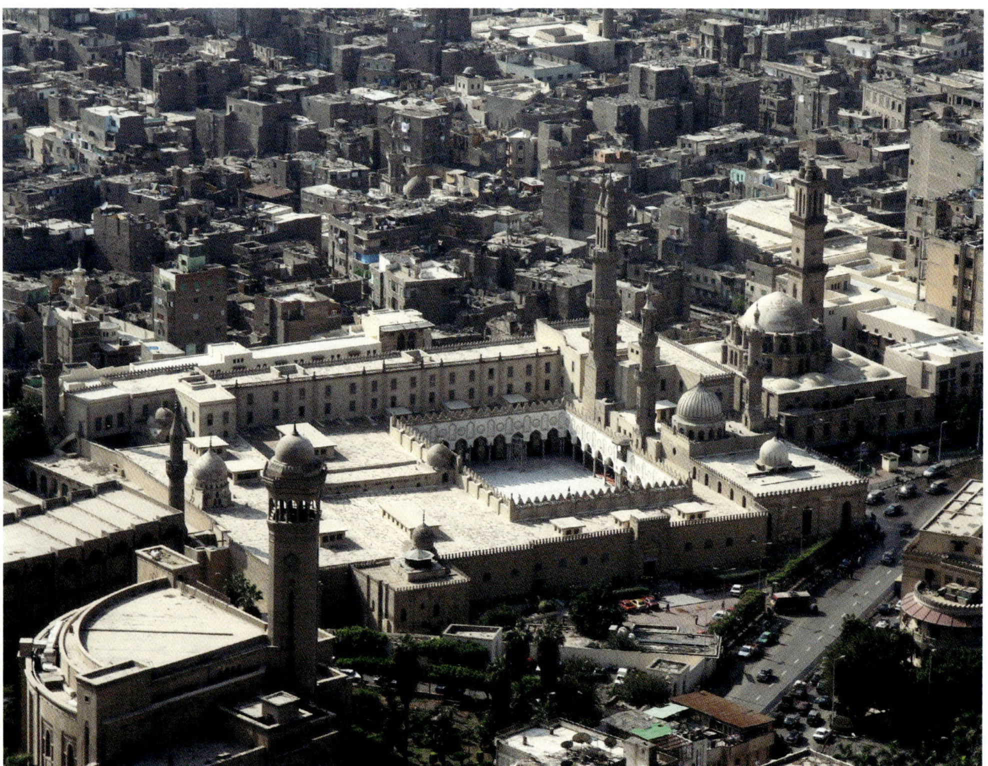

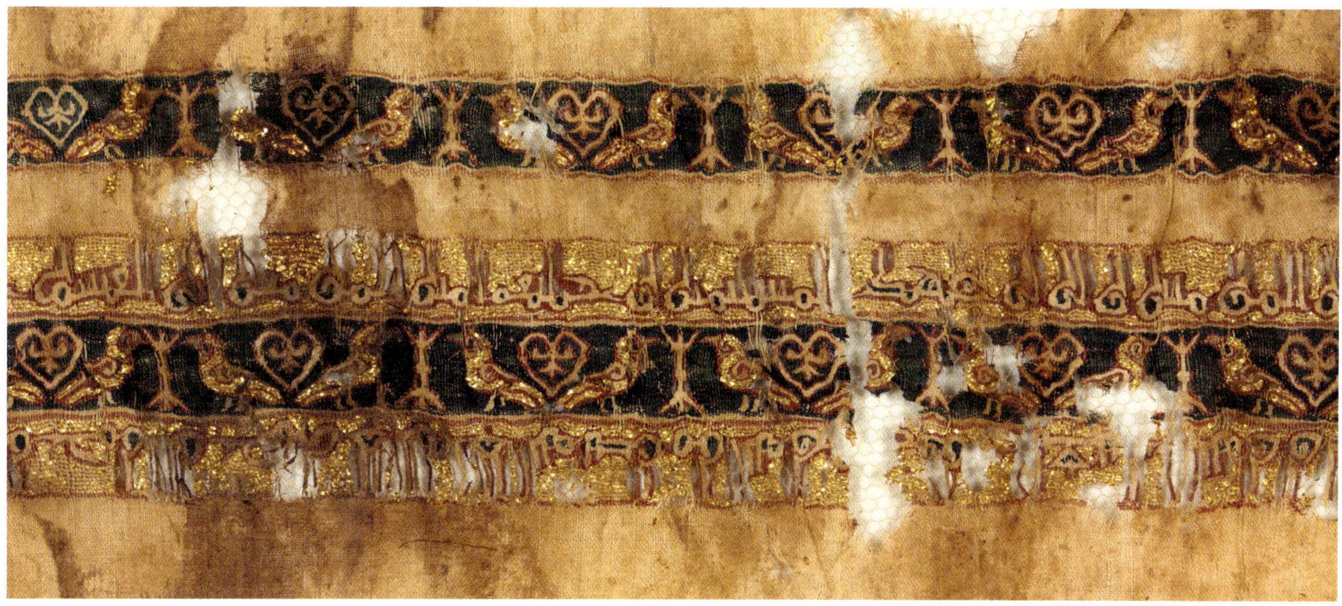

Fig. 6 Detail of cat. 17, tiraz textile naming the Fatimid caliph al-Hakim.

building — religious, commemorative, or palatial — the formal and spatial relationships between them, their monumental architecture and furnishings (such as richly carved wooden panels, silver lanterns, incense burners, carpets, curtains, and candles), and the use of inscriptions on their facades were coordinated by a complicated symbolic program centered on the imam-caliph, who was the ultimate temporal and religious authority.[17] The program was enacted through caliphal processions on Fridays and on historical and religious holidays, when the ceremonial spatial map of the capital, or specific portions of it, came to life. Throughout the Fatimid period, for instance, the caliph led the Friday prayers alternately from al-Azhar Mosque, al-Hakim Mosque, and the two older mosques of al-Fustat, but al-Azhar played a larger ceremonial role in most other caliphal processions, which variously started, ended, or made a stop there (Fig. 5).[18] The symbolic importance of processions was enhanced by the hierarchical arrangement of the participants around the caliph, their color-coded and richly ornate dresses, headgears, and robes of honor embellished with tiraz in the name of the caliph, and the paraphernalia they carried (Fig. 6).

Cairo also became the center of the sophisticated global network of proselytizing (*markaz al-da'wa*) the official Isma'ili creed, where new missionaries (*du'at*, singular *da'i*) were trained before being sent out to the various regions of the Islamic world. The *da'wa* (literally, call), which had been the organizational structure of Isma'ilism when it operated underground, continued unabated after the establishment of the Isma'ili caliphate, with its formal diplomatic and administrative apparatus. It in fact peaked in the mid-eleventh century, especially in Iran and farther east, after the caliphate began its political and territorial retreat, and survived the fall of the Fatimids, though no longer under a unified authority.[19] In Cairo, al-Azhar Mosque, which had served as a center of teaching practically since its completion, vied for the position of supreme foundation of Fatimid propaganda with the more specialized learning institution, Dar al-'Ilm or Dar al-Hikma (House of Wisdom), founded by the third caliph, al-Hakim bi-Amr Allah (r. 996–1021), in 1005. Dar al-'Ilm, whose history is somewhat ambiguous, ultimately became the official headquarters of Isma'ili teaching and jurisprudence, with instruction in rhetoric, logic, and philosophy.[20] Al-Azhar Mosque, on the other hand, retained its role as a center of Isma'ili religious learning for members of the ruling class. This was not a status al-Azhar shared with the other mosques in Cairo and al-Fustat, probably because most Egyptians remained Sunnis under the Fatimid regime, which does not seem to have put as much effort into proselytizing at home as it did abroad.

The Fatimids at first presented a serious threat to the Abbasid caliphate centered in Baghdad, as they managed to extend their realm over much of Syria, the Hijaz, Yemen, and large parts of North Africa in addition to Egypt. But by the late eleventh century, they had lost most of their domains outside Egypt aside from parts of Palestine. Even their hold over what remained under Fatimid control was weakened by the severe crisis known as *al-shidda al-Mustansiriyya* (the

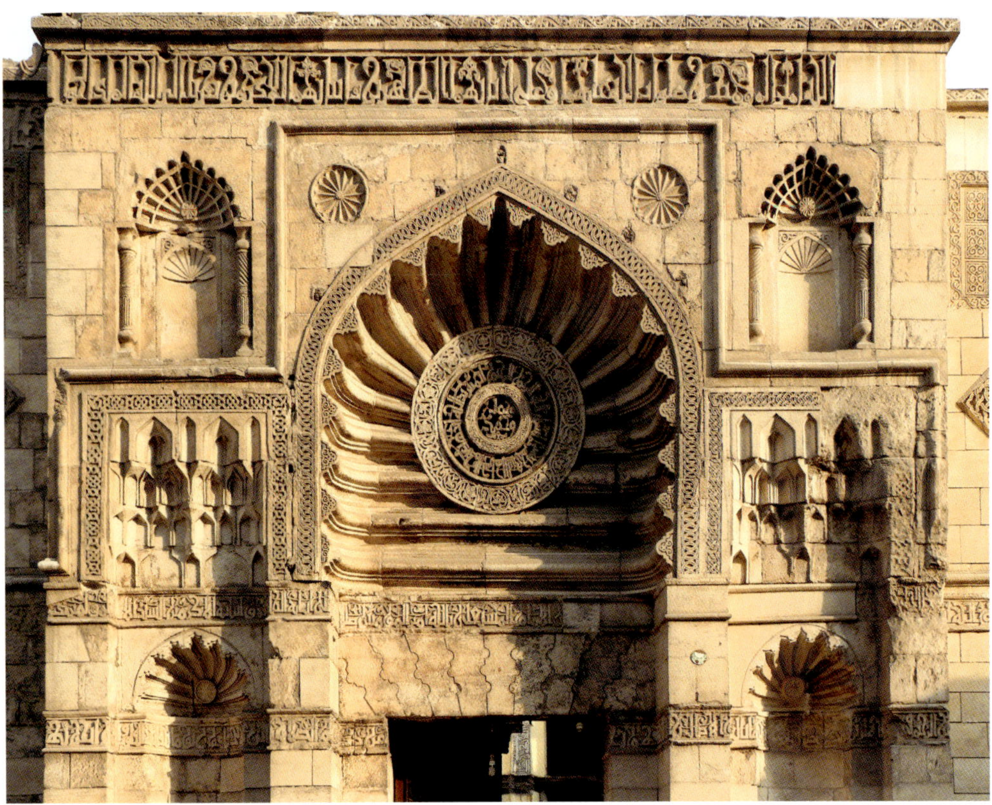

after the removal of his patrons, the Shiʿite Buyids, in 1055, Turkic military officer Arslan al-Basasiri switched loyalties and occupied several Iraqi cities, including Baghdad, under the banner of the Fatimids. Al-Basasiri held Baghdad for less than a year (January–September 1059) before being defeated and executed by the Seljuqs in December 1059.[23] Mired in turbulence at court and existential challenges abroad, the Fatimids subsequently focused their energies on rhetorically reasserting their credentials as descendants of the Prophet and therefore as the legitimate rulers of the Islamic world. This anxious message was inscribed on various media, from architecture to tiraz textiles. In 1125, for instance, al-Ma'mun al-Bata'ihi, vizier to Caliph al-Amir from 1121 to 1125, constructed one of the most intriguing surviving Fatimid buildings, the Mosque of al-Aqmar (Fig. 7). Its stone facade is ornamented with bands of superbly carved, floriated Kufic that invokes the Prophet's family (*ahl al-bayt*) and calls for divine blessings upon the Fatimid caliph and his "pure ancestors and descendants" (see also cats. 15–16).

In 1153, the Fatimids lost their last Palestinian foothold in Ascalon to the Crusaders and ceased to be an active player in the power struggles in the eastern Mediterranean. Their vulnerability attracted the attention of Amalric, king of Jerusalem (r. 1163–1174), and Nur al-Din ibn Zengi (r. 1146–1174), the champion of both the counter-crusade and the Sunni revival in Syria and a partisan of the Abbasid caliphate. From 1164 to 1169, the two rivals fought over Egypt. Two campaigns, in 1164 and 1167, ended in stalemates. After the third, in October 1168, the army of Nur al-Din forced the Franks to retreat without a fight, seizing control of the country. The Syrian amir, Shirkuh, was installed as the vizier of the Fatimid caliph al-ʿAdid li-Din Allah (r. 1160–1171). Shortly afterward, Shirkuh died suddenly, and in January 1169, his nephew Salah al-Din, then a recently minted amir of the Syrian detachment, succeeded his uncle as vizier of Egypt. In 1171, Salah al-Din eliminated the Fatimid caliphate after the premature death of al-ʿAdid and restored the Abbasid caliphate in Egypt.[24]

Salah al-Din instigated a concerted effort to erase all traces of the Fatimids immediately after their downfall.[25] Separated according to gender, members of the Fatimid family were sequestered in perpetuity to prevent their propagation. Ismaʿilis in the army and the administration were purged on accusation of sedition; many were killed in battle, executed on the gallows, or expelled from the country. The royal city

calamity of al-Mustansir; 1054–72), a period of famine and fighting between the various factions of the Fatimid army in the middle of the long reign of al-Mustansir bi-Allah (r. 1036–1094) that ruined the countryside, depleted the treasury, and upended the balance of power at the top.[21] Beginning with the vizierate of the Armenian general Badr al-Jamali (r. 1074–1094), who was called from Syria to restore the caliphate, political power fell into the hands of viziers. Badr initiated modifications to the state structure, fortified Cairo anew — this time with stronger brick walls and monumental stone gates — and rehabilitated the old neighborhoods within the city limits that had deteriorated before his arrival.[22] But his reforms only slowed the decline. For the remainder of the Fatimid caliphate, Egypt faced mounting external threats (from the Seljuqs in Syria and the Crusaders in Palestine) and internecine struggles among rival groups, each trying to install its leader in the vizierate, while the caliphs became mere symbols confined to their palaces save for Friday prayers and ceremonial processions, when they were paraded in lavish regalia.

Ironically, it was during the calamity that the Fatimids fleetingly realized their dream of having the khutbah (Friday sermon) in Baghdad pronounced in the name of their caliph:

was stripped of its exclusivity and opened to the Egyptian population. Its Fatimid palaces were distributed among the Ayyubid amirs and ultimately demolished to make room for religious complexes in the thirteenth and fourteenth centuries (Fig. 8). Some Fatimid mosques were closed off for almost a century, such as al-Azhar, or neglected so that they fell into disuse, such as the Mosque of al-Qarafa, and tombs of the Fatimid caliphs were dug out and built over. Fatimid archives were deliberately destroyed and their libraries and artifacts sold at auction. Finally, the Fatimids' name was changed in later Egyptian sources to *al-'ubaydiyyuun*, after 'Ubayd Allah al-Mahdi (r. 909–934), the founder of the caliphate, in a bid to denigrate their claim of descent from Fatima. A new chapter in Egyptian history was thus opened, one that would see the country turning its back on the Isma'ili episode and becoming the center of the Sunni world under the Mamluks (1250–1517).

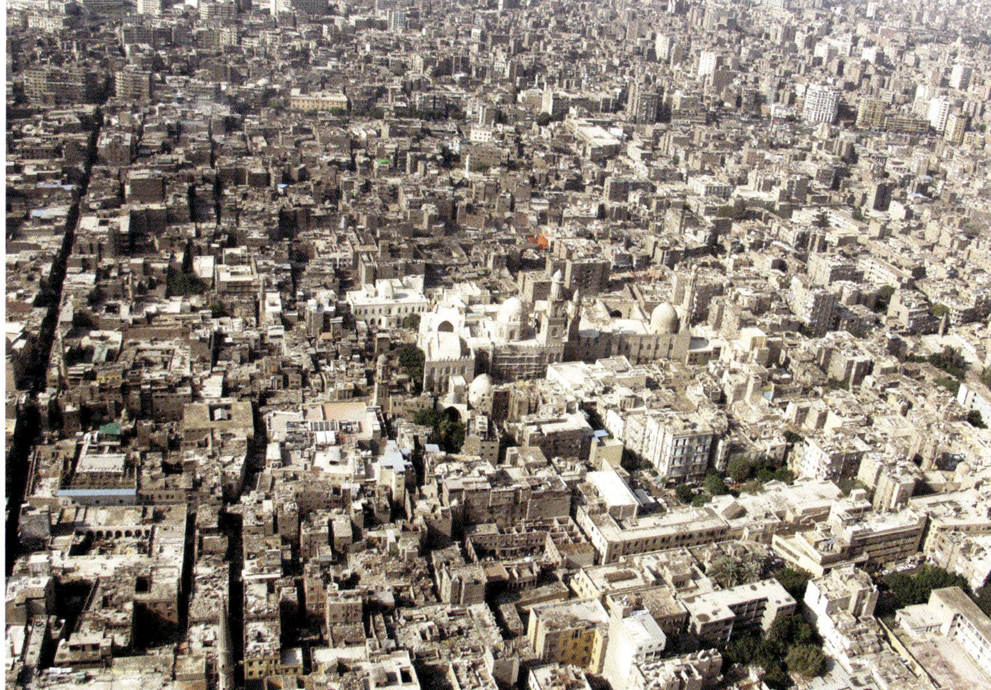

Fig. 8 Aerial view of the site of the two Fatimid palaces overbuilt with Mamluk religious complexes.

1   Haarmann 1980; Abulhimal 2011; and Antrim 2012, 11–29, 61–83.
2   The idea that Egypt was a clearly defined entity with a unique identity is the theme of many nationalist historical studies. Hamdan 1980–84 pioneered this area of investigation; see also Hanna 1994. 'Ashur and 'Ashur 1999 takes the argument to its logical end by characterizing the history of the country from 332 BCE to 1952 CE as a long period of occupation and acculturation of Egypt by "foreigners," including the Arabs — now a hot-button topic.
3   The rhyming aphorism, which goes on to say "Its women are dolls, and its men are slaves to whoever conquers them," has not been conclusively attributed to any known figure in Islamic history. Bits of it, however, appear in various aphorisms and poetic citations on the character of the Egyptians, many indeed negative. For a collection, see al-Maqrizi 1853, 1:49–50, 366–68.
4   Allen 1997; Ibrahim and Ibrahim 2003, 1–37, 57–66; and Haas 1997, 1–89.
5   Wheatley 2000, 39–42, 49–53.
6   Abu-Lughod 1971, 13–20; Raymond 2000, 7–30; and AlSayyad 2011, 39–54.
7   Leiser 1985. For an examination of the various opinions about conversion to Islam in Egypt, see O'Sullivan 2006.
8   Brett 2005, 1–32, republished in Brett 2019; and Décobert 1992, 273–300, esp. 278–80.
9   Rapoport 2004.
10 For a review of the debates over Fatimid lineage, see Brett 2001, 29–49; and Daftary 1990, 118–23.
11 Al-Maqrizi 1853, 1:348, 359, 377.
12 Ibn 'Abd al-Zahir 1996, 13–74; Ibn al-Dawadari 1961, 137–42; and ibid., 2:138.
13 Goitein 1969, 80–96.
14 Al-Muqqadasi 1906, 200; and al-Maqrizi 1853, 1:451–57. The *musalla* lost its ceremonial role after Fatimid times and became a space of prayer for the dead, known as the *musalla* of Bab al-Nasr; al-Maqrizi 1853, 2:5, 138.
15 Rabbat 1996.
16 Sanders 1994, 5–81.
17 Behrens-Abouseif 2018, 44–67; and O'Kane 2018b, 142–59.
18 For a detailed description of the four nights of illuminations (*layali al-wuqud*) and the procession of the caliph and his family to al-Azhar, see al-Maqrizi 1853, 1:362, 465–67.
19 Daftary 2018, 280–91; Halm 1997, 71–78; and Stern 1972, 437–50, reprinted in Stern 1983, 234–56.
20 Al-Maqrizi 1853, 1:458–60; and Walker 1997.
21 Elbendari 2002, 67–83.
22 Al-Maqrizi 1853, 1:381. The three gates, Bab al-Nasr, Bab al-Futuh, and Bab Zuwayla, resemble contemporary north Syrian architecture and are said to have been built by three Armenian brothers from Edessa; see Tabbaa 1993, 33–36.
23 Daftary 1990, 193–222, 238–54; and Lev 1991, 38–63.
24 Ibn-Shaddad 1964, 36–41; Elisséeff 1967, 627–40; Ehrenkreutz 1972, 50–68; and Lev 1999, 45–94.
25 On the actions against the Fatimids taken by Salah al-Din, see Abu Shama 1956–62, 2:506; al-Maqrizi 1853, 1:396–98; Lev 1999, 116–36; and Bora 2015.

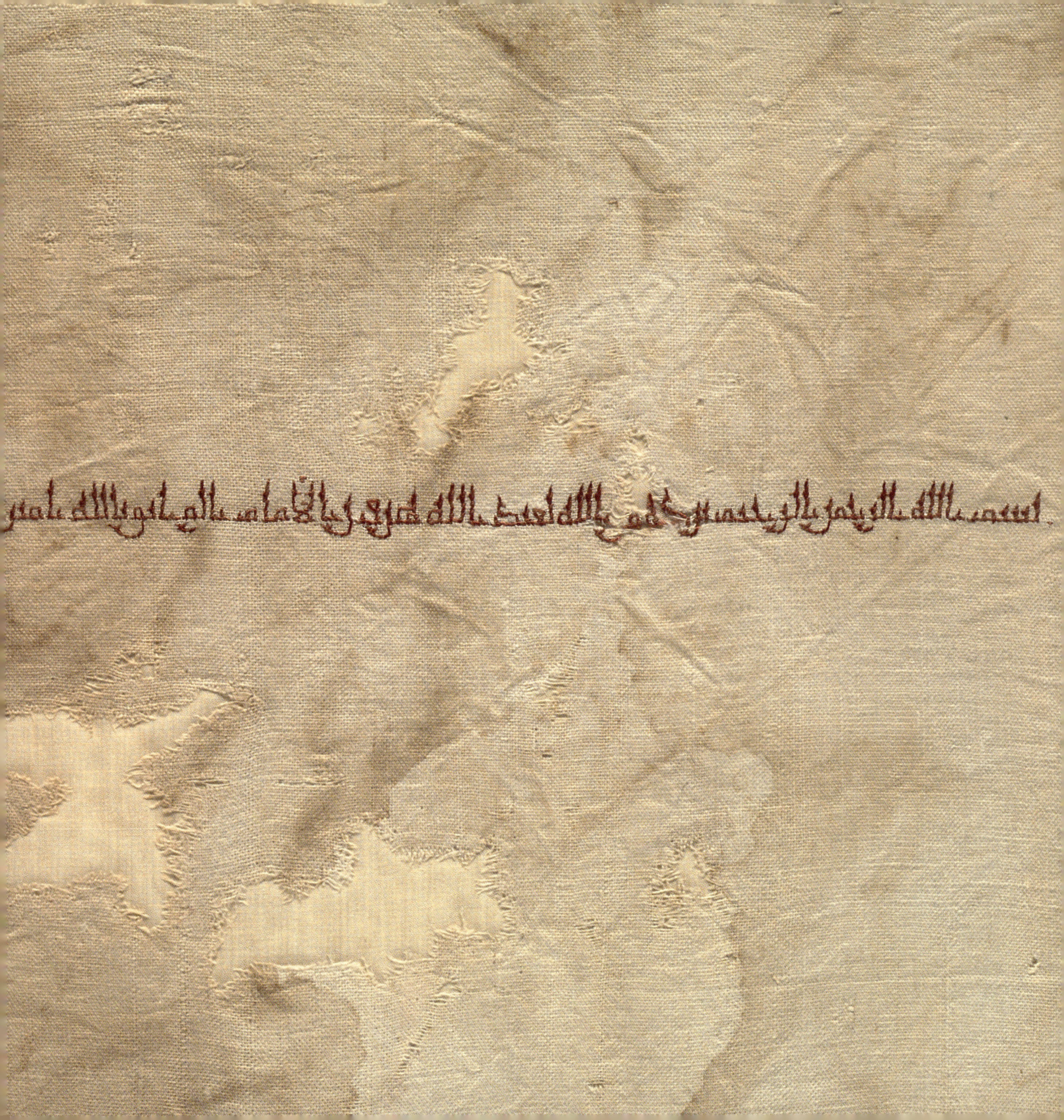

JOCHEN SOKOLY

Social Fabrics: Early Islamic Egypt through the Lens of Inscribed Tiraz Textiles

The conquest of Egypt by Islamic forces between 639 and 646, just a few years after the death of the Prophet Muhammad in 632, was a watershed for the establishment of an early Islamic empire. Since antiquity, Egypt had been an economic powerhouse in the eastern Mediterranean, with an advanced system of government and administration reflecting the wealth and complexity of its economy. Egypt's agriculture produced food crops plus the raw materials for sophisticated textile production, such as linen and wool, and its coastlines on the Mediterranean and Red Seas allowed participation in international trade networks. Because its revenues were indispensable, control over Egypt's economy became key to the political success of the early Islamic caliphates. This is partly the reason why the state's political and economic history is so well documented in administrative texts surviving on papyrus, coinage, and thousands of textiles.

Inscribed textiles have been largely overlooked as primary sources for studying the sociopolitical history of the early Islamic caliphates, unlike papyri and coins, which have been central to its investigation. Referred to as tiraz, the inscriptions were embroidered, painted, or in the case of larger swaths of cloth, woven into the fabric. The concepts behind the creation and use of tiraz textiles evolved as the centuries unfolded, but initially the texts were of a protocolary nature, recording administrative information such as the names and titles of the ruling caliph, the officers of procurement — for example, a vizier or financial administrator — and the type of workshop where the textile was created, its location, and the year of production.[1] Although the term "tiraz" eventually came to refer exclusively to inscribed textiles, at the beginning of the Islamic era these texts appeared on diverse objects and mediums, most notably papyri (Fig. 1) and coins, but also architectural foundation stones, glass weights, ceramics, and carved ivory.[2]

Tiraz textile inscriptions, like other types of public text, carried political messages that underlined and announced a ruler's right to exercise control. Inscribing the name and titles of a caliph was a highly coveted and jealously guarded prerogative granted by the ruler himself to high-level administrators, who often added their own names and titles as well as their roles in the procurement of these prized textiles. The inscriptions can therefore be read like historical tracks of the many constellations of control over government administration, or of the relationship between the caliphate's central government and that of the provinces. In subtle ways, tiraz reveal the political and economic ambitions of the individuals, groups, and dynasties that ruled Egypt. But the story does not end there.

Tiraz textiles had a double life that was closely connected to the significance of the texts. Once inscribed with the names of the authorities who enabled their production, the textiles were then dispersed by the central government to favored courtiers, administrators, and soldiers, much as robes of honor (*khilaʿ*) were gifted by the caliph to high-ranking courtiers in public investitures. To receive a tiraz textile with a caliphal inscription signified integration in a network of the ruling elite. The prestigious textiles were then made into clothing or

Opposite: Detail of cat. 1.

Fig. 1 Papyrus tiraz, Egypt, al-Ashmunein, c. 864–73. Papyrus and ink, inscribed in Arabic, 7.6 × 16.9 cm. Austrian National Library, Vienna, Archduke Rainer Collection, A.P. 04057 (R/V).

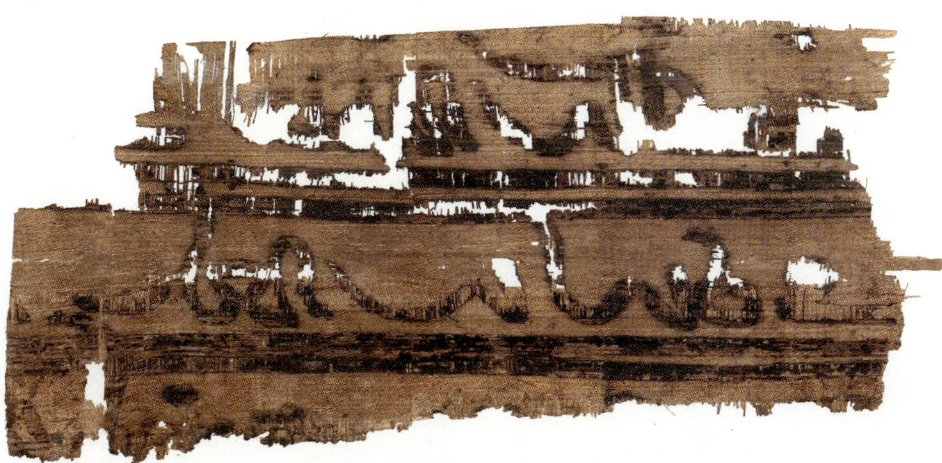

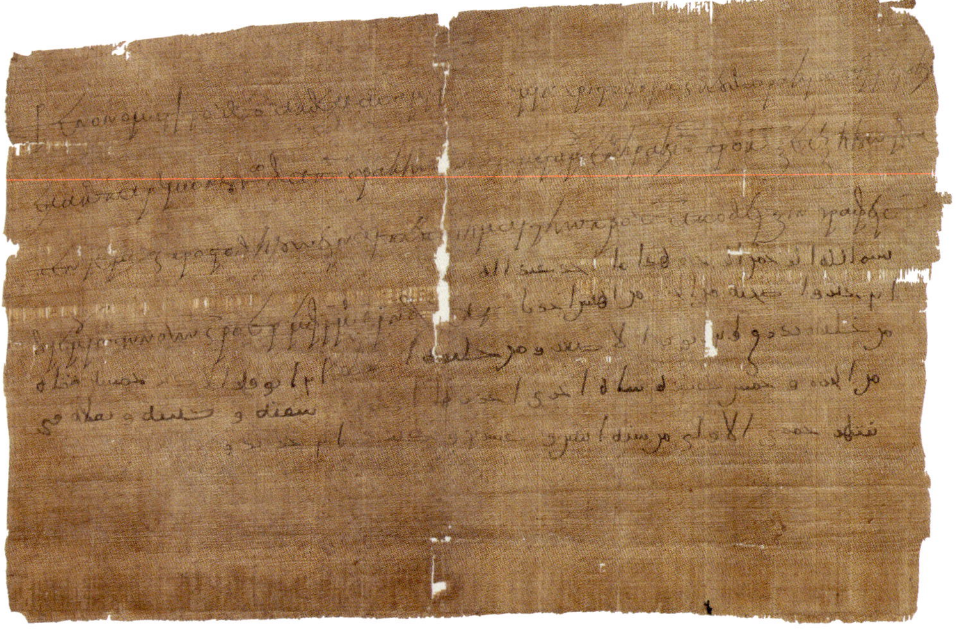

kept for later use. In Egypt, many were employed as shrouds. There is literary evidence from the Fatimid period (969–1171) that textiles inscribed with a caliph's name, or from a caliph's treasury, became symbolic of caliphal benevolence and could transmit religious blessings to a Muslim. This notion provides a way to interpret surviving Egyptian tiraz textiles, almost all of which have been found in human burial sites. However, recent excavations of Christian graves have shown that the textiles were not limited to Muslim burials, demonstrating that the relationship between Muslims and Christians — and between the Islamic state and Christian institutions — was dynamic.

TEXT AS EXPRESSION OF POLITICAL POWER

While public texts were ubiquitous as a statement of imperial power in antiquity, they were largely confined to architecture, proclaiming a ruler's political ambition, military strength, and religious piety. With the arrival of Islam in the Mediterranean world, text took on another level of symbolism. The revelation of the Qur'an to the Prophet Muhammad in Arabic had elevated both the Arabic language and script to carriers of the divine message: inscribed text was no longer just a means of conveying content, it also held religious significance.

Post-conquest, Egypt's largely Christian administration was subjected to incremental change by Muslim governors. A mere two years after the siege of Alexandria, Arabic began to rival Greek as the language of government, a shift reflected in an important surviving papyrus document from 22/643 (Fig. 2). The document records an economic transaction between the Muslim conquerors and the resident Christian population in both Greek and Arabic.[3] Eventually, Arabs filled the upper levels of government and supervised the executive levels still staffed by Coptic- and Greek-speaking Egyptians. Arabic came to replace Greek as an administrative language completely and permanently through centralizing reforms issued in the 690s by Caliph 'Abd al-Malik (r. 685–705), who ruled from the Umayyad capital in Damascus. Henceforth, public inscriptions on buildings as well as state documents were no longer bilingual. 'Abd al-Malik also introduced a new form of Islamic coinage, replacing earlier models that had merged Arabic text with Byzantine and Sasanian elements — a portrait of the ruler, for example, or religious symbols such as the cross or fire altar. New Islamic coinage featured only text: on one side the *shahada*, a proclamation of belief in the unity of God and the prophethood of Muhammad, and information relating to the coin's mint and commission on the other (Fig. 3). This became the standard in the Islamic lands for centuries to come (see cats. 4–5).

These reforms did not eradicate entirely the use of Greek and Coptic in Egypt, but Christians who continued to work in the provincial administration were forced to adapt. Many eventually became Muslim. Still, it took several hundred years for Egypt to become majority Muslim, and for Christians and Jews to adopt Arabic as their vernacular and eventually as the language of religious expression (cats. 31–32). Other predominantly Christian regions conquered by Arab Muslims, such as al-Andalus, Iran, Syria, Palestine, and Yemen, underwent similar cultural transformations.

Textiles are key indicators of socioeconomic change. In pre-industrial societies, they formed one of the most important cornerstones of economic output, linking agriculture, industry,

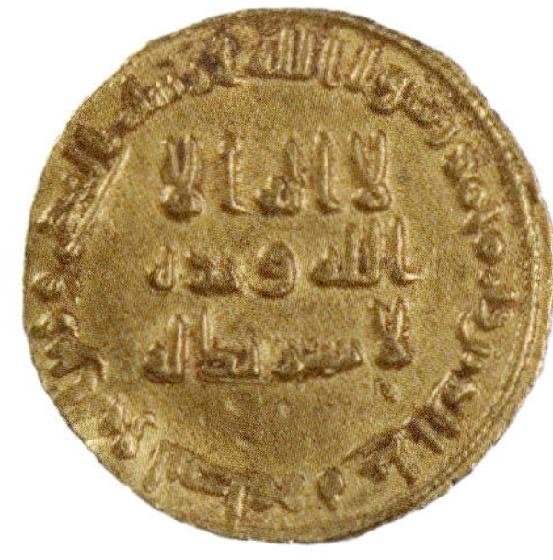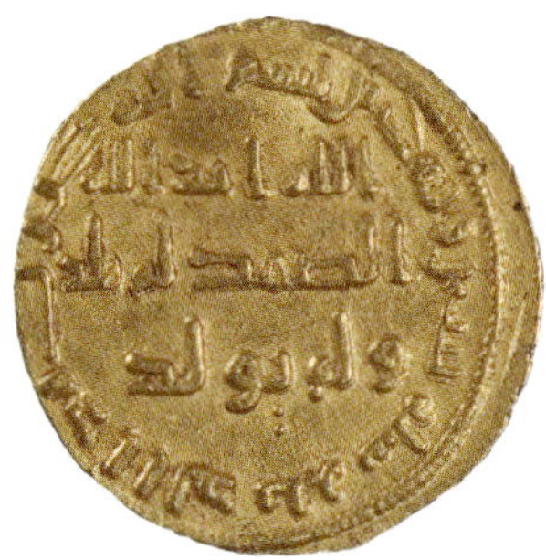

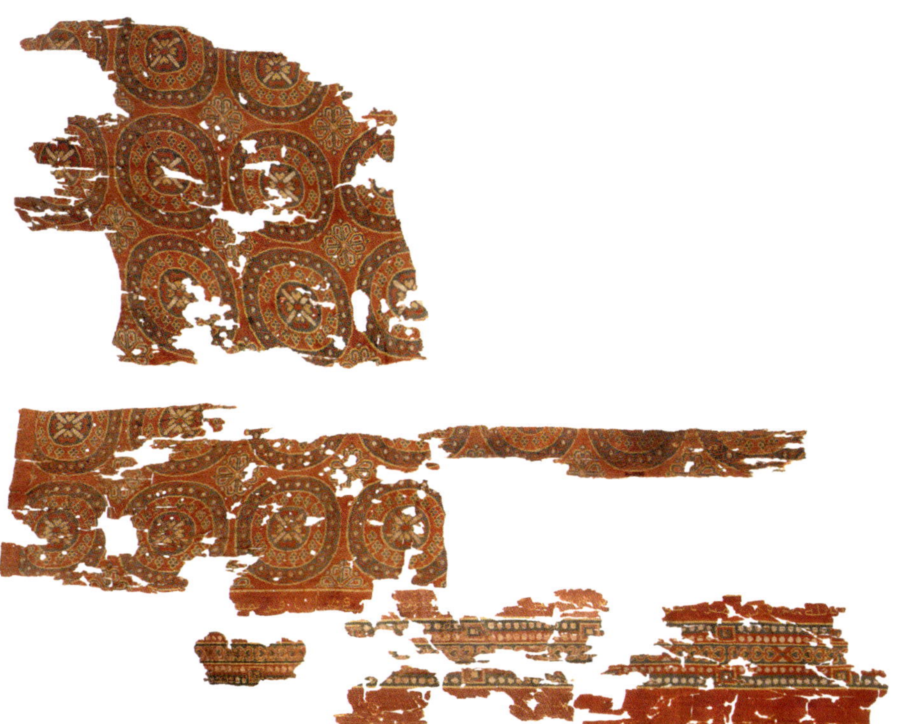

trade, and finance in one dynamic system. Since pharaonic times, linen and wool had been the mainstays of Egyptian textile production. In Egypt, as in Byzantium and Sasanian Iran, the state closely monitored the various constituents of the textile industry for quality control and taxation purposes, but also to ensure the proper division of state production versus that for the open market. Materials such as silk, for example, were often subject to state monopolies. This was the case in Byzantium, where imperial silks were produced in workshops attached to the palace in Constantinople and from there sometimes distributed as diplomatic gifts to foreign states.

The earliest known example of a tiraz textile — now dispersed as fragments between four museums — is a luxury item reportedly recovered in the late nineteenth century from a cemetery in Akhmim, the ancient Panopolis in Upper Egypt (Fig. 4).[4] The fragments are tattered remnants of a once magnificent compound-woven silk fabric with designs in mustard and muted blue on a dark-red ground.[5] Two are inscribed in an early form of Arabic script, embroidered in yellow silk between the border and the main field of beaded roundels. The now incomplete inscription follows a formal sequence that gives the name and titles of the caliph Marwan, states that the piece was commissioned or ordered by an administrator whose name and title are now lost, and cites the location

of the tiraz workshop as Ifriqiya, a province spanning most of the North African Mediterranean coast between eastern Algeria and western Libya, with its capital at Kairouan, in modern-day Tunisia. The creation date could fall into the reign of one of two Umayyad caliphs called Marwan: Marwan ibn al-Hakam (r. 684–685) or Marwan ibn Muhammad (r. 744–750), the last ruler of the Umayyad dynasty (661–750). Although the text names Ifriqiya, the silk fabric itself was not necessarily woven there; the inscription was added in embroidery after weaving. It has been suggested that stylistically the beaded roundels reflect Sasanian influence, which could indicate a weave center to the east, possibly Iraq or Iran.[6] Wherever its place of production, the Marwan textile's embroidered inscription makes clear that in Umayyad times, the concept of tiraz as a marker of administrative requisition extending to textiles was already well established.

While the language reforms of 'Abd al-Malik clearly resulted in the Arabization of the upper levels of bureaucracy and, in effect, of all written government output, surviving textiles from the early Islamic period show that the same was not necessarily true of the lives of ordinary Egyptians, the majority of whom were Christian. Particularly illuminating is a turban dedicated to a certain Samu'il ibn Murqus (Fig. 5): the ambiguity of its inscription has allowed for a range of scholarly interpretations, but a more recent reading of the name as Samu'il ibn Murqus (Samuel, son of Mark) clearly identifies the patron as Christian.[7]

A full loom width and length of the linen ground fabric survives. The inscription, written in an unadorned, early type of Arabic script, and the colorful, ornamental band below, with small birds set inside diamond-shaped cartouches, are woven in wool. The inscription tells us that the piece was a wraparound turban cloth (*imama*) made in a tiraz workshop in Sanhur, in the Fayyum Oasis. The text also places its time of manufacture in the month of Rajab in the year 88/707–8, seemingly dating the turban to the Umayyad period. More likely, the maker omitted the hundreds digit, a common practice in early Islamic inscriptions, and did not finish the word for eighty (*thamanin*). This would date the piece to either 188/804–5 or 288/901–2, when Egypt was under Abbasid rule. The diamond-shaped lozenges with small birds are indeed more reminiscent of Abbasid ornament than Umayyad; they evoke the architectural decorations of luster ceramics from the later period in particular.[8] In script and ornamental band,

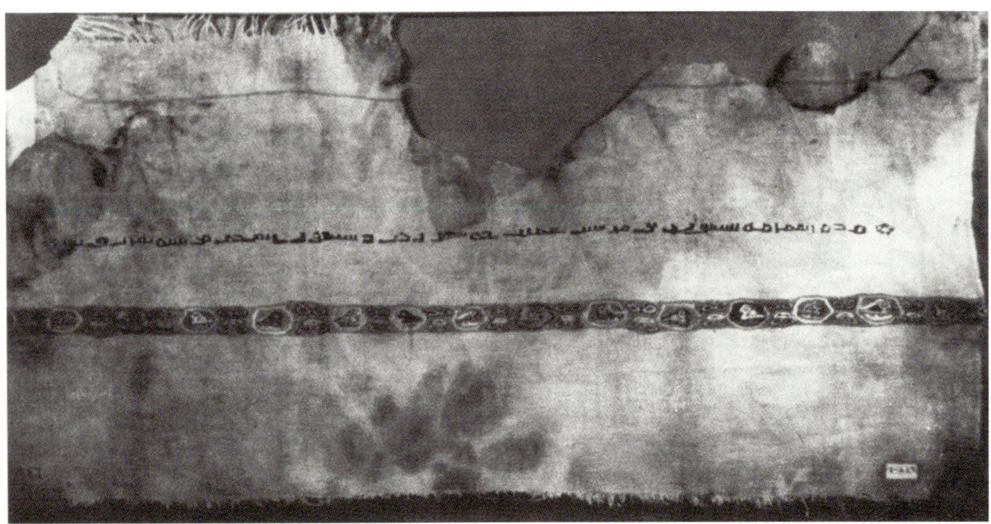

Fig. 5 Textile fragment from the turban of Samu'il ibn Murqus, Upper Egypt, Sanhur in Fayyum, 88/707 or 188/804–5. Linen with wool tapestry. Museum of Islamic Art, Cairo, 10846. Image after 'Abbās Muḥammad Salīm 1997, 66, Fig. 22.

Fig. 6 Two shawl fragments with bilingual inscription in the name of Raphael, Upper Egypt, private tiraz workshop in Tutun in Fayyum, c. 9th–10th century. Wool and linen tapestry on wool, 85 × 57 and 30 × 57 cm. Musée du Louvre, Paris, Gift of Mme. David Weill, 1955, E 25405.

the turban relates well to a shroud in the Textile Museum (cat. 35) that bears an inscription recording its manufacture for an unnamed patron in the private tiraz workshop (*tiraz al-khassa*) of Misr, the provincial capital of Egypt in the early Islamic period. Based on their epigraphic styles, both textiles are datable to the early Abbasid period (c. 750–850), and from the formal protocols of their inscriptions, the naming of tiraz locations, and the exactness of their execution, it can be argued that both were produced in workshops supervised by the provincial administration. That the turban bears a Christian name demonstrates that such workshops filled not only governmental orders but also commissions for private, even non-Muslim, patrons.

Additional textiles produced or recovered in the Fayyum provide further evidence that, in Egypt, the gifting of textiles bearing personalized inscriptions quickly generalized beyond the elite network of caliphal patronage discussed above. Situated about 62 miles south of Cairo, the Fayyum is one of Egypt's oldest settlements, going back to pharaonic times, and a site well known for the finds of Roman period painted mummy portraits. Called Arsinoë in Arcadia when the Romans ruled, it became a suffragan bishopric to the bishop of Oxyrhynchus with the rise of Christianity and was named al-Fayyum after the Muslim conquest.

A large textile in the Louvre with a bilingual inscription in Arabic and Coptic offers an important example of non-caliphal production (Fig. 6). The Arabic text states that it was made for an unnamed owner in a private workshop in the city of Tutun within the governate (*kurat*) of al-Fayyum (see the map on p. 7). Its Coptic inscription is a religious invocation to Christ to help a certain Raphael, son of Ganarkhou.[9] A related piece with the same line in Arabic, albeit without a Coptic inscription, is in the Museum of Islamic Art in Cairo.[10] Interestingly, in the Louvre piece the Coptic and Arabic inscriptions are clearly demarcated by content: the Coptic, a personalized prayer; the Arabic outlining the textile's production in much the same way as the shroud from Misr.[11] Given that these textiles were excavated as funerary shrouds, it is tempting to assume that the Coptic prayers were intended to protect the deceased from evil, yet the Arabic inscriptions are clearly rooted in the temporal world. It has been suggested that such textiles were inscribed to record a gift from father to child during their lifetimes or a gift to members of the clergy, such as priests or monks.[12]

ABBASID TIRAZ

The high point of tiraz textile production extended from the ninth through the mid-twelfth century, when Egypt was ruled first by the Abbasid caliphate, with its capital in Iraq, and then by the rival Fatimid caliphate, which established a capital in Egypt.[13] (The majority of the textiles in the Harvard Art Museums exhibition date to these periods.) It is clear when one looks at figural representations such as those on Abbasid luster ceramics that the Abbasids were fashion conscious. A bowl in the Harvard Art Museums (cat. 7) shows a figure holding a beaker seated cross-legged in patterned trousers and a monochrome shirt, a tiraz armband prominently displayed on his right arm. An architectural fragment from an eleventh-century bathhouse in al-Fustat, painted in fresco,

Fig. 7 Architectural fragment from a bathhouse in al-Fustat, with fresco-painted figure, 11th century. Stucco painted in red and black pigments, 24.5 × 60 cm. Museum of Islamic Art, Cairo, 12880.

Fig. 8 Funerary tunic with pseudo-inscription, 11th century. Linen embroidered with blue, pink, and undyed silk, 120 × 153 cm. Ashmolean Museum, University of Oxford, Purchased with the assistance of the Art Fund, the MLA/V&A Purchase Grant Fund, and the Friends of the Ashmolean, 1998, EA1998.210.

features a seated, turbaned figure whose sleeves and scarf are adorned with decorative bands (Fig. 7). And a folio from an illustrated manuscript of the *Khawass al-Ashjar* (*De Materia Medica*) by Dioscorides, probably copied in late Abbasid Baghdad and dated 1224 (cat. 8), shows two figures in brightly colored robes accentuated by golden tiraz bands, thus demonstrating the enduring taste for inscribed clothes.

Although perhaps not as ostentatious as these pictorial representations of tiraz bands, a piece of clothing in the Textile Museum (cat. 6) constitutes a rare example of an extant tailored child's garment. Made out of a larger sheet, the garment takes the shape of a short, buttonless tunic or shirt, with tapering sleeves and body. The inscription appears upside down on the back of the left sleeve. It is dated 306/918–19, during the reign of the Abbasid caliph al-Muqtadir (r. 908–932), and was made in Misr, the capital of Abbasid Egypt. Remarkably few complete garments carrying Arabic inscriptions or decorated with tiraz bands have survived from Islamic Egypt. A fine and rare adult's tunic in the Ashmolean Museum featuring pseudo-Kufic bands of letters on the sleeves and the front and back of the torso has been radiocarbon dated to the eleventh century (Fig. 8).[14]

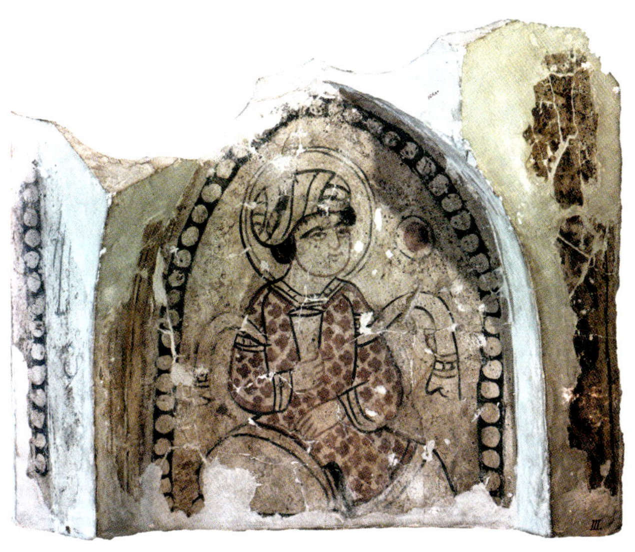

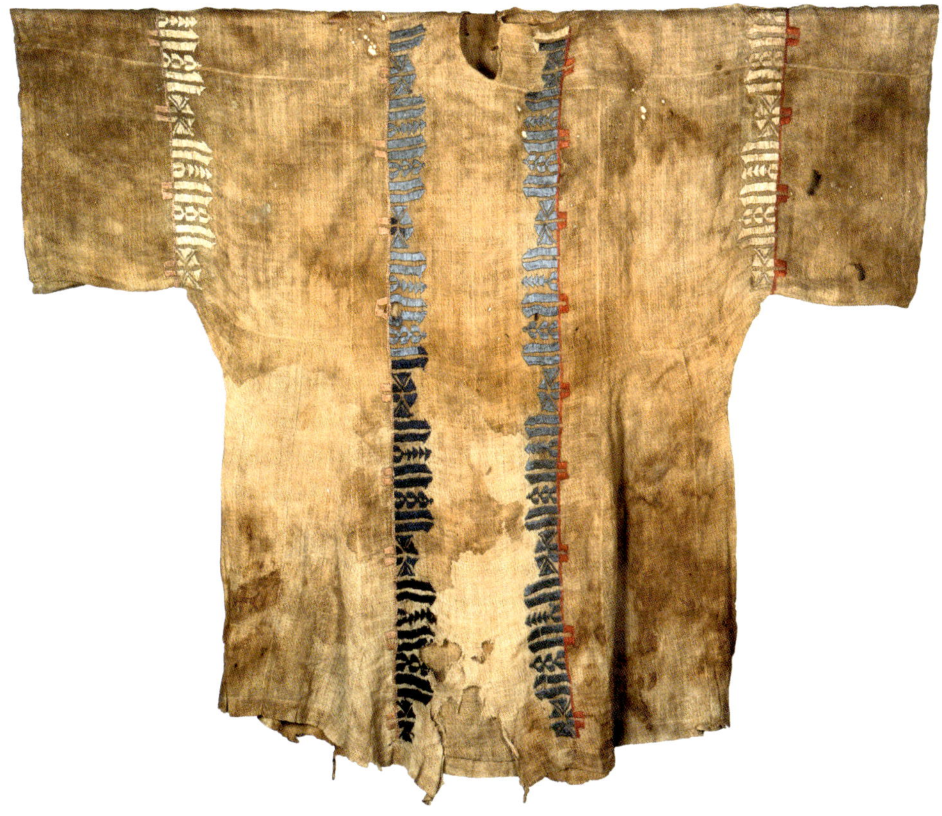

The variety of fabrics and materials, styles and execution of inscriptions, and changing color preferences all speak to the vibrant exchange among the various provinces of the Abbasid caliphate and its center. The textiles unearthed from Egyptian graves in the late nineteenth and early twentieth centuries provide a clear picture of the region as the heart of political and trade networks stretching from the Indian Ocean and eastern Iran to the Mediterranean and North Africa. In addition to linen cloths with embroidered and tapestry-woven inscriptions from Egypt and woolen fabrics from Upper Egypt, the graves contained cottons from Iraq (cats. 2, 10), embroidered *mulham* and silk textiles from Khurasan (cat. 9), ikats from Yemen (cats. 11–12), and woven mats from Palestine (cat. 38).

Several Abbasid examples in the exhibition bear inscriptions that reflect the struggles of the caliphate to manage and hold together a vast and disintegrating empire riddled by growing regionalism, showing clearly how control over the production of tiraz textiles was an expression of political status quo and a right to rule. The years from roughly 868 to 969 formed a pivotal century in which the governors of Egypt carved out a degree of independence from Abbasid authority. Prior to this, governors loyal to the central authority were appointed from Baghdad, often for very short terms. But in the last hundred years of Abbasid rule, hereditary governorships began to develop and redirect provincial taxation to benefit the Egyptian peoples, agriculture, and industries, as opposed to meeting the needs of the empire. Tiraz inscriptions of this era continue to make evident the tight control of procurement and payments by powerful Abbasid viziers and finance directors, but they also reveal challenges to caliphal authority from provincial governors as well as from within the caliphal family.

In 868, Caliph al-Mu'tazz (r. 866–869) ordered Ahmad ibn Tulun, a member of his Turkish guard, to travel to Egypt to suppress a series of disturbances and establish himself as regional governor. After restoring order and gaining control of the Egyptian economy, Ibn Tulun instituted himself as de facto ruler, with the aim of withholding tax payments to the central government. Ibn Tulun and his descendants governed Egypt for almost forty years (868–905), although very few buildings in Cairo, among them the large Mosque of Ibn Tulun (see p. 12) and the Nilometer on Rawda Island, have survived as testimony to the ambitious building program that manifested his power.

A tiraz textile in the Dumbarton Oaks collection (cat. 13) exemplifies the relationship between the central government and the province of Egypt during Tulunid rule. In a departure from precedent and as an assertion of independence, Tulunid governors had their own names inscribed in the chain of delegation, usurping the place usually held by Abbasid viziers. Embroidered in red silk on a linen ground fabric, this highly informative inscription includes the names and titles of Caliph al-Mu'tadid (r. 892–902) and states that the amir (governor) Harun bin Khumarawayh bin Ahmad ordered the textile's manufacture in the Nile delta city of Tinnis in the year 285/898–99. The order was executed (*'ala yaday*), the inscription tells us, by an individual named Fa'iq.[15] The grandson of Ibn Tulun, Harun was heir to the governorship that his forebears had founded and strengthened through military campaigns and treaties that extended their authority into Syria and Iraq, guaranteeing their status as vassals of the caliphate. In this tiraz, Harun is styled with a pompous

title — "client of the Commander of the Faithful" (*mawla amir al-mu'minin*) — that professes his nominal allegiance to the Abbasid caliph, who alone could claim the title Commander of the Faithful. The term *mawla* referred to former non-Arab slaves or dependents who needed the protection of an Arab to function in the highly tribal and hierarchical society of the early Islamic period. To be a *mawla* of a ruling caliph was an impressive honor bestowed on a chosen few.[16] The appearance of the title in a tiraz inscription indicated that its recipient had major political clout, and its use in this particular case might well have been negotiated as part of a treaty with the ruling caliph. Unluckily, Harun was no longer in the seat of power at the time this textile was made. By 898, the affairs of his largely bankrupt state were run by slave-soldiers, and in 904 he was assassinated. The Tulunid governorship was soon crushed, and Egypt returned to direct Abbasid control.

Two textiles in the Harvard exhibition, produced in the aftermath of the upset, testify to the altered relationship between the Abbasid central government in Baghdad and the province of Egypt — and to the power of high-ranking Abbasid administrators. The textiles were produced one year apart, during the reign of al-Muqtadir. The first (cat. 3), embroidered in red silk on a linen ground fabric, is dated 309/921–22 and was created in a tiraz workshop in Tinnis. The second (cat. 2), embroidered in black silk on a cotton ground fabric, was made a year later in a private tiraz workshop in Baghdad (Madinat al-Salam). Both bear inscriptions concerning the chain of delegation that are illuminating. Significantly, the Egyptian textile no longer names an Egyptian governor; instead, both the Tinnis and the Baghdad tiraz identify an Abbasid vizier at the head of the sequence, followed by an Abbasid administrator responsible for carrying out the order. Each names the vizier Hamid bin al-'Abbas, but differences in the language accorded to him and to the administrators who executed the orders offer clues to the real exercise of power in the central government at this time.

Al-Muqtadir ascended the throne in 908, at the age of thirteen. During his twenty-year reign, the Abbasid state slid into fiscal and political decline. He was essentially a figurehead, with affairs of state run by his ministers, who in turn were controlled by his mother. The instability of al-Muqtadir's rule is made plain when one considers that no fewer than fourteen changes to the position of vizier are recorded during his reign.[17] The vizier Hamid bin al-'Abbas mentioned in both inscriptions

Fig. 9 Detail of cat. 3.

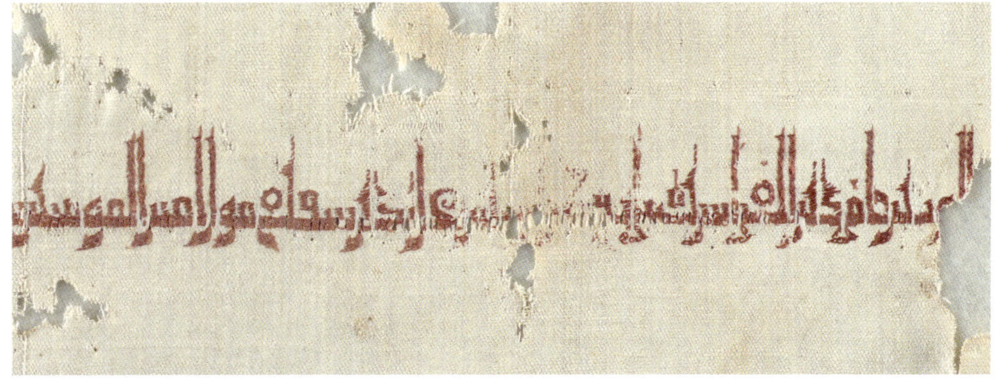

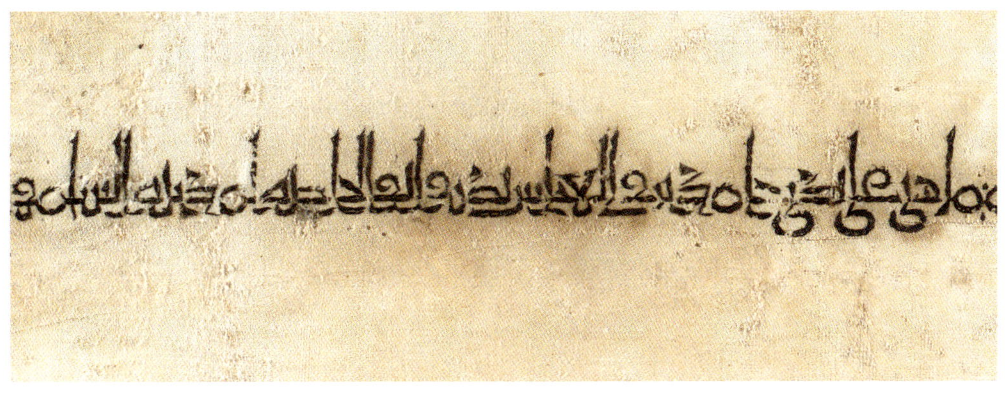

was in office from 918 to 923. Over eighty years old and inexperienced as an administrator when he assumed office, his affairs were in reality handled by his deputy, ʿAli bin ʿIsa (859–946), a Persian from a distinguished family of Abbasid officers. Both men were members of the *kuttab* (scribes), a class of administrators akin to bookkeepers and accountants who also received an education in the art of calligraphy.[18]

Tiraz inscriptions are generally brief but carefully composed. In these two inscriptions, the differences in the descriptions of Hamid bin al-ʿAbbas's involvement are telling. In the Tinnis textile, he is credited with placing the order (the inscription, partially lost, uses the formula *amara bi-ʿamalihi*; Fig. 9), while in the Baghdad piece, he is relegated to an inferior role: the textile is merely part of what was cared for (*jariʾa*) under his direction (Fig. 10). Although the vizier occupies the high position in the Tinnis inscription, his status appears to be undermined by the surprisingly prestigious title awarded to the Abbasid administrator, a certain Shafiʿ, tasked with executing (*ʿala yaday*) the order. In a manner that far outstrips his inferior position in the chain of delegation, Shafiʿ is styled "client of the Commander of the Faithful" (*mawla amir al-muʾminin*), similar to the Tulunid governor discussed above. Earlier scholars posited that Shafiʿ was a factory supervisor of a tiraz workshop in Tinnis, but as such, he never could have used this title. Historical sources show that he was in fact an officer in the central administration and a military commander, a non-Arab who had entered service as a slave.[19] In some inscriptions, Shafiʿ is further honored with the title *al-muqtadiri*, indicating that he enjoyed a bond with the caliph that was perhaps much closer than his honorific *mawla amir al-muʾminin* alone would suggest — or that his elevated titles are a projection altogether, rather than a reflection of true status. Either

way, they were deployed as a way of jockeying for power at the heart of the Abbasid central government. These two textiles provide evidence that orders for tiraz, as well as the composition of their inscriptions, were tightly controlled and monitored by the central government, and that the real powers behind these requisitions were high-ranking administrators of the *diwan*, the office of government, who saw in these texts a way to promote their own social status within the court hierarchy.

After al-Muqtadir's reign ended in 932, Abbasid hegemony continued to disintegrate, and Egypt returned to a semi-autonomous state. First in 933 and then again in 935, Caliph al-Radi (r. 934–940) appointed a Turkish mamluk (slave) named Muhammad ibn Tughj al-Ikhshid as governor of Egypt.[20] Having previously governed Damascus, Muhammad ibn Tughj commanded an army with which he successfully invaded Egypt by land and sea in 935. The title al-Ikhshid, a Persian honorific referring to the ancient king of Farghana (a province in eastern Iran), was awarded to him by the caliph in 939, and in 944 he was granted a hereditary governorship over Egypt, Syria, and the Hijaz that endured for almost thirty years.

A tiraz textile in the Museum of Fine Arts, Boston (cat. 14) demonstrates that Ikhshidid governors maintained nominal allegiance to the caliphate, but in subtle ways it also reveals Egypt's increasing separation from the Abbasid realm. It was manufactured in a private tiraz workshop in the Nile delta city of Shata in 350/961–62, while Muhammad ibn Tughj's younger son, Abu al-Hasan ʿAli (r. 961–966), was governor of Egypt. The inscription names the reigning Abbasid caliph, al-Mutiʿ li-Allah (r. 946–974), and unlike the Tulunid tiraz omits the name of the Egyptian governor. The ordering of the textile is instead ascribed to a vizier, although he is not named, and the execution of the order is attributed to a certain Faʾiz, who is again given the prestigious title *mawla amir al-muʾminin*. Thus, the procedure of procurement is credited in a fashion that suggests a close relationship between central government and provincial place of manufacture. The reality was far from it. State affairs in Egypt at this time were run by the Ethiopian eunuch Abu al-Misk Kafur (905–968), who had been bought by Muhammad ibn Tughj in 923 and promoted to the rank of provincial vizier in 946.[21] It seems likely that the unnamed vizier mentioned in the tiraz inscription was not an Abbasid administrator but Kafur himself, maintaining through anonymity the appearance of a close alliance with the Abbasid

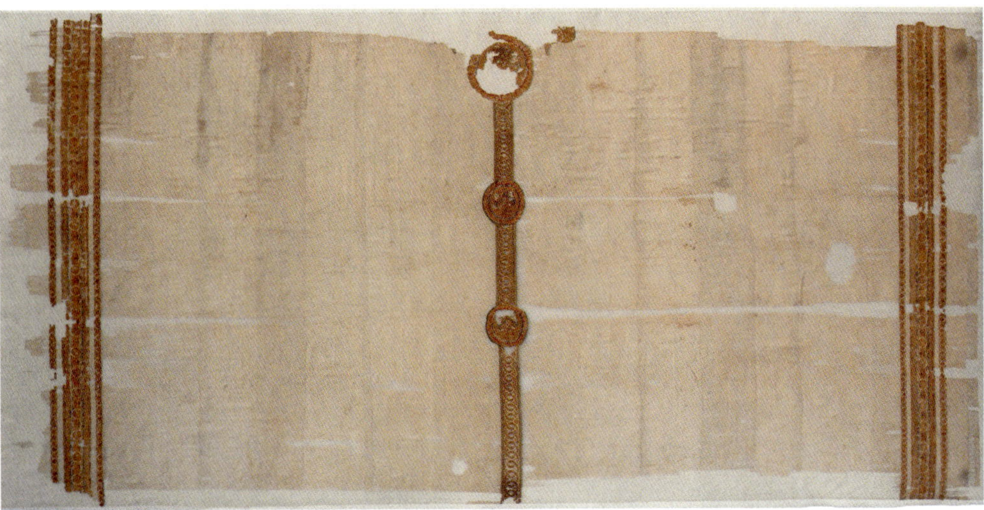

Fig. 11 The Veil of Saint Anne, Lower Egypt, private tiraz workshop in Damietta, 489/1096–97 or 490/1097–98. Silk tapestry on linen, 310 × 150 cm. Church of St. Anne, Apt, France.

caliphate. Unlike the aforementioned Shafiʿ, whose biography shows that he worked for the central government in Baghdad, Faʾiz was probably an administrator working in the Egyptian administration, whose grand title, though perhaps awarded to him from Baghdad, was more likely bestowed by Kafur himself, usurping caliphal authority.

Superficially, the inscription on the MFA textile looks very similar to the three Abbasid era tiraz discussed immediately above, but it signals a significant departure in that it was rendered in tapestry, a technique favored in Egypt since antiquity (see p. 53). By contrast, embroidery appears to have been an eastern technique made fashionable in Egypt under Abbasid rule, which lasted only briefly after the MFA textile was made. Kafur died in 968, and the following year Egypt fell to the Fatimids, a dynasty from North Africa, thus cutting Egypt's ties with what was left of the Abbasid caliphate.

FATIMID TIRAZ

The Fatimids belonged to the Ismaʿili branch of Shiʿa Islam and traced their ancestry back to Fatima, daughter of the Prophet Muhammad. Under the first Fatimid caliph, al-Mahdi (r. 909–934), they established a counter-caliphate in North Africa, thus challenging the Sunni Abbasids. In 969, the army of Fatimid caliph al-Muʿizz (r. 953–975) conquered Egypt and formed a new capital, al-Qahira (Cairo). The caliphate remained stable until the 1020s, when the multiethnic nature of the Fatimid army gave rise to infighting among the soldiers, culminating eventually in civil war. During that initial period of stability, Egypt became a powerful political and economic player in its own right in the Mediterranean and the Near East. The Fatimid court exerted significant cultural influence over the arts and sciences throughout the Mediterranean region and was famous for luxuries procured from faraway lands. Only when the Fatimid treasury was plundered by mutinous soldiers demanding payment of salaries in 1068–69 did the immense wealth of the caliphs become known.[22] The treasuries were subsequently opened and their contents sold on the open market. It is very likely that many of the extant textiles from Egypt came into circulation during this period. Two important Fatimid tiraz textiles inscribed with the name and titles of Caliph al-Mustaʿli (r. 1094–1101) — the so-called Veil of Saint Anne, made in Damietta in 489/1096–97 or 490/1097–98 (Fig. 11), and the so-called Suaire de Cadouin — were brought to France by Crusaders who must have acquired them in the Holy Land during or shortly after the First Crusade (1095–99).[23] Others were used as shrouds in Egyptian burials in the later Fatimid and Ayyubid (1169–1250) periods, as discussed below.

When one looks at the content of Fatimid tiraz inscriptions, it becomes clear that previously established administrative traditions carried on, yet at the same time, decisive changes reflecting a shift in the religious climate were introduced. Three Fatimid textiles in the Harvard exhibition, from the reigns of al-Muʿizz (cat. 15), al-ʿAziz (r. 975–996; cat. 16), and al-Hakim (r. 996–1021; cat. 17), allude to the caliphs within the context of their ancestry and their special relationship to God. The inscriptions go beyond their administrative nature to record and embrace a level of religiosity not seen in Abbasid tiraz. The Fatimid caliphs are described as "friends of God" (*wali Allah*) in addition to being "servants of God" (*ʿabd Allah*). The inscriptions, furthermore, make mention of the "pure forefathers" (*al-aʾimma al-tahirin*; Fig. 12), the "people of the House" (*ahl al-bayt*), and "proximate victory" (*futuh qaribun*), all references to the claim that the Fatimids descended from the Prophet Muhammad's bloodline or to their ambition of conquering the holy places of Mecca and Medina.

However, just like Abbasid tiraz inscriptions, Fatimid ones also manifest a caliph's authority to rule and his administrators' right to issue orders for procurement on his behalf. The textile made during the reign of al-ʿAziz mentions his vizier, Abu al-Faraj Yaʿqub bin Yusuf ibn Killis (930–991), who was descended from a Jewish family in Baghdad and had previously served under the Ikhshidid governors of Egypt. Ibn Killis was a close companion of al-ʿAziz, and this is reflected in the inscription, where he is referred to by name. In addition to naming al-Hakim, the later textile offers a rare variant by mentioning the heir apparent (*wali ʿahd al-muslimin*), Abu al-Qasim ʿAbd al-Rahim ibn Ilyas. A great-grandson of al-Mahdi and cousin of al-Hakim, ʿAbd al-Rahim was installed by al-Hakim as his successor to the caliphate and de facto co-regent in 404/1013–14. However, when al-Hakim disappeared on the night of 27 Shawwal 411/February 13, 1021, his sister Sitt al-Mulk declared her protégé Abu al-Hasan ʿAli, son of al-Hakim's wife Ruqayya, as the new caliph al-Zahir (r. 1021–1036), and just over one month later had her cousin ʿAbd al-Rahim arrested in Damascus and transferred to a dungeon in Cairo, where he died (most likely murdered).

As caliphs, Fatimid rulers were revered not only as temporal leaders of the Muslim community but also as imams appointed by God himself and imbued with infallible secret knowledge derived from their kinship with the Prophet's family (*ahl al-bayt*). This relationship ensured their spiritual and physical purity and allowed their participation in the names and attributes of God, putting an imam on a plane of existence far beyond that of a normal believer. Indeed, according to Ismaʿili doctrine, an imam was a source of God's blessing and could intercede on behalf of believers on the Day of Judgment — an important point to remember when interpreting the use of Fatimid tiraz in burials.

Fig. 12 Detail of cat. 16.

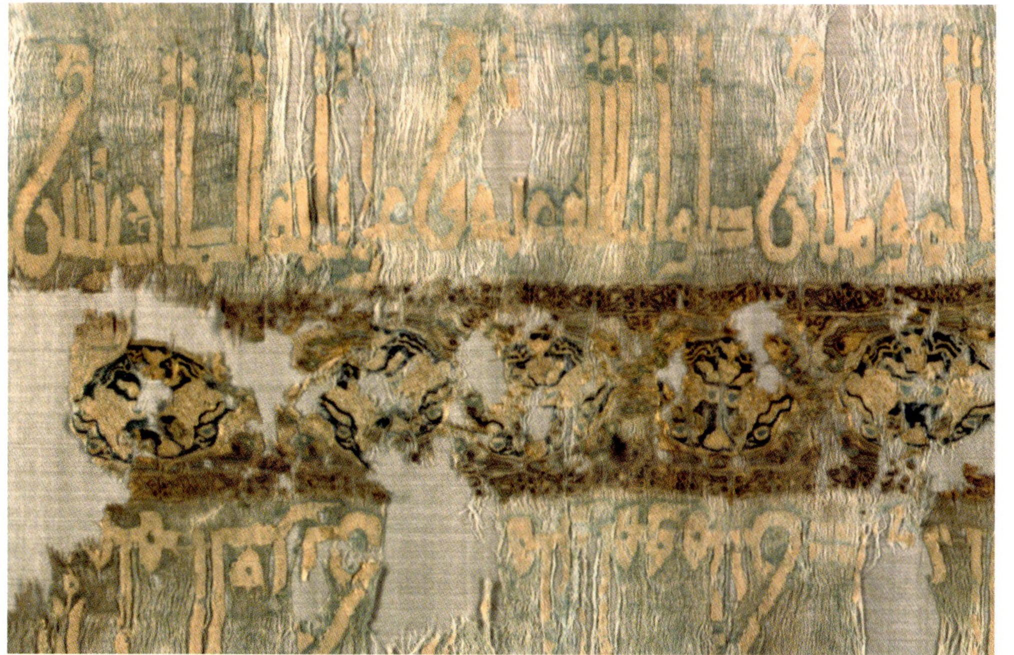

TEXT AS BENEDICTION

Fatimid tiraz inscriptions contained many religious components that underlined the ancestral link of the dynasty to the Prophet Muhammad's family. A Dumbarton Oaks textile (cat. 37) carries an inscription invoking God's help for Caliph al-Hakim and confers God's blessings upon him and his father al-ʿAziz, as well as their forefathers, to satisfy them until the Day of Judgment. In fact, much of Fatimid theological doctrine was concerned with the Day of Judgment and the imams' powers of intercession. Two passages by Fatimid theologian Qadi al-Nuʿman (d. 974) relating statements by al-Muʿizz mention that Fatimid imams were God's portals and mediators who could absolve sins.[24] An anecdote recorded in the biography of al-Muʿizz's secretary Jawdhar describes a letter in which he asked the caliph for one of his garments so that he could use it as his burial shroud, on account of its sacral properties. Al-Muʿizz sent him elaborate outfits owned by the four caliphs under whom Jawdhar had served, along with a note in which he stressed the blessing attached to the gift and the hope that Jawdhar would visit Mecca and the Prophet's grave in Medina in the afterlife.[25] In doing so, al-Muʿizz followed the precedent of the Prophet Muhammad and members of his family who, as told in hadith literature, shared their own clothes with close companions to be used as shrouds.[26]

The majority of surviving tiraz textiles are shrouds or funerary garments excavated from graves, first at the instigation of art dealers (see Mary McWilliams's essay in this volume) and later by the Egyptian Antiquities Organization (Fig. 13). In both circumstances, the methods of excavation lacked the rigor of modern archaeological science. Valuable data concerning findspots, the manner of wrapping the corpse, and the environment of deposition have been lost forever. Only within the last thirty years have a number of scientific excavations been able to contribute important new data. From 1992 to 1994, a French team of archaeologists under the leadership of Roland-Pierre Gayraud excavated a mausoleum in the Southern Cemetery of Cairo in an area called Istabl ʿAntar, an Abbasid necropolis.[27] The mausoleum could be associated with the Fatimid dynasty: a foundation stone names Taghrid, wife of al-Muʿizz. When the caliph moved from his base in Mahdia in North Africa to Cairo, he brought with him coffins containing the remains of his three predecessors and other important members of the dynasty.[28] In one

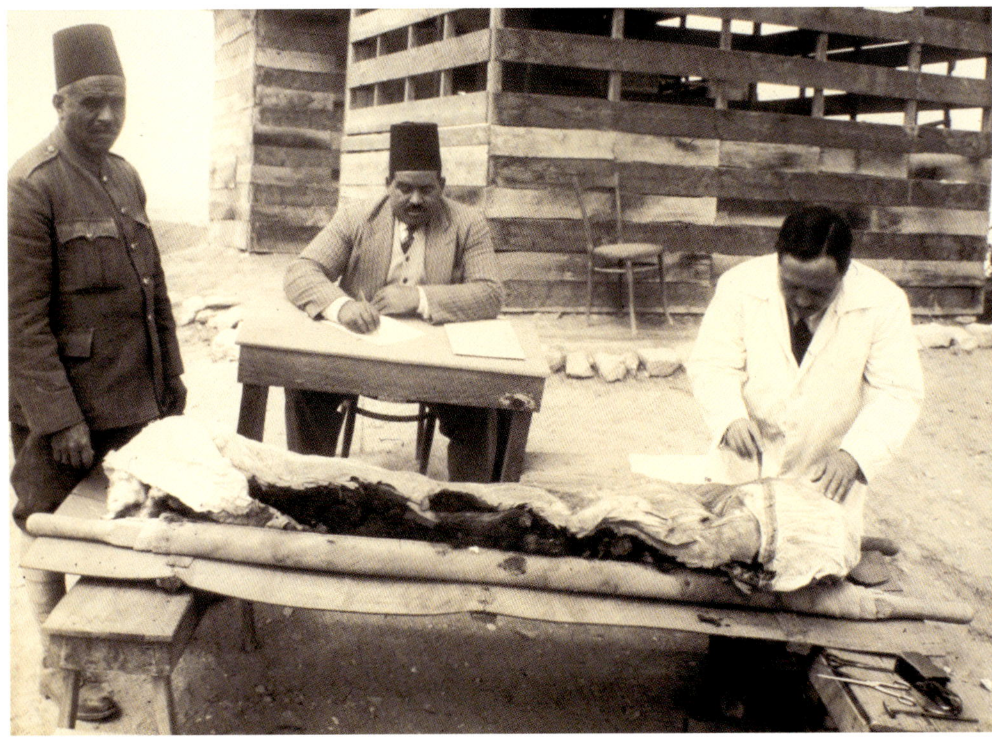

of the tombs, the team excavated a body enveloped in a mat and wrapped tightly in a sequence of sheets with tiraz bands (Fig. 14).[29] In this instance, the various burial cloths appeared to have been made for both Abbasid and Fatimid regimes. The uppermost shroud comprised a fabric of silk and cotton (*mulham*) produced in Iraq or Khurasan and was embroidered in dark-blue chain stitch with an inscription dated to 932–33 (see cat. 10 for similarly styled embroidery). Another layer carried a tapestry band inscribed with the *kunya* (given name) Maʿad, which could point to either al-Muʿizz or al-Mustansir (r. 1036–1094).[30] Both inscriptions were placed so that they encircled the head of the deceased.

This find raised many questions, particularly how one might now interpret the archaeological context of the massive numbers of surviving inscribed textiles. Perhaps tiraz inscriptions manifested the physical presence of the Fatimid imam-caliphs as carriers and dispensers of divine blessing. The names and titles of the caliphs, invocations of their relationship to God and the family of the Prophet, would have made these textiles mediators of caliphal blessing, and so too would the fact that the textiles once belonged to the caliph's treasury or were gifted by him through his administration, like those bestowed by al-Muʿizz on his secretary.

In the 1990s, excavations by a Polish team of archaeologists at a Christian monastery at Naqlun, in the Fayyum Oasis,

added another layer of context for the presence of inscribed textiles in medieval burials.[31] The individuals buried there — both male and female, including a mother and small child — were wrapped in linen sheets decorated with tapestry-woven and embroidered bands, some with epigraphic designs, others only zoomorphic. The textiles are generally of very fine quality and relate in type to examples in the Cleveland Museum of Art (cats. 18, 23) and Museum of Fine Arts, Boston (cat. 19). The burials were largely contained in coffins, some of which were themselves wrapped in inscribed sheets (Fig. 15).[32] The earliest firmly datable textiles found at Naqlun were created during the reigns of al-Hakim and his successor, al-Zahir.[33] Most of the tiraz bands, however, could be dated to around 1050–1150. The bodies were accompanied by grave goods, including crosses clearly identifying them as Christian, but also necklaces comprised of Abbasid silver dirhams.[34]

These finds help us see that inscribed textiles were revered as luxury items by different social groups. Perhaps they had played a role in the lives of the deceased on whose bodies they were found and were cherished and kept safe to be used after death. For a follower of the Fatimids, the inscribed text would have been a link to the divine effulgence of the imam-caliph, a mediator of God's blessing and intercessor on the Day of Judgment. For a Christian, the inscriptions would not necessarily have had religious significance themselves but perhaps were indicators of how special, expensive, fashionable, and sought-after these textiles were. Furthermore, they show the extent to which the Christian population of Egypt had integrated with Muslim society by the time of the Fatimids, creating a unique Egyptian identity.

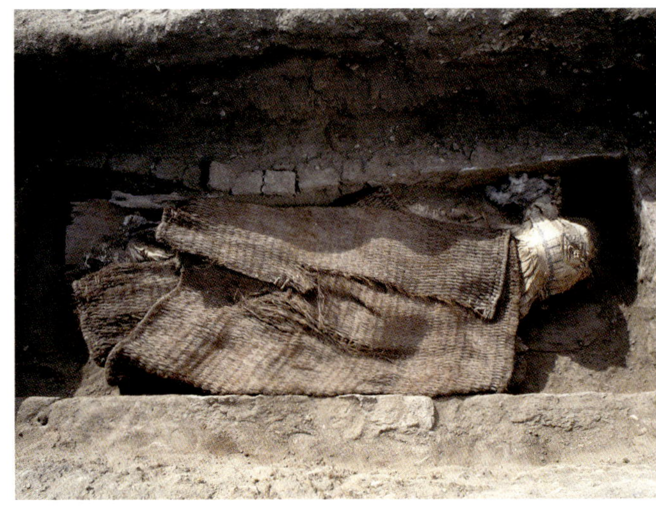

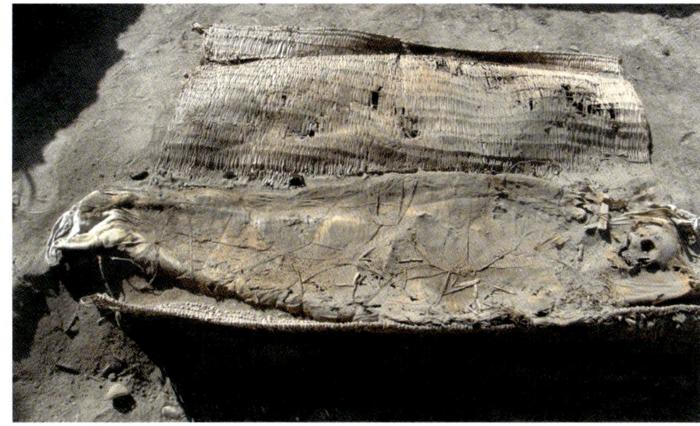

Fig. 15 Enshrouded corpse from a Christian cemetery in Naqlun, Fayyum, Upper Egypt, c. 11th–12th century.

1   For a general discussion of the topic, see Sokoly 2017, 275–99; for a summary of the scholarship, see Sokoly 2006. See also Stillman and Sanders 2000.

2   For two papyri at the Austrian National Library, Vienna, see Von Karabacek 1909, 24, P.II. No. 2163, inscribed *mimma amara* [. . .] *bi-'amalihi fi tir(az)*; Grohmann 1924, 199–200, no. 204 (illustrated as pl. 30a); and Von Karabacek 1909, 24, Per. Inv. No. Ar. P. 4057 (formerly P.III. No. 51), inscribed *fi tiraz (al-'far* [. . .]). Recent work on the epigraphy of papyri inscriptions published in Khan 1992 (at 37–38) suggests that these papyri were created in the seventh or first half of the eighth century, given that the final *ya* is extended backward underneath the word (for example, under *fi* in the last of the examples cited here). The inscription on an unglazed ceramic flask in the L. A. Mayer Memorial Museum, Jerusalem, mentions its manufacture in a tiraz workshop in Jurjan, possibly modern Gorgan in Iran (*baraka wa khayr li-sahibihi* [. . .] *ishrab haniyan mariyyan* [. . .] *mimma 'amala Muhammad* [. . .] *bi-tiraz Jurjan*). See Baer 1989, 85–86, Figs. 4–5, 17.

3   Rāġib 2009. The bilingual papyrus documents the receipt of a herd of sixty-five sheep by Islamic troops under the commander 'Abdallah bin Jabir from local Christian administrators at Heracleopolis in the Fayyum on 27 Jumada al-awwal 22/April 25, 643; for a comprehensive discussion of this topic, see Sijepestein 2007.

4   Day 1952; and Evans and Ratliff 2012, 238–41, cat. 173A–C. A recent article considers the textile fragments in more detail; see Cabrera-Lafuente and Rosser-Owen 2020.

5   Attempts at digital reconstruction based on the surviving fragments can be found in Evans and Ratliff 2012, 238–39; and Cabrera-Lafuente and Rosser-Owen 2020, 70–71.

6   Evans and Ratliff 2012, 239.

7   Earlier scholars interpreted the name of the dedicatee as Samu'il ibn Musa; see Marzouk 1954. The scholarship that has revised "Musa" to "Murqus" includes 'Abbās Muḥammad Salīm 1997, 65–66, Figs. 22–25; and Van der Vliet 2006, 32n41. Van der Vliet's reading of a *ra* instead of *waw*, *qaf* instead of *sad*, and *sin* instead of a final *ya* can be confirmed by the present author.

8   'Abbās Muḥammad Salīm 1997, 65–66, Figs. 22–25.

9   David-Weill 1957, 74–76, pls. 2–4; and Durand and Rettig 2002, 167–68, 198–99, cat. 165.

10   Grohmann 1971, 112bn1, pl. 23, Fig. 1.

11   See Van der Vliet 2006, 33–34, where the deployment of Coptic/Greek bilingual inscriptions is discussed further.

12   Ibid., 36–37. The practice of a father giving textiles to his sons or daughters is recorded in the wealth of documents from the Cairo Genizah. For more on this custom in both Christian and Jewish communities in Egypt, see Elizabeth Dospěl Williams's essay in this volume and the references cited therein.

13   In 762, twelve years after the Abbasid revolt against the Umayyads, Abbasid caliph al-Mansur (r. 754–775) moved the central government from Damascus to the newly founded capital Baghdad (then Madinat al-Salam). The period of almost a hundred years that followed witnessed a flourishing in architecture, arts and sciences, diplomacy, and trade due to Abbasid patronage that would shape Islamic culture for centuries to come. In 836, however, Caliph al-Mu'tasim (r. 833–842) decided to relocate the seat of the caliphate to the recently established city of Samarra, some 125 kilometers north of Baghdad. It remained the Abbasid capital for almost sixty years, until 892, when Caliph al-Mu'tadid (r. 892–902) moved the government to Baghdad once again.

14   A comparable example in terms of cut and decoration is a long linen shirt in the Al-Sabah Collection in Kuwait (LNS 57 T).

15   Fa'iq, a *mawla* of Khumarawayh ibn Tulun, is called *al-khadim* in al-Kindi's work on the governors and judges of Egypt. See al-Kindī, Guest, and al-'Asqalānī 1912, 237, 242, 246, 517; and Sokoly 2002, III, app. 59, no. 11.

16   The term *mawla* (client) originates from the early Islamic legal concept of *wala'* (proximity) and in later Islam designates an unequal relationship between a master or patron on the one hand and a freedman, protégé, or client on the other. See Crone 1991, 874.

17   Zetterstéen and Bosworth 1997.

18   It was indeed the Abbasid vizier Ibn Muqla (886–940) who is credited with reforming the Arabic script to embrace a system of proportion based on the size of a reed pen's nib.

19   For a biography of Shafi' al-Muqtadiri, see Sokoly 2002, III, app. 59, no. 18.

20   Bacharach 1993.

21   Ehrenkreutz 1997, 418–19.

22   For a discussion of this event as told in historical literary sources, see Kahle 1935.

23   Cornu 1999a, 331–37; and Cornu 1999b.

24   Sokoly 2017, 294–95.

25   Ibid., 285; see also Bloom 1985, 32, 37, no. 112.

26   Sokoly 2017, 286; see also Halevi 2007, 106–13.

27   Gayraud, Björnesjö, and Speiser 1994; and Gayraud et al. 1995.

28   Gayraud suggested that the caliph and his predecessors were buried in a mausoleum called Turbat al-Za'faran, while members of the family were subsequently buried at Istabl 'Antar, where they remained until the graves were plundered and mostly destroyed during al-Mustansir's reign (1036–1094).

29   Gayraud et al. 1995, 6–10; and Gayraud 2002, 172–73. For further discussion, see Sokoly 2017, 278–88.

30   Gayraud et al. 1995, 8, 19, Figs. 16–17; for further discussion, see Sokoly 2017, 288.

31   Godlewski 2002, 100–104.

32   Godlewski 2004, 144, Fig. 3; and Godlewski 2011, 474, Fig. 5.

33   Helmecke 2004, 196–97, Figs. 1–2; and Godlewski 2004, 142–43, Figs. 1–2.

34   Godlewski 2014, 186, Fig. 15; and Godlewski 2004, 145, Fig. 4.

Adoption, Adaptation, Reinterpretation: Inscribed Textiles in Medieval Egypt's Christian and Jewish Communities

Because the majority of surviving tiraz textiles from medieval Egypt name caliphs, are written in Arabic, and feature Islamic phrases and prayers, we tend to think first of their Muslim makers and users. Yet Christian and Jewish communities thrived in Egypt for centuries before and after the spread of Islam in the seventh century, and these groups, too, greatly valued tiraz. Scholars long viewed tiraz as a Muslim innovation introduced to Egyptian society, with the underlying idea that local communities had minimal cultural context for inscribed textiles before the arrival of Islam.[1] Following this logic, it would be easy to assume that Christians and Jews using the textiles in the later medieval period were imitating the practices of their Muslim neighbors.

However, historical images, texts, and objects present a different picture of the appreciation for tiraz among Egypt's Christian and Jewish communities. The practice of inscribing textiles with words and phrases can indeed be traced in late Roman and Byzantine Egypt (c. 3rd–7th century), allowing us to perceive continuities with past traditions in medieval examples while at the same time recognizing the novelty of Islamic tiraz.[2] As the institution of tiraz became ever more established in Egypt in the medieval period, Christian and Jewish uses of inscribed fabrics became at once reactionary

and adaptive, a point of cultural convergence and a marker of difference. These complexities reflect the status of Christian and Jewish communities in medieval Egypt more generally, as textiles present a microcosm of broader attitudes about the processes of cultural adoption, adaptation, and reinterpretation at the heart of these groups' interactions with the Muslim population.

INSCRIBING AND DESCRIBING

Textiles from late antique and Byzantine Egypt are usually identified in art historical scholarship as "Coptic," though it is difficult at times to determine whether Copts were uniquely responsible for the manufacture of such artifacts. While pieces inscribed in Greek and Coptic account for only a small portion of late antique and Byzantine textiles, one can surmise that inscribed fabrics represented a meaningful subset of textile production at the time. These include examples of all sorts: garments and furnishings in tapestry weave and silk, sometimes even inscribed in pen ink.[3] Scholars have presented case studies of specific collections or examples; to date, however, there has been no comprehensive consideration of evidence for inscribed textiles in Egypt before the arrival of Arabic tiraz. Yet a survey of the inscriptions on these textiles — and a consideration of the relationships between the text and images they present — is essential background for understanding the range of associations embedded in Egyptian culture in the centuries immediately preceding the arrival of Islam.

Inscriptions on late antique and Byzantine textiles from Egypt tend to be limited to single words or simple phrases; extended biblical quotations appear only rarely.[4] Most common are brief inscriptions that identify mythological figures, saints, or allegorical figures. For example, numerous representations of biblical scenes survive on late antique and Byzantine

Opposite: Detail of cat. 28.

Fig. 1 Tunic fragment showing David presented to Saul, Egypt, 7th–8th century. Linen and wool, tapestry weave, 64.5 × 25.8 cm. Walters Art Museum, Baltimore, Museum purchase, 1977, 83.728.

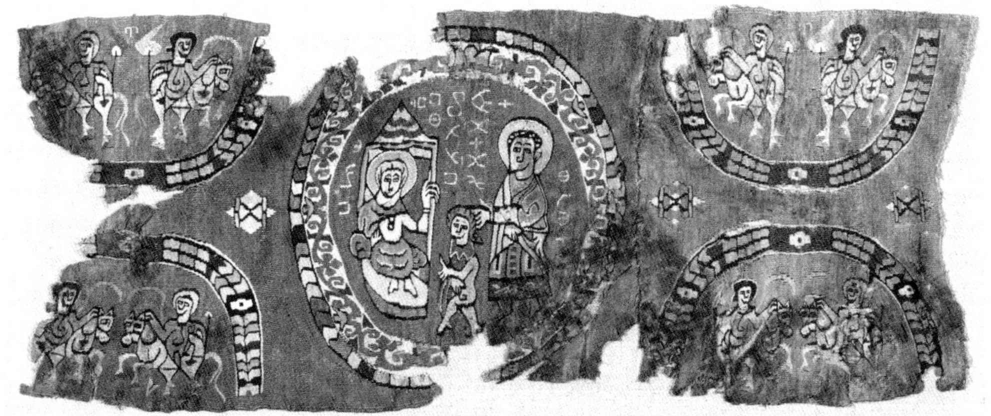

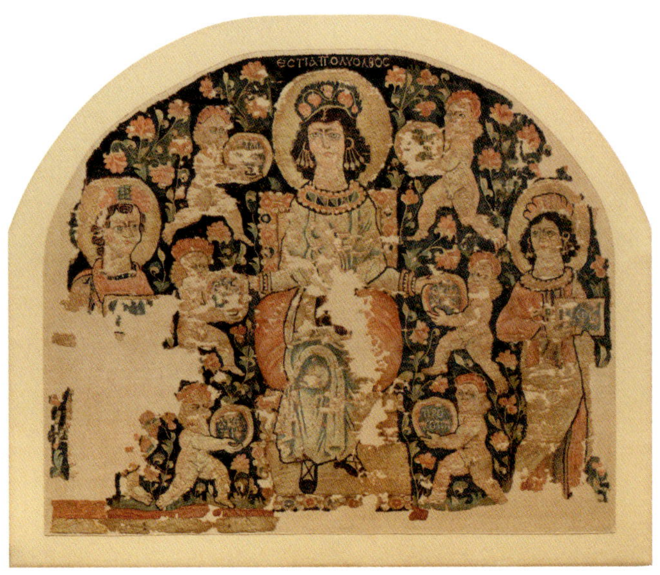

Fig. 2 Hanging with Hestia Polyolbus, Egypt, c. 6th century. Wool, tapestry weave, 114.5 × 138 cm. Dumbarton Oaks Research Library and Collection, Washington, D.C., BZ.1929.1.

Fig. 3 Sleeve band with personification of Gaea, inscribed "George," Egypt, 6th–9th century. Wool and linen, tapestry weave, 32.5 × 17.4 cm. Harvard Art Museums/Arthur M. Sackler Museum, Gift of Charles Bain Hoyt, 1931.43.

textiles, often labeled with basic information about the figures. A group of such textiles featuring scenes set in roundels — usually interpreted as depictions of the life of David — survive in bands that once bordered tunics (Fig. 1).[5] Inscriptions could also appear on furnishing textiles, as in a unique extant example of a monumental sixth-century hanging that represents the ancient goddess of the hearth, Hestia. The regal figure is labeled simply but boldly in Greek, while tiny genii offer the goddess plates or disks inscribed with attributes or blessings, such as wealth, mirth, and virtue (Fig. 2).[6] In this first category of inscribed textiles, then, the words directly describe the imagery they accompany. We might therefore understand these inscriptions as part of established iconographic traditions that deploy similar strategies of labeling — that of wall paintings, for example, or wooden icons.

A second category of inscribed late antique and Byzantine textiles features protective or aspirational messages, often single words or short phrases. A fourth- or fifth-century fragment depicting a flowering tree (cat. 25), for instance, includes the Greek word *EUPHORIA* (fertility or flourish) down the center of the tree's trunk. In this textile, the inscription is incorporated into the imagery itself, rendering the tree a visual embodiment of the otherwise abstract concepts of growth and rejuvenation. Such blessings indeed appear on late antique and Byzantine furnishings and garments alike. A particularly interesting example of a large-format cover dating to the fifth or sixth century and now in the Harvard Art Museums (cat. 24) includes Greek inscriptions at its ends, possibly the name of its owner. Ankh crosses that frame the writing amplify the blessings and protection conveyed by the words themselves.

Individuals' names are not uncommon on late antique and Byzantine textiles. A sixth- to ninth-century sleeve band from a tunic, completed in tapestry weave, features a personification of the earth goddess Gaea, along with an inscription in Greek naming "George" (Fig. 3). Perhaps the most intriguing late antique textiles bearing names are two-toned silks from the Byzantine period, with horsemen appearing below the names "Zachariah" and "Joseph" in Greek (Fig. 4).[7] These fragments are associated with Akhmim, in Upper Egypt, and can be dated to the early Islamic period thanks to their stylistic and technical similarities with Arabic-inscribed textiles. It is difficult to tell the relationship between word and image in these examples. It seems unlikely that the inscriptions relate in a straightforward manner to their accompanying images: George does not correspond in any obvious way to Gaea, for instance, and the names Zachariah and Joseph are interchangeable across textiles. It may be that the inscriptions reference the wearer, though this is also highly speculative, since the range of names is very limited. Another possibility is that the names refer to the maker or weaver, as a kind of logo or label that conveyed meaningful information about production.

In the broadest sense, however, such a precise relationship of image and text may have been beside the point. Compare, for one, the sleeve band depicting Gaea in the

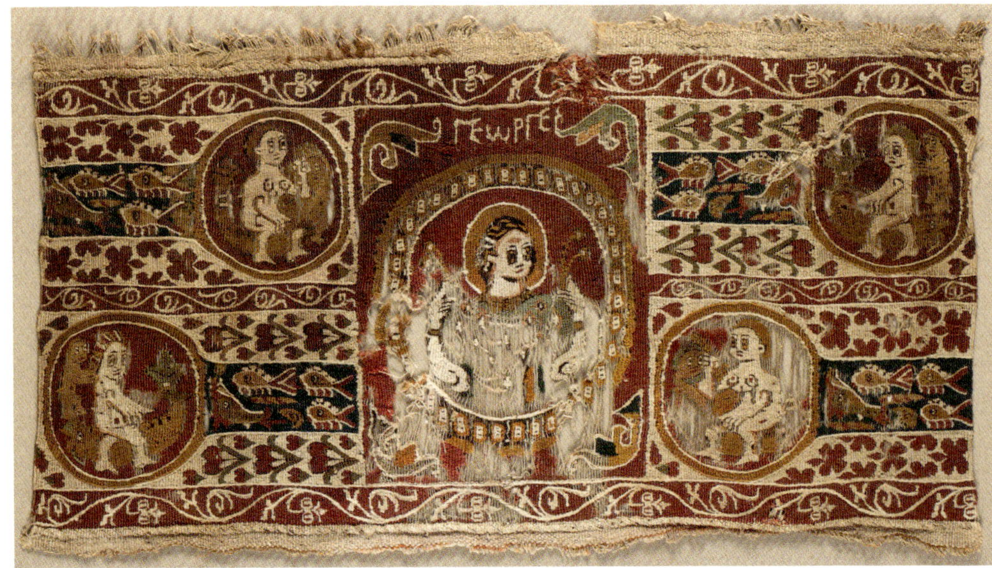

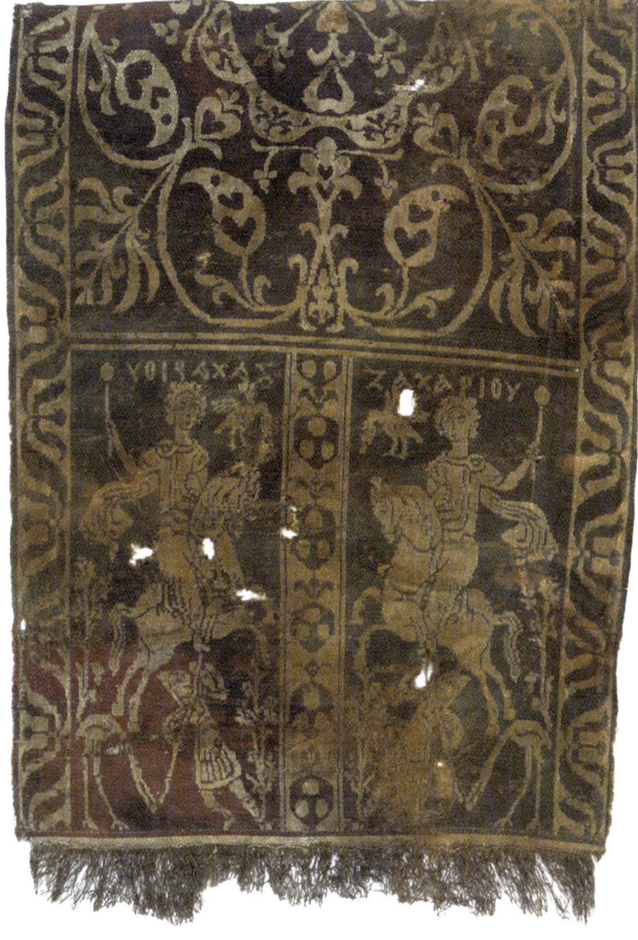

example above with a fragment of similar design now in the Dumbarton Oaks collection (Fig. 5).[8] In place of the elegantly rendered Gaea, an awkward figure now stares out at the viewer with wide, dark-rimmed eyes. Squiggly beige lines above the figure's shoulders and running top to bottom in the space immediately to the left recall letters, though their highly abstracted forms lack specificity. The comparison of these two tunic sleeve bands indicates that legibility itself was perhaps not entirely necessary to a late antique viewer; instead, the mere suggestion of an inscription seems to have been enough to convey protective powers or prestige, among other possible meanings.[9]

Taken as a whole, this survey of inscribed textiles in late antique and Byzantine Egypt leads us to appreciate the fertile ground in which the later traditions of tiraz took root. First, late antique and Byzantine Egyptians were accustomed to seeing script-bearing textiles and were therefore attuned to a wide range of associations conveyed by these fabrics. The relatively small numbers of textiles with truly legible inscriptions suggest that they were considered special or unusual, and perhaps as a result particularly valuable. Second, with the exception of very few embroideries and penned inscriptions, the vast majority of texts on late antique textiles were inscribed as part of the weaving process itself and were thus integral to the structure of the fabric. This means that words and phrases were imagined into the weaving process from the start, copied as part of a predetermined design rather than in the spontaneous gesture of an individual weaver. Finally, we can guess that late antique and Byzantine Egyptians did not necessarily expect image and text to correspond directly. While the prominent use of labeling in depictions of holy figures or mythological beings shows an appreciation for the one-to-one relationship of image and text, in other examples it is apparent that the very hint of legibility was sufficient in itself. These trends carry through to the Islamic period, suggesting that the phenomenon of inscribing textiles popularized in tiraz was not entirely alien to Egyptians, but rather capitalized on and drew from longstanding attitudes about the relationship between sign and meaning, material and message, language and power.[10]

A MESSAGE TO THE COMMUNITY

Although there was an established tradition of inscribed textiles in late antique and Byzantine Egypt, Islamic-era tiraz textiles were indeed novel on many accounts: earlier examples never name specific rulers, rarely include scriptural quotations, and do not feature dates, all of which are innovations of tiraz. The adoption and adaptation of Islamic practices by medieval Egypt's subordinate Christian and Jewish communities must thus be situated as part of broader cultural shifts,

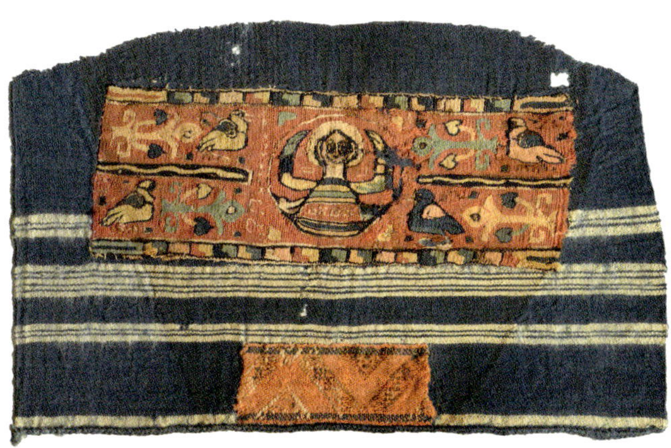

particularly in how these groups defined and presented their individual and group identities within Muslim society. Those practicing Christianity and Judaism (themselves multifarious faiths with a spectrum of beliefs) were considered "protected people" (*ahl al-dhimma*, or dhimmis) in recognition of their monotheism and adherence to scriptural traditions. As a result, these groups were not required to convert to Islam. It is tempting to view this quasi-acceptance of the dhimmis as a kind of religious tolerance or coexistence as we understand these terms today. In practice, however, Christians and Jews in Muslim Egypt were subjected to numerous rules and regulations: dhimmis were required to pay a penalty tax and adhere to ordinances controlling aspects of their daily life. Dress, too, was regulated, as dhimmis were expected to wear different colors than Muslims, though the extent to which such laws were enacted remains unclear.[11]

Visual, material, and textual evidence for the use and production of tiraz by Christians and Jews indeed reflects some of the complexities of living as a dhimmi in a predominantly Muslim society. On the one hand, the sheer cultural force of tiraz was such that Christian and Jewish communities in Egypt used these textiles in a manner similar to their Muslim neighbors in daily dress, interior decor, and even burial garb. The association of tiraz with courtly status, for example, seems to have been a particularly powerful draw among Egypt's non-Muslims. Eloquent testimony to the use of tiraz among dhimmis is found in the shreds of documents preserved in the attic of a synagogue in Cairo, the so-called Cairo Genizah. The items in this hoard, some dating to the eleventh and twelfth centuries, are written in a variety of languages, including Hebrew and Judeo-Arabic, thus giving a vivid sense of Jewish life around the medieval Mediterranean (cat. 31). The texts include many references to inscribed textiles. Jewish bridal dowries, for instance, specifically mention *khilaʿ* (robes of honor, singular *khilʿa*) as some of the most valuable garments in a woman's possession.[12] The Genizah texts also preserve numerous records of Jewish traders across the Mediterranean, showing the purchase and sale of tiraz over vast distances: in one particularly intriguing example dating to the twelfth century, a merchant in India ordered from Egypt a turban with his son's name written on it.[13] References to orders for Egyptian-made prayer shawls and other garments inscribed with biblical verses in Hebrew also appear scattered throughout the Genizah documents, though the practice is so far known only from these textual sources.[14]

If texts like those found in the Genizah attest to the adoption of tiraz among Egypt's Jewish communities, significant archaeological evidence points to its popularity among medieval Christians as well. The graves at Naqlun, a Christian necropolis with burials from roughly the tenth to the thirteenth century, reveal much about how Egyptian Christians wore and used tiraz (see also Jochen Sokoly's essay in this volume).[15] The textiles found in these graves compare closely to those found in Egypt's Muslim cemeteries, a testimony to the shared popularity of inscribed textiles among Christians and Muslims alike. Arabic tiraz appeared in graves of individuals of all ages — a middle-aged man, a young mother with her toddler and newborn, and an elderly woman, to name only a few.[16] The exceptional fineness of the woven linen and silk examples demonstrates that Christians had access to the highest quality tiraz, a reflection perhaps of their participation in (or aspirations to join) elite society. The graves thus intimately and poignantly testify to the Christian use of tiraz in life and death, across age, gender, and social status.[17]

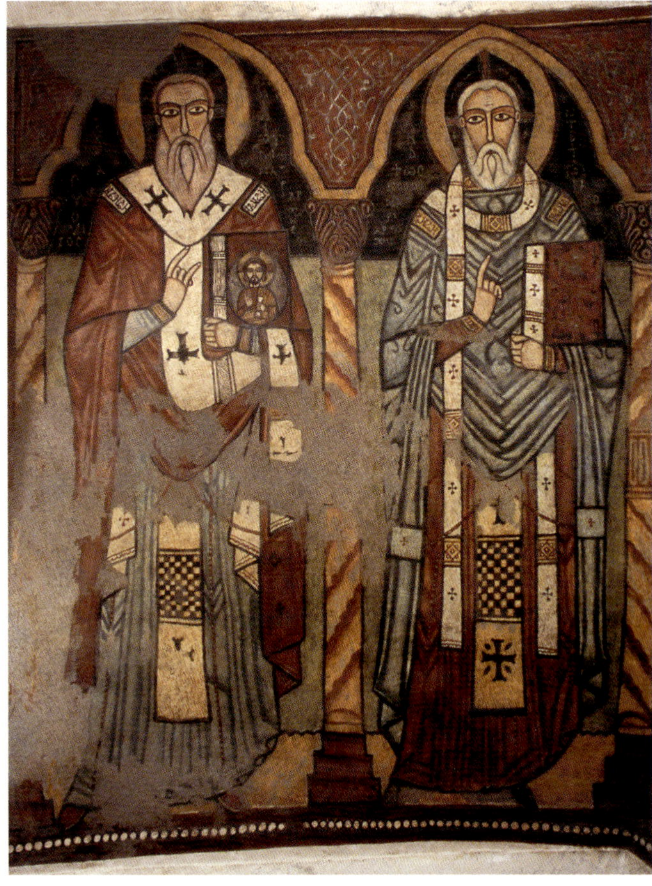

Fig. 6 Wall painting of Severus of Antioch and Dioscorus of Alexandria, Egypt, 1232–33. Secco. Monastery of Saint Anthony by the Red Sea, ADP/ SA 11S 98.

At first glance, the texts from the Cairo Genizah and the graves at Naqlun suggest a certain détente, a sharing of cultural practices despite religious difference. The powerful allure of luxury goods like tiraz, in this interpretation, would have been enough to unite the varied communities. In reality, dhimmis needed to constantly negotiate their positions in Muslim society. Textual, visual, and archaeological records are valuable witnesses to this fraught cultural interaction: we see that the Arabic-inscribed tiraz were objects not only to be desired by dhimmi communities, but also to be replicated and adapted as a vehicle for differentiating themselves from the dominant culture.

The thirteenth-century wall paintings at the Monastery of Saint Anthony by the Red Sea testify to the twin poles of integration and separation that characterized medieval Christian communities in the Middle East.[18] These brightly hued paintings are exceptional in that they are associated with an artist, named Theodore, and given a precise date, 1232–33. The works evince the wealth of the community: the church was repainted several times over a short period, and the quality of the paintings is very high. They depict holy figures, biblical scenes, and the lives of saints, with a particular emphasis on popular warrior and monastic saints. Tiraz textiles appear in numerous depictions of historical bishops and patriarchs at the monastery: a painting of the early patriarchs Severus of Antioch and Dioscorus of Alexandria, for example, shows the saintly figures with bands of tiraz at their shoulders (Fig. 6).

This is an anachronistic detail for late antique ecclesiastics, of course, but its inclusion in these portraits speaks to the use of tiraz among contemporary Coptic priests.[19] Indeed, a portrait of the Coptic patriarch Mark III (investiture 1167–1189) in a Gospel book copied in 1180, during the priest's lifetime, in Damietta, Lower Egypt, portrays the bearded bishop wearing a hooded garment with bands prominently inscribed in Arabic at his shoulders (Fig. 7).[20] These images thus offer evidence for the incorporation of tiraz in ecclesiastical garb, possibly as a sign of rank. Visual depictions attesting to church use of tiraz are corroborated by the archaeological record: in the early twentieth century, a hoard of tiraz was discovered in a genizah in the monastery of Dabra Dammo in Tigray, northern Ethiopia, including rare Abbasid and Fatimid examples.[21] The textiles likely arrived there as gifts sent along the close-knit ecclesiastical channels that ran through Egypt; the portrait page depicting Mark III, for example, features

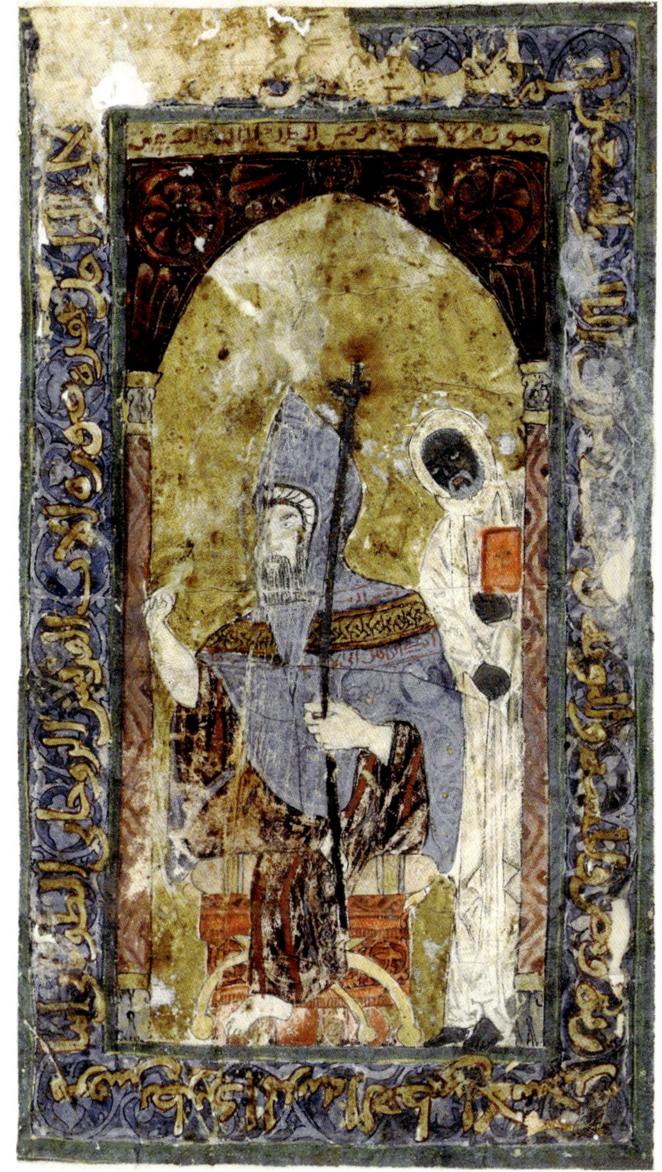

a dark-skinned acolyte possibly intended to represent an Ethiopian.[22] That the textiles were kept in the monastery's treasury and eventually ritually stored in a genizah suggests they were considered of particular value to the community.

At the same time, however, it is important to contextualize monastic or ecclesiastical admiration for tiraz within the broader religious and political realities faced by dhimmis in Muslim society. The wall paintings at Saint Anthony's were intended for a monastic community; warrior saints and monks were meant to inspire viewers to contemplate the struggles of the figures against spiritual oppression past and present.[23] There is some irony in the inclusion of such detailed visualizations of secular luxuries in the paintings of a monastery

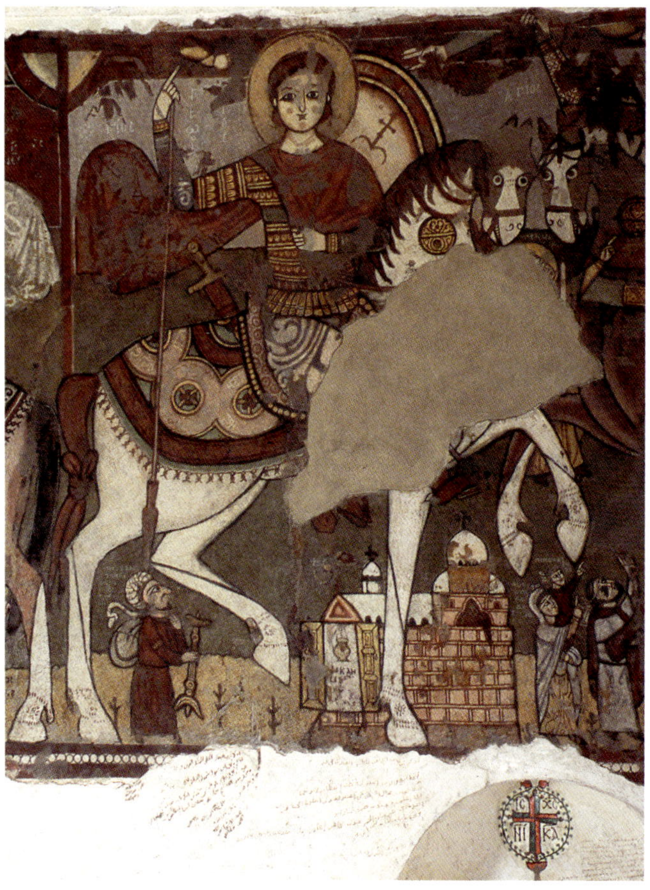

whose members were actively fighting for their spiritual souls and for the supremacy of their religious community. That tiraz inscriptions appear on the saddle cloths of numerous warrior saints, like George, seems significant: these Christian warriors battled historically for the faith, and the viewer is perhaps meant to understand that these beautiful young men are splendorous in the trappings of secular wealth and virtuous in their efforts to assert Christian legitimacy and even primacy (Fig. 8).

The tension between integration and distinction that characterized dhimmi status in medieval Egyptian society is perhaps best seen in the development of what might be called Christian tiraz. As Arabic tiraz gained in popularity, Coptic inscriptions on textiles became longer and more formulaic, emulating the tone and content of Muslim examples. In some instances, these Christian inscriptions are candid requests for God's help or direct biblical quotations. Because the Coptic inscriptions are frequently written in dialect and often feature individuals' names, it is even possible at times to identify specific owners and locations through comparison with

documentary texts (including tax receipts, letters, and the like). A fragment from a garment or furnishing fabric now in the Dumbarton Oaks collection, for instance, includes a prayer for the succor of a certain Viktor, son of Meus (cat. 27). The unusual name Meus can in turn be independently traced to a person mentioned on papyri and ostraca (clay pot sherds bearing text) from eighth-century Upper Egypt, in Djeme or Aphrodito.[24] Textiles inscribed in Coptic are rarely studied alongside quotidian texts like these, yet the comparison is invaluable in revealing patterns of use, production, and ownership.

By the ninth century, the increasingly regulated existence of dhimmis is apparent from changes in the production of inscribed textiles. It is around this time that a new kind of Christian tiraz developed, one featuring lengthier biblical inscriptions and sometimes even bilingual texts in Coptic and Arabic (see p. 22). The large size of many surviving examples stands out, and scholars often refer to the pieces as shawls.[25] Similarities in the textiles' technique, style, and overall aesthetic — dark-blue backgrounds, with red, green, and beige decoration in tapestry weave clustered at the short edges — are noteworthy. A few of the more complete fragments from this group include references to a private workshop (*tiraz al-khassa*) in Tutun, in the Fayyum, a site well known in the Middle Ages as a major producer of luxury textiles.[26]

These new developments in tiraz reveal much about the status of Christians in medieval Egyptian society. While some feature generic blessings and translate phrases in both Arabic and Coptic (see, for example, cats. 28–29), others declare more elaborate and contentious views. For instance, many feature psalms, which themselves often include statements about the struggle against powerful enemies and proclamations about just kingship or dominion. The relevance of such statements to Christian communities in medieval Egypt is self-evident.[27] A spectacular, nearly complete textile (Fig. 9a–b) now held by the Phoebus Foundation, for example, features a citation from Psalm 17 in a Fayyumic dialect: "It is God who girds me with strength. He made my way spotless. Who strengthens my feet as those of the hind." The inscription continues with an extratextual addition, not part of any psalm: "You made me superior over all my adversaries. And humiliate all my enemies behind my [*sic*]."[28] The Coptic text is lined with stylized, pseudo-Arabic lettering. Here we are left

Fig. 9a–b Shawl with Coptic inscription (and detail of upper inscription), Egypt, Tutun, 1029–1219 (radiocarbon dated with 95% probability). Wool and linen, tapestry weave, 220.5 × 105 cm. The Phoebus Foundation, Antwerp, 711/DM 159b.

with questions about the relationship between text, message, wearer, and audience: Did the makers and wearers of such textiles view the inclusion of pseudo-text as a reference to Arabic tiraz? Was the illegibility of the pseudo-epigraphy meant to evoke protective powers? Or is the combination of Coptic and unreadable Arabic meant as a provocation, deliberately suggesting inaccessibility to an Arabic reader illiterate in Coptic? The belligerent text of the chosen psalm hardly seems accidental; we can understand it instead to reflect a milieu in which Christians understood themselves to be engaged in a deeper spiritual battle with larger societal forces.

The embrace of tiraz by Christians and Jews — and the development of their own forms of inscribed textiles — testifies to the complex status of these faith communities in medieval Egypt. On the one hand, the very act of making a Coptic-language textile can only be seen as a direct response to Arabic tiraz, and in this sense reflects a shared appreciation for inscribed fabrics that transcended confessional divide. But we must complicate this interpretation by digging deeper into the conflicts, compromises, and responses that these textiles and their inscriptions reveal: far from projecting a convivial coexistence, the Christian engagement with tiraz declares that group's distinctive identity and traditions. In the end, by considering Christian and Jewish uses of tiraz, we gain insight into the constant negotiations that these communities made in their movements through Muslim society, as they adopted, adapted, and reinterpreted inscribed textiles on their own terms.

1   For a discussion of inscribed textiles both before and after the arrival of tiraz in Egypt, see Fluck and Helmecke 2006. Maximilien Durand outlines a critical note about the relationship of late antique and Byzantine inscribed textiles in his contribution to that volume; see Durand 2006, 83–94, esp. 83–84.

2   For the purposes of this essay, I use "tiraz" to refer to textiles inscribed in Arabic; I define "Christian tiraz" as those examples bearing Greek or Coptic text made in response to the influx of the former following the Muslim conquest of Egypt.

3   For a discussion of late antique textiles inscribed in pen, see Bénazeth and Dal-Prà 1995.

4   One exception is a small fragment (18.2 × 4.5 cm) likely dating to the fifth or sixth century, with an extract from the apocryphal Gospel of Thomas. Its use as a burial shroud is supposed because it cites a passage referring to Christ raising the dead. Luijendijk 2011.

5   Dale 1993; for a critique, see Nauerth 2006, 94–105.

6   For more on this hanging, see the discussion by Gudrun Bühl, Kathrin Colburn, and Elizabeth Dospěl Williams on the object page on the Dumbarton Oaks website, https://www.doaks.org/resources/textiles/catalogue/BZ.1929.1.

7   See Thomas 2012, 154–59, cat. 103A–G.

8   For more on this fragment, see my discussion on the object page on the Dumbarton Oaks website, https://www.doaks.org/resources/textiles/catalogue/BZ.1953.2.104.

9   For a discussion of the magical associations of Greek, Coptic, and Arabic texts from the fourth through thirteenth centuries, see Van der Vliet 2006.

10 Ongoing evaluation of the relationship of material and inscription is being conducted by the Materiale Textkulturen group (SFB933) at the University of Heidelberg (https://www.materiale-textkulturen.org). In December 2019, I joined this group as a Mercator Fellow, which allowed me to focus in greater detail on the relationship between inscription and image in Egyptian textiles. I thank Julia Lugovaya and Rodney Ast for the invitation to participate in the research group.

11 For dhimmi dress regulation, see Stillman 2003, 39–40.

12 Ibid., 55–61. For a discussion of *khila'*, see Sanders 2001, 225–39.

13 Stillman 1995, 134. The turban was said to be *dabiqi*, a very fine linen.

14 Goitein 1983, 197–98.

15 Helmecke 2004; Godlewski 2002, 100–104; and Godlewski 2005, 173–83.

16 Godlewski 2002, 103–4.

17 Winnik, forthcoming. Winnik's dissertation addresses the material culture of Christian burials in medieval Egypt, especially textiles.

18 Lyster 2002, 103–25.

19 Ibid., 111.

20 For a discussion of the portrait and a complete bibliography, see Thomas 1998, 368–70, 380–81, cat. 251. The Gospels are copied in Boharic dialect, with Arabic inscriptions throughout.

21 I thank Finbarr Barry Flood for drawing my attention to these tiraz. A description of the discovery of the textiles and photos of examples can be found in Mordini 1957.

22 Thomas 1998, 370.

23 See Badamo 2019. I thank Heather Badamo for sharing with me her article on the paintings ahead of its publication and for many years of conversation about the status of eastern Christian communities in the medieval Middle East.

24 For more on this fragment, see the discussion by Elizabeth Dospěl Williams and Marek Dospěl on the object page on the Dumbarton Oaks website, https://www.doaks.org/resources/textiles/catalogue/BZ.1953.2.3.

25 Julia Galliker and Ines Bogensberger are conducting research on these large-format textiles inscribed in Coptic. Their preliminary results will appear in Galliker and Bogensberger, forthcoming.

26 Durand and Rettig 2002, 167–70.

27 See Van der Vliet 2006, 42–47; a list of textiles and corresponding psalms is at 52–57.

28 Published in De Moor et al. 2008, 204–5.

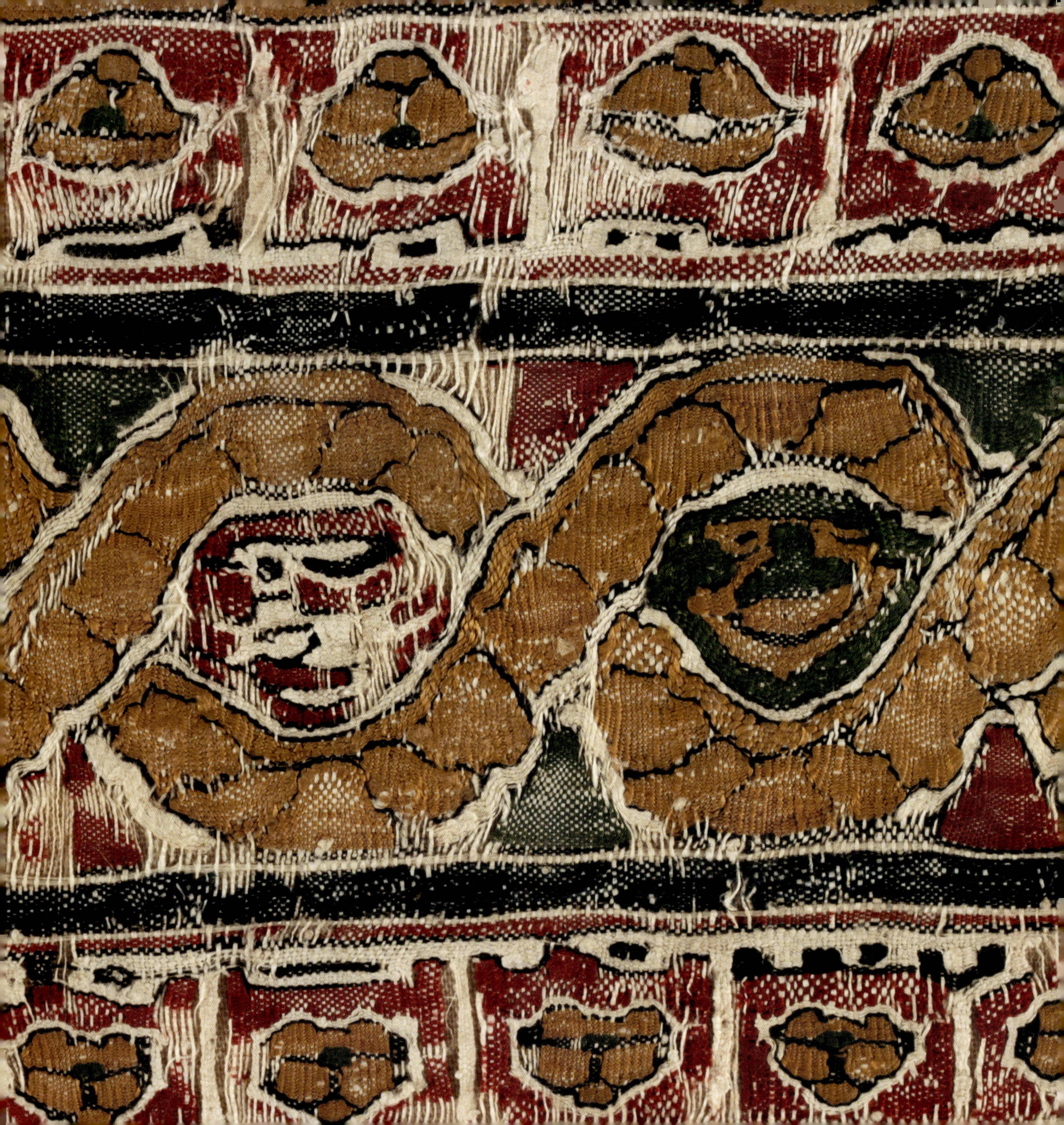

MARY MCWILLIAMS

Interwoven Motives: Collections of Tiraz Textiles in American Museums, c. 1890–1950

In the medieval era, Egypt's fine linen textiles, whether gossamer sheer or vibrantly patterned, were coveted internationally by the well-connected and well-to-do. The Egyptian textile industry engaged a diverse labor pool, generating and distributing wealth — albeit unequally — along an elaborate production chain that included dyers, weavers, embroiderers, and merchants, overseen and taxed at various stages by government administrators.

Some thousand years later, remnants of this medieval industry again found an international market and generated new wealth. In the late nineteenth and early twentieth centuries, innumerable textiles emerged from Egypt's long-abandoned cemeteries, sometimes through clandestine digging. As before, the enterprise required a complex interplay of producers, merchants, government officials, and consumers, but with profound differences. Fragmentary and discolored, the textiles were no longer functional fabrics, but objets d'art, while the actions of producers and merchants had merged in the antiquities trade. The role of government officials was now to protect Egypt's artistic heritage and to control export permits. Consumers were now "collectors," an elite though permeable group. The most radical shift came in the purported terminus of the textiles, which was no longer the personal burial, but the museum collection, at a time when public museums were emerging as a game-changing development for the art market. Toward this end converged, if not always deliberately, the actions of individuals from many walks of life — professors, philanthropists, businessmen, diplomats, artists, archaeologists, and curators.

The largest single collection of tiraz textiles, numbering more than a thousand, entered the Museum of Arab Art (now the Museum of Islamic Art) in Cairo, but from the 1890s to 1950s, many hundreds crossed the Atlantic, awakening American audiences to a rich artistic heritage beyond mummies and pyramids. This essay focuses on five museum collections drawn upon for the Harvard exhibition, briefly surveying the collectors primarily responsible for their formation. By order of founding, they are the Museum of Fine Arts, Boston (MFA) and the Metropolitan Museum of Art in New York, both founded in 1870; the Cleveland Museum of Art (CMA), 1916; the Textile Museum in Washington, D.C., 1925; and the Dumbarton Oaks Research Library and Collection, also in Washington, D.C., 1940.[1] By birth order, the collectors are Denman Waldo Ross (1853); George Dupont Pratt (1869); George Hewitt Myers (1875); Robert Woods Bliss (1875), usually acting in concert with Mildred Barnes Bliss (1879); and Émil Delmár (1876). Insofar as their paper trails allow, I consider the collectors' actions, motivations, and connections.

In the five museums, textiles bearing inscriptions in Arabic are a subset of much larger holdings of Egyptian textiles from the late antique through early Islamic eras (c. 3rd– 12th century). Inevitably, given the dearth of archaeological context for thousands of fragmentary textiles, terminology for both the broad and narrow group has varied among institutions and evolved with research.[2] For simplicity, in this essay I use the outmoded classification "Coptic" for Egyptian textiles from the third through roughly the seventh century, because this was the most commonly used term when the majority of these fabrics entered American institutions. Similarly, textiles with Arabic inscriptions dating from the eighth through the twelfth century are referred to as "tiraz," although the character of their texts ranges considerably, from legible, to garbled, to seemingly ornamental. As we will see, tiraz initially entered collections on the coattails of Coptic textiles and ancient Egyptian art.

By the end of the 1950s, these five institutions held more than 750 tiraz: the Textile Museum with more than 400, the Metropolitan Museum with more than 130, the CMA and MFA with just over 100 each, and Dumbarton Oaks with more than 20.[3] By the close of the 1930s, almost all of these objects

Detail of cat. 19.

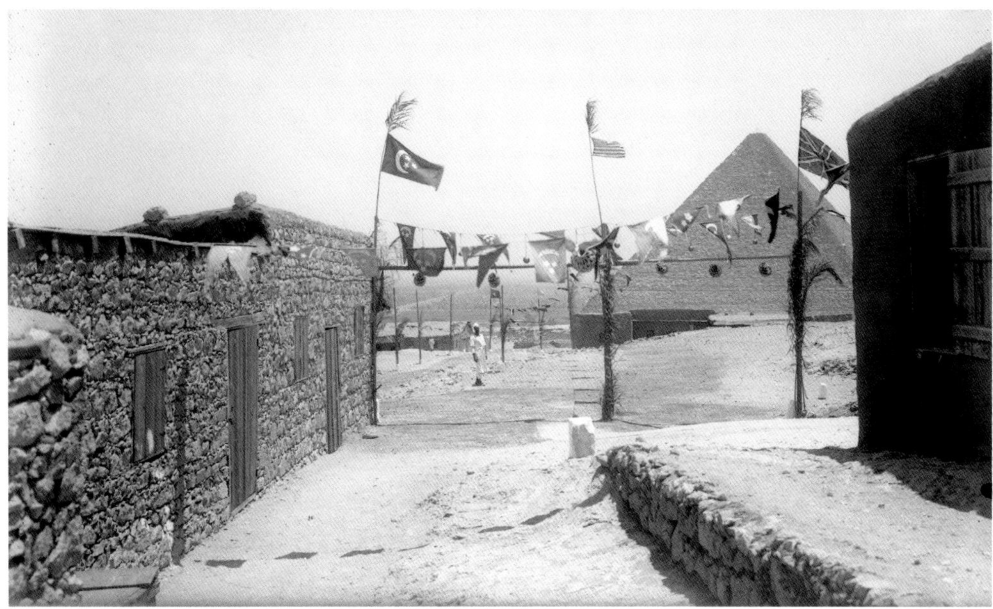

were in private hands, if not yet in museums. Their passage and the interactions of the collectors were propelled by broad economic and historical developments. A class of philanthropists — either creators of or heirs to the titanic fortunes of America's Gilded Age — competed to enrich their favored institutions with rare and valuable collections to advance the culture and industry of their fellow citizens. If their motives seem narrow today, their efforts were nevertheless influential in enlarging the worldview of a nation defined by geographical separation. As Myers expressed:

> The province of Museums of Art is certainly to preserve free from harm the best examples of artistic creations that they can obtain by gift or afford to purchase. But it is more certainly their duty, and on them most of all falls the responsibility to show these things to the public so as best to educate the public taste and set constantly higher standards in art. To give pleasure to the initiated is of less importance, especially in a country like the United States which we must admit is comparatively both "nouveau" and "riche."[4]

Works of art were on the move because people were circulating more than ever before. The structures of European colonialism, especially the British occupation of Egypt that began in 1882, facilitated access for Americans with little or no knowledge of Arabic. In January 1905, American painter and amateur Egyptologist Joseph Lindon Smith (1863–1950)

noted in his diary the swarms of tourists traveling on houseboats with names like *Mayflower* and *Puritan*, operated by the Anglo-American Steamer and Hotel Company: "Big Anglo American crowd at Karnak this mornin[g]. a poor helpless aimless seeming herd of people — all looking here — now there. Now the other way at command Same crowd. Somewhat thinned out. Came to Luxor in the afternoon after their tea."[5] An idea of how the upper crust experienced a Nile cruise can be gleaned from a film made in 1921 by Metropolitan Museum trustee and amateur filmmaker George Pratt, in which his companions grapple with the scale of Egypt's monuments and history.[6] And by 1913, on his third trip to Egypt, MFA trustee Denman Ross groused in his diary: "Everybody travels these days whether he has a reason to travel or not."[7]

These trips invariably included visits to antiquities dealers, whose offerings usually originated in Egypt's pharaonic through Islamic eras. The dealers whose names appear most frequently in the museums' provenance records for Coptic and tiraz textiles were wealthy Cairenes: Maurice Nahman and the multigenerational Tano and Abemayor families. That the world came to Cairo in the early twentieth century can be confirmed by Nahman's guest book, an international who's who of archaeologists, professors, museum professionals, government officials, minor aristocrats, collectors, and dealers.[8]

The most intense period of American collecting of Coptic and tiraz textiles aligns with the foundational decades of American Egyptology. In the first decades of the twentieth century, the Egyptian government granted archaeological concessions to foreign cultural institutions, including the MFA and the Metropolitan Museum, and departments of Egyptology were established in American museums and universities. The joint Harvard University/MFA expedition that began in 1902 became the longest-running excavation at the Giza Necropolis (Fig. 1). Foreign domination of Egyptian art and archaeological institutions declined throughout the 1930s, as Egyptians increasingly exerted political and cultural independence. The coming of World War II, followed by the Egyptian government's termination of most foreign concessions, brought sharp declines in the number of Americans in Egypt — and concomitantly their collecting of tiraz.

Well-heeled and well-educated, the collectors in this study operated within the social and economic elite. The top collectors of tiraz textiles never formed a large group, and this essay can only hint at the ways in which those examined here were directly and indirectly linked across philanthropic and professional networks. With the exception of Delmár, all connected in some fashion — through gifts, study, or correspondence — to Harvard University.

DENMAN WALDO ROSS (1853–1935)

Denman Ross (Fig. 2) donated fifty-five tiraz to the MFA between the years 1896 and 1931, representing the earliest and longest period of giving among our collectors. Ross began collecting tiraz when the field was hardly in its infancy, and his involvement ended before 1934, the year Adolf Grohmann published a typological definition of tiraz that most scholars would follow for the next six decades.[9] Another two generations passed before scholarship offered a comprehensive assessment of the place of tiraz in medieval Islamic societies.[10] To consider Ross a pioneer in this specialized field, however, would misrepresent his interests, which were encyclopedic, encompassing all manner of media and more of the globe than even he was able to cover in a lifetime of relentless travel. His collecting crossed boundaries of time, space, and medium because his primary concern lay not in the historical, cultural, or literary associations of the visual arts, but in universal principles of design.[11]

Ross was educated at Harvard (A.B. 1875; Ph.D. 1881) and by the mid-1880s had determined to devote his life and resources to the fine arts — to collecting, investigating the properties of great art, and formulating an analytical terminology to express and teach his findings. In 1899, he began a twenty-five-year career teaching design at Harvard and the MFA. His 1907 publication *A Theory of Pure Design* encapsulated his principles and enfolded them in a moralizing philosophy:

> Our object, then, in the study and practice of Pure Design is, not so much the production of Works of Art, as it is to induce in ourselves the art-loving and art-producing faculties. With these faculties we shall be able to discover Order and Beauty everywhere, and life will be happier and better worth living.[12]

Ross's formalist system used dots, lines, shapes, tones, and color values to demonstrate the principles of design. For Ross, design meant harmony, balance, and rhythm. He directed his students to analyze and paint copies of original artworks, including textiles from the Ross Collections at both the MFA and Harvard's Fogg Museum.

Undoubtedly inspired by the Arts and Crafts movement, Ross had a deep, although far from exclusive, interest in the

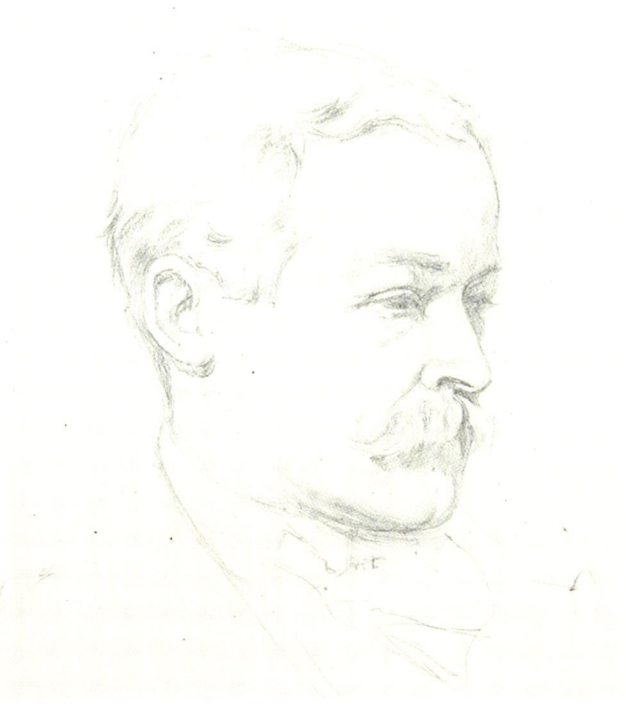

Fig. 2 Joseph Lindon Smith, *Dr. Denman W. Ross* (detail), August 4, 1887. Graphite on heavy off-white wove paper, 17.8 × 26.4 cm. Harvard Art Museums/Fogg Museum, Gift of Dr. Denman W. Ross, class of '75, 1919.290.

Fig. 3 Denman W. Ross, *Study of a Coptic Tapestry in the Cluny Museum*, 1893. Opaque watercolor on paper, 35.2 × 25.4 cm. Harvard Art Museums Archives, Denman Waldo Ross Papers, Box 33.

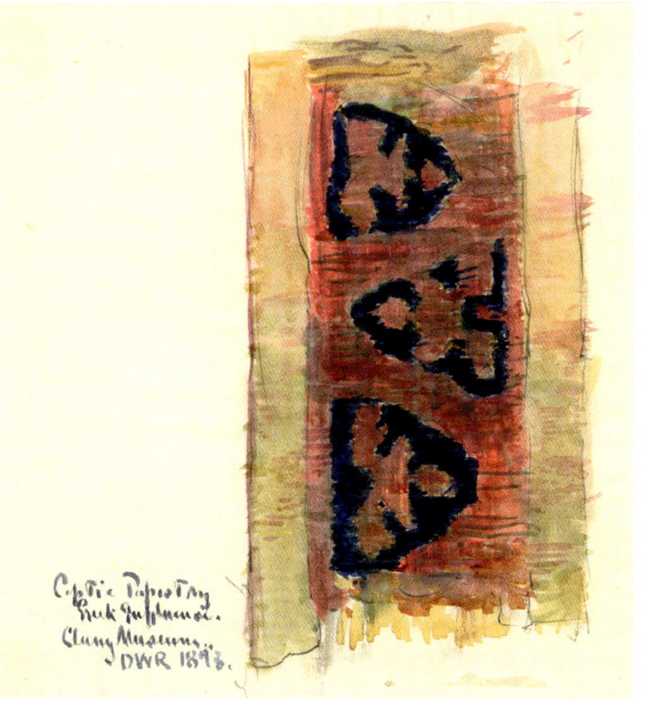

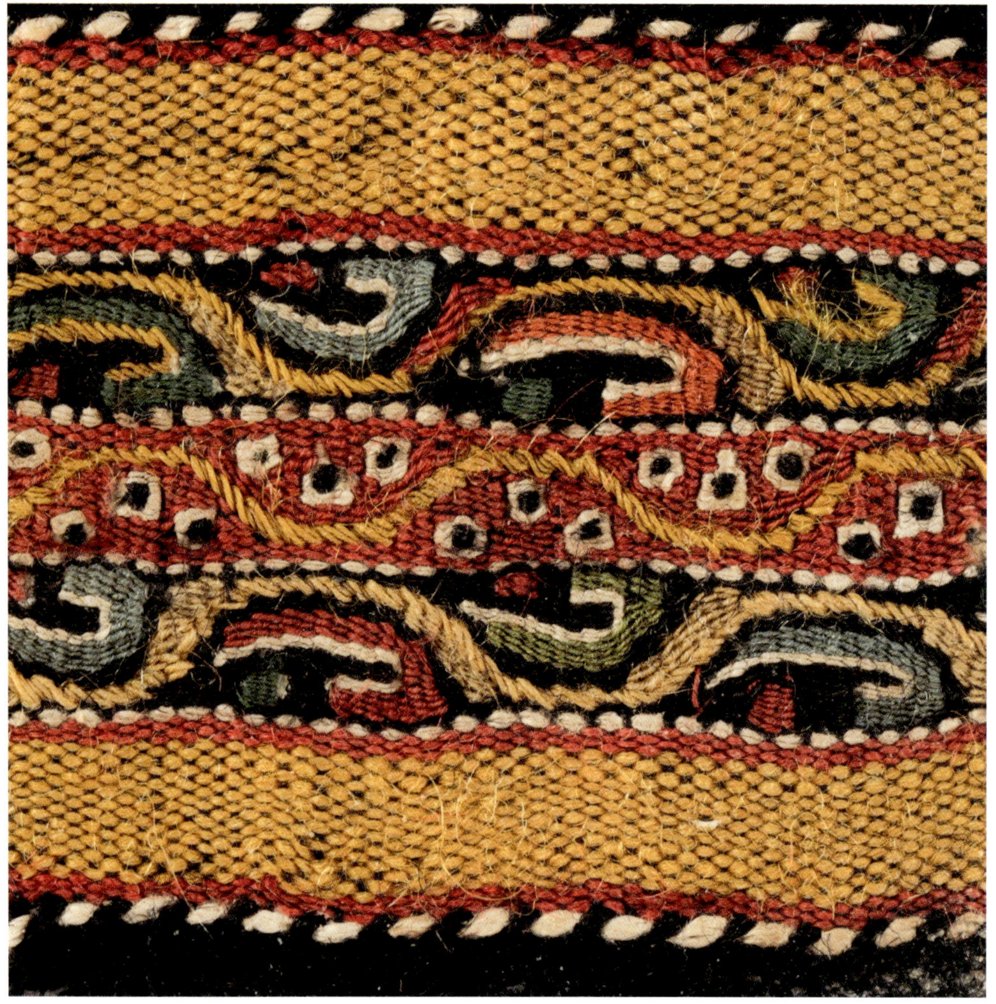

Fig. 5 Tiraz textile, Iraq, first half 10th century. Cotton with silk embroidery, 8.5 × 20.5 cm. Museum of Fine Arts, Boston, Denman Waldo Ross Collection, 15.761.

textile arts. He donated more than 6,000 textiles to the MFA and 330 to the Fogg. Coptic tapestries caught his attention early, as evidenced by his 1893 study of a fragment in the Musée de Cluny (Fig. 3), and he eventually donated more than 800 to the MFA and 36 to the Fogg (see cats. 22, 25). In the late nineteenth century, Coptic (and pre-Columbian) tapestries were esteemed as the earliest examples of woven patterns; that is, textiles in which the design is created during the weaving process itself (see the essay by Julie Wertz et al. in this volume). Ross's study only minimally suggests surface texture, for his interest lay in pattern rather than technique.

Coptic tapestries may have been foundational for the development of Ross's design theories, and they certainly informed his early tiraz purchases. A Fayyum tapestry donated to the MFA in 1911 probably intrigued him not because of its Coptic and Arabic inscriptions, but because of its bands of Coptic-style designs (cat. 29; see Fig. 4 for a detail). These illustrate multiple Rossian principles: harmony of curvature through alternation of directions; balance through inversion and opposition of attitudes and directions; and rhythm through repetition of contrary movements at equal intervals along an imaginary axis.

Ross's early tiraz donations are notable chiefly for Coptic-style patterns, rather than inscriptions, which usually land on the decorative end of the spectrum. Although dating was speculative in this period, most of Ross's tiraz are from the Fatimid era, perhaps reflecting the influence of Gaston Migeon, curator at the Louvre and a pioneering scholar of Islamic art. Migeon's 1907 *Manuel d'art musulman* singled out Fatimid textiles for praise and sketched a royal context through accounts of the fabulous wealth of Fatimid palaces and references to the *Arabian Nights*.[13]

Two textiles gifted in 1915, however, stand out among Ross's early donations as the first purely epigraphic tiraz to enter the collection.[14] Particularly interesting is a small, monochromatic Abbasid embroidery with exaggerated verticals and sublinear curves (Fig. 5). The twenty years since Ross's first tiraz purchases had been powerfully formative for Islamic art history, with advances in scholarship and ambitious, international exhibitions. Among the most notable was the monumental 1910 exhibition *Meisterwerke Muhammedanischer Kunst* in Munich. One of the tiraz illustrated in its multivolume catalogue (published in 1912) is strikingly similar to Ross's 1915 gift.[15] An even more direct influence on Ross was surely Hervey Wetzel, with whom he toured Egypt in the spring of 1913. Wetzel had studied with Ross as an undergraduate (Harvard 1907). His graduate work in "Muhammadan art" was interrupted by World War I, and at his untimely death in 1917, his impressive collection of Arabic calligraphy passed to the Fogg.

Ross's final tiraz gifts in 1931 are dominated by Arabic inscriptions, signaling a change for a collector hitherto unconcerned with content. Much credit for the growing appreciation of tiraz is due to European scholars, especially A. F.

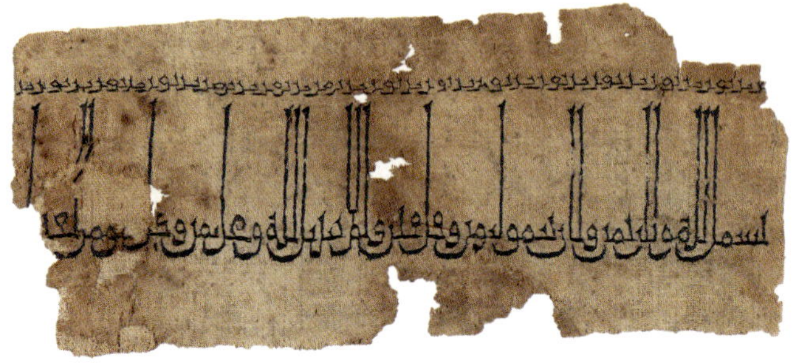

Kendrick of the Victoria and Albert Museum in London and
Ernst Kühnel of the Kaiser-Friedrich Museum in Berlin. Their
illustrated catalogues from 1924 and 1927, respectively, put in
place a five-hundred-year scaffold from the Umayyad through
Fatimid eras and outlined a system of private and public workshops (see Jochen Sokoly's essay in this volume).[16] Kendrick
further hinted that tapestry technique provided a continuum
with Coptic and ultimately pharaonic weaving traditions, thus
positioning tapestry tiraz as the final chapter.

Although Ross was disinclined to purchase collections formed by others, preferring to acquire "one thing
after another,"[17] his last tiraz donation was assembled by
a well-connected and well-informed individual in Egypt:
Joseph Lindon Smith, the American who had mused in his
diary about the tourists on the Nile.[18] An instructor in painting
and drawing at Harvard and the MFA, Smith is best known
for meticulous paintings of newly excavated Egyptian tomb
reliefs, produced in the brief period before their surface
polychromy faded (Fig. 6). For nearly fifty years, beginning
in 1898, Smith wintered in Egypt, painting antiquities and
becoming thoroughly integrated into the society of archaeologists and artists.[19]

A self-described "persona grata with some of the big dealers,"[20] Smith augmented his income by serving as an art agent,
advising Isabella Stewart Gardner, Ross, and the MFA on a wide
range of purchases. Ross's 1914 letter to Frederic Allen Whiting,
founding director of the Cleveland Museum of Art, reveals the
basis of his connoisseurship and his esteem for Smith's eye:

> [Y]ou want, not all kinds of things, but only the best
> of every kind. You want not examples but master-
> pieces . . . if you are a Museum of Art, and not a
> Museum of Anthropology. To get these first class
> things you must have in your employ the men who
> know them — men who have used their eyes; dis-
> criminating, judging, detecting. . . . The best person
> I know, and I know him well, the most all-round
> person who has been everywhere and seen all kinds
> of things who knows the good things from the bad
> thing, almost unerringly, is Joseph Lindon Smith.[21]

In subsequent purchases, Smith's eyes served the MFA's
tiraz collection well (see cats. 12, 14, 19, 26).[22] In 1937, he gifted
a Fatimid tiraz to the museum and also squired MFA president

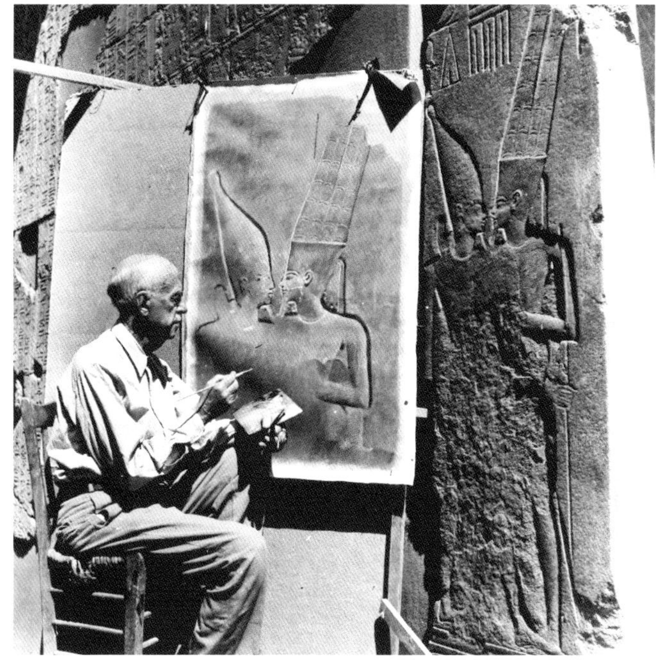

Edward Jackson Holmes through Cairo's antiquarian shops,
assisting his purchases of "Arabic textiles."[23]

By the mid-1930s, the MFA's tiraz collection had attained
sufficient depth and quality that a catalogue was planned.
Published in 1938 and modeled after the format of Kendrick's
publications, Nancy Britton's excellent monograph *A Study of
Some Early Islamic Textiles in the Museum of Fine Arts Boston*
was the first of its kind from an American museum.[24]

GEORGE DUPONT PRATT (1869–1935)

By the time New Yorker George D. Pratt began donating tiraz
textiles in 1927, they were gaining in status as museum-quality
artifacts. The son of one of John D. Rockefeller's early
associates in the petroleum industry, Pratt devoted his life
to numerous and diverse philanthropic pursuits, including
co-founding the Boy Scouts of America and serving as conservation commissioner of New York. He also held various offices
for the Pratt Institute in Brooklyn (founded by his father) and
served as trustee for his alma mater, Amherst College (1893),
and for the Metropolitan Museum.

Pratt's art donations were similarly wide-ranging and
enriched multiple museums. To the Met alone he gifted more
than one thousand objects, including American painting,
Romanesque stained glass, Chinese cricket cages, Persian
painting, and Peruvian tapestry. A small subset of his largesse,

Pratt's donations of approximately ninety tiraz stand out in a series of gifts made over five years to two museums: the Metropolitan Museum (1927, 1929, 1931) and the Cleveland Museum of Art (1932).[25] Overall, the tiraz credited to Pratt form a superb selection in terms of quality and range (see cats. 1, 9). The number of embroidered Abbasid tiraz among his gifts is unusual for a time when most collectors were focused on Fatimid tapestries.

Little of Pratt's own thinking on art can be gleaned from his surviving correspondence with recipients, in part because he was of modest temperament, if not means, but also because his practice included purchasing collections formed by others. For at least one of his groups of tiraz — more than thirty fragments gifted in 1929 — Pratt revealed his source in a letter to Metropolitan Museum curator of decorative arts Joseph Breck: "In regard to the Arabic textiles, I made Prof. Whittemore an offer for these textiles, which he cabled to Europe, and the last time I heard from him, he had had no reply."[26]

The professor in question was the elusive yet consequential Thomas J. Whittemore (1871–1950).[27] Whittemore's long and varied career included teaching at his alma mater, Tufts College (1894), and at Columbia University and New York University. He was soon swept into the growing enthusiasm for Byzantine art, and after viewing the 1910 Munich exhibition, for Islamic art as well. In 1911, Whittemore joined a British archaeological expedition sponsored by the Egypt Exploration Fund and worked at various Coptic and ancient Egyptian sites over the next fifteen years.

After witnessing the suffering and destruction caused by World War I and the Russian Revolution, Whittemore immersed himself in relief and preservation projects. He developed and managed a complex patronage network to raise funds for his philanthropic programs, and among his staunch supporters was George Pratt. In a 1923 photograph (Fig. 7), they are seen with Russian and Bulgarian monks on Mount Athos, home to an Orthodox community in Greece impoverished after the fall of the Russian imperial family. By 1930, Whittemore's various philanthropic efforts had coalesced into the Byzantine Institute. After his death in 1950, his institute was absorbed into Dumbarton Oaks, founded by his friends and devoted supporters Mildred and Robert Bliss. Whittemore is most celebrated today for heading up and funding the enormous project of uncovering and consolidating the Byzantine mosaics at the Hagia Sophia. Less well known are his activities as an art agent and a collector. Among other gifts, he willed to Harvard his extensive collections of Byzantine coins and seals and early Islamic coins (see cats. 4–5 and p. 20).[28]

Pratt's tiraz gifts to the Metropolitan Museum had an immediate impact. In a brief article in 1927, Maurice Dimand, curator of the newly established sub-department of Islamic art, signaled the museum's interest in "Egypto-Arabic textiles," prominently positioning them in the crosscurrents of art history: "[T]hese fragments are of great importance to students of textiles and of Near Eastern art, as they show not only the continuation of the Coptic tradition, but the rise of a New Arabic style which later influenced European weaving to a high degree." Dimand concluded by declaring Egypt "the textile country of perfection."[29]

In 1930, Dimand showcased the Pratt/Whittemore group in a special exhibition of Coptic and tiraz textiles. While praising the quality of Fatimid tapestry weaving, he also emphasized the importance of the inscriptions, both for their historical content and the quality of the calligraphy, proudly stating, "These Egypto-Arabic textiles will be a novelty to most visitors to the Museum, and it may be noted, not without a little gratification, that our collection of these interesting textiles is

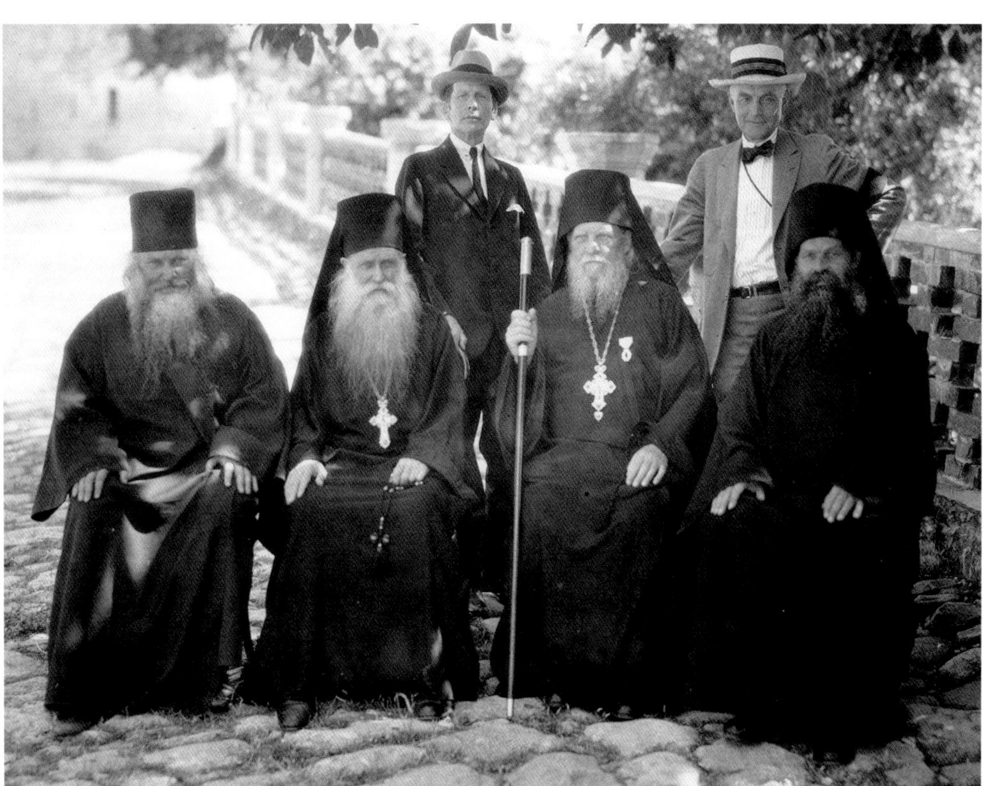

Fig. 7 Thomas J. Whittemore (left) and George D. Pratt (right) with four seated monks on Mount Athos, Greece, 1923. Dumbarton Oaks Research Library and Collection, Washington, D.C., Thomas Whittemore Papers c. 1875–1966.

Fig. 8 Mildred Barnes and Robert Woods Bliss in the Rose Garden at Dumbarton Oaks, c. 1938.

very representative in its variety and quality."[30] More detailed cataloguing, with transcriptions and translations, appeared the following year in an article by archaeologist Joseph Upton for *Metropolitan Museum Studies*.[31] Tiraz textiles, with an emphasis on legible inscriptions, had now definitively entered the canon for American museums.

ROBERT WOODS BLISS (1875–1962) AND MILDRED BARNES BLISS (1879–1969)

Robert Bliss (Harvard 1900) caught the "incurable malady" of the "collector's microbe" in 1912, when his diplomatic career brought him and wife Mildred Barnes to Paris (Fig. 8).[32] The couple formed an intense and mutual interest in Byzantine art during their seven years in the French capital. As with many others, their artistic pursuits were pushed aside by the outbreak of war in 1914, and both played important roles steering committees for relief work in Europe. Among the many acquaintances Mildred Bliss pulled in to raise funds for these efforts were Joseph Lindon Smith and his wife, Corinna.[33]

Soon after the war, Robert Bliss was posted to the State Department in Washington, D.C., where he and Mildred purchased the 54-acre estate to be named Dumbarton Oaks. The Blisses resumed collecting art, deepening their involvement in two principal areas — pre-Columbian and Byzantine works.

With faint Rossian echoes, Robert Bliss summarized his collecting philosophy: "I have collected . . . objects that gave me pleasure — a sculpture boldly conceived; a gold object delicately wrought; a fabric of good design, well woven; ceramics with interesting iconography; metal work of quality — a rhythm here, a form there."[34] The Blisses often went to extreme lengths to secure an object whose beauty moved them, but they were not tempted by "an object representing a link in the long chain of evolution, but without inherent quality."[35]

Declining multiple offers for tiraz textiles throughout the 1920s and 1930s, the Blisses nevertheless made a substantial purchase of twenty-one examples in 1933 (see cats. 10–11, 13, 15, 30, 37). Most came from Cairo dealer Nicolas Tano, often through the intermediary Frances Morris, an independent scholar and former assistant curator of textiles at the Metropolitan Museum. Although comprising the smallest group in our study, the Bliss tiraz textiles form a fine selection whose taxonomic range and diversity reflect the previous decade's scholarship. The inscriptions — embroidered,

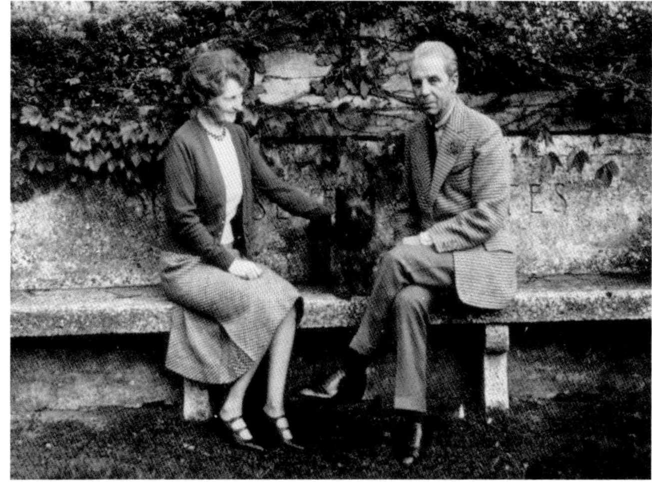

painted, and tapestry woven — are mostly legible, and many provide historical information. Five years after the purchase, Mildred Bliss engaged Morris and historian of Islamic art Richard Ettinghausen "to make a little 'catalogue raisonné' of our small textile collection."[36]

Tiraz textiles were ancillary to the Blisses' collecting interests — a postscript to Egyptian textiles of the Byzantine era. Their place may be gauged by a broader project the couple conceived in the late 1930s, the "Census of Byzantine, Early Christian and Related Arts in American Collections." As Dumbarton Oaks librarian Barbara Sessions explained to Morris, that census would include "all textiles which could have influenced either the 'Byzantine' or Coptic styles as well as all later designs derived from those of the Sasanian and Byzantine periods."[37]

Many collectors are tempted to fill gaps as their treasures are being catalogued, but the Blisses adhered to aesthetic value as their chief criterion. Declining yet another offer of tiraz in 1940, Sessions wrote to Morris:

[T]he textiles at Dumbarton Oaks have been chosen with an eye to their beauty and interest of design as much as for their interest as documents. We shall never have an exhaustive study collection here, and even though Mrs. Bliss realized the interest attached to some of these pieces on account of the fact that the inscriptions localized the manufacture, she found them aesthetically in quite a different class from the more handsome pieces for which the Collection is indebted to you already.[38]

In 1936, the Blisses determined that their estate, collections, and vast libraries should eventually become part of Harvard University, to serve as a cultural and educational institution, the Dumbarton Oaks Research Library and Collection. With war clouds gathering in the late 1930s, they accelerated their plans and put their beloved "Home for the Humanities" under Harvard's trusteeship. In the words of Mildred Bliss, "If ever the Humanities were necessary . . . it is in this epoch of disintegration and dislocation."[39]

ÉMIL DELMÁR (1876–1959)

Émil Delmár's collection of tiraz textiles (see cat. 17) opens another window onto the tremendous dislocations caused by World War II. In the early twentieth century, Delmár enjoyed a high position in Hungarian society due to family wealth, his education, and his reputation as a distinguished art collector (Fig. 9).[40] By 1910, his collecting interests had somewhat narrowed to medieval European sculpture and decorative arts. Delmár's tiraz textiles appear to have been an outlier within his collecting portfolio. Perhaps they caught his attention because Kufic inscriptions sometimes appear along the garments of religious figures in medieval European painting and sculpture. Delmár probably purchased his tiraz on business trips to Egypt in 1934 and 1937, years that his signature appears in Nahman's guest book. He promptly loaned his tiraz to the Staatliches Kunstgewerbemuseum in Vienna, where they were juxtaposed with late antique and medieval art.

Of Jewish origin, Delmár reacted quickly to the waves of anti-Semitism boiling through Europe in the late 1930s. Immediately after the passage of the first "Jewish Law" in Hungary in 1938, he began systematically relocating his

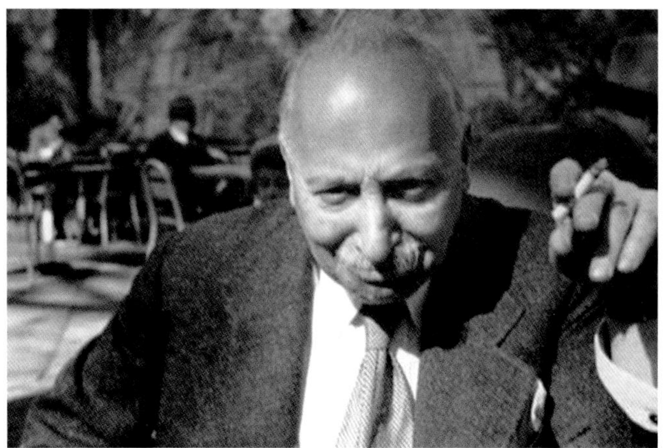

collection to avoid confiscation or destruction. Portions were shipped to Switzerland, ostensibly for an exhibition at the Kunstmuseum in Bern.[41] Delmár himself escaped war-torn Europe, entering the United States in 1941. He served as a volunteer assistant to the American Council of Learned Societies, which advised the Monuments, Fine Arts, and Archives section of the Allied Armies, better known as the Monuments Men. A refugee in his mid-60s, Delmár surely valued his art objects as precious survivors of a devastating war and as financial assets. In 1950, he sold fifty-six Coptic and tiraz textiles to the Cleveland Museum of Art, whose curator of textiles Dorothy G. Shepherd may have known him through her work as a Monuments Officer. A letter to Delmár from December 1950 reveals Shepherd's genuine excitement — as well as a generous helping of curatorial competitiveness:

> I cannot tell you how happy I am that we are going to be able to buy your superb collection. As we had so little in the field of Egypto-Arabic material it is of special importance and I think that the quality of the group is superior to any other collection that I know. . . . It is going to be a most interesting and exciting thing for me studying them and publishing them.[42]

Shepherd received a head start in studying the Delmár tiraz: along with the textiles, the CMA also acquired a detailed catalogue of the holdings prepared years earlier by Kühnel, presumably when the collection was still in Europe.[43] One of the foremost experts on early Islamic textiles, Kühnel would later help realize the ambitions of the last collector in our study, George Hewitt Myers.

GEORGE HEWITT MYERS (1875–1957)

If Ross began acquiring tiraz textiles in a period of scholarly innocence, Myers's collecting was informed by experts from the outset. His twenty-five-year involvement with tiraz culminated in 1952 with a substantial contribution to scholarship, a catalogue of dated tiraz textiles authored by Kühnel and Louisa Bellinger.[44]

Similar to the Blisses, with whom he was acquainted as fellow Washingtonians, Myers (Fig. 10) concentrated on an area of intense personal interest and founded a private museum, the Textile Museum, for his collection. Like the

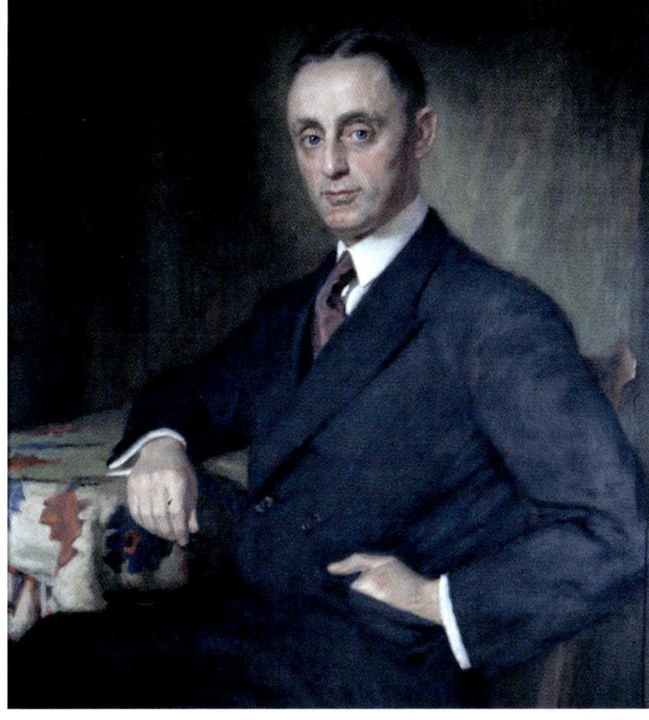

Blisses, he did not collect encyclopedically in his chosen field, but focused on specific areas. Most notably, he eschewed the European textile tradition, which he considered derivative of "eastern textiles."[45] Egypt appeared on his collecting horizon after a Coptic tapestry captured his attention. By 1931, in an article for the *American Magazine of Art* in which he offered "a hasty glimpse" of the Textile Museum's collection, Myers could describe his holdings of Egyptian tapestries as spanning the "Graeco-Roman, Coptic, Arabian, and transition periods."[46]

Something of Myers's collecting philosophy — and independent streak — is expressed in his 1931 article:

> As the collection increased there came to be a more and more conscious effort to seek objects for their intrinsic beauty and to avoid buying on a basis of rarity or of purely archaeological interest. This effort was not always successful, and if space permitted it would be interesting to go into the question of buying from the viewpoint of resistance to the dealer's ability to sell something by means of his cleverness in showing that nobody else has anything like it.[47]

If, like the Blisses, Myers could resist mere rarity or archaeological interest, he was nonetheless more susceptible to "the long chain of evolution." Connections and continuity

intrigued him from his earliest collecting years, when "the only underlying thought, 'if any,' was to find out what went before a certain piece to make it what it was."[48] Tiraz textiles with datable inscriptions fitted this preoccupation and meshed well with his developing interest in technical examination.[49]

In 1930, the year before his article appeared, Myers made his first serious foray into Egyptian textiles. He traveled to Cairo and purchased more than one hundred examples from the Islamic era, most from the Abemayors, the Tanos, and Nahman. His report to the Board of Trustees reveals that the independent-minded Myers nevertheless valued scholarly advice:

> In Cairo in the Spring of 1930, with the assistance of Mr. Winlock of the Metropolitan Museum and Prof. Newberry of the University at Cairo, I got a number of tapestry weavings ranging from Greco-Roman through the Coptic period and a larger number of woven stuffs from the Arabian period. These are of silk, linen and cotton and give the collection a fairly complete and representative series of Egyptian textiles — the more so because they include a number of early embroidered pieces which are scarce.[50]

In 1930, Herbert Winlock, soon to become director of the Metropolitan Museum, was head of its Egyptian expedition. The mention of Percy Newberry is particularly interesting. A British Egyptologist whose career, like Whittemore's, began with the Egypt Exploration Fund, Newberry was an expert in, and collector of, Islamic embroideries, then an underappreciated field.[51] To catalogue his various collections, and particularly to transcribe and translate inscriptions, Myers would later engage Islamic art historians, including Ettinghausen, Kühnel, and Mehmet Aga-Oğlu.

Myers's attention to inscriptions increased significantly and consistently. To give but one comparison, texts played a relatively minor role in the Egyptian textiles of the early Islamic period that he purchased in 1930: most are uninscribed, and less than 10 percent have historical texts. In contrast, of the fifty-nine textiles he acquired in 1951, 90 percent carry inscriptions with historical content. His trajectory reflects broader developments in the field, especially in the study of Arabic epigraphy. The year 1931 brought the first of many volumes of the *Répertoire chronologique d'épigraphie*

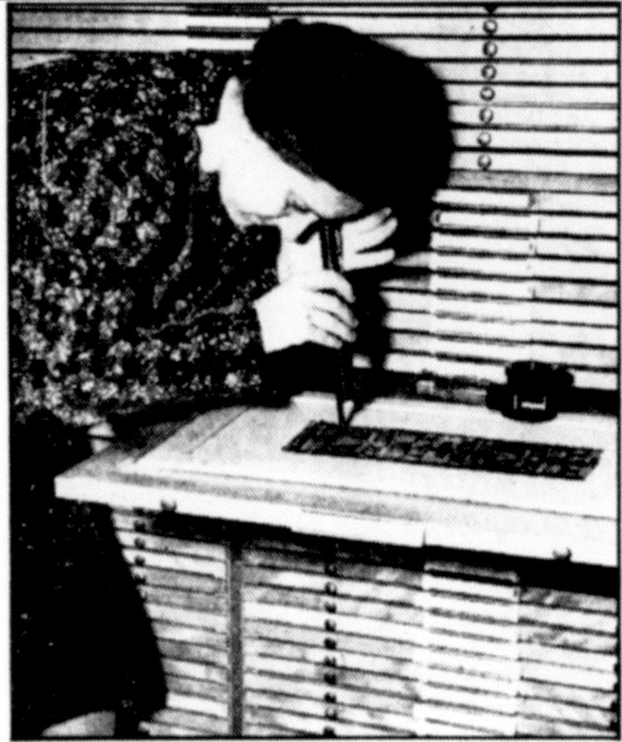

RESEARCH AT DUMBARTON OAKS—Miss Louisa Bellinger, research assistant specializing in early textiles, analyzes weave and spinning with a 20-power, wide-field textile tube at the Dumbarton Oaks Research Laboratory.   —Star Staff Photo.

catalogue, which presents 138 textiles with historical inscriptions in chronological order. A landmark in the field, the publication illuminates Myers's tremendous collecting achievement through Kühnel's careful study and translation of the inscriptions coupled with Bellinger's comprehensive analysis of fibers, embroidery techniques, and weave structures.

———

The collections of tiraz textiles in American museums were constructed from a complex interplay of professions, approaches, and motivations. The players, while competitive, were also collaborative, and the fluid overlapping of the antiquities dealer with the archaeologist, college professor, artist, curator, and collector is almost unfathomable in our age of increased specialization, narrowed professional ethics, and more regulated procurement of art.

With no known personal identification with Islam or Egypt, our collectors were drawn to art as a broadening experience, and their efforts significantly expanded the canon for the type of art that would be studied in American museums and universities. For globe-trotter Denman Ross, collecting was a journey of discovery, tempered by rigorous, if idiosyncratic, formal analysis. The Blisses' approach to art was also essentially visual, but theirs was an acute and personal aesthetic response. If the aesthetic inclinations of serial philanthropist George Pratt remain obscure, his generous gifts to several museums elevated tiraz to museum status in America. Buffeted by the century's cataclysms, Émil Delmár and Thomas Whittemore found a different purpose for an art collection's value. The datable character of tiraz had an intrinsic appeal to George Hewitt Myers, whose collecting efforts married aesthetic appreciation, technical analysis, and scholarship to form the most ambitious and systematic collection.

Having dedicated considerable personal wealth to tiraz textiles, these collectors entrusted their treasures to museums to be preserved, but not re-entombed. They believed in art's power to uplift contemporary culture and in the value of connecting the "everchanging present" to the achievements of past civilizations.[55] While Ross expected his collections to enable him "to speak to the people of Boston long after [his] death," he and his fellow collectors accomplished something far more generous by allowing tiraz textiles to address the questions and interests of every subsequent age.[56]

arabe, supervised by French linguist Gaston Wiet, then director of the Museum of Arab Art. Closer to home, Myers hired Florence Day, a specialist in Islamic art, as curator. Together, they conceived of a related project "which [they hoped] may be of value in clarifying the problem of dating textiles in the period of the 6th to the 12th centuries, A.D. . . . In brief, our idea is that an adequate sequence of dated inscriptions from all sources can make it possible by epigraphy to assign approximate dates to undated pieces."[52]

Pursuant to this goal, the Textile Museum acquired through trade eighteen tiraz textiles from the Detroit Institute of Arts: "This fortunate transaction along with 16 from Miss Frances Morris gives us examples from every Califate, except one or two from the mid 9th Century to the 13th Century and a few between the 7th and 9th Centuries."[53] Simultaneously, Bellinger, who worked at both Dumbarton Oaks and the Textile Museum, was engaged in a multiyear project to analyze more than one thousand Egyptian textiles, including the collections at the Victoria and Albert Museum (Fig. 11).

Since Day's tenure at the Textile Museum was short,[54] the most complete expression of Myers's project was the 1952

1   This space is wholly inadequate to express my debt of gratitude for the generosity and encouragement of curators, conservators, technicians, librarians, and archivists who aided my research at these institutions. Their names appear in the acknowledgments in this catalogue. Any errors are mine alone.

2   The textiles have been described as Saracenic, Copto-Arabic, Egypto-Arabic, Copto-Oriental, and Egypto-Islamic, among other terms.

3   All counts are approximate, because tallying these objects is an admittedly subjective exercise. In addition to visiting museums, I consulted online collections databases, which are continuously being updated.

4   Textile Museum Archives, George Hewitt Myers, typescript for a lecture (undated and untitled), 1.

5   Smithsonian Archives of American Art, Joseph Lindon Smith Diary, entries for January 6 and January 22, 1905, "The account of the short voyage of the dahabeah 'Aboo-Simbel' from Elephantine Island — [Assouan] to Luxor. Winter 1904–05 and the time spent there. on the West bank of the river." Available at https://transcription.si.edu/view/7501/ECjKx.

6   Pratt's film is preserved in the Field Museum of Natural History in Chicago, http://cdm17032.contentdm.oclc.org/digital/collection/p17032coll5/id/3.

7   Harvard Art Museums Archives, Box 119, DWR Diaries 1912–1916, entry for Friday, March 28, 1913.

8   Recent appraisals of Nahman's activities in the formation of international collections include Pintaudi 1993, Williams 2014, and Abdulfattah 2020. I am grateful to Kathrin Colburn and Jochen Sokoly for the references. Nahman's guest book is now in the Brooklyn Museum's Wilbour Library of Egyptology, https://archive.org/details/bml-SCR_N362_N14. See also Williams 2014.

9   Grohmann 1934, 785. For a detailed discussion of the historiography of tiraz studies, see Sokoly 2002, esp. chaps. 1, 3.

10   For example, Bierman 1980.

11   Recent studies of Ross's design theories and collecting include Frank 2011; and Meyer and Brysac 2015, 48–56.

12   Ross 1907, 194.

13   Migeon 1907, xxxv–xxxvii, 382–84.

14   MFA 15.761, 15.767.

15   Meisterwerke 1912, vol. 3, pl. 178, no. 2274. See also Vernoit 2000, Roxburgh 2000, and Lermer and Shalem 2010.

16   Kendrick 1924; and Kühnel 1927, 9.

17   Museum of Fine Arts, Boston, Archives, Directors' Correspondence 1901–54, Charles Greely Loring, letter DWR to CGL, 1897.

18   Museum of Fine Arts, Boston, Archives, Correspondence Joseph Lindon Smith, radiograms between JLS (Cairo) and DWR (Boston), November 22, 1930, requesting and granting permission to acquire "cufic inscriptions textiles."

19   A member of the Harvard/MFA expedition from 1910 to 1939, Smith was appointed honorary curator of the MFA's Egyptian department in 1927.

20   Museum of Fine Arts, Boston, Archives, Directors' Correspondence 1901–54, Edward Jackson Holmes, letter JLS to EJH, April 28, 1933.

21   Cleveland Museum of Art Archives, Directors' Correspondence, Frederic Allen Whiting, Box 12, Folder 131, letter DWR to FAW, May 31, 1914.

22   Museum of Fine Arts, Boston, Archives, Directors' Correspondence 1901–54, radiograms between JLS (Cairo) and DWR (Boston), November 4 and 6, 1931, requesting and granting permission to purchase "inscribed textiles." Although approved by Ross, the tiraz acquired in 1932 were purchased through the Marie Antoinette Evans Fund.

23   The tiraz is MFA 37.634. Museum of Fine Arts, Boston, Archives, Directors' Correspondence 1901–54, Harold Edgell, letter Corinna Putnam Smith to HE, February 22, 1935. Holmes's purchases surely included the eleven tiraz he donated to the MFA in 1937 and 1938.

24   Britton 1938.

25   Another important group of forty tiraz textiles was gifted to the Detroit Institute of Arts in 1932 by a certain George Dwight Pratt of New York. These tiraz are very similar in character to those donated to the Metropolitan Museum and the CMA by George Dupont Pratt. It was not possible to conduct further archival research to determine whether there is a connection between the two George Pratts while museums were closed due to the COVID-19 pandemic. As discussed below, eighteen of the Detroit tiraz were acquired by the Textile Museum through exchange in 1951 (see cat. 3).

26   Metropolitan Museum of Art Archives, Office of the Secretary, George Pratt (Folder P8882), letter GDP to JB, October 1, 1929.

27   See, for example, Klein 2011, 466–80; Labrusse and Podzemskaia 2000; Nelson 2004, 155–86; and Major 2010.

28   At the Fogg, Whittemore was appointed honorary keeper of Byzantine coins and seals.

29   Dimand 1927.

30   Dimand 1930.

31   Upton 1931.

32   See Carder 2008, 10–15; and Nelson 2005, 39–51.

33   Smith 1962, 271–81.

34   Carder 2008, 11.

35   Ibid., 15.

36   Dumbarton Oaks Archives, Morris Folder, letter MB to FM, March 11, 1938.

37   Dumbarton Oaks Archives, Morris Folder, letter BS to FM, March 17, 1939.

38   Dumbarton Oaks Archives, Morris Folder, letter BS to FM, March 12, 1940.

39   This statement is engraved on the exterior of the Dumbarton Oaks Library, as Mildred Bliss to Paul Sachs, May 9, 1942.

40   See Rózsavölgyi 2013, 225–39; and Rózsavölgyi 2010, 177–81.

41   Delmár's tiraz textiles were exhibited in 1947; see Altislamische 1947. For this reference, I am grateful to András Riedlmayer, bibliographer in Islamic art and architecture at Harvard's Fine Arts Library.

42   Cleveland Museum of Art Archives, Box 13, Records of the Director's Office, William Milliken, Folder: Delmár, Émil, letter DGS to ED, December 9, 1950, l F.

43   In the ensuing years, Shepherd used Kühnel's notes as the basis for a catalogue of the CMA's textile collection, which remains unpublished.

44   Kühnel and Bellinger 1952.

45   Textile Museum Archives, George Hewitt Myers, undated typescript "Draft of Introduction to Catalogue," 2.

46   Myers 1931, 336.

47   Ibid., 335.

48   Textile Museum Archives, George Hewitt Myers, typescript "Brief Statement re Textile Museum to the Oriental Society," January 1949, 1.

49   Myers 1931, 337, 344.

50   Textile Museum Institutional Archives, Notebook: Board of Trustees Meeting Minutes & Reports 1925–1940, "Additional report made by Mr. Myers at the meeting of the Board of Trustees . . .," December 20, 1930, 2.

51   Barnes and Ellis, n.d.

52   Textile Museum Institutional Archives, Notebook: Board of Trustees Meeting Minutes & Reports October 1942–November 1952, "Report of the President to the Board of Trustees of the Textile Museum, District of Columbia Covering Period from December 5, 1947 to October 17, 1948," 2.

53   Textile Museum Institutional Archives, "Report of the President to the Board of Trustees of the Textile Museum Covering Period from January 30, 1951 to January 30, 1952," 3. The eighteen tiraz in question include cat. 3. All had been gifted to the Detroit Institute of Arts by George Dwight Pratt in 1932; see note 25 above.

54   Day served as curator from April 1947 until her resignation in May 1949.

55   Carder 2010, 110.

56   Museum of Fine Arts, Boston, Archives, Directors' Correspondence, Samuel D. Warren, letter DWR to Morris Gray, August 15, 1912.

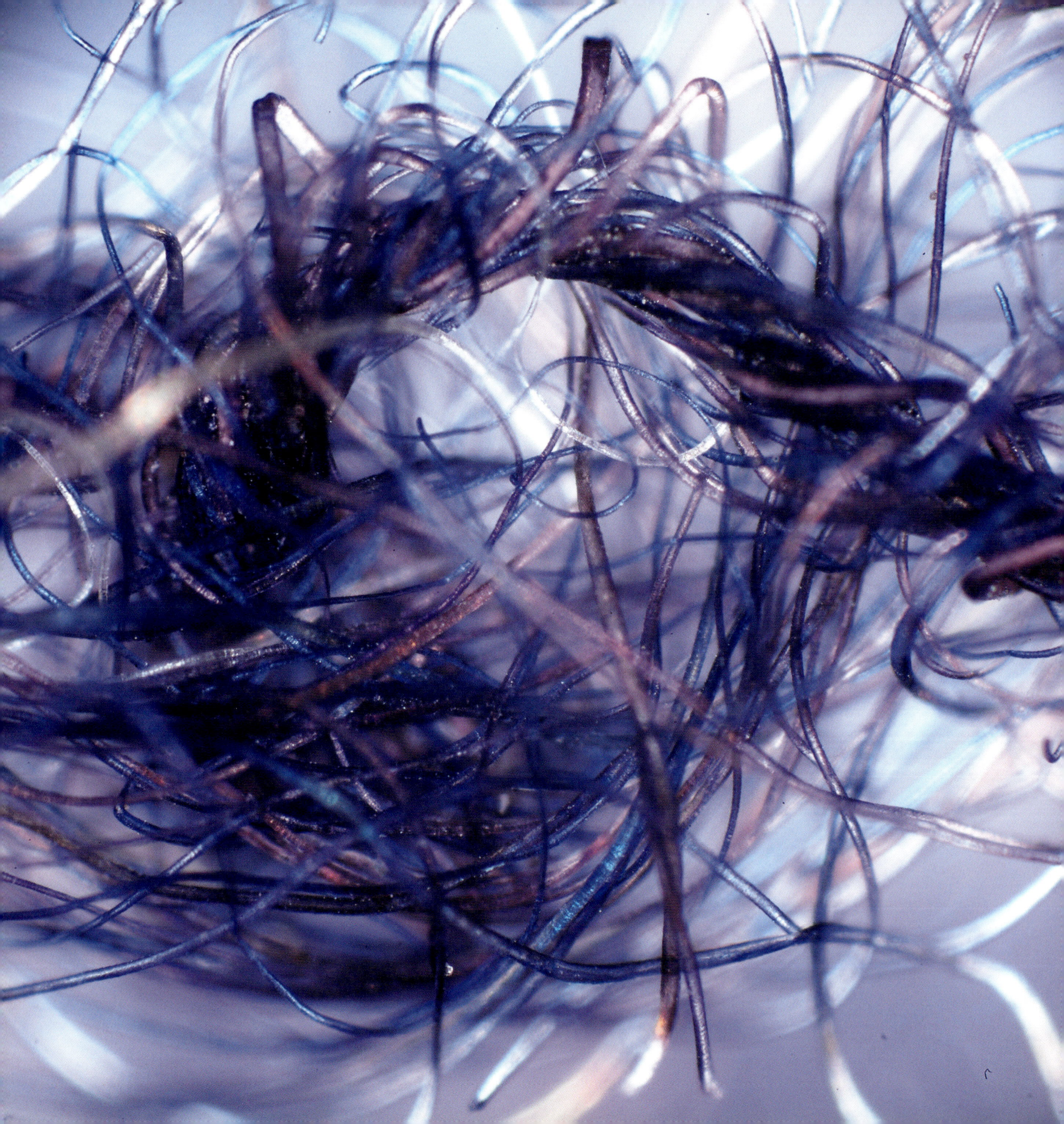

JULIE H. WERTZ, MEREDYTH LYNN WINTER, ROBIN HANSON, AND MEREDITH MONTAGUE

Beyond the Surface: Technical Analysis of Egyptian Textiles, c. 4th–12th Century

The interpretation of historical objects, particularly those stripped of archaeological context, can often be enhanced through technical study. Fundamentally, an understanding of the materials and their properties offers a framework that can illuminate the possibilities and limitations faced by an artisan. The identity of raw materials may indicate the social status of a textile, where or by whom it was made, or how populations interacted and operated. With textiles, for example, the use of S- or Z-twist yarn could place the weaver in a region where that technique was more prevalent, or the presence of a material associated with documented trade routes or conquests might help map the life of an object. This data is revealed through technical study, which demands that one look beyond the surface, perhaps setting aside assumptions based on aesthetic observations, to get (literally and metaphorically) close to the object.

Analytical techniques provide information not visible to the naked eye, contributing to a more rigorous interpretation of both individual textiles and textile collections as a whole. This essay discusses aspects of making and materials that were investigated for the exhibition *Social Fabrics: Inscribed Textiles from Medieval Egyptian Tombs* and the conclusions that can be drawn from this study.

WEAVING AND PATTERNING TECHNIQUES

A comparison of the numerous methods of weaving and finishing in the exhibition textiles highlights the repeated intersection and interaction of the two halves of the Islamic world, east (*mashriq*) and west (*maghrib*), which met in Egypt in the medieval period. Over and over, their respective textile traditions emulated one another.

One explanation for these two zones of influence is geography. Louisa Bellinger, examining the collection of tiraz in the Textile Museum in Washington, D.C., divided the linen spun from Egyptian-grown flax from the cotton cultivated in Iran.[1] Others have ascribed the phenomenon to the lasting impact of historical geopolitical factors on the Islamic world and its material culture. For example, coinage — a conservative medium with an administrative function not unlike tiraz (see the essay by Jochen Sokoly in this volume) — presented a challenge for early Islamic rulers. By adopting a Byzantine-inspired gold (dinar) and copper (fals) currency alongside a Sasanian-style silver (dirham) currency, they upheld both precedents.[2] The coming together in Egypt of the Byzantine tradition of tapestry weaving with the embroidery tradition of Iran and Iraq at this time seems at first to mirror these narratives.

Yet the textiles assembled in *Social Fabrics* tell a more complex version of the story. In this instance, it is not the rise and fall of empires or differences in climate that forged a new style or aesthetic, but communities of textile workers who, trained in distinct textile traditions and confronted with one another's products, emulated visual effects and adapted their techniques to suit the challenges at hand. What is more, we see this exchange crossing back and forth in textiles from Egypt and Iraq and Iran. An innovative blending takes place at multiple intervals in this period of sustained exchange, resulting in the birth of a tiraz aesthetic that was itself imitated.

The textiles in *Social Fabrics* are all constructed in the simplest form of interlacing — under one/over one — known as plain weave.[3] Whether the resulting weave is open, tight, weft-faced, warp-faced, or evenly balanced depends on the setup of the loom, the actions of the weaver, and the properties of the threads. The two contrasting textile traditions both used color change for patterning. Plant-based linen and cotton fibers were difficult to dye, while the animal-based fibers of wool and silk accepted colors more readily. These inherent characteristics contributed to the predominant use of wool to pattern linen fabrics in Egypt and silk to pattern cotton fabrics in Iran and Iraq.

Photomicrograph of purple fiber samples from cat. 21.

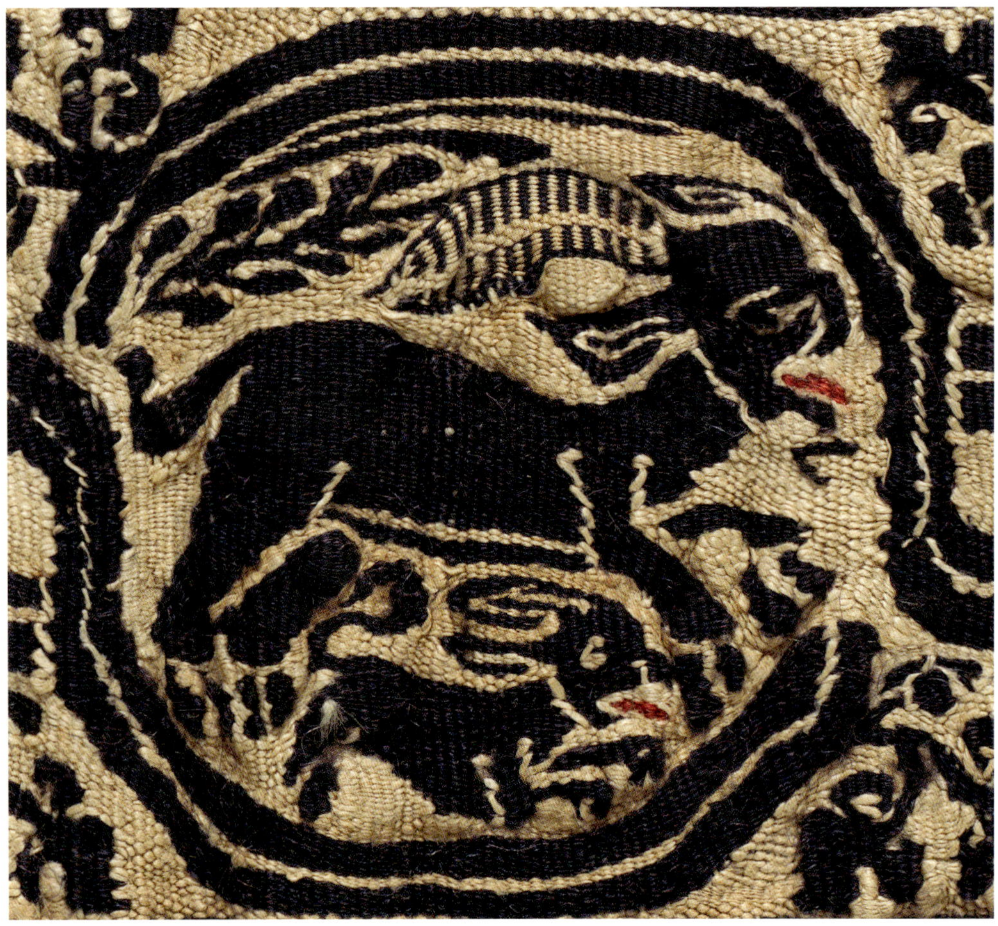

densely as to largely or entirely obscure the warp. A detail from a Byzantine era tapestry in the Harvard Art Museums (cat. 21) shows that the ecru-colored warp almost disappears behind the weft, especially in the densely compressed areas of purple (Fig. 1). This detail also illustrates the freedom of the tapestry technique: in a feature described as "non-horizontal" or "eccentric" weft, the weft deviates from the rectilinear grid of the loom to create sinuous curves.

When the tapestry structure is carried out from end to end and from selvedge to selvedge, it is called "allover tapestry" (see cats. 24, 27, 34). In the tradition prevalent in late antique and medieval Egypt, textiles with a plain weave ground were also embellished with sections of tapestry weave in contrasting colors. The tapestry-woven pattern could be sewn onto a finished ground fabric as an appliqué or woven directly into the fabric as bands or inserts, known as in-woven tapestry.

When weft yarns of wool were used to weave tapestry into a linen ground textile, weavers had to make accommodations for the greater thickness of the wool yarns, lest their interlacing with the slender linen warp create too concentrated a structure. One solution to smooth the passage of the weft was to reduce the number of over/under movements it had to negotiate. Details of the front and back of a fourth- or fifth-century textile in the Museum of Fine Arts, Boston (cat. 25) show the weaver accomplishing this in two ways: by grouping the warp yarns into twos and threes and by dropping selected warp yarns out of the tapestry structure, allowing them to float on the back as "surplus" (Fig. 2a–b). These details also illustrate a strategy to anchor the dense tapestry weave within the looser plain weave: above and below the tapestry segment, the weaver has crossed warp yarns one over another at set intervals. In this object, there is

The longstanding tradition of tapestry weaving in Egypt dates to the pharaonic era. The term "tapestry" denotes both a weaving technique (or method by which the textile is made) and a fabric structure (how the elements within the textile interact). The technique involves introducing colored threads in the weft direction with needles, shuttles, or quills in the precise areas needed to create the desired design. The structure is a weft-faced textile with the weft yarns woven so

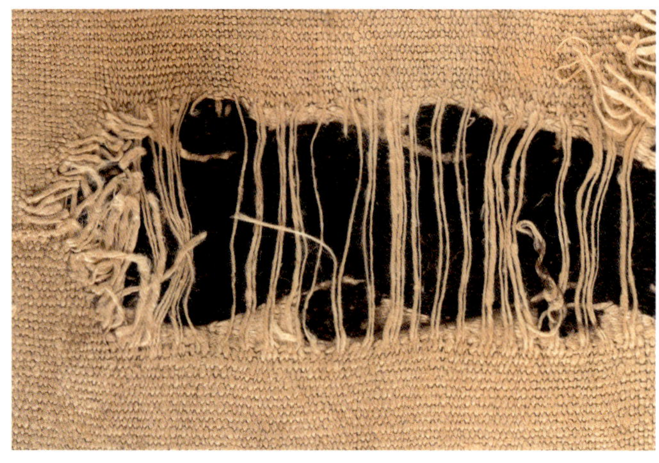

Fig. 1 Detail of cat. 21.

Fig. 2a–b Details of cat. 25 (front and back).

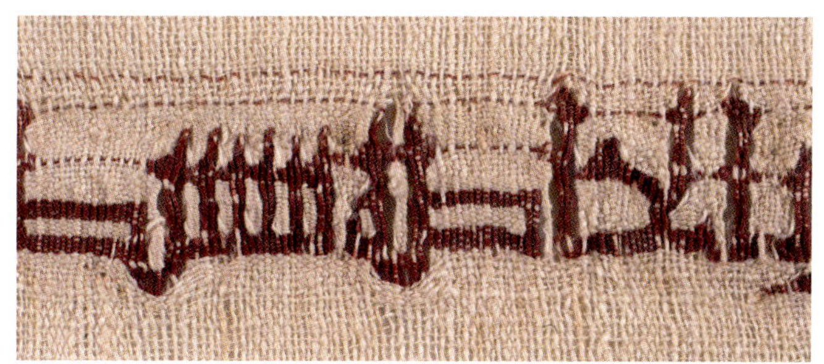

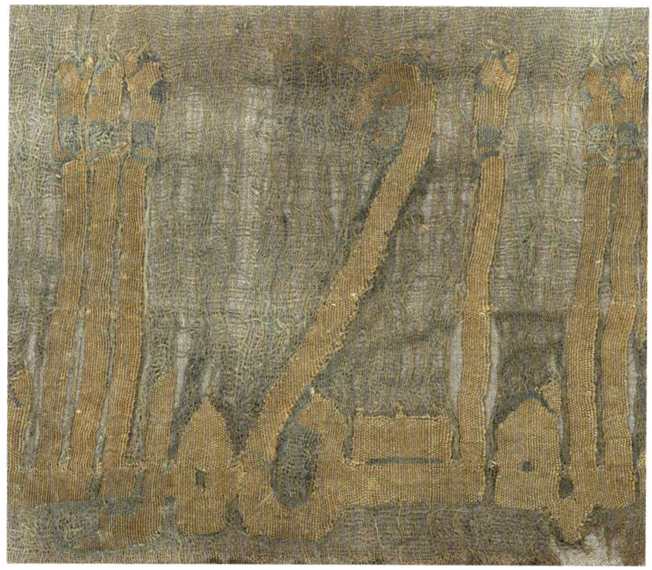

marked contrast between the plain-weave ground fabric and the in-woven tapestry (for a more detailed example of warp crossing, see Fig. 9 in the glossary).

With the rise of the Abbasid empire in Iraq, a wealth of textiles with administrative texts inscribed in silk embroidery made their way from textile centers in Iraq and Iran to far-flung provinces like Egypt (see cats. 2, 9–10). A post-weaving surface embellishment added to a finished textile, embroidery, as a structure, is quite distinct from tapestry. The silk filament — thin and smooth — is ideal for pulling through a woven structure. As a technique, on the other hand, embroidery and tapestry share something in common: both introduce threads via a needle or quill to create the desired design. Thus, when Egyptian workshops began to produce embroidered textiles, such as a ninth-century example in the Cleveland Museum of Art (cat. 1; see p. 18 for a detail of the embroidery), they did so in a way that recalled the tapestry technique. A single weft was drawn from the ground fabric, baring the warps just enough to introduce a baseline for embroidery (see, for example, Fig. 1 in the glossary), not unlike the transition from plain weave to in-woven tapestry. Bellinger noted that Egyptian embroideries employ a wider variety of stitches than those produced in Abbasid centers.[4] She attributed the Egyptians' more experimental approach to their relative unfamiliarity with the technique, but it also recalls the way in which tapestry weavers approach design.

Tapestry, likewise, came to resemble embroidery. A tiraz in the exhibition made in the second half of the tenth century (cat. 14) is distinguished by its inscription, executed in a single color of silk against an undyed ground, as in Abbasid embroideries. A detail (Fig. 3) shows that the weaver has minimized the contrast between the tapestry band that holds the inscription and the overall plain weave of the ground fabric (compare, for example, the clear distinction maintained in cat. 37). Making the linen tapestry weft blend into the ground

weave was particularly difficult, since the primary challenge of tapestry weaving is to maintain an even loom tension despite the varying densities of the different areas of the textile. Here, the weaver has gradually increased the compression of the linen weft to avoid sharp delineation. This detail highlights another aspect of the weaver's adaptability: the density of the silk wefts in the tapestry is higher than the surrounding linen ground weave, a feature that approximates the earlier practice in Egyptian tapestry of using a weft of thick wool yarns.

In addition, the weaver ingeniously supported the long tapestry slits created by the letter shafts by instituting a system of self-bands that carried the colored silk yarns from section to section. The tidy efficiency of these tiraz textiles with in-woven tapestry approximated the Abbasid embroidery aesthetic, while enriching the local tapestry tradition.

Around this time, in the second half of the tenth century, another type of tapestry was drawing on the embroidery aesthetic to become its own kind of luxury textile. The "floating" tapestry technique (see cats. 15–16) required weavers to lay a ground weft every few sheds, creating an open structure, while also working letter shafts in a densely beaten tapestry weft (Fig. 4). By this method, weavers emulated to some degree the way in which embroiderers placed letters directly within the ground weave. No longer embedded in a dense band, the tapestry-woven letters stand like silhouettes against the gossamer ground. This difficult technique created a delicate and sumptuous textile favored under the Abbasid caliph al-Muti' (r. 946–974), and when Egypt was conquered

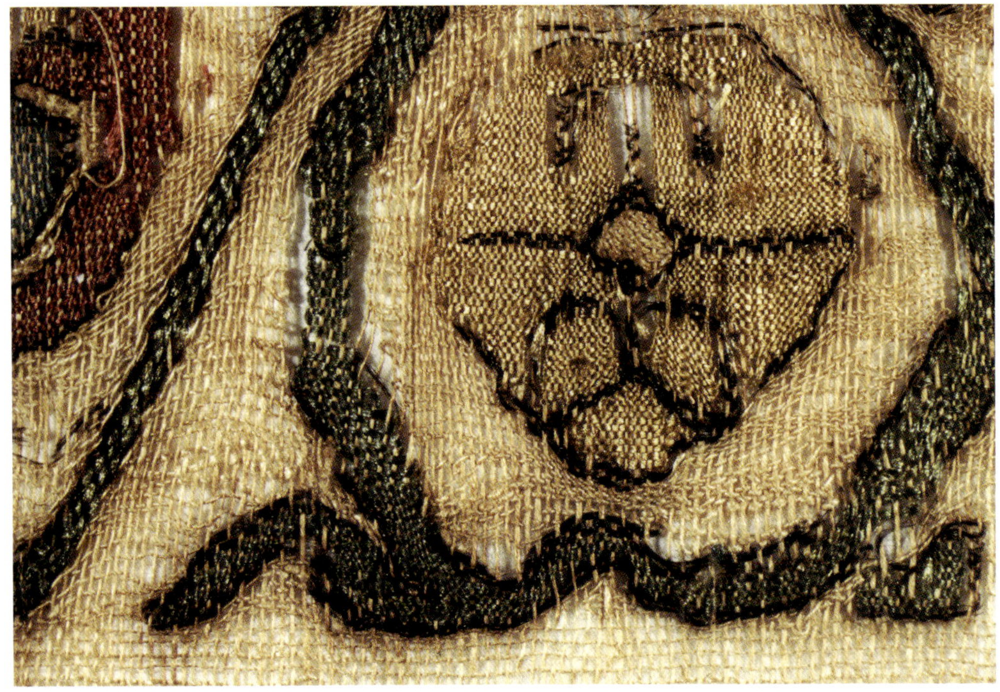

fell out of use as the fine diameter of silk yarns permitted Egyptian weavers to render even minute designs directly into the tapestry. As a close detail from a late eleventh-century textile (cat. 18) shows, Egyptian tapestry weavers blended silk and other fibers with virtuosic skill and sensitivity (Fig. 5).

The sustained presence of Abbasid protocollary textiles in Egypt allowed for a fruitful artistic interaction between textile-making traditions in the ninth and tenth centuries. The status of tiraz textiles in Abbasid administrative life pushed tapestry weavers in Egypt to adapt and innovate, learning from the imported embroideries. While the rise of the Fatimids and their distinctive dynastic style took tapestry weaving back to ornament rooted in Egypt's late antique and Byzantine past, the sway of Iraqi and Iranian embroidery left an indelible mark on the weaving tradition. The two regions of the Islamic world came to share the tiraz aesthetic, and their traditions of making textiles would become inextricably interwoven.

by the Fatimids, al-Muʿizz (r. 953–975) and his son al-ʿAziz (r. 975–996).

Although silk was not unknown in Egyptian textiles of the Byzantine era, it increasingly appeared in tapestry from the tenth century onward. Previously, when Egyptian weavers working in colored wools wanted to create a linear design, they employed the labor-intensive technique of supplementary weft wrapping (see Fig. 5 in the glossary). This practice

GOLD

Egyptian textiles of the medieval era show a remarkable sensitivity to fiber types, textures, weave density, and shading and juxtaposition of color. Egyptian weavers were masters at using pattern, color, and combinations of fibers to create diverse visual and tactile effects. The inclusion of gold in particular adds a striking dimension of luster and richness to the textiles.

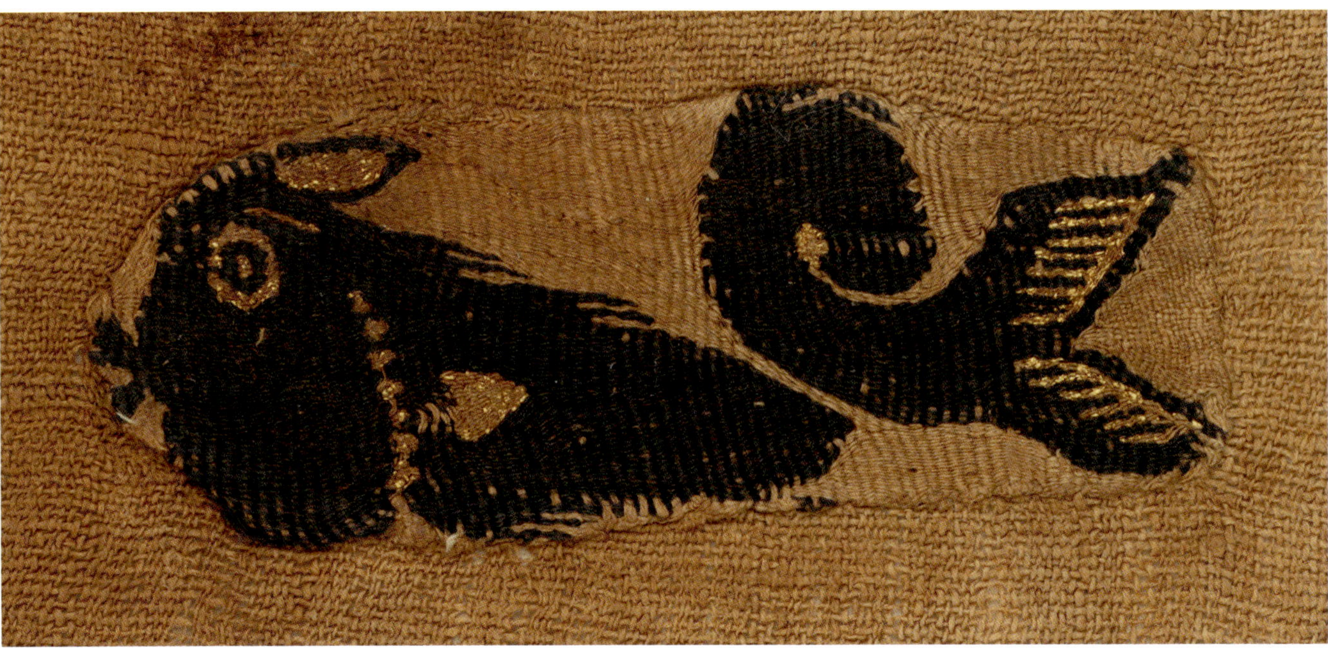

Fig. 5 Detail of cat. 18.

Fig. 6 Fragment from a curtain with dolphins (detail), Egypt, 5th–6th century. Plain weave with in-woven tapestry weave; linen, wool, linen or silk, and gold *filé*, 26.2 × 11 cm. Cleveland Museum of Art, Andrew R. and Martha Holden Jennings Fund, 1982.82.

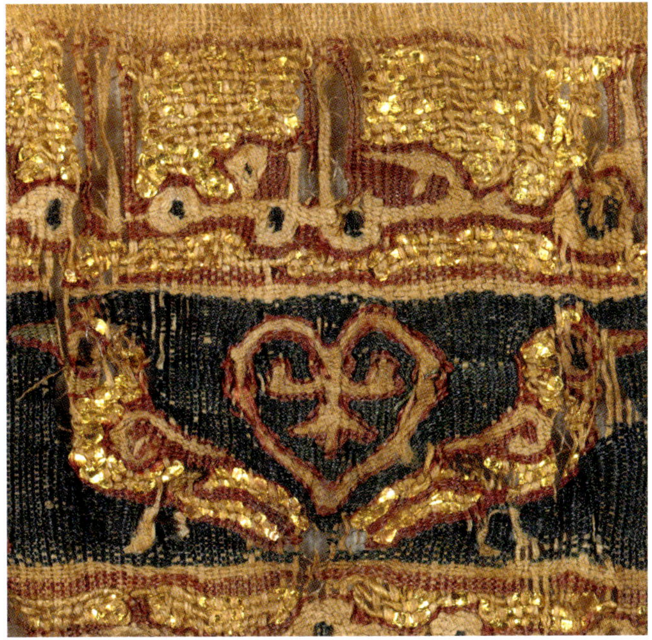

For this study, the collection of the Cleveland Museum of Art (CMA) was surveyed to better understand the use of gold in eastern Mediterranean textiles made in the centuries before and after the Arab Muslim conquest. The CMA has a rich corpus of twenty textiles with gold, from the Byzantine through Fatimid periods (5th–12th century), that can be attributed to Egyptian or Yemeni manufacture.[5] One of these is featured in the Harvard exhibition (cat. 17). Because gold does not tarnish, the bright, glittering nature of these decorative elements, some of which are sixteen centuries old, is as remarkable today as it was at the time of manufacture.

Seven of the CMA textiles with gold were made in pre-Islamic Egypt (c. 4th–5th century).[6] A small fragment of a linen curtain decorated with motifs in-woven in linen and wool tapestry is representative of the group (Fig. 6). Here the gold is used only as a weft yarn in the tapestry section; it is wound in narrow strips of foil around a fiber core (*filé*).[7] In an otherwise monochromatic design, the gold is used sparingly but to great effect, highlighting the eyes, gills, and fins of a dolphin. The glittering gold contrasts dramatically with the dark-purple wool yarns of the tapestry.

The CMA has no examples of tiraz textiles with gold thread that can be dated to the first three centuries of Islamic rule in Egypt. From the eleventh century, during the reign of the Fatimids, the collection has eleven fragments.[8] As in the Byzantine examples above, the precious metal takes the form of "gold threads" constructed of thin gold *filé* and again is used only in tapestry-patterned sections that are woven into the plain weave linen ground. Compared to its spare presence in the Byzantine dolphin, a more generous use of gold can be seen in the early eleventh-century textile naming the Fatimid caliph al-Hakim (r. 996–1021; cat. 17), where it is deployed in two ways: in the blue-green band, it highlights the bird motifs; and in the inscription bands, it fills the negative space around the letters (Fig. 7).[9] An image of the inscription taken under higher magnification better reveals the construction of the gold *filé* and shows how the weaver has contrasted the surface qualities of the threads (Fig. 8). The letters themselves are rendered in a relatively matte white linen, outlined in shiny red silk, while interstitial space is filled with lustrous gold. Other examples from the Fatimid period demonstrate that by varying the color of the core in the *filé* from cooler to warmer hues, the apparent tone of the gold itself could be subtly shifted.

Some tiraz textiles from the Fatimid period merely create the appearance of gold. Many of the design elements in three CMA textiles (cats. 16, 18, 23) are woven from a shiny yellow silk like that used for the *filé* cores (see Fig. 5). In the right lighting conditions and at a distance, the yellow silk effectively suggests the use of the precious metal.

In contrast to the *filé* technique, artisans in medieval Yemen applied gold leaf to textiles that were fully woven (see

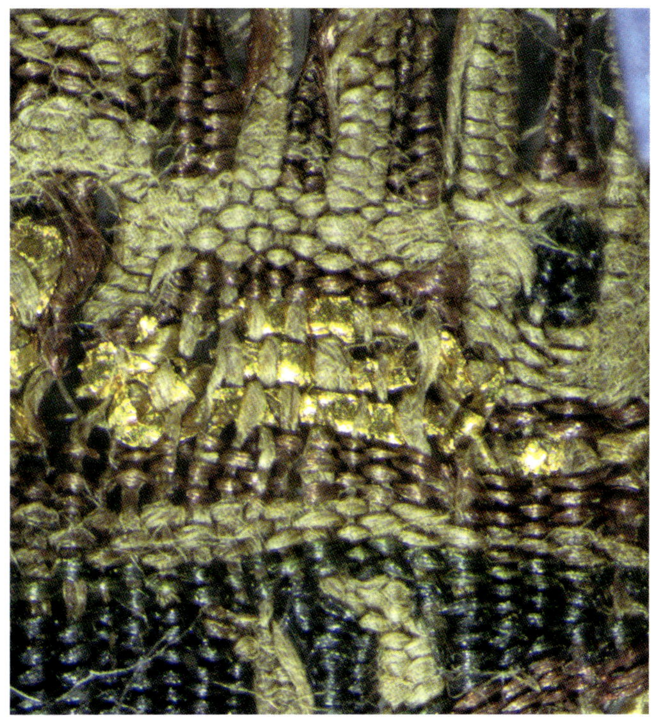

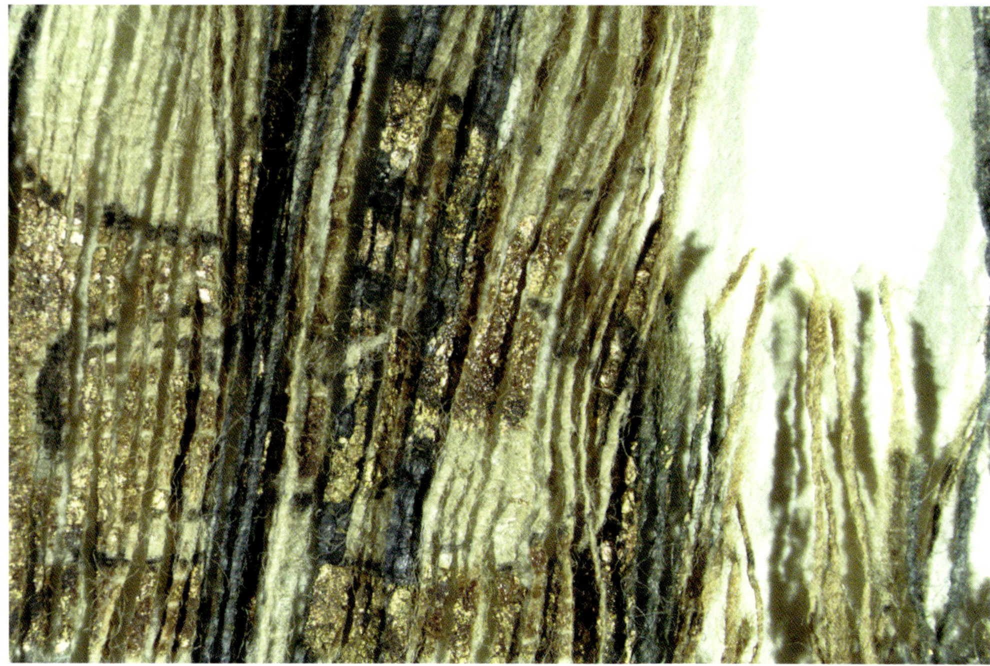

for comparison, the thickness of copy paper is about 0.1 millimeters, or roughly 140 times that of the gold layer.

DYES AND RADIOCARBON DATING

For most of human history, textile dyes were sourced from nature — specifically, from plant or animal material. The vivid colors of the tiraz in the Harvard exhibition are a testament to the skill of the dyers, who worked with a palette of primarily red, yellow, and blue to obtain the desired shades. In most cases, secondary colors required successive dyeings, because dye baths cannot be mixed in the same manner as pigments. Dyeing could easily account for a large portion of the price of a new textile.[13] It is a common misconception that coloring textiles with natural dyes could not achieve the same depth of hue or brilliance to which we are accustomed today. The less vibrant appearance of many ancient textiles is possibly the result of centuries of light exposure and fluctuating climatic conditions. The arid, archaeological environment of the Egyptian tombs from which the textiles in the exhibition were excavated allowed the dyers' work to be preserved more completely, as the richness and variety of colors attest.

Natural dyeing by hand is a labor-intensive process requiring time, skill, large volumes of water, fuel for heat, and additives to the dye itself, which in turn must be cultivated, harvested, and processed before use. Many natural materials will impart some color to textile fibers; however, the majority will not be particularly colorful or fast, meaning resistant to fading. Robust colorants are conventionally referred to today as *grands teints*, in contrast with the cheaper, lower-quality *petits teints*,[14] though both require considerable labor and resources. *Grand teint* reds and yellows typically need the fibers to be mordanted with a metal ion, most commonly iron or aluminum, to aid dye uptake and retention, while *petits teints* might be applied directly. Blue, sourced from woad or indigo, is imparted via a reduction-oxidation reaction that dyers induced by fermenting the dye vat and maintaining it much like a sourdough starter.

Technical studies of dyes on Egyptian textiles date from at least the mid-1930s, when Rudolf Pfister tested red colorants in fibers in a range of solvents to examine solubility and color change.[15] Dye identification is still of significant scholarly interest, though scientists today use instrumental methods for less invasive, more robust results. Notably, the

cats. 11–12). The CMA holds two fine examples of plain-weave cotton Yemeni textiles from the late tenth century, which were produced using the ikat technique, where the yarn is resist-dyed before weaving to produce variegated patterns in light brown, blue, and white.[10] As seen in a photomicrograph of one of these examples (CMA 1950.524), a very thin layer of gold leaf was adhered to the woven ikat with a gummy, resinous substrate to form the Arabic inscription (Fig. 9; see also Jochen Sokoly's essay in this volume). The material, now reddish-brown, was painted directly onto the woven textile before the leaf was applied. After the gold leaf was adhered, the script characters were outlined in black ink to further delineate them.[11] Fourier-transform infrared spectroscopy (FTIR) analysis of a sample from the resinous layer determined it is consistent with gum ammoniac (*Dorema ammoniacum*), which was also identified in a Yemeni textile in the Museum of Fine Arts, Boston (cat. 12).[12] The gold leaf is so thin it appears slightly red, owing to the hue of the resin beneath. A sample of the gold leaf and resin layer was made into a cross-section and examined by scanning electron microscopy with energy-dispersive X-ray spectroscopy (SEM-EDS). In the resulting SEM image (Fig. 10), the gold leaf shows as the ragged, light-gray line atop the resin layer. SEM-EDS determined the leaf was approximately 90 percent gold and 10 percent silver, with some trace elements present. Its variable thickness was measured at 500–900 nanometers;

technical literature on materials from this period most often categorizes textiles as "Coptic," "Byzantine," or "Egyptian," and rarely "Islamic." The data is often not directly linked to museum accession numbers, further complicating a broad understanding of production and consumption in this period. Art historical literature provides a context for analytical data, making it a valuable complementary resource in technical studies. For example, curator and textile historian Louise Mackie observed a taste for color and variegated or iridescent shades in Egypt. She further noted that cotton fibers were more common in textiles from Iran and Iraq, and that a red and yellow palette emerged with the Fatimids, for whom redwood dye was a popular choice.[16] These informed observations are essential to understanding the significance and implications of results from technical studies.

Decades after Pfister's technical investigation of red dyes, André Verhecken conducted a large survey that supported Pfister's conclusion that lac was introduced to Egypt in the Islamic period. Verhecken compared analyses of dye components in Egyptian textiles to the ages of the textiles as determined by radiocarbon dating,[17] a technique that measures the amount of ^{14}C isotope in a material to ascertain when it was alive. With textiles, this provides the date range in which the fibers were harvested — for example, when the flax was cut or sheep sheared. The method was first applied to textiles in the 1950s by Pierre du Bourguet, working with the collections at the Louvre, and more recent re-investigations have validated the technique as a tool for studying textiles, though the sample mass required may be prohibitive for some objects.[18] The results provide a concrete link between the object age and the dyes present and also indicate that art historical methods to determine creation date may be less accurate than previously thought, stymied by long-lived styles and weaving techniques. More recently, Monica Gulmini identified a combination of madder and lac on red threads in textiles attributed to the late antique and Byzantine era.[19] The results contradict Verhecken and Pfister, but it must be noted that there is no corresponding radiocarbon date for these pieces, and their age is presumably based on art historical methods of dating. In 2019, six Egyptian textiles were dated by radiocarbon content (see Table 1 for results), further contributing to the body of knowledge linking art historical methods to physical age. Although

Table 1 Results of radiocarbon analysis. Objects marked with an asterisk appear in the exhibition.

OBJECT	CALIBRATED ^{14}C DATE (95.4% PROBABILITY)
HAM 1924.124*	435–608
HAM 1975.41.25	256–393
HAM 1975.41.28	417–545
HAM 2004.204*	346–528
CMA 1956.330*	770–887
DO BZ.1933.25*	901–1023

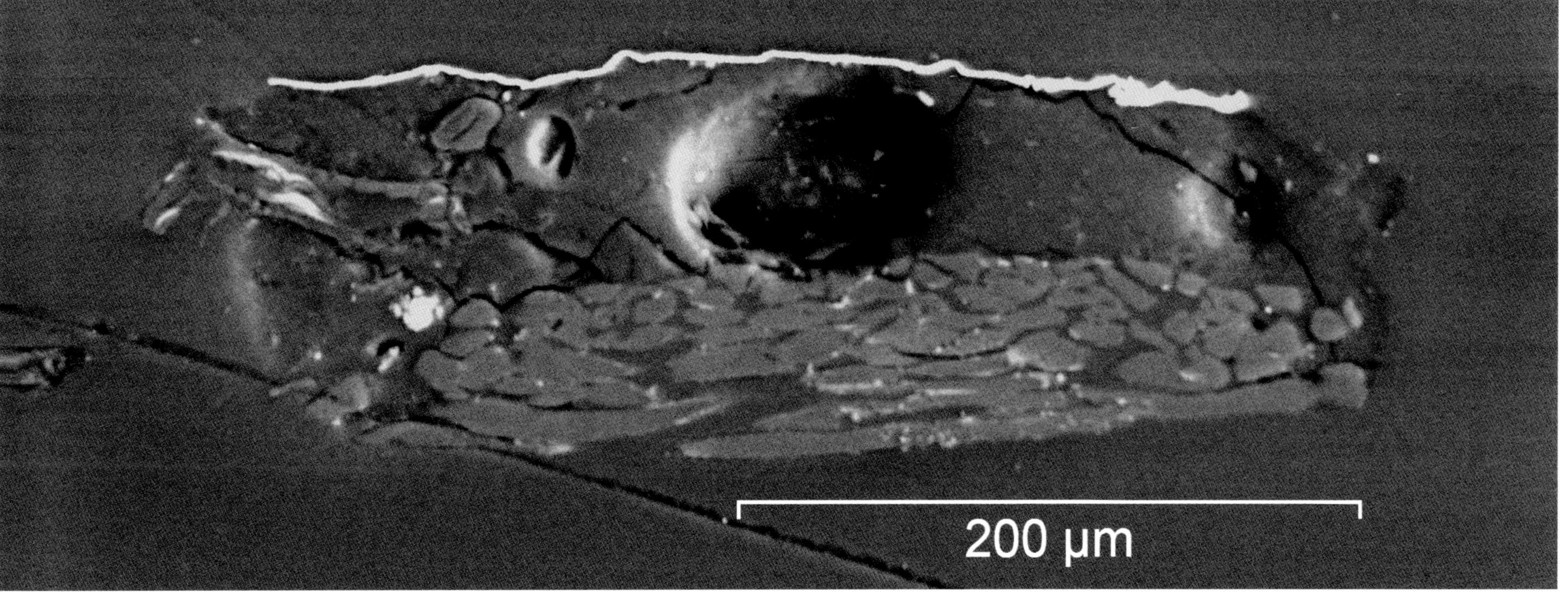

Fig. 10 Scanning electron microscope image of gold leaf/resin cross-section from CMA 1950.524.

Table 2 Results of analysis of extracted dyes. Objects are arranged in approximate chronological order. Those marked with an asterisk appear in the exhibition.

OBJECT	COLOR	DYES	DATE
HAM 1975.41.25	purple	madder, indigoids	late 3rd–4th c.
MFA 23.177*	purple	madder	4th–5th c.
HAM 2004.204*	red	wild madder	late 4th–early 5th c.
HAM 2004.204*	purple	wild madder, indigoids	late 4th–early 5th c.
HAM 1975.41.28*	blue	indigoids	5th–6th c.
HAM 1975.41.28*	green	flavonoids	5th–6th c.
HAM 1975.41.28*	red, bright	wild madder	5th–6th c.
HAM 1975.41.28*	red, light	wild madder	5th–6th c.
HAM 1975.41.28*	purple	wild madder	5th–6th c.
HAM 1924.124*	purple	wild madder, indigoids	mid-6th–7th c.
DO BZ.1953.2.3*	red	lac, madder	8th c.
DO BZ.1953.2.3*	pink	madder	8th c.
DO BZ.1953.2.3*	yellow	flavonoids	8th c.
DO BZ.1953.2.3*	green	flavonoids, indigoids	8th c.
MFA 11.1398*	red	wild madder, lac	late 8th–9th c.
MFA 11.1398*	yellow	flavonoids	late 8th–9th c.
MFA 11.1398*	green	flavonoids, indigoids	late 8th–9th c.
MFA 11.1398*	blue	indigoids	late 8th–9th c.
CMA 1956.330*	yellow	flavonoids, tannins	late 8th–late 9th c.
CMA 1956.330*	green	flavonoids, indigoids	late 8th–late 9th c.
CMA 1956.330*	brown	flavonoids	late 8th–late 9th c.
CMA 1956.330*	red	lac	late 8th–late 9th c.
CMA 1956.330*	black	madder, indigoids, tannins	late 8th–late 9th c.
CMA 1959.48*	green	flavonoids, tannins	early 9th c.
CMA 1959.48*	yellow	flavonoids	early 9th c.
CMA 1959.48*	red	lac, madder	early 9th c.
MFA 03.1879d	red	lac	9th–11th c.
MFA 03.1879d	blue	indigoids	9th–11th c.
MFA 03.1879d	brown	tannins	9th–11th c.
MFA 34.115*	brown	tannins	late 9th–early 10th c.
MFA 34.115*	blue	indigoids	late 9th–early 10th c.

OBJECT	COLOR	DYES	DATE
CMA 1950.524	brown	tannins	960–80
CMA 1950.524	blue	indigoids	960–80
MFA 34.118*	red	lac, tannins	962–63
DO BZ.1933.37*	brown	tannins	c. 980
DO BZ.1933.37*	blue	indigoids	c. 980
DO BZ.1933.25*	yellow	flavonoids	10th–early 11th c.
DO BZ.1933.25*	red	lac, madder	10th–early 11th c.
DO BZ.1933.25*	black	indigoids	10th–early 11th c.
DO BZ.1933.25*	brown	flavonoids	10th–early 11th c.
DO BZ.1933.25*	green	flavonoids, indigoids	10th–early 11th c.
MFA 34.116*	black	tannins	c. 996–1021
DO BZ.1933.22*	red	lac, madder	1008–9
CMA 1965.313*	blue	indigoids	c. 1094–1101
CMA 1965.313*	black	tannins	c. 1094–1101
CMA 1965.313*	green	flavonoids, indigoids	c. 1094–1101
CMA 1965.313*	yellow	flavonoids	c. 1094–1101
CMA 1965.313*	red	lac	c. 1094–1101
CMA 1929.937	yellow	tannins	1130–49
CMA 1929.937	red	madder, lac	1130–49
CMA 1982.291*	green	flavonoids, indigoids	12th c.
CMA 1982.291*	blue	indigoids	12th c.
CMA 1982.291*	black	tannins	12th c.
CMA 1982.291*	yellow	flavonoids	12th c.
CMA 1982.291*	red	lac, madder	12th c.
CMA 1982.303	blue	indigoids	12th c.
CMA 1982.303	yellow	flavonoids, tannins	12th c.
CMA 1982.303	red	lac, madder	12th c.

DO = Dumbarton Oaks Research Library and Collection, Washington, D.C.
CMA = Cleveland Museum of Art
HAM = Harvard Art Museums
MFA = Museum of Fine Arts, Boston

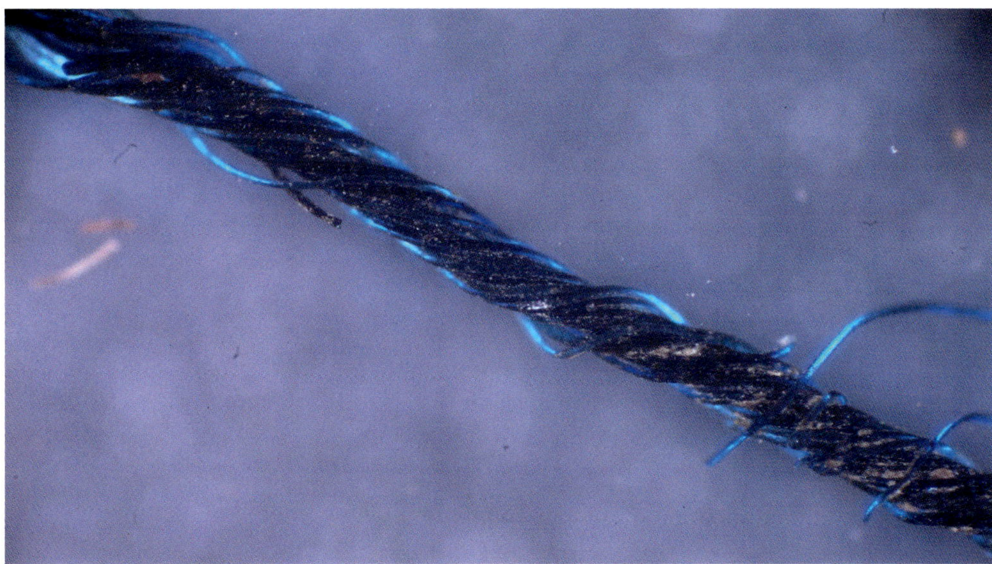

Fig. 11 Photomicrograph (at 50x magnification) of a sample from the ground of cat. 30, which appears black but is actually deep blue.

Fig. 12 Photomicrograph (at 50x magnification) of purple fiber samples from cat. 21.

this represents a small sample set, the findings are consistent with Verhecken and Pfister.

Previous analyses of "Coptic" textiles have identified red dyes from madder, Armenian cochineal, kermes, lac, and soluble redwood; yellow dyes from weld, yellow larkspur, Persian berries, and young fustic; and blue from indigo or woad; as well as henna, safflower, and tannins.[20] The dye composition of fifty-eight colored fiber samples from Egyptian textiles dating from the late third through twelfth centuries was analyzed using high-performance liquid chromatography-mass spectroscopy (HPLC-MS). The results, shown in Table 2, reveal the variety of skillful ways in which dyers created blacks and intermediate colors like purple and green.

The dye sources described in this table were determined based on the occurrence and relative abundance of characteristic components in the colorant extracted from fiber samples. The precision of an assignment depends on the concentration of dyes in the extract, which in turn depends on the sample and therefore the object. Madder (*Rubia*) is a genus of plant with a few species that have tinctorial properties, the source of a ubiquitous red dye. The major components of madder dye are alizarin and purpurin, which vary in relative abundance to each other and other minor components. Minor components may reveal whether a particular species of *Rubia* was used — for example, *R. peregrina* and *R. cordifolia*, sometimes called "wild madder," have a higher ratio of purpurin to alizarin and contain other components, such as munjistin and xanthopurpurin. Cultivated madder (*R. tinctorum*) was bred for its higher abundance of alizarin, which produces a purer

red, and tends to have fewer minor components. In the results presented here, an assignment of "wild madder" indicates enough components were detected to identify the dye as such, whereas "madder" implies that a characteristic marker such as alizarin was detected but the dye concentration is too low for minor components to be useful. It should be noted that a compound can be present but below the limit of detection, so results improve with further analytical innovation. Indigo and woad, used to create a blue dye, cannot yet be distinguished analytically,[21] since the dye components in both plants are indigotin and indirubin; in this work, they are grouped together as "indigoids." The precise identification of yellows is often complicated for similar reasons — many dye sources contain the same, primarily flavonoid components. Yellow dyes can be better characterized through minor components, which are frequently in the form of glycosides, or sugars, though these compounds are also susceptible to degradation during the extraction process. In this investigation, major components such as luteolin, fisetin, apigenin, sulfuretin, and quercetin are identified as "flavonoids." Tannins are a broad class of compounds abundant in the natural world, often presenting in yellow, black, and brown dye extracts. They are similarly identified as "tannins" in this work.

The dark border of the decorative bands of a shawl in the Dumbarton Oaks collection (cat. 30 [DO BZ.1933.25]) was created by dyeing the wool a velvety, deep blue-black

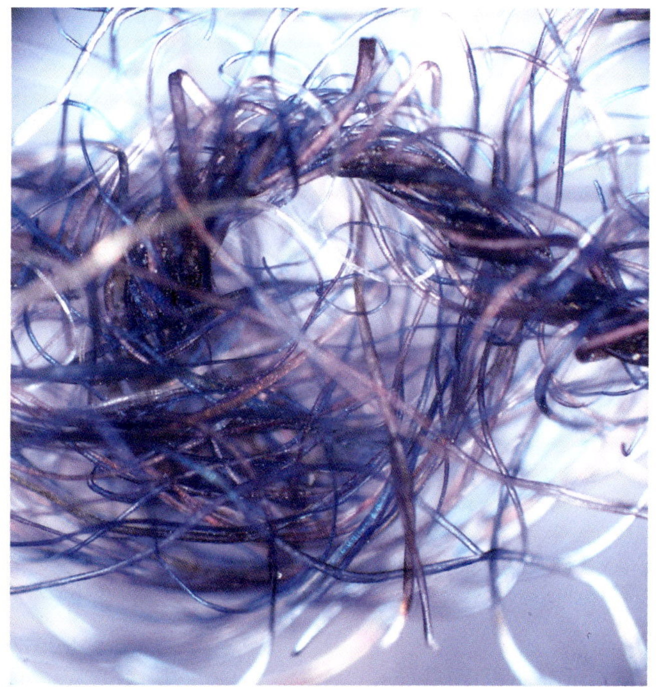

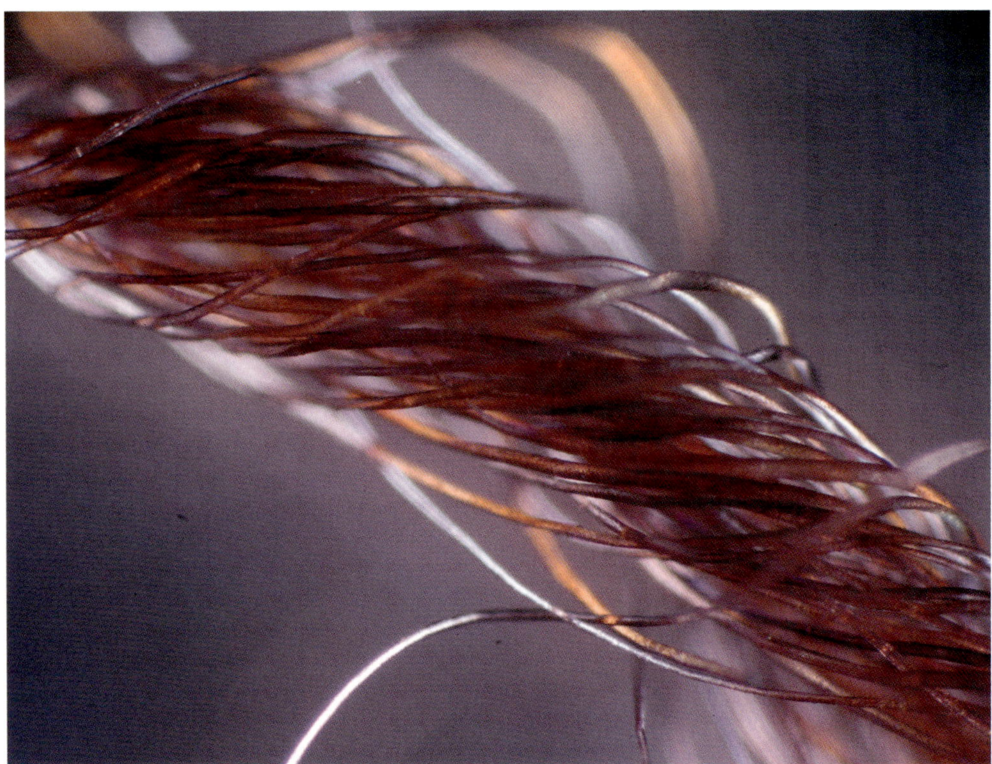

Fig. 13 Photomicrograph (at 50x magnification) of purple fiber samples from cat. 24.

is complicated, especially on archaeological materials that are contaminated by the burial environment, but the dye's makeup and hue are consistent with iron-mordanted wool dyed with madder.

As discussed above, reds dyed with lac are associated more with the Islamic period in Egypt, reflecting trade with eastern lands. The use of lac in the border of a shawl in the Museum of Fine Arts, Boston, bearing inscriptions in Coptic and Arabic (cat. 29 [MFA 11.1398]) manifests the mixture of people, cultures, languages, and beliefs in Egypt during this era. The red threads in two other Islamic era textiles in the exhibition (cats. 23, 27 [CMA 1982.291, DO BZ.1953.2.3]) contain components from both lac and madder, as observed in earlier examples by Gulmini et al., showing the precise way dyers used two reds to obtain the desired shade. The increase in red and yellow pieces during the reign of the Fatimids noted by Mackie may also originate from improved access to lac through trade. Certainly, the makers and wearers of these textiles had a true appreciation for color and could create an impressive range of shades with relatively few raw materials.

with indigo/woad (Fig. 11). Two pieces from the Cleveland Museum of Art reveal different ways to achieve black: one (cat. 28 [CMA 1956.330]) uses a combination of indigoids, madder, and tannins; while the other (cat. 18 [CMA 1965.313]) produces a similar shade using only tannins, requiring fewer materials and less time.

Purple appears more frequently in pre-Islamic Egyptian textiles, and the color could be produced a few ways. The scarcity and status of Tyrian purple, harvested from the glands of certain seashells of the genus *Murex* and considered the only "true" purple dye found in nature, means it rarely appears on anything other than imperial objects or textiles of religious significance. Verhecken found Tyrian purple in textiles made prior to roughly 600, after which its occurrence tails off.[22] An affordable purple could be made by overdyeing fibers red after blue, as seen in a cuff in the Harvard Art Museums (cat. 21 [HAM 2004.204]) whose purple bands were made with a combination of indigo or woad and madder (Fig. 12). By contrast, the purple in a large cover or shroud at Harvard (cat. 24 [HAM 1975.41.28]) contains only madder and no indigoid dyes (Fig. 13). Madder is a polygenetic dye, yielding different shades depending on the mordant used. In conjunction with aluminum, madder dyes a bright red hue, but with iron the color is a deeper, reddish-purple. Mordant identification

ANALYTICAL NOTES

Dye extraction was performed by Julie Wertz, the Beal Family Postgraduate Fellow in Conservation Science in the Straus Center for Conservation and Technical Studies at the Harvard Art Museums, with Richard Newman, head of scientific research at the Museum of Fine Arts, Boston. Samples were analyzed using HPLC-MS at the Harvard Center for Mass Spectrometry with the support of senior director Sunia Trauger. SEM-EDS was performed on a cross-section at the MFA with support from Katherine Eremin, the Patricia Cornwall Senior Conservation Scientist in the Straus Center. FTIR analysis was performed by Wertz in the Straus Center. Accelerated mass spectrometry (AMS) radiocarbon analysis was performed at the University of Georgia Center for Applied Isotope Studies by Alex Cherkinsky. The results were calibrated on the IntCal13 curve using the OxCal interface.[23]

1   Kühnel and Bellinger 1952, 101ff. Bellinger likewise associated embroidery with an "Asiatic" tradition that she saw as a response to Chinese warp-faced compound silk weaving.

2   Heidemann 1998.

3   For definitions of textile terms, see the glossary at the end of this volume.

4   Kühnel and Bellinger 1952, 102–6.

5   Egyptian textiles with gold in the CMA are 1948.258, 1950.541, 1950.549, 1950.550, 1950.555.a–b, 1950.556, 1968.248, 1971.172, 1982.79, 1982.82, 1982.103, 1982.105, 1982.106, 1982.109, and 1983.140.a–c. Yemeni textiles are 1950.353 and 1950.524.

6   1982.79, 1982.82, 1982.105, 1982.106, and 1983.140.a–c.

7   It has not been possible to identify the fiber around which the gold foil in this textile is wrapped. Analysis of an Egyptian tapestry of similar date (4th–5th century) with gold *filé* in the Museum of Fine Arts, Boston (46.401) revealed that the fiber core was silk. The metal was analyzed in 2004 using scanning electron microscopy with energy dispersive X-ray spectroscopy (SEM-EDS) and found to be 99.2 percent gold and 0.7 percent silver, with a trace of copper. SEM images show tool markings that appear to indicate hammering of the foil as well as a bur along the edge of the gold that makes it appear as if cut. The silk was identified using polarized light microscopy and micro-chemical tests.

8   1946.258, 1950.541, 1950.549, 1950.550, 1950.555.a–b, 1950.556, 1968.248, 1971.172, 1982.103, and 1982.109.

9   This textile also continues the pre-Islamic workshop practice of warp-grouping and warp-crossing in the transition between the plain weave of the ground fabric and the bands of in-woven tapestry. Perhaps the need to reduce the number of interlacings of the tapestry weft reflects the thickness of gold-wrapped threads, or maybe the weaver judged that the tapestry band needed to be secured by warp-crossing due to the weight of the gold *filé* threads.

10   1950.353 and 1950.524.

11   Bier 2001 and Bier 2014.

12   Results of the FTIR analysis of the MFA textile were documented in an unpublished report by Michele Derrick, "FTIR Analysis of Resin Coating over Gold Threads (MFA 34.115)," in 2003.

13   Mackie 2015, 105.

14   The French classifications of *grands* and *petits teints* are anachronistic for medieval Egyptian tapestries, but are used here simply to illustrate dye substantivity. See Brunello 1973.

15   Pfister 1936a and Pfister 1936b.

16   Mackie 2015, 120.

17   Verhecken 2007, 206–13.

18   Van Strydonck, De Moor, and Bénazeth 2004; and Van Strydonck and Bénazeth 2014.

19   Gulmini et al. 2017.

20   Ahmed et al. 2017; Gulmini et al. 2017; Hofmann-de Keijzer, Van Bommel, and De Keijzer 2007, 214–28; Shibayama, Wypyski, and Gagliardi-Mangilli 2015; and Wouters 1993, 53–64.

21   Gulmini et al. 2017, 487.

22   Verhecken 2007, 211.

23   Bronk Ramsey 2009 and Reimer et al. 2013.

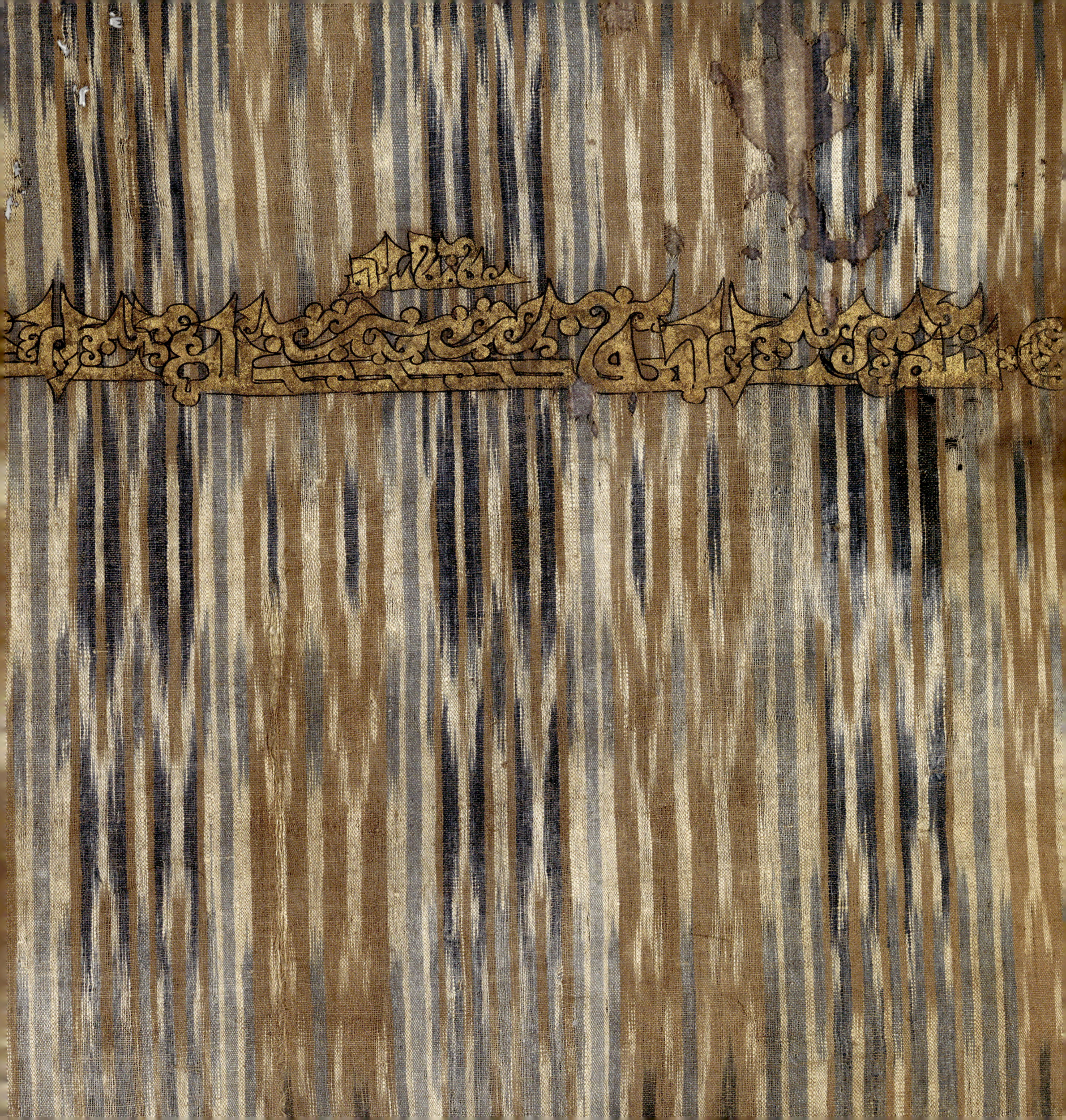

1   Expressions of the State: The Abbasid Era

The suite of tiraz textiles exhibited in *Social Fabrics: Inscribed Textiles from Medieval Egyptian Tombs* reveals a dynamic institution that, as an organ of the state, expressed evolving hierarchies, politics, and fortunes. Examples in this section that date from the mid-ninth to mid-tenth century span the last century of Abbasid rule in Egypt. By this time, tiraz had fully matured both as a concept and as an industry. Control of inscriptions — who was named, in what sequence, and in what capacity — was a closely guarded prerogative of the caliph and his immediate administrators. Similar to texts struck on Islamic coins or spoken in the khutbah (the Friday sermon), tiraz inscriptions acknowledged the sovereignty of the reigning caliph and invoked divine blessings upon him.

Whether gifted as robes of honor or as part of annual salary disbursements, caliphal tiraz were a concrete manifestation of a network of patronage. As furnishing fabrics or clothing, their display communicated membership in the ruling class. Only a handful have survived as complete garments, but pictorial representations help us re-embody the many fragments under study.

The fabrics in this section are all said to have been recovered from Egyptian burial grounds, and many were produced in Egyptian workshops. Their texts, appearance, construction, and materials vary in meaningful ways that speak to Egypt's status as a province within the Abbasid empire. With the caliph and central administration headquartered in Iraq, Abbasid tiraz reflect an eastern aesthetic. Typically, the primary decoration is the Arabic inscription itself, often comprising red, blue, or black letters on a plain white ground — echoing, in a sense, calligraphy on a manuscript page. The inscriptions are usually rendered in embroidery, an eastern technique favored in Iraq and Iran, rather than in the indigenous Egyptian tapestry technique. Egyptian weavers assimilated eastern tastes and methods, readily incorporating imported silk into tapestry weaving. A few of these tiraz hint at a two-way dialogue between eastern and western traditions.

The prestige of the imperial capital in Baghdad influenced practices in other provincial courts as well, such as that of Yemen, even as the caliphate's power collapsed inward. As the periphery inevitably began to break away from central rule, one of the first provinces to establish a degree of autonomy was Egypt, under the governorship of the Tulunid dynasty (868–905). Not surprisingly, this assertion of independence found expression in the language of tiraz.

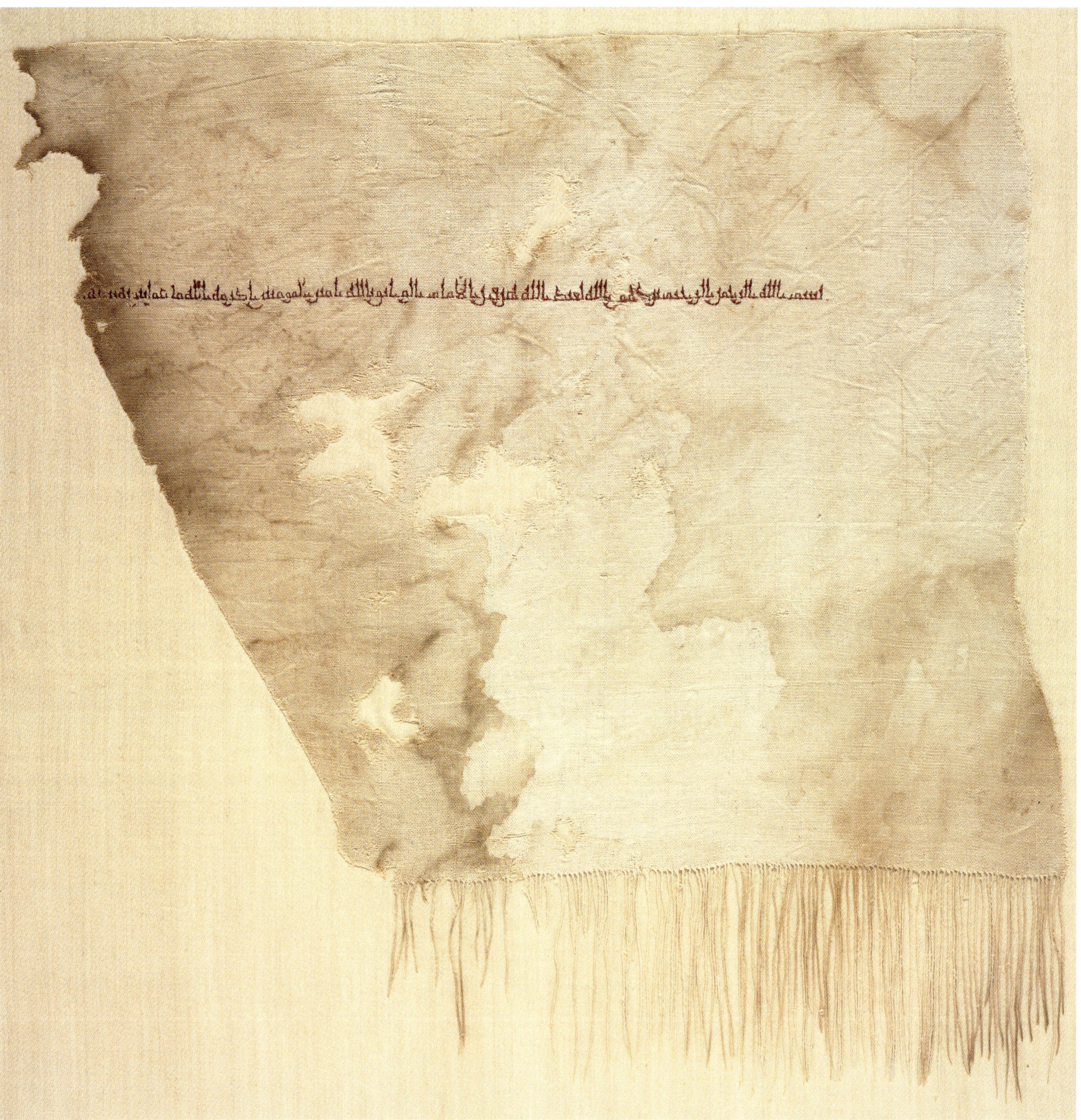

1

Tiraz textile naming the Abbasid caliph al-Wathiq bi-Allah

Egypt, Tuna, c. 842–47

Cleveland Museum of Art, Gift of George D. Pratt, 1932.25

1   Kühnel and Bellinger 1952, 105.
2   Al-Yāqūt 1906, 435ff.
3   Ibn Ḥawqal 2001, 150.
4   Thread count by Dorothy Shepherd, unpublished manuscript, cat. 95.

This rare early example of embroidery from Egypt reveals the intersection of Abbasid administrative practices and the local weaving tradition. The inscription bears the name of Caliph al-Wathiq (r. 842–847) and features relatively short script, measuring less than an inch in height. This aesthetic emphasizes the functional over the ornamental: the inscription was meant to convey information. Its visual form derived not from local artistic tradition but an epigraphic style aligned with Abbasid imperial textiles. Nevertheless, the couching stitch used in this piece bears little resemblance to the chain stitch commonplace in Iraq and Iran, suggesting that Egyptian textile workers were accommodating the eastern aesthetic indirectly (see the detail on p. 18). It is unlikely that the makers of this piece had any immediate contact with Iraqi or Iranian embroiderers. In assimilating new techniques into the Egyptian repertoire, the weavers made adjustments for local materials and practices: here, the weft yarn pulled out at the baseline of the script continued the use of preparatory indications on linen, recalling the method with which western weavers transitioned a ground fabric to tapestry while maintaining even tension throughout the piece. This may reflect differences in properties between linen and the cotton used in the eastern part of the Abbasid empire.[1] Alternatively, it may suggest that Egyptian workshops divided the tasks of situating and applying the inscription. Once "drawn," the baseline could subsequently be embroidered in red silk, with the ascending and descending lines couched after.

The city where this textile was produced, Tuna, located on an island in the eastern Nile delta, appears to have developed lasting ties to the Abbasids.[2] In 978, almost a decade after the Fatimid conquest and nearly a half-century after the first incursions into Egypt, geographer Ibn Hawqal noted that the city still supplied significant numbers of textiles to Iraq.[3]

— MLW

INSCRIPTION (ARABIC)

بسم الله الرحمن الرحيم بركه من الله لعبد الله هرون الامام الواثق بالله امير المؤمنين أكرمه
الله ما عمل بتونة سنة [. . .]

In the name of God, the Merciful, the Compassionate. Blessing from God to the servant of God, Harun, the imam al-Wathiq bi-Allah, Commander of the Faithful, may God be generous to him. Of what was made in Tuna in the year [. . .]

TECHNICAL DESCRIPTION[4]

Overall: 41.6 (warp) × 44.5 (weft) cm
Linen and silk: plain weave with embroidery
Plain weave: off-white linen, S, single, 14 warp × 22 weft/cm; embroidery: red silk, thrown, single, couching stitch
Baseline of inscription established by a drawn weft. Warp fringe at bottom edge. Reverse inaccessible.

SELECTED REFERENCES

Mackie 2015, 91–92

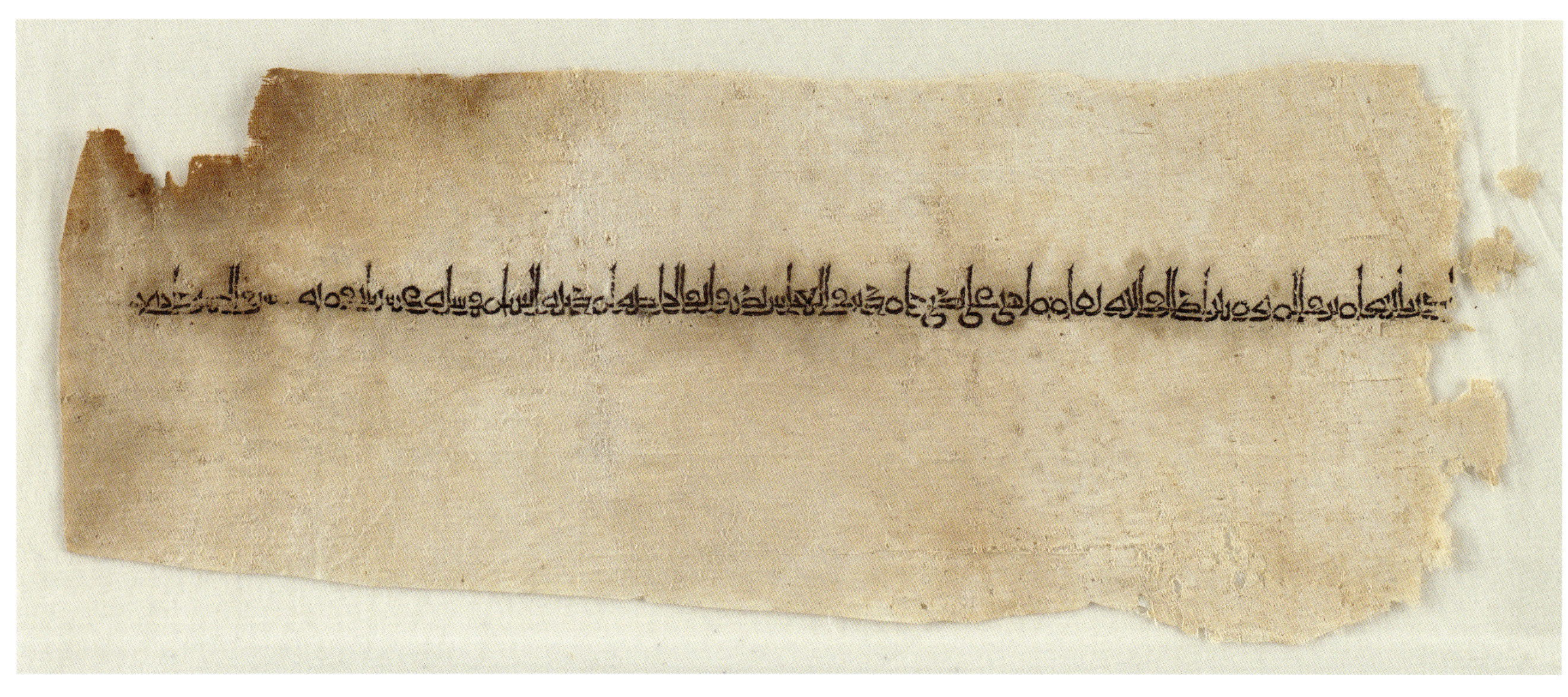

2

Tiraz textile naming the Abbasid caliph al-Muqtadir bi-Allah

Iraq, Baghdad, 310/922–23

The Textile Museum, Washington, D.C., Acquired by George Hewitt Myers in 1931, 73.17

1   Textile Museum 73.14. See Kühnel and Bellinger 1952, 27, pl. XII. Kühnel attributed the piece to Bishapur, but left open the possibility that it was made in Nishapur. See cat. 9 in this volume, attributed to Nishapur based on a historical connection between Khurasan and the Abbasid viceroy mentioned there.

2   All edges of this textile have been cut; the horizontally oriented yarns have a slightly tighter twist.

The embroidered inscription on this textile, which states that the work was completed in Baghdad (Madinat al-Salam), the Abbasid capital, is a good example of the imperial epigraphic style developed in the central Islamic lands. The chain-stitched letters typify the so-called eastern style of tiraz found on textiles from Iraq, Iran, and Khurasan. Empty needle holes suggest that some of the silk has been lost (see the detail on p. 25). The cotton ground fabric was sized, or glazed, and some of this agent appears over the inscription, indicating that the embroidery was already present. Thus, we can hypothesize that the weaving and embroidery were carried out in the same workshop, before finishing techniques were applied.

Evidence of the westward spread of embroidery at this time has supported the view that Abbasid administrative textiles exerted influence in Egypt. Much rarer is evidence of the reverse. Here, however, a limited use of blanket stitch, seen more typically in Egyptian embroideries, indicates that western Islamic techniques were indeed used in Iraq. While it seems that fewer western tiraz were making their way from Egypt to the central Abbasid lands than were entering the province, this small detail nonetheless attests to an exchange of technique and ideas in the early tenth century.

The vizier identified in the inscription, Hamid bin al-'Abbas, held that office from 306/918 to 310/923. He is named on a significant number of tiraz from both Iraq and Egypt (see also cat. 3; for a discussion, see Jochen Sokoly's essay in this volume). Interestingly, the inscription here credits him with executing the commissioning of the piece (*'ala yaday*), rather than initiating its order (*amara*). The individual mentioned after the date at the end of the inscription, a certain al-Husayn bin Ahmad, is likely the same person inscribed on another textile from al-Muqtadir's reign (908–932) made in Bishapur, or possibly Nishapur, in 309/921–22.[1] That the two textiles were created in separate locations undermines a previous interpretation that the name could be a workshop supervisor's signature. While his exact role is yet to be understood, Husayn bin Ahmad, like the vizier alongside whom he is named, may have held a managerial position within the Abbasid administration in Baghdad.

— MLW

[. . .] (al-Muq)tadir bi-Allah, Commander of the Faithful, may God prolong his existence. What was cared for under the direction of Hamid bin al-'Abbas in the private factory at Madinat al-Salam. Year ten and three hundred [. . .] al-Husayn bin Ahmad.

TECHNICAL DESCRIPTION

39.5 (length) × 16.3 (width) cm^2
Cotton and silk: plain weave with embroidery
Plain weave: off-white cotton, Z, single, 20–24 vertical × 20–22 horizontal/cm; embroidery: black silk, thrown, single, chain and couching stitch
Glazed and burnished

PROVENANCE

Purchased April 1931 from L. J. Moutafoff, Paris. In February 1931, Moutafoff shipped to George Hewitt Myers a parcel of 75 "Arabian textiles," purchased from Mr. J. O. Mardik of Egypt and said to have been found in the "*nécropoles d'Égypte* 1930–31." Myers acquired the majority of the Moutafoff textiles over the next decade.

SELECTED REFERENCES

Kühnel and Bellinger 1952, 28–29, pl. XII

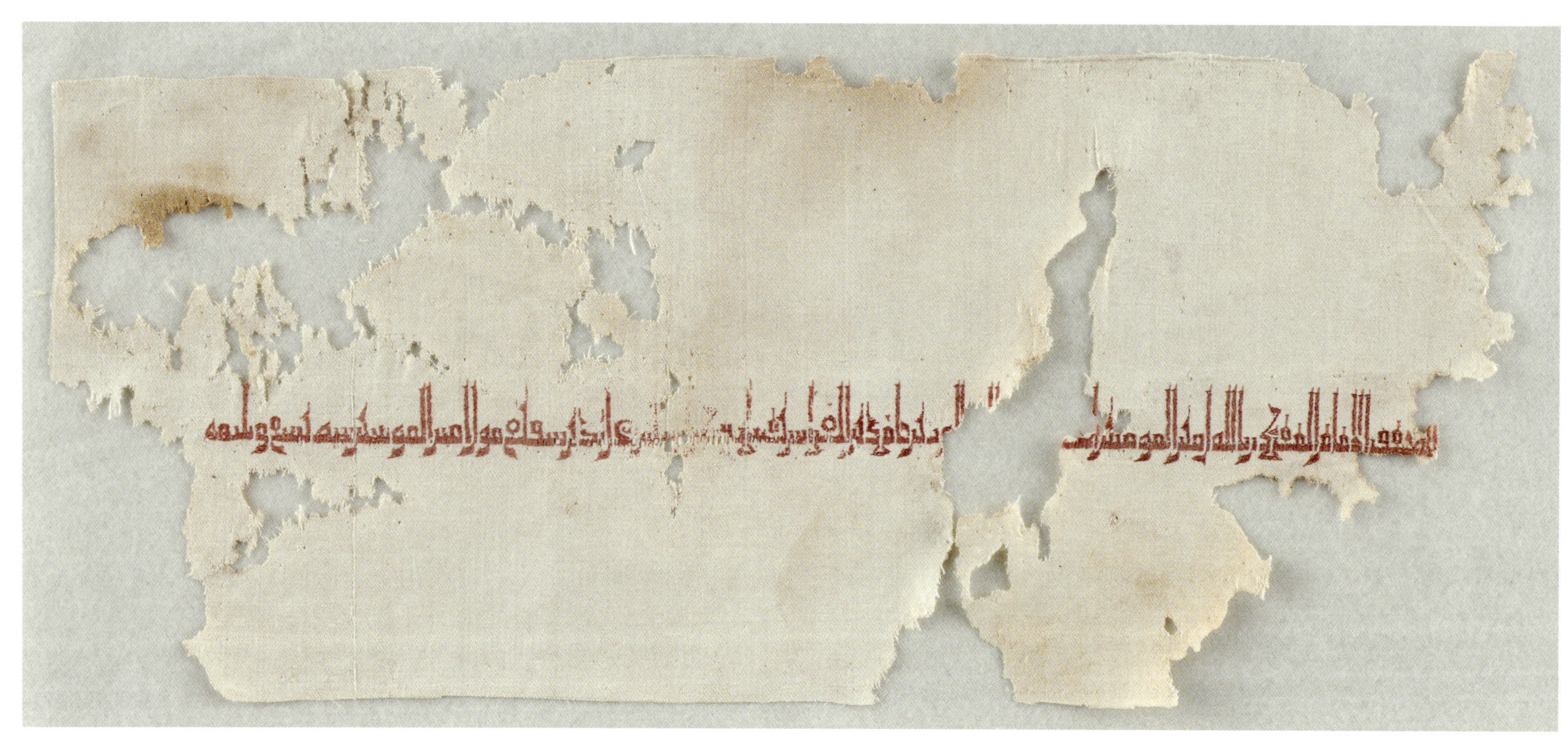

3

Tiraz textile naming the Abbasid caliph al-Muqtadir bi-Allah

Egypt, Tinnis, 309/921–22

The Textile Museum, Washington, D.C., Acquired by George Hewitt Myers in 1951, 73.660

1 Kühnel and Bellinger 1952, 29.
2 All edges of this textile have been cut.
3 I am grateful to Amy Dunn, assistant registrar at the Detroit Institute of Arts, for providing the invoice of purchased merchandise from Phocion J. Tano to Wilhelm Valentiner dated November 1929.

The exceptionally complete inscription embroidered in silk on this linen cloth preserves the names of the caliph, vizier, and a possible commissioner, as well as the place and year of production. While the caliph, vizier, and year conform to the previous Iraqi tiraz (cat. 2), this example was made in Tinnis, in the Nile delta, and names an additional individual: Shafi'. Comparison of the two contemporary pieces reveals an ongoing Egyptian production of Abbasid-style tiraz. Yet Egyptian weavers were not simply copying Abbasid models. Instead, they adapted local tapestry weaving techniques to the medium of embroidery and brought about a new style and aesthetic of distinctly Egyptian embroidery. The diversity of stitches — particularly counted stitches — distinguished Egyptian embroidery from its Iraqi and Iranian counterparts. By this period, Egyptian embroidery had developed into its own visual idiom marked by "barber poles" and "braided" lines, both variations of a satin stitch visible here (see the detail on p. 24).

The use of the phrase *'ala yaday* (literally, at the hands of) adds an extra layer of depth to ordering procedure in the tiraz system. Whereas the phrase occurs in conjunction with the vizier in the previous example from Baghdad, here it precedes the name of Shafi', who carries the honorific *mawla amir al-mu'minin* (client of the Commander of the Faithful). While it has been suggested that the term *'ala yaday* introduces the superintendent of a workshop, it appears in addition to the phrase crediting the act of ordering itself. Thus, it is more likely that *'ala yaday* refers to a further step in commissioning an item, perhaps on behalf of the vizier, who in turn represented the caliph (see the essay by Jochen Sokoly).[1] This may point to different ordering procedures in Egypt and Iraq. Since this Egyptian textile does not specify the role of the vizier, however, and the Baghdadi textile makes no mention of an additional individual, any conclusions drawn remain conjecture.

— MLW

INSCRIPTION (ARABIC)

[..] (بركة من الله لعبد) الله جعفر الامام المقتدر بالله امير المؤمنين [اطال الله بقاه ما امر] الوزير حامد
بن العباس بعمله في طراز تنيس على يدى شفيع مول امير المومنين سنة تسع وثلثمئة

[. . .] (Blessing from God to the Servant of) God Ja'far, the imam al-Muqtadir bi-Allah, Commander of the Faithful, [may God prolong his existence. What has been ordered] by the vizier Hamid bin al-'Abbas to be made in the factory at Tinnis, under the direction of Shafi', client of the Commander of the Faithful, year nine and three hundred.

TECHNICAL DESCRIPTION

50 (length) × 21.2 (width) cm^2
Linen and silk: plain weave with embroidery
Plain weave: off-white linen, S and Z, single, 30 warp × 16 weft/cm; embroidery: red silk, thrown, single; flat, back, braid, and split-chain stitch
Baseline of inscription established by drawn yarn. Burnished.

PROVENANCE

Acquired May 1951, by exchange with the Detroit Institute of Arts (formerly DIA 32.46, Gift of George Dwight Pratt of New York). One of forty tiraz textiles originally shipped to Detroit in 1929 by Cairo dealer Phocion Tano, who purchased them from Samaan Mellawi c. 1925.[3]

SELECTED REFERENCES

Kühnel and Bellinger 1952, 28, pl. XIV

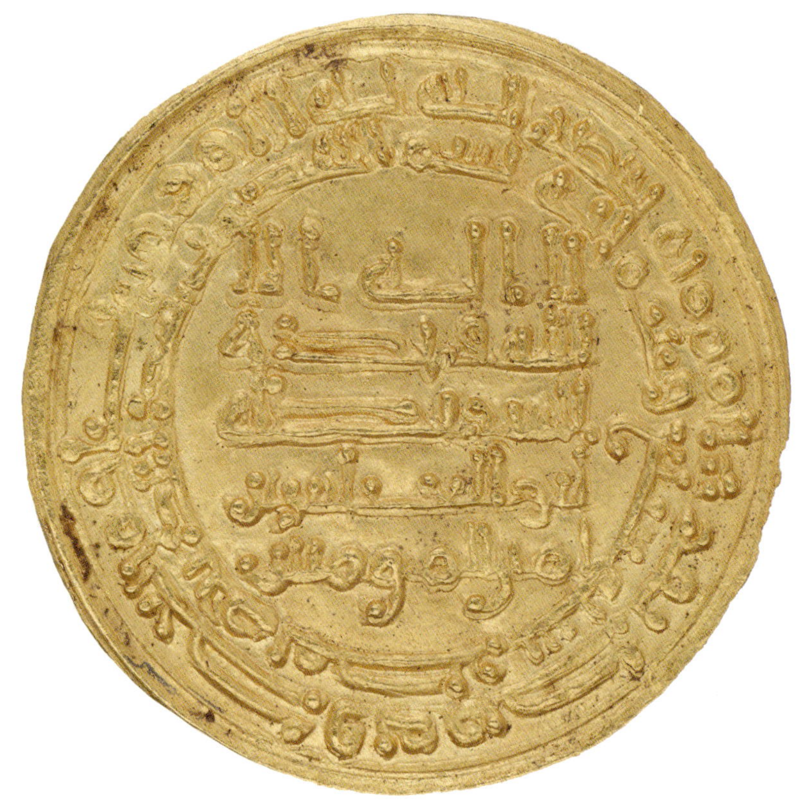

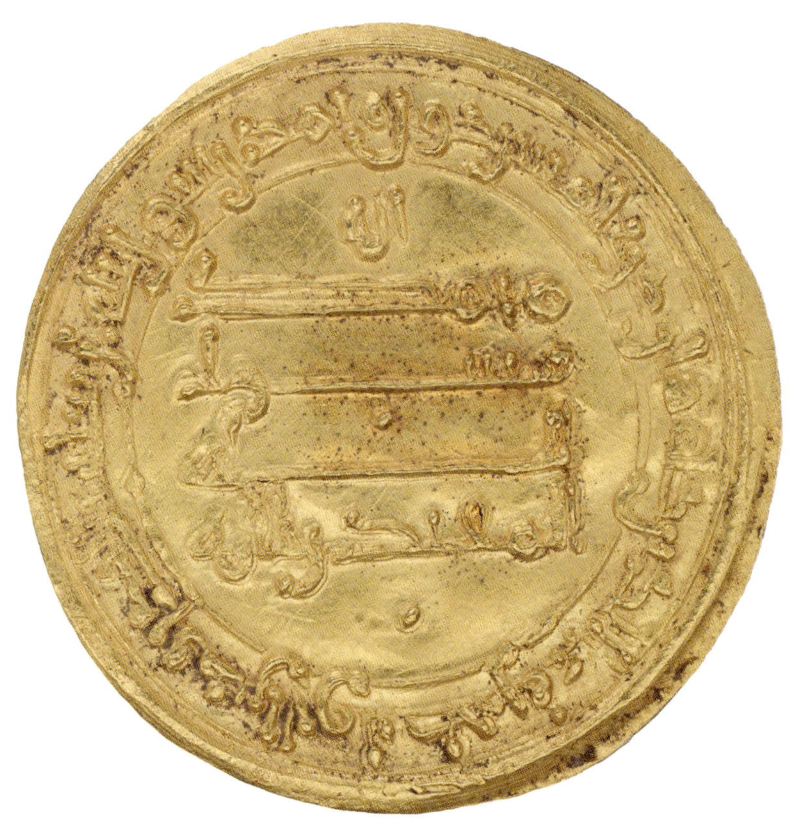

4–5

Dinar of the Abbasid caliph al-Muqtadir bi-Allah (obverse)

Egypt, Misr, 307/919–20

Gold, 4.01 g

Dinar of the Abbasid caliph al-Muqtadir bi-Allah (reverse)

Egypt, Misr, 311/923–24

Gold, 4.29 g

Harvard Art Museums/Arthur M. Sackler Museum, Bequest of Thomas Whittemore, 1951.31.4.2315–16

1   Bosworth 1996, 591–92; and Darley-Doran 1996, 592–99.

2   For the complexity of monetary matters in the early Islamic era, see Heidemann 1998.

3   Darley-Doran 1996, 594.

4   Abu al-ʿAbbas eventually took the throne in 934 as Caliph al-Radi bi-Allah.

To explain the importance of inscribing the caliph's name on tiraz textiles, Islamic historians often draw a parallel with the more familiar example of coinage, for many cultures have struck coins in the name of a ruler as a sign of authority and a guarantee of quality (see Jochen Sokoly's essay in this volume). In the Islamic caliphate, the right of the ruler to place his name on coinage was known as *sikka*.[1] During the centuries considered in the Harvard exhibition, both caliphal tiraz textiles and coinage were state-controlled products, and inscribing names within their formulaic texts was an exercise of royal power. In practice, the operation of *sikka* was often an arena for the competing interests of caliphs, independent-minded governors, challengers, and administrators, especially as the central authority of the caliphate deteriorated from the mid-ninth century onward.

The purely epigraphic character of these two Abbasid coins reflects the dramatic coinage reform of 696 under the Umayyad caliph ʿAbd al-Malik (r. 685–705), in which Arabic texts asserting the Islamic faith replaced portraits of rulers and religious symbols on dinars (the gold unit of currency; see example on p. 20).[2] Following this rupture with past practice and non-Muslim neighbors, the overall appearance of Umayyad and Abbasid dinars changed little for centuries. Coinage is an especially conservative form of material culture because it must be widely recognized and accepted to undergird economic activity. Nevertheless, the texts within the central field and circular margins of dinars changed with the imperatives and needs of those in power.

The inscriptions on these coins, minted in Egypt, are identical except for the dates. The texts, which include Qurʾanic verses, affirm the oneness of God and the prophetic mission of Muhammad. Because the legitimacy of their rule was continually challenged, the Abbasids inserted language to imply that their right of *sikka* derived from God.[3] On the obverse, they added the expression "In the name of God" before the date and mint; on the reverse, they capped the legend with the phrase "For God," so that the chain of authority was seen to pass down from God through the Prophet Muhammad to the caliph. The caliph al-Muqtadir, in whose name these coins were issued, was a notably weak ruler who was temporarily deposed twice during his twenty-five-year reign (908–932). In an attempt to designate his successor, he put forth the name of his son Abu al-ʿAbbas on the obverse, just above his own title as "Commander of the Faithful." This effort was unsuccessful in the short term: at al-Muqtadir's death

in 932, powerful viziers imprisoned Abu al-ʿAbbas and engineered the accession of the late caliph's brother.[4]

— MMcW

INSCRIPTION (ARABIC)

1951.31.4.2315, OBVERSE

Field

لا اله الا الله وحده لا شريك له ابو العباس بن امير المؤمنين

There is no god but God, the One, with no partner. Abu al-ʿAbbas son of the Commander of the Faithful.

Inner Circular Margin

بسم الله ضرب هذ[ا] الدينر بمصر سنة سبع وثلثمائة

In the name of God, th[is] dinar was struck in Misr, year seven and three hundred.

Outer Circular Margin

لله الامر من قبل ومن بعد ويومذ يوفرح المؤمنون بنصر الله

To God is the command before and after. And that day the faithful will rejoice in the victory of God. (partial, Qurʾan 30:4–5)

1951.31.4.2316, REVERSE

Field

لله محمد رسول الله المقتدر بالله

For God. Muhammad is the Messenger of God. Al-Muqtadir bi-Allah.

Circular Margin

محمد رسول الله ارسله بالهدى ودين الحق ليظهره على الدين كله ولو كره المشركون

Muhammad is the Messenger of God. He sent him with guidance and the religion of truth to manifest it over all religion, even though the polytheists dislike it. (adapted from Qurʾan 9:33)

SELECTED REFERENCES

Unpublished

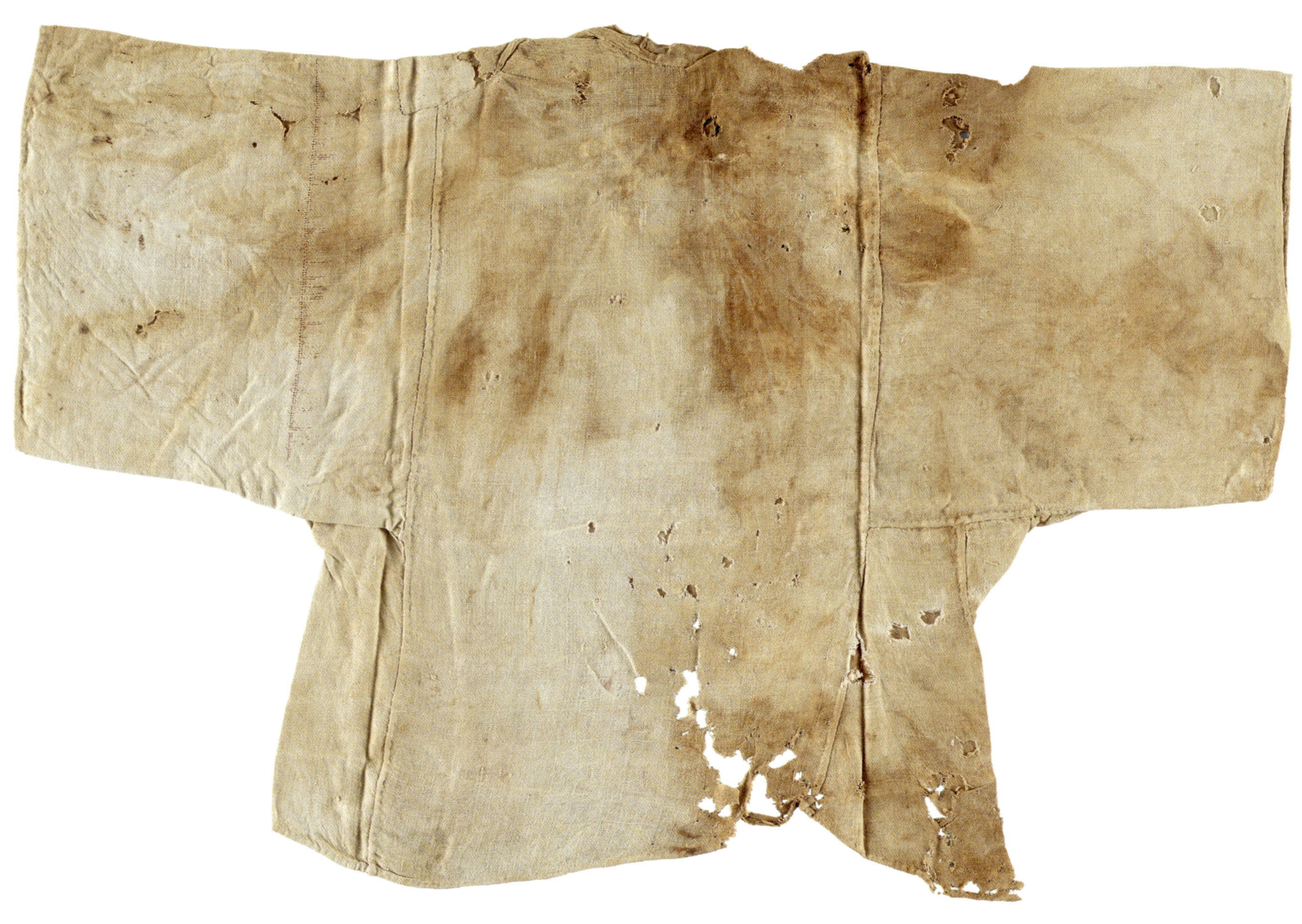

Tunic with tiraz inscription naming the Abbasid caliph al-Muqtadir bi-Allah

Egypt, Misr, 306/918–19

The Textile Museum, Washington, D.C., Acquired by George Hewitt Myers in 1936, 73.444

1 Museum of the Faculty of Archaeology at Cairo University +17. See Sokoly 2002, vol. 2, pl. 33.

2 Ashmolean Museum EA1998.210; Al-Sabah Collection, Kuwait, LNS 57 T.

3 Designation of warp direction follows that of Louisa Bellinger in Kühnel and Bellinger 1952, 25. Examination of this object in 2017 did not extend to opening the garment to search for selvedge or finish treatments.

This tunic is a rare example of a surviving tailored garment. Its small size suggests that it was once worn by a child. A large rectangular piece of cloth runs from front to back to form the body of the tunic, while two smaller rectangular pieces attached at the left and right shoulders fashion the sleeves. On the back of the left sleeve, an embroidered tiraz inscription mentions the Abbasid caliph al-Muqtadir (r. 908–932) and gives the date as 306/918–19. Two additional rectangular panels inserted below the sleeves form the lower sides of the tunic. On the right side, a small trapezoidal piece has been inserted under the sleeve to provide volume. A collar added to the shoulder of the tunic allowed the head to pass through and could be closed with a small button (Fig. 1).

It is curious that the inscription appears on the back; given the caliphal content, one would expect to find the text on the front of the garment. It is likely that the tunic was tailored out of a large sheet of linen similar to that of a shroud in the exhibition (cat. 35), as all parts conform in terms of yarn type and weave. The inscription, which would have been placed at one end of such a long stretch of fabric, was then reserved for the sleeve when the tunic was tailored. The same construction can be found in another child's tunic from the Fatimid period in the museum of the Faculty of Archaeology at Cairo University.[1] This, too, features tiraz bands, albeit tapestry-woven on the sleeves. Furthermore, two almost intact adult tunics from the Fatimid period, one in the Ashmolean Museum, Oxford (see p. 23), the other in the Al-Sabah Collection, Kuwait, feature similar construction on a larger scale.[2] The latter two are decorated with large-scale tiraz-style bands on both the main body and sleeves.

—JS

بسم الله الرحمن الرحيم بركة من الله لعبد الله جعفر الامام المقتدر بالله امير المؤمنين ايده الله مما عمل بمصر سنة ست و ثلثمائة

In the name of God, the Merciful, the Compassionate. Blessing from God to the servant of God Ja'far the imam al-Muqtadir bi-Allah, Commander of the Faithful, may God strengthen him. From what has been made in Misr in the year six and three hundred.

TECHNICAL DESCRIPTION

Overall: 98 (warp) × 63 (weft) cm[3]
Linen and silk: plain weave with embroidery
Plain weave: ecru linen, S, single, 12 warp × 13 weft/cm; embroidery: red silk, thrown, single, back and couching stitch
Baseline of inscription established by drawn weft

PROVENANCE

Purchased July 1936 from L. J. Moutafoff, Paris. In February 1931, Moutafoff shipped to George Hewitt Myers a parcel of 75 "Arabian textiles," purchased from Mr. J. O. Mardik of Egypt and said to have been found in the "*nécropoles d'Égypte* 1930–31." Myers acquired the majority of the textiles over the next decade.

SELECTED REFERENCES

Kühnel and Bellinger 1952, 25–26, pl. XI
Mackie 1996, 83, Fig. 58

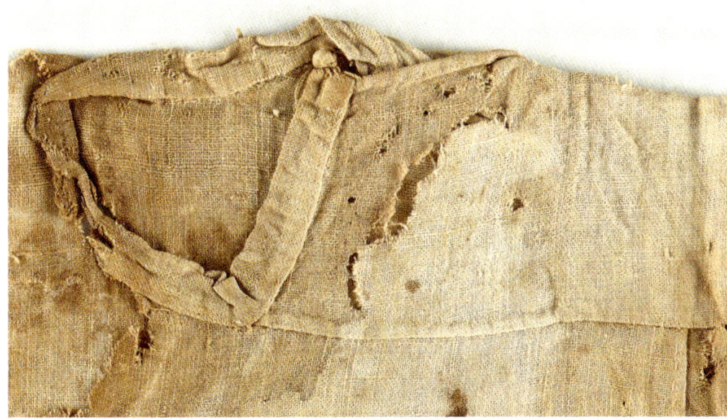

Fig. 1 Detail of collar

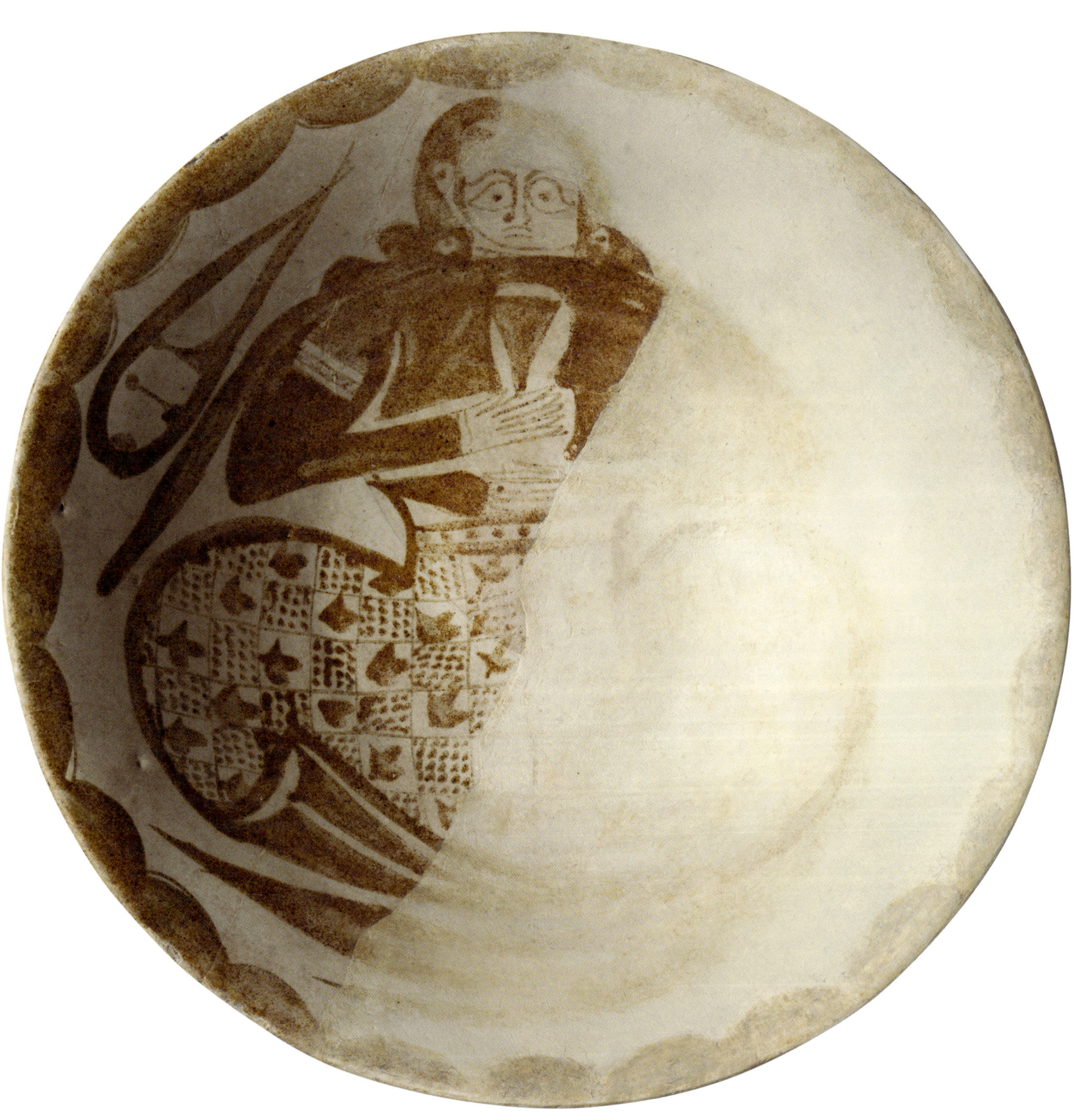

7

Fragmentary bowl with seated figure holding a beaker

Iraq, Basra, 10th century

Earthenware, luster-painted over opaque white glaze

Height: 6.8 cm; diameter: 22.2 cm

Harvard Art Museums/Arthur M. Sackler Museum, Norma Jean Calderwood Collection of Islamic Art, 2002.50.84

1   Mason 2004, 23–60.
2   Saba 2012.
3   Victoria and Albert Museum C.62-1981.
4   On the enigmatic iconography of these wares, see al-Khamis 1990 and Daneshvari 2005.
5   Pancaroğlu 2013; Watson 2004, 247–52; and Wilkinson 1973, 3–53.
6   See, for example, British Museum 1964,0713.1; Museum of Fine Arts, Boston, 57.684; and Museum of Islamic Art, Doha, PO.428.2006.

Similar to tiraz textiles, the luster ceramics of the early Abbasid era were an elite product. But whereas tiraz were produced in numerous centers across the empire, luster painting was a craft secret in the ninth and tenth centuries, when it appears to have been practiced exclusively in the Basra region of southern Iraq.[1] This costly technique involved painting metallic oxides onto an already glazed ceramic surface, which was then fired again in an anaerobic kiln. When successful, the metallic particles adhered to the glaze as an iridescent film imperceptible to the touch. Photography rarely captures the shifting reflections of a well-preserved luster surface, whose ephemeral qualities enthralled contemporary viewers.[2]

This fragmentary bowl features a seated figure holding a beaker in one hand and a leaf-shaped object in the other. Comparison with a closely related but more complete bowl in the Victoria and Albert Museum suggests that the drinker is male.[3] In both vessels, a wide-eyed figure with long, wavy tresses wears earrings, knee-high boots, a belted garment, and armbands. Although not inscribed, the armbands surely represent tiraz.

These vessels belong to a fascinating phase of luster production that favored large, centrally placed humans and animals (see the example on p. 4).[4] Many of the pictorial elements of such lusterwares find parallels in a contemporary and equally vibrant ceramic tradition located farther east: the potteries of Nishapur in northeastern Iran (Fig. 1).[5] Tenth-century potters in both regions produced exuberant designs with goggle-eyed figures holding goblets or ewers, branch or leaf forms, musical instruments, or weaponry. It is only in the Basra lusterwares, however, that the figures are occasionally distinguished by tiraz bands.[6] Perhaps this restricted usage indicates that the association of tiraz textiles with the caliphal entourage was relatively strong in this period, for Basra lay at the heart of the Abbasid empire, while Nishapur was in the realm of the Samanid amirs. In later centuries, artists would adopt tiraz bands more generally as a shorthand for wealth and status (see cat. 8 and the essay by Elizabeth Dospěl Williams in this volume).

Around the year 975, as the Abbasid economy plummeted and the fortunes of the Fatimid dynasty rose, Basra potters immigrated to Egypt. There they began a new and vivid chapter in lusterware ceramics (see p. 5).

— MMcW

Fig. 1 Shallow bowl, Iran, Nishapur, 10th century. Earthenware decorated with purplish-black slip on a white ground under a clear, transparent glaze with green and yellow staining, 9.5 × 22.1 cm. The Nasser D. Khalili Collection of Islamic Art, London, POT 389.

PROVENANCE

Purchased before 1992 by Norma Jean Calderwood from Hadji Baba Rabbi Antiquities of London and Tehran.

SELECTED REFERENCES

McWilliams 2013, cat. 4, p. 172

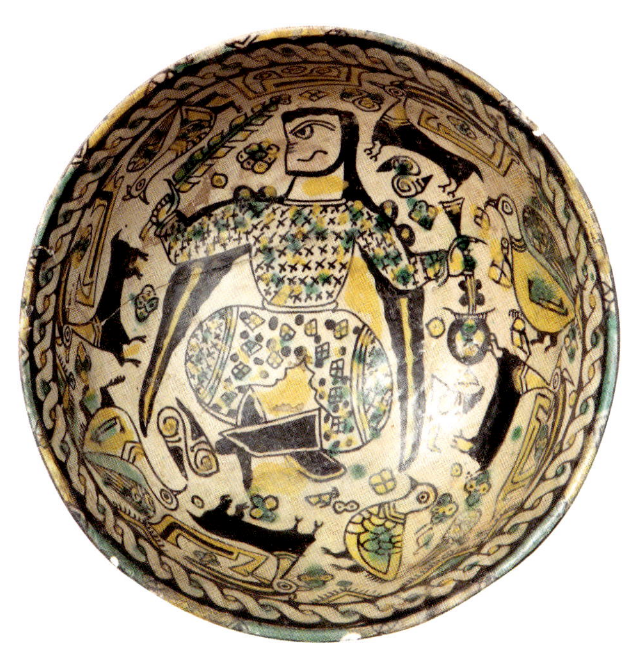

خو من ذراع أو أكثر من نبع وورق طوال لينة شبيهة في شكلها
... الموط ... شرفه طيبه الرائحة وما للي الأرض من
ورق ... بعضم من سائر الورق ... غير في الساق بزر

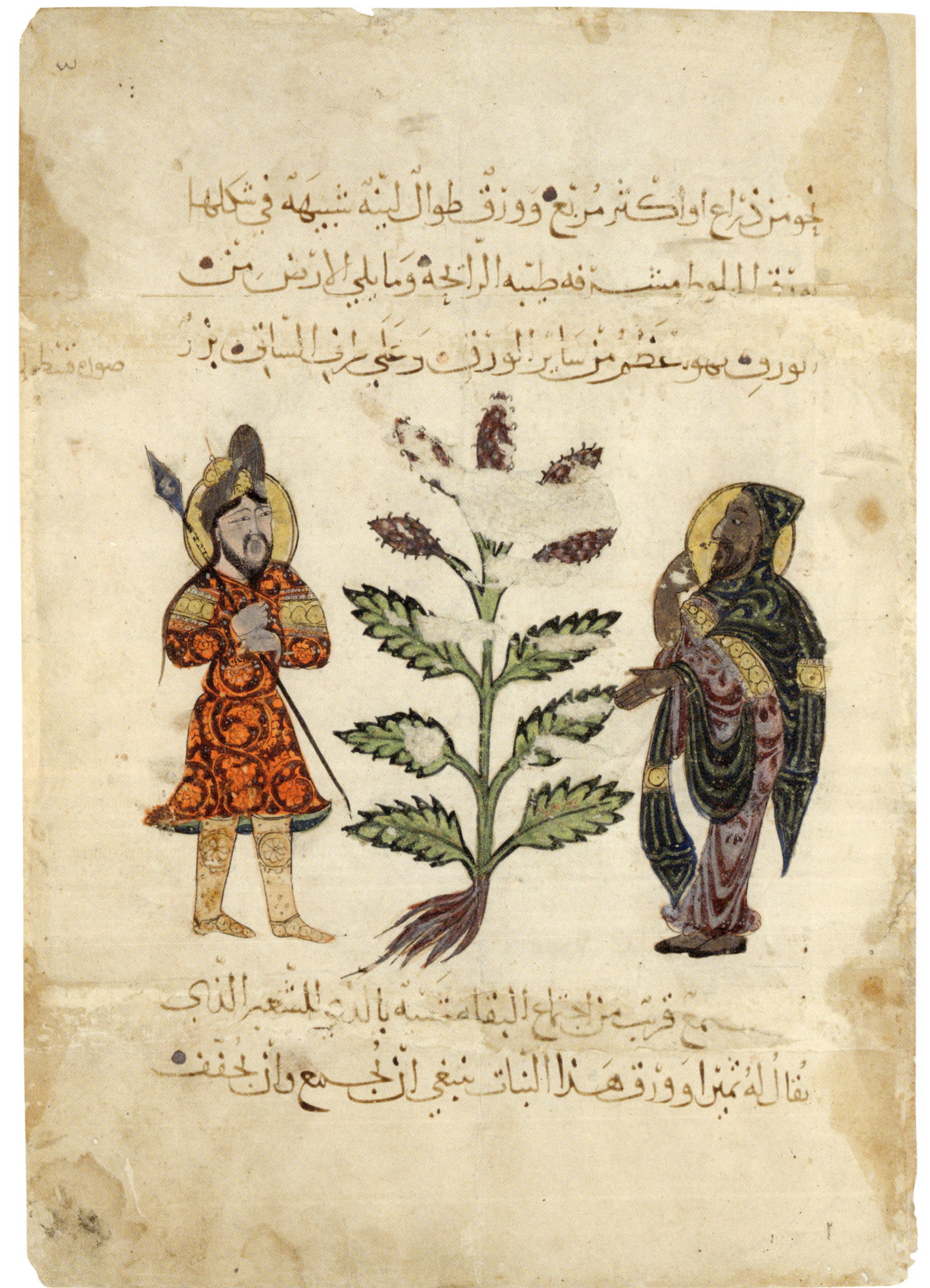

... مع قريب من ذراع البقا ... سه بالدي للشعر الذي
نقاله ثمنا وورق هذا النبات ينبغي أن يجمع وأن يجفف

8

Warrior and physician with the plant kestron

Folio from an illustrated manuscript of *Khawass al-Ashjar* (*De Materia Medica*) by Dioscorides

Probably Iraq, Baghdad, 621/1224

Ink, colors, and gold on paper

32.8 × 23.7 cm

Harvard Art Museums/Arthur M. Sackler Museum, Bequest of Abby Aldrich Rockefeller, 1960.193

1   Ettinghausen 1962, 67–74.
2   Ettinghausen, Grabar, and Jenkins-Madina 2001, 260–61; and ibid., 104–24.
3   Ettinghausen 1962, 64–65.
4   Romberg 1985, 77, Table 1.
5   Serjeant 1972, 147.

This page from a manuscript of an Arabic translation of *De Materia Medica* by the first-century Greek physician, pharmacologist, and botanist Pedanius Dioscorides was copied and illustrated by 'Abd Allah ibn al-Fadl in 1224, during a revival of Abbasid culture in northern Iraq just before the Mongol invasion. Another surviving manuscript of the same work is dated 1229.[1] Both relate in their style of painting and calligraphy to a famous 1227 manuscript of the *Maqamat* (Assemblies) by al-Hariri, now in the Biblothèque nationale in Paris (see p. 6), and another in the Russian Academy of Sciences, St. Petersburg.[2] Late Abbasid Baghdad was a vibrant place of exchange of knowledge and goods, with a rising middle class that could afford manuscripts such as this one. The costumes and fabrics worn by the individuals populating the illustrations are a reflection of the affluence and fashion consciousness of late Abbasid society in Baghdad. They are characterized by an abundance of color and ornament but also by lavish accents of gold. In a famous portrait from the frontispiece of a copy of the *Kitab al-Aghani* (Book of Songs) by Abu al-Faraj al-Isfahani dated 1217–19, Badr al-Din Lu'Lu' (d. 1259), successor to the Zengid amirs of Mosul, wears a robe with armbands inscribed with his name in cursive script on a gold ground (Fig. 1).[3] The figures on the present page wear garments with gold-ornamented bands reminiscent of tiraz. Particularly striking is the figure at right, who wears a robe with golden armbands but also a shawl with bands at either end draped over the head and shoulders.

During the medieval period, textiles woven with gold thread were some of the most highly prized commodities. The most sumptuous descriptions of garments woven or embroidered with gold thread are perhaps in accounts of the contents of the Fatimid treasury. The sheer weight of the gold used in the decoration of some of the garments mentioned is staggering. A shirt (*thawb*) and turban composing a caliphal ceremonial costume, for example, contained a documented 375.5 mithkals (1.589 kg) and 325 mithkals (1.486 kg) of gold, respectively.[4] Since gold was a precious commodity, it is not surprising that textiles woven or embroidered with gold thread were very expensive. Looking back to the Fatimid period, the Mamluk author Ibn Duqmaq described the products of the various textile centers in the Nile delta. He stated that in Tinnis and Damietta, a cloth or garment embroidered in gold could be worth about a thousand dinars, whereas one without was priced at only one or two hundred dinars.[5]

—JS

SELECTED REFERENCES
Martin 1912, pl. 6b
Simpson 1980, cat. 1, pp. 9–11, 15–17
Touwaide 1992–93, 76, Fig. 69

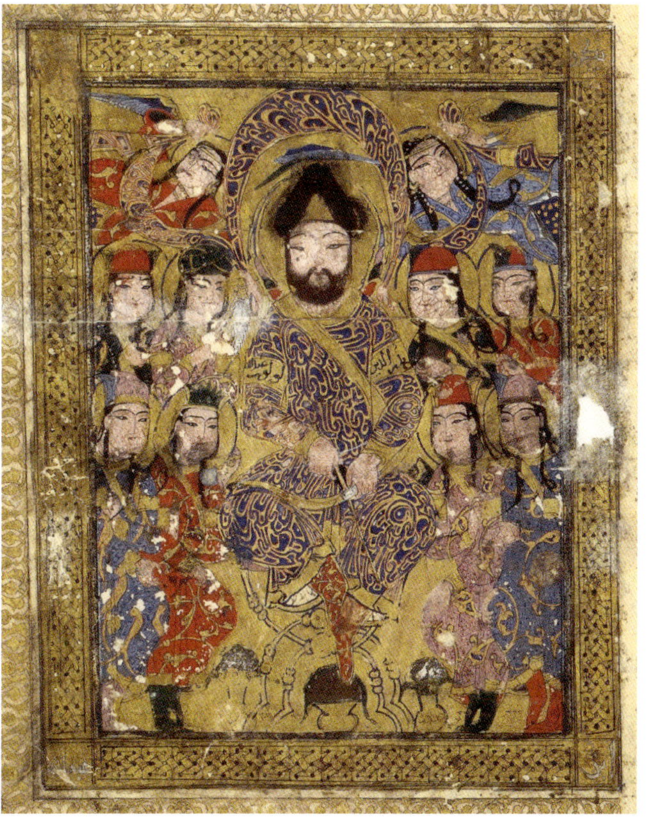

Fig. 1 Portrait of Badr al-Din Lu'Lu', frontispiece to a manuscript of the *Kitab al-Aghani* (Book of Songs) by Abu al-Faraj al-Isfahani, probably Iraq, Mosul, 1217–19. Opaque watercolor and gold on paper, painting: 17 × 12.8 cm. Millet Kütüphanesi, Istanbul, Feyzullah Efendi no. 1566.

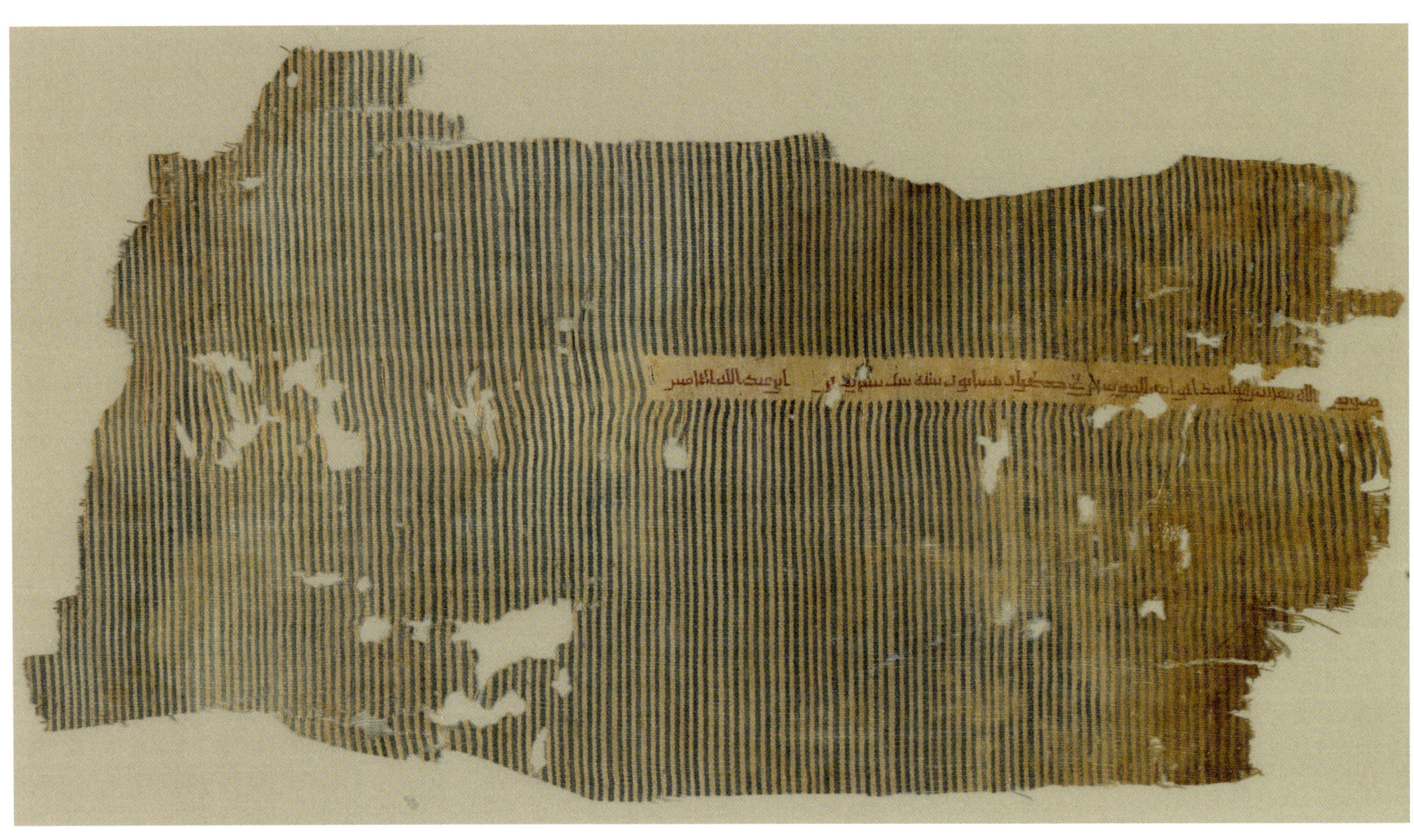

9

Tiraz textile naming the brother of the Abbasid caliph al-Muʿtamid ʿala-Allah

Iran, Nishapur, 266/879–80

Metropolitan Museum of Art, New York, Gift of George D. Pratt, 31.106.27

1 Kennedy 1993, 777–78.

2 Textile Museum 73.4. See Kühnel and Bellinger 1952, 10, pl. V.

3 Combe, Sauvaget, and Wiet 1931–37, 2:246, no. 753.

4 Jaubert 1836–40, 1:352–53.

5 Because the fragment is mounted under plexiglass, it was not possible to obtain an accurate thread count or to examine the reverse. According to notes in the object folder made by Nobuko Kajitani in 1974, the blue yarns "are floated on the reverse of the white ground." All edges of this fragment are cut, so warp and weft direction cannot be determined with certainty. The determination offered in this catalogue — which places the inscription along the warp axis — was made by Milton Sonday, Elena Kanagy-Loux, and Mary McWilliams, who examined the textile with a binocular microscope in the laboratory of the Antonio Ratti Textile Center in June 2019. The yarns here identified as weft have definite Z-twist, while the yarns identified as warp have little or no twist and appear to be held in greater tension. Furthermore, it was thought that the manipulation of the yarns that create the off-white band to hold the inscription would have been easier to carry out with weft yarns.

This textile fragment is important not only for the details of its manufacture, but also because of the historical data recorded in its inscription. The silk fabric is striped all over save for a band reserved for the line of inscription, embroidered in red silk. The name of the ruling caliph is lost, but the text states that the textile was ordered by a certain Abu Ahmad, brother of the *amir al-muʾminin* (Commander of the Faithful; that is, the caliph) in the tiraz of Nishapur in 266/879–80. The inscription ends with the name Abu ʿAbd Allah al-Khamis. Abu Ahmad (full name Abu Ahmad al-Muwaffaq) was viceroy of the eastern provinces and, as brother of the caliph, a contender for al-Muʿtamid's (r. 870–892) throne. He commanded an army of Turkish mamluks during the Zanj rebellion in Iraq (869–83) and in the years of unrest caused by the Saffarid uprising against the caliphate in Iran.[1] Two further textiles bear al-Muwaffaq's name, one in the Textile Museum dated 260/873–74,[2] the other formerly in the Tano collection dated 277/890–91.[3] Both were made in Merv, the provincial capital of Khurasan, suggesting that al-Muwaffaq exercised control of the vital structures of administration there. Nishapur was an important trade emporium in Khurasan known for its rich archaeological record; it was the site of a mint and was famed in medieval literature for its textiles. Indeed, the twelfth-century author al-Idrisi mentioned in his *Geography* that Nishapur possessed a tiraz workshop.[4]

—JS

INSCRIPTION (ARABIC)

[. . .] [اميرالـ]ـمؤمنين ايد[ه] الله مما امرابو احمد اخو اميرالمؤمنين في طراز نيشابور

سنة ست و ستين [؟] مئتين أبي عبدالله الخامس

[. . .] [Commander of the] Faithful, may God strengthen [him].
What was ordered by Ahmad, the brother of the Commander of the Faithful, in the tiraz of Nishapur in the year six and sixty(?) (and) two hundred. Abu ʿAbd Allah al-Khamis.

TECHNICAL DESCRIPTION[5]

30.5 (warp) × 15.9 (weft) cm
Silk: plain weave with embroidery
Warp: off-white silk, thrown, single; weft: off-white and blue silk, Z, single; embroidery: variant of chain stitch
Burnished. Reverse inaccessible.

SELECTED REFERENCES

Ekhtiar et al. 2011, cat. 26, pp. 48–49

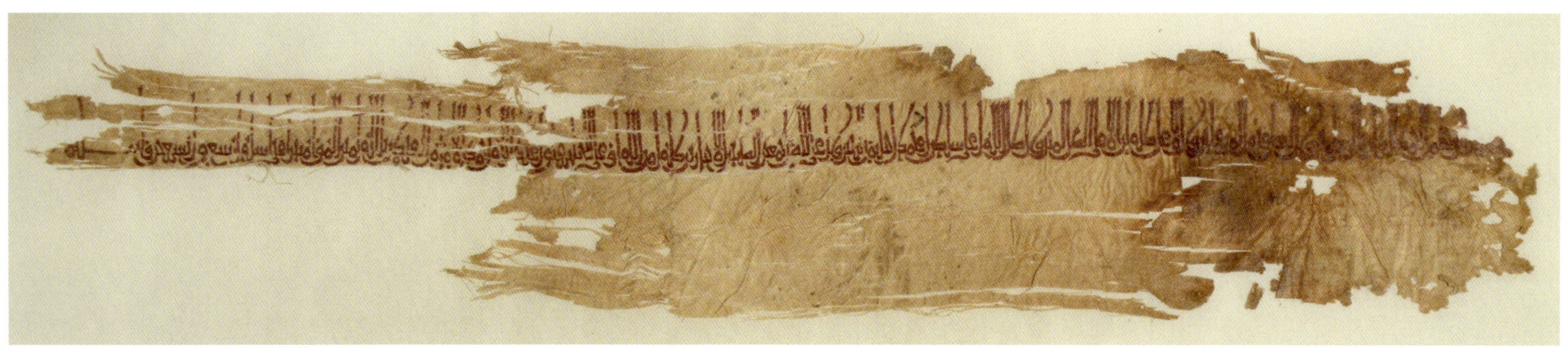

10

Tiraz textile naming the Abbasid caliph al-Qadir bi-Allah

Probably Iraq, 399/1008–9

Dumbarton Oaks Research Library and Collection, Washington, D.C., BZ.1933.22

1   Al-Ṭabarī 1987, 61–64.

2   For results of dye analysis, see Table 2 on p. 58.

3   Because all edges have been cut, dimensions and thread count for this fragment are oriented according to the direction of the inscription, in which case the silk yarn runs in warp direction, and the cotton yarn in weft direction.

This textile dates to the year before the Abbasid caliph al-Qadir (r. 991–1031) penned the so-called Baghdad Manifesto, denouncing the claims of the rival caliphate in Cairo and specifically of the Fatimid imam-caliph al-Hakim (r. 996–1021). The inscription provides a sense of how the threatened Abbasid caliphate adapted official textiles. First, the aphoristic phrase *al-ʿaqiba li al-muttaqiyyin* (good things come to those who fear God) occurs twice in the Qur'an (28:82; 7:125). Juxtaposed with verse 193 of the sura (chapter) al-Baqara, concerning the fate of unbelievers, this may constitute a veiled allusion to the righteousness of the Abbasids over the Fatimids. Referring to the Prophet Muhammad as the "seal" (*al-khatim*) of the prophets — in other words, the last and greatest — underlined Abbasid sovereignty, refuting Fatimid claims to revelation as Muhammad's descendants (Fig. 1). The reverence paid to the Prophet's family likewise emphasized the *ashraf* (those who traced their lineage to the prophet) over the Fatimids, whose ʿAlid lineage the Abbasids challenged.

Blending a silk warp and burnished cotton weft, this *mulham* fabric aesthetically parallels the fusion of different textual elements. An emphasis on upward strokes and lower dashes takes precedence over legibility, so that some letters are shortened, whereas others are lengthened or added in a seemingly superfluous manner, mirroring Fatimid tiraz's aesthetic turn in the Abbasid context. The inscription's form may have also evoked sound. The phrases selected would have been commonly recited: the opening through *rab al-ʿalamin* (literally, Lord of the Worlds) comes directly from the first sura of the Qur'an, al-Fatiha. By orally invoking the verses' inherent virtue, as the tenth-century exegete al-Tabari explained, one could acknowledge the vastness of creation despite mankind's inability to conceive of it wholly.[1] The repeated omission of the doubled *ya* as well as the use of a long *alif* rather than the dagger *alif* in *zalimin* (the unjust) resonates with the way such terms were spoken. Overall, the orthographic peculiarities in this inscription, combined with a seemingly unorthodox blend of Qur'anic quotations, highlight the ways in which tiraz,

as both a form of public self-fashioning and an element of administration, continued to develop.

— MLW

INSCRIPTION (ARABIC)

[بسم الله الـ]ـرحمن الرحيم الحمد لله رب العـ(ـا) لمين والعاقبة للمتقيين ولا عاد لولن
(عدوان) الا على الظالمين وصل (صلى) لله على سيدنا محمد خاتم النبيـن (النبيين) وعلى اهله
الجمعين الطيين (الطيبين) الاخيار بركة من الله و العز على الخليفة عبد الله احمد الامام
القادر بالله امير المؤمنين في سنة تسع و تسعون و ثلثمـ(ـائة)

[In the name of God, the] Merciful, the Compassionate. Praise be to God the Lord of the Worlds. Good things come to those who fear God, for (God) is hostile only to those who practice oppression. May God bless our lord Muhammad, the Seal of the Prophets, and all his goodly and excellent family. Blessing and glory from God to the caliph and servant of God, Ahmad, the imam al-Qadir bi-Allah Commander of the Faithful. In the year nine and ninety and three hund(red).

TECHNICAL DESCRIPTION[2]

48.2 (length) × 8.7 (width) cm[3]

Silk and cotton (*mulham*): plain weave with embroidery

Warp: off-white silk, Z, single, 44/cm; weft: off-white cotton, Z, single, 36/cm; embroidery: red silk, thrown, chain stitch

Reverse inaccessible

PROVENANCE

Reportedly found in Egypt. Acquired from Tano Collection, Cairo, via Frances Morris, 1932.

SELECTED REFERENCES

Combe, Sauvaget, and Wiet 1931–37, 6:70, no. 2130

Glidden and Thompson 1989, 93–97, no. 15, Fig. 15

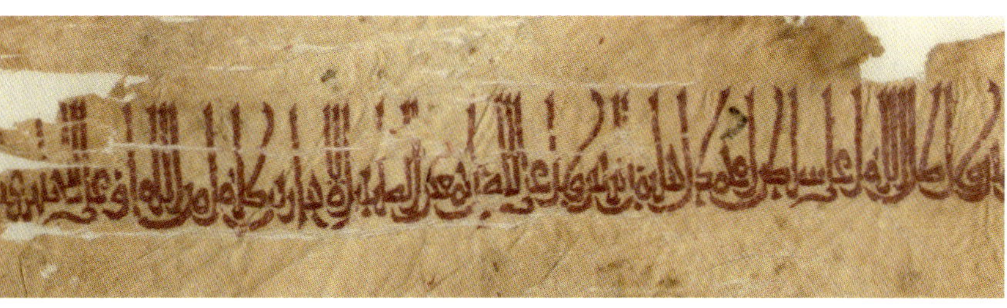

Fig. 1 Detail

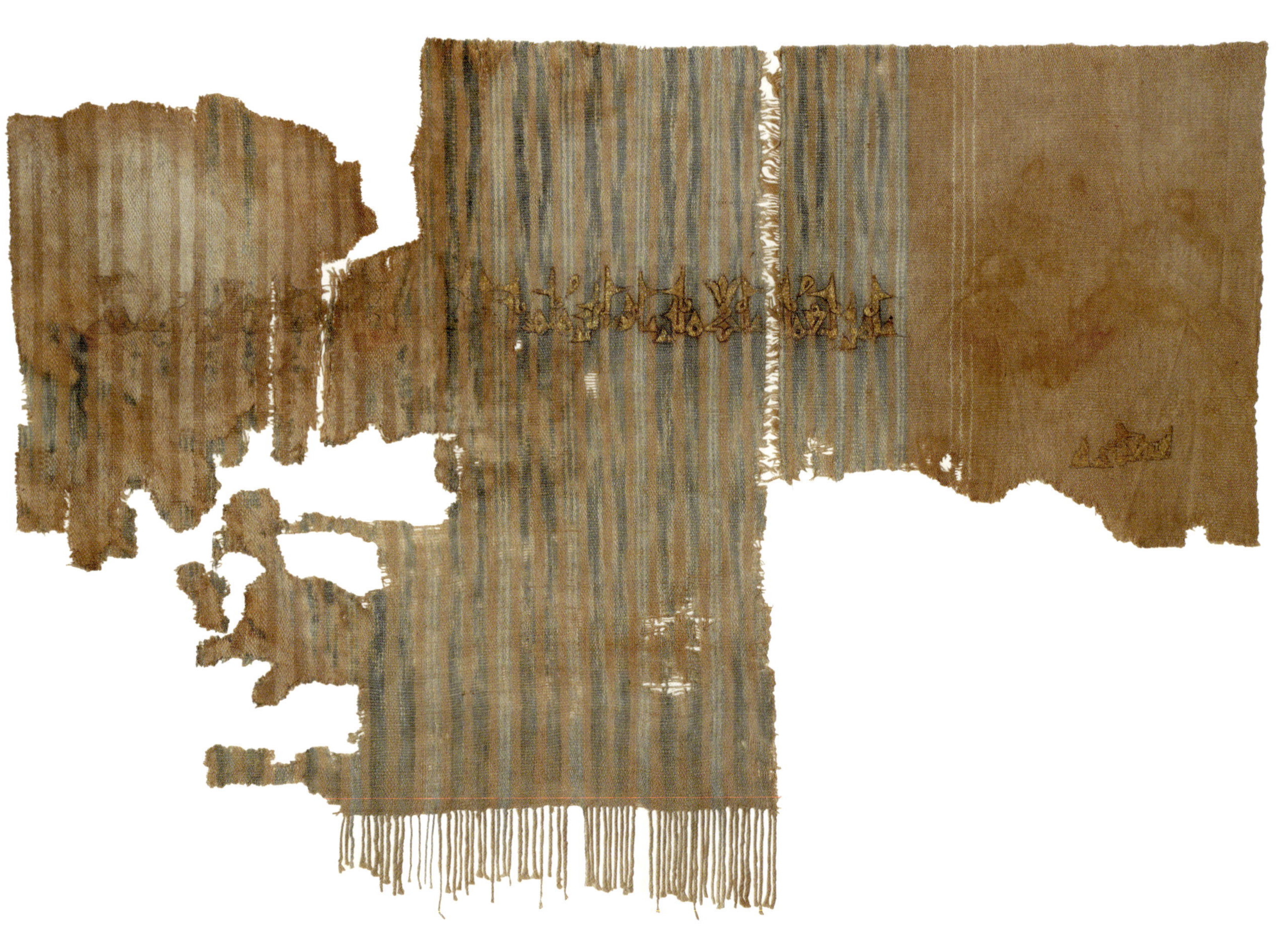

11

Tiraz textile naming the Zaydi imam Abu Ibrahim bin al-Muntasir bi-Allah al-Jamr bin Muhammad

Yemen, c. 980

Dumbarton Oaks Research Library and Collection, Washington, D.C., BZ.1933.37

The "striped" cotton cloths of Yemen were widely appreciated in Islamic lands. In some examples, the effect is achieved by setting up the warp threads of the loom to create simple bands in alternating colors.[1] In this instance, however, the patterning is carried out in a technique commonly called ikat, in which the yarns are tie-dyed to create gradations of blue, tan, and the white of the undyed cotton (Fig. 1). The resist-dyed yarns fluctuate like flames, separated by stripes of solid tan. The ikat technique originated in Southeast Asia and spread to the Islamic world via Indian Ocean trade routes. Literary sources from the early Islamic period attest that it was a specialty of Yemen, where it was called *'asb*, the root of which means to bind or tie.

This fragment is a magnificent example of Yemeni ikat textiles, in both its manufacture — the fineness of its cotton threads, the regularity of the weave with its pattern, and the delicately twisted fringe — and the beautifully elaborated inscription. The text is rendered in gold leaf outlined in black ink in Kufic script, with letters that occasionally loop back on themselves or break into foliate terminals.[2] The piece is also of great historical value: while a number of similar gold leaf inscriptions comprise merely benedictory phrases, the name mentioned here refers to an amir of the Zaydi imamate, Abu Ibrahim bin al-Muntasir bi-Allah al-Jamr bin Muhammad. He is likely the same individual known from another surviving ikat in the Pfister Collection at the Vatican Library.[3] An ikat tiraz in the Cleveland Museum of Art carries the name of the Zaydi imam al-Da'i Yusuf ibn Yahya ibn al-Nasir (r. 980–1003), who is well known from literary sources and who attempted to claim the Zaydi imamate in San'a several times.[4] All three inscriptions share a well-defined and minimally embellished angular style of script that contrasts with the heavily ornamented styles of purely benedictory inscriptions on ikats. Emerging in the eighth century, the Yemeni Zaydiyyah was a Shi'a sect named after Zayd bin 'Ali, grandson of Husain ibn 'Ali and son of the fourth imam, 'Ali ibn Husain.[5] Textiles such as this are evidence of the changing nature of power and control in Yemen, one of the most significant Abbasid provinces in terms of long-distance trade, and its growing religious and ultimately economic independence from Abbasid hegemony in the tenth century.

—JS

INSCRIPTION (ARABIC)

The amir A[bu?] Ibrahim bin al-Muntasir bi-Allah al-Jamr bin Muhammad ordered [it] to be made.
Felicity.

TECHNICAL DESCRIPTION[6]

33.3 (warp) × 55.3 (weft) cm, excluding fringe
Cotton (plain weave), gold leaf, and black ink
Plain weave: cotton, Z, single; warp: ecru and resist-dyed light blue and tan, 19–20/cm; weft: ecru, 8–9/cm
Selvedge on right. Warp fringe at bottom edge. Reverse inaccessible.

SELECTED REFERENCES

Kühnel and Bellinger 1952, 91
Glidden and Thompson 1989, 89–91, no. 12, Fig. 12
Mackie 2015, 480, no. 148

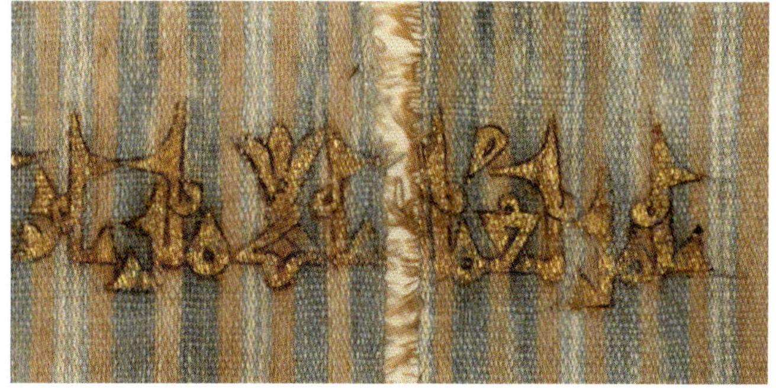

Fig. 1 Detail

---

1   This technique was used for Dumbarton Oaks BZ.1933.40.

2   For a technical discussion of an undated Yemeni ikat in the Cleveland Museum of Art (1950.524), see the essay by Julie Wertz et al.

3   Biblioteca Apostolica Vaticana 6744, published in Cornu 1992, 63–65; Pfister 1945–46, 70, no. 46, pl. XIII; and Pfister 1936b, 78–79, pl. XXX D1. Here the individual is named [Allah] ibn al-Muntasir bi-Allah. It is noteworthy that "al-Muntasir bi-Allah" is followed by a benedictory formula, rather than the formula *amir al-mu'minin* (Commander of the Faithful), normally indicating a caliphal patron. M. M. Sauvaget and Gaston Wiet originally suggested that this could possibly point to a son of the Abbasid caliph al-Muntasir (r. 861–862), but acknowledged that the usage is curious. On the basis of an unpublished catalogue by Richard Ettinghausen at Dumbarton Oaks, Sheila Blair suggested that the name must be that of Zaydi amir 'Abdallah ibn Muhammad al-Muntasir, who, according to literary sources quoted in Madelung 1965 (at 194), took the title of amir in San'a in 369/980. See Blair 1992, 68–70. Blair posits that the names on the textiles at Dumbarton Oaks and the Vatican refer to the same individual and that both date no earlier than 980.

4   Cleveland Museum of Art 1950.353 (formerly collection of Maurice Nahman), published in Combe, Sauvaget, and Wiet 1931–37, 4:174, no. 1544; Wiet 1935c, 287, pl. XLVIIIb; and Lamm 1937, 146. See Table B in Zambaur 1927 for Yusuf ibn Yahya's genealogy. Carl Johan Lamm suggested in 1937 that this individual can be identified as the Zaydi imam of San'a after 344/955–56 and before 393/1002–3. Based on a study of historical texts, Madelung 1965 shows more concretely (at 194–95) that Yusuf ibn Yahya first conquered San'a in Sha'ban 369/February 980, then ruled again from 391/1001 to 393/1003. Blair 1992 states (at 68) that the amir 'Abdallah ibn Muhammad al-Muntasir discussed above was a second cousin once removed of Yusuf ibn Yahya ibn al-Nasir.

5   For a general discussion of the Zaydiyyah, see Madelung 2002.

6   For results of dye analysis, see Table 2 on p. 58.

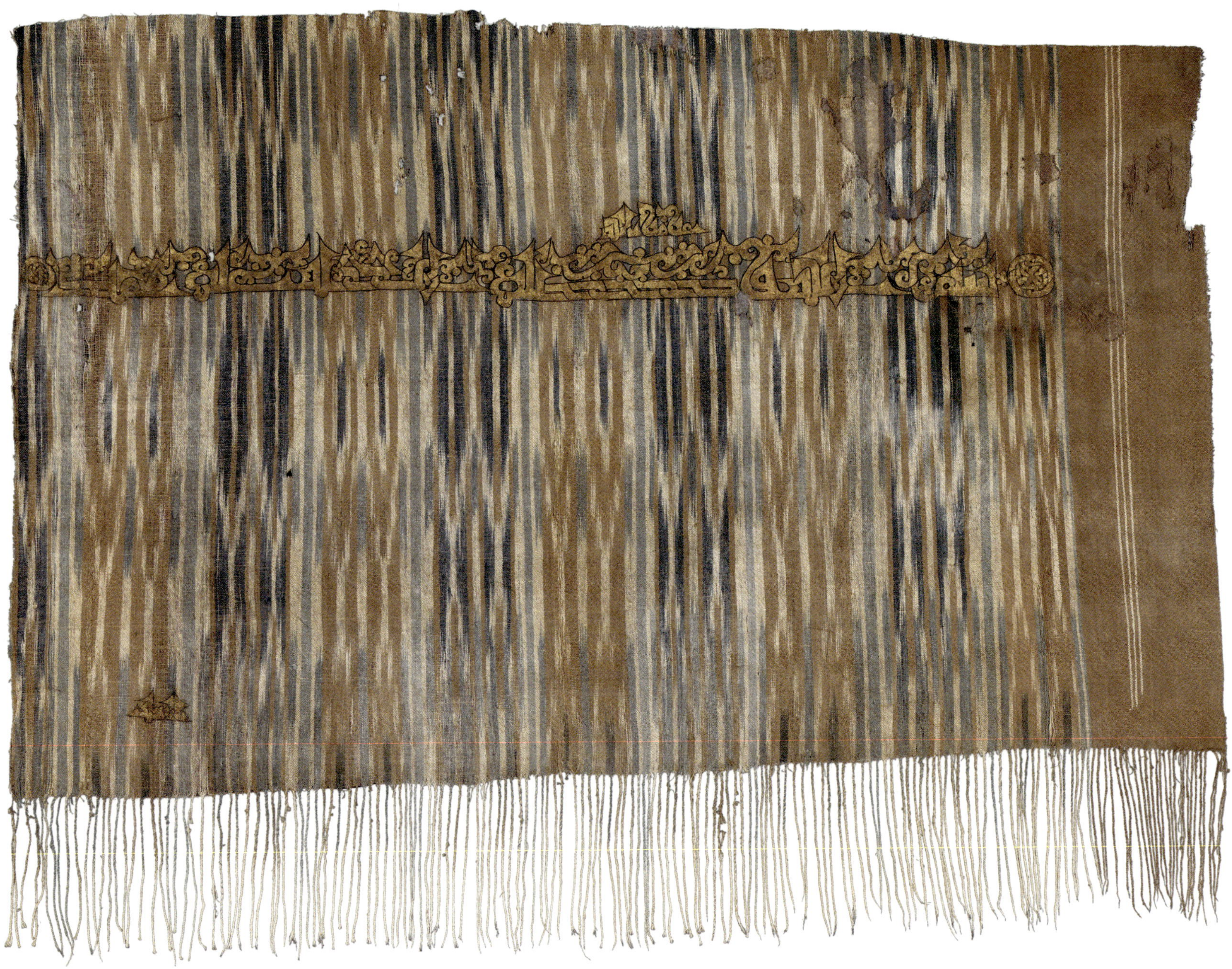

12

Shawl fragment with benedictory inscription

Yemen, late 9th–early 10th century

Museum of Fine Arts, Boston, Helen and Alice Colburn Fund, 34.115

SELECTED REFERENCES

Britton 1938, 75, Fig. 92

Weinstein 2015, cat. 10, p. 36

1   For results of dye analysis, see Table 2 on p. 58.
2   The gold leaf on this textile contains small amounts of silver and copper.

This fragment, like the previous one (cat. 11), belongs to a group of ikat textiles produced in Yemen in the late ninth and tenth century, during the reign of the Zaydi dynasty. Its inscription is comprised of benedictory phrases in a style of Kufic script characterized by foliations and floriations at the letter ends and by complicated and exaggerated interlacing of letters, to the point where legibility is compromised. The base fabric is of high quality, with the ikat stripes carefully laid out (see the detail on p. 62). It seems that the inscription was first outlined in ink or a black pigment, then filled in with gum ammoniac, to which gold leaf was then applied. Microscopic analysis of the inscription has shown that the gold leaf has flaked off in some areas, revealing the glue below. The glue is a mixture of gum, oil, and resin extracted from the stem sap of plants such as *Dorema ammoniacum* (a type of parsley), *Senegalia senegal* (an acacia tree), or *Vachellia seyal* (the shittah tree), all native to the Indian Ocean region. Stored dry, it was later diluted in water to produce an emulsion that could then be applied to organic surfaces, such as textile weaves, vellum, or paper. The calligraphy of the famous Blue Qur'an, a ninth- or tenth-century manuscript with text copied in gold on indigo-dyed blue vellum, was produced in a similar way (Figs. 1–2). Instead of shell gold (gold leaf diluted in a suspension of water and resin), the Kufic text of the Blue Qur'an is made of leaf gold applied to a sticky resin substrate.

—JS

UPPER

بسم الله وصلى الله على محمد
عز من الله

In the name of God, and the blessing of God be upon Muhammad. Glory from God.

LOWER

Undeciphered

TECHNICAL DESCRIPTION[1]

55 (warp) × 73 (weft) cm

Cotton (plain weave), gold leaf,[2] and black ink

Plain weave: cotton, Z, single, 22 warp × 16 weft/cm; with three rows of supplementary warp insertion of ecru cotton (two-ply: Z-twist, S-ply); warp: ecru and resist-dyed light blue and light brown; weft: ecru

Inscription rendered in gold leaf over ammoniac adhesive and outlined in black ink. Warp fringe at lower edge. Burnished. Reverse inaccessible.

PROVENANCE

Purchased December 1933 with a group of "fine textiles cufic inscriptions" in Cairo by Joseph Lindon Smith for the Museum of Fine Arts, Boston; the purchase was approved by Edward Jackson Holmes and Gertrude Townsend through cablegram.

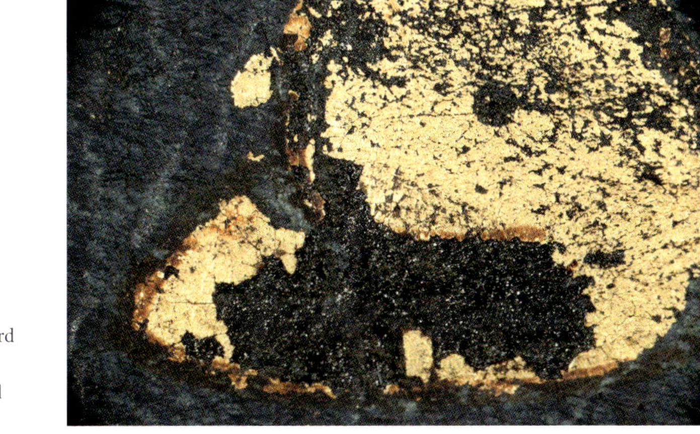
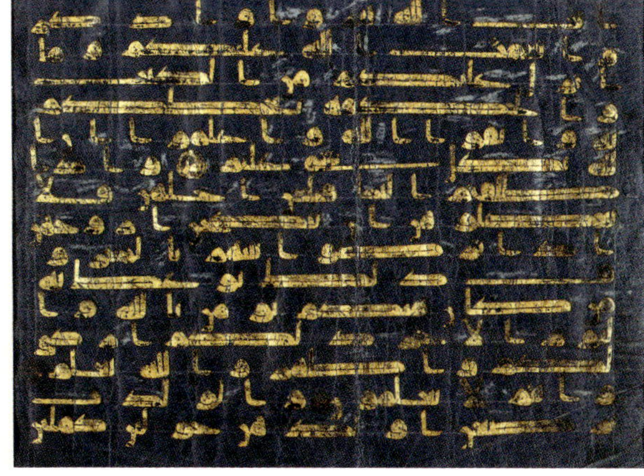

Figs. 1–2 Folio from a manuscript of the Qur'an (details), Iraq or Tunisia, 9th–10th century. Ink, color, gold, and silver on vellum dyed blue, 28.73 × 37.62 cm. Harvard Art Museums/Arthur M. Sackler Museum, Francis H. Burr Memorial Fund, 1967.23.

13

Tiraz textile naming the Abbasid caliph al-Muʿtadid bi-Allah

Egypt, Tinnis, 285/898–99

Dumbarton Oaks Research Library and Collection, Washington, D.C., BZ.1933.32

1   Bianquis 1998, 105–6.
2   Kennedy 2004, 181–85.
3   Textile Museum 73.11 and 73.639. See Kühnel and Bellinger 1952, 17–18, pls. VIII, XL.

This textile is a fragment of a once much larger sheet that was likely plain and undecorated, save for the caliphal inscription at top. The excavator or dealer who removed the fragment was careful to cut a square around the inscription, preserving the surviving fringe as well. The intact textile would have enveloped an entire body in burial. The fact that the area around the inscription is so well preserved is probably due to its placement on the upside of the corpse, perhaps similar to the treatment of the bodies shown in Figures 13 and 14 in Jochen Sokoly's essay (p. 28), where the inscription is carefully folded around the head. The straight edges of the fragment seen here, meticulously cut with scissors, remind us that the object as it exists today was edited largely to meet the demands of a commercial market in which the inscription, not its historical context or the history of the textile at large, was the sole point of interest.

Aesthetically, the minimalist inscription is characteristic of Abbasid tiraz. The content, however, is historically significant. In addition to the caliph, the inscription names the de facto independent Tulunid governor of Egypt, Harun bin Khumarawayh bin Ahmad ibn Tulun (in office 896–904), in the place usually reserved for the Abbasid vizier as commissioner of the textile. Although it may seem subtle, this usurpation is tantamount to an assertion of autonomy. Further, Harun is here styled with the honorific *mawla amir al-mu'minin* (client of the Commander of the Faithful). This title, used to honor non-Arab bureaucrats at the Abbasid court, suggests a close connection with the caliph. In fact, the date of the inscription falls in the period when the Abbasid caliph al-Muʿtadid (r. 892–902) had reconciled relations with the descendants of Ahmad ibn Tulun, the Turkish administrator who had been sent to Egypt under the caliph al-Muʿtazz (r. 866–869), by recognizing them as governors in return for an annual tribute as well as continued control over the tiraz factories in Alexandria and al-Fustat.[1] It is possible that the use of the honorific was part of the bargain. However, under Harun, a grandson of Ahmad ibn Tulun, the state of affairs in Egypt declined: beginning in 897, a year before this textile was made, the Abbasids gained ground in Syria, where the Tulunids had extended their authority, and only seven years after that, al-Muʿtadid's successor, al-Muktafi (r. 902–908), invaded Egypt and re-established direct Abbasid control over the province.[2] The use of Harun's title in this inscription is therefore a political statement suggesting goodwill at a time when the relationship between the provincial government and the Abbasids was in fact in steep decline. Interestingly, the inscriptions on two tiraz textiles in the Textile Museum from 289/902–3 and 290/903–4 name al-Muktafi in the main text, with Harun's name and title appearing below, separated from the mention of the caliph and the administrative protocol.[3] It is as if his name were relegated to a subordinate position, a visual reflection of the reversal of power and Harun's fall from grace. Harun was killed in an army mutiny in 904.

—JS

INSCRIPTION (ARABIC)

بسم الله و الحمد لله و صلى الله على محمد خاتم النبيين نصر من الله لعبد الله احمد الامام المعتضد بالله امير المومنين ادام (ادام) الله بقاه مما امر الامير هارون بن خمارويه بن احمد مولى امير المومنين بعمله بتنيس على يدى فائق سنة خمس [و] ثمانين [و] مائتيـ[ن] [ال]خير مقبل

In the name of God. And praise be to God, and may God bless Muhammad, the last of the prophets. Help from God to the servant of God, Ahmad the imam al-Muʿtadid bi-Allah, Commander of the Faithful, may God cause him to endure. Of that which the amir Harun bin Khumarawayh bin Ahmad, client of the Commander of the Faithful, ordered to be made in Tinnis through the agency of Fa'iq in the year five [and] eighty [and] two hundred.
Good is at hand.

TECHNICAL DESCRIPTION

37.5 (warp) × 45 (weft) cm, excluding fringe
Linen and silk: plain weave with embroidery
Plain weave: off-white linen, Z, single, 27–30 warp × 16 weft/cm; embroidery: red silk, thrown, single; back, stem, couching, and running stitch
Baseline of inscription established by drawn weft. Warp fringe at bottom edge. Burnished. Reverse inaccessible.

PROVENANCE

Reportedly found in Tinnis. Acquired from the Tano Collection, Cairo, via Frances Morris, 1932.

SELECTED REFERENCES

Glidden and Thompson 1988, 120–21, Fig. 1

14

Tiraz textile naming the Abbasid caliph al-Muti' li-Allah

Egypt, Shata, 350/961–62

Museum of Fine Arts, Boston, Helen and Alice Colburn Fund, 34.118

1   Wiet and Halm 2012.
2   For results of dye analysis, see Table 2 on p. 58.

Medieval Arab geographers praised the fineness of textiles such as this, calling them *shatawi* after the village of Shata where they were first woven in the Nile delta.[1] The inscription tells us this example was woven in the name of the Abbasid caliph al-Muti' (r. 946–974), who ruled from Baghdad. It is interesting that the weavers created the inscription in tapestry weave, following a long Egyptian tradition, yet the result looks more like the embroidered Abbasid inscriptions with administrative formulae seen elsewhere in this catalogue. The restrained red palette assimilates the aesthetic of embroidered tiraz fabrics, while the overall simplicity disguises the technical prowess needed to masterfully maintain an even tension between the plain weave ground and tapestry (see the detail on p. 53). A system of three self-bands comprising both linen and red silk weft yarns, which appear as parallel red lines, allowed the linen tapestry yarns to be worked in small sections and the red silk yarns to be carried where needed. Furthermore, by wrapping a linen weft yarn around the warp yarns preceding the long, vertical slits formed by the red letter stems, the weavers anchored the linen yarn before floating it behind the slits at a roughly 45 degree angle to support the slit while simultaneously moving to the next section (Fig. 1). That the tapestry emulates embroidery may reflect an aesthetic desire to express a formal connection to the Abbasid caliphate in Baghdad. Egypt was, at this time, quasi-independent politically and economically, but it still relied on Abbasid symbols to justify sovereignty. The textile thus communicated its official nature visually: even without reading the content of the inscription, its larger message was clear.

— MLW

INSCRIPTION (ARABIC)

[. . .] سعادة لعبد الله الفضل الامام المطيع لله امير المومنين اطال الله بقاه امر الوزير بعمله في طراز الخاصة بشطا على يدى فائز مولى امبر المؤمنين اطال الله بقاه سنة خمسين و ثلثمئة

[. . .] Good fortune to the Servant of God, al-Fadl, the imam, al-Muti' li-Allah, Commander of the Faithful, may God prolong his life. The vizier ordered [this] to be made in the royal workshop of Shata by the hands of Fa'iz, the client of the Commander of the Faithful. May God prolong his life. The year fifty and three hundred.

TECHNICAL DESCRIPTION[2]

23.5 (warp) × 48 (weft) cm

Linen and silk: plain weave with in-woven tapestry weave

Plain weave: off-white linen, S, single, 26 warp × 25 weft/cm; tapestry: 1 tapestry, slit, with non-horizontal weft and weft wrapping (warp: same as plain weave; weft: red silk, thrown, single; and off-white linen, S, single, thicker than weft of plain weave)

Transition to tapestry marked by a self-band (paired weft: one silk, one linen). Additional self-bands (also paired weft: one silk, one linen) run width of tapestry band, connecting the slits and calibrating the letters. Open-weave band and warp fringe preserved at upper edge.

PROVENANCE

Purchased December 1933 with a group of "fine textiles cufic inscriptions" in Cairo by Joseph Lindon Smith for the Museum of Fine Arts, Boston; the purchase was approved by Edward Jackson Holmes and Gertrude Townsend through cablegram.

SELECTED REFERENCES

Britton 1938, 48, Fig. 28

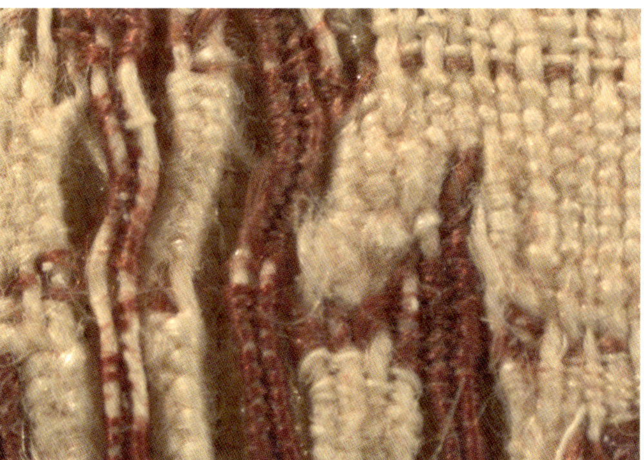

Fig. 1 Detail

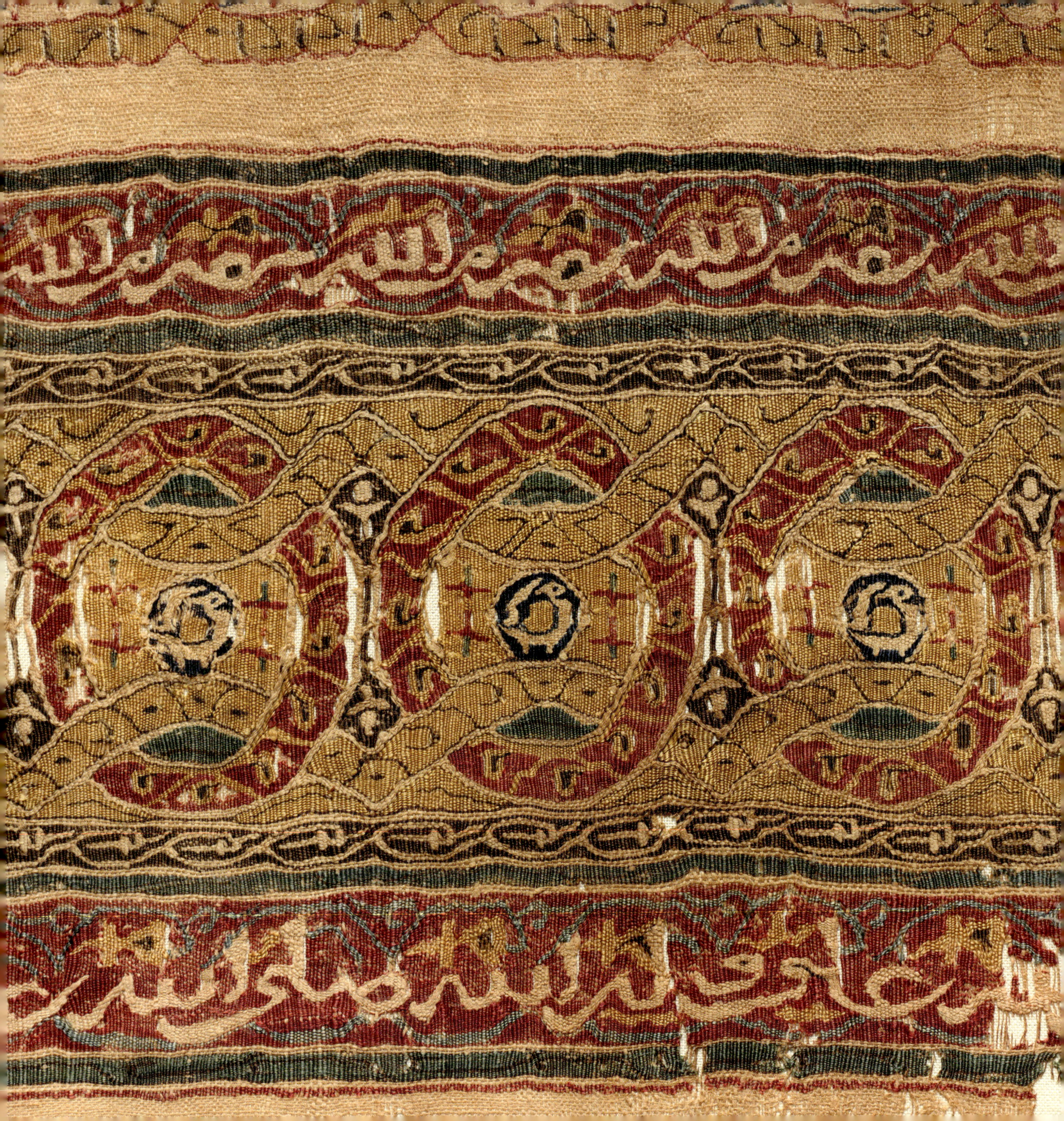

Schism and Assimilation: The Fatimid Era

The schism between the Shiʿi and Sunni branches of Islam propelled the rulers of the Fatimid dynasty to extend their realm into a far-flung empire along the southern and eastern Mediterranean. In a direct challenge to the Sunni Abbasids, the Fatimids claimed to be rightful leaders of the Islamic world, professing descent from the Prophet Muhammad through his daughter Fatima. They established their imperial capital in Cairo in 969 and held it for two centuries, with profound implications for Egyptian politics and for the textile industry. Fatimid caliphs immediately expressed their ancestral right to rule in tiraz inscriptions.

As a rival caliphate, the Fatimids were largely cut off from the luxury textiles produced in Abbasid territories. To meet the reportedly extravagant needs of their court for luxury fabrics, they expanded the Egyptian textile industry, with spectacular results. The majority of Egyptian weavers in this period were Christian Copts who brilliantly adapted their traditional repertory of designs and indigenous tapestry technique for the tiraz context. In this section, Fatimid tiraz are juxtaposed with Byzantine Egyptian textiles to demonstrate the reinvention and reinterpretation of pre-Islamic compositions and motifs. In the earlier works, animal, vegetal, geometric, and interlace patterns were the primary carriers of meaning. In the Fatimid textiles, Arabic inscriptions, which take the place of the reciprocal designs in the triple bands found on pre-Islamic textiles, literally spell out wishes for prosperity and protection.

The primacy of Arabic—the language of the Islamic revelation and of the Muslim ruling class—is inherent in the concept of tiraz. The prestige of these textiles and the distinctive appearance of their prominent inscription bands inspired emulation beyond court circles. From the Fatimid era, we find a proliferation of textiles with inscriptions that are non-caliphal, sometimes non-sectarian, and occasionally illegible. Even further removed from the administrative network that originally defined the tiraz industry are what may be called Christian tiraz; that is, textiles with Coptic or Coptic and Arabic inscriptions. In the medieval era, Arabic became the vernacular and eventually the predominant language of religious expression for Egypt's Christian and Jewish communities.

Integrating Egypt's weaving traditions into the tiraz industry enriched both art forms immeasurably. Masters of the craft exploited the freedom of the tapestry technique to create inscribed fabrics of varied textures and weights with richly colored designs woven in threads of silk and gold.

Detail of cat. 23.

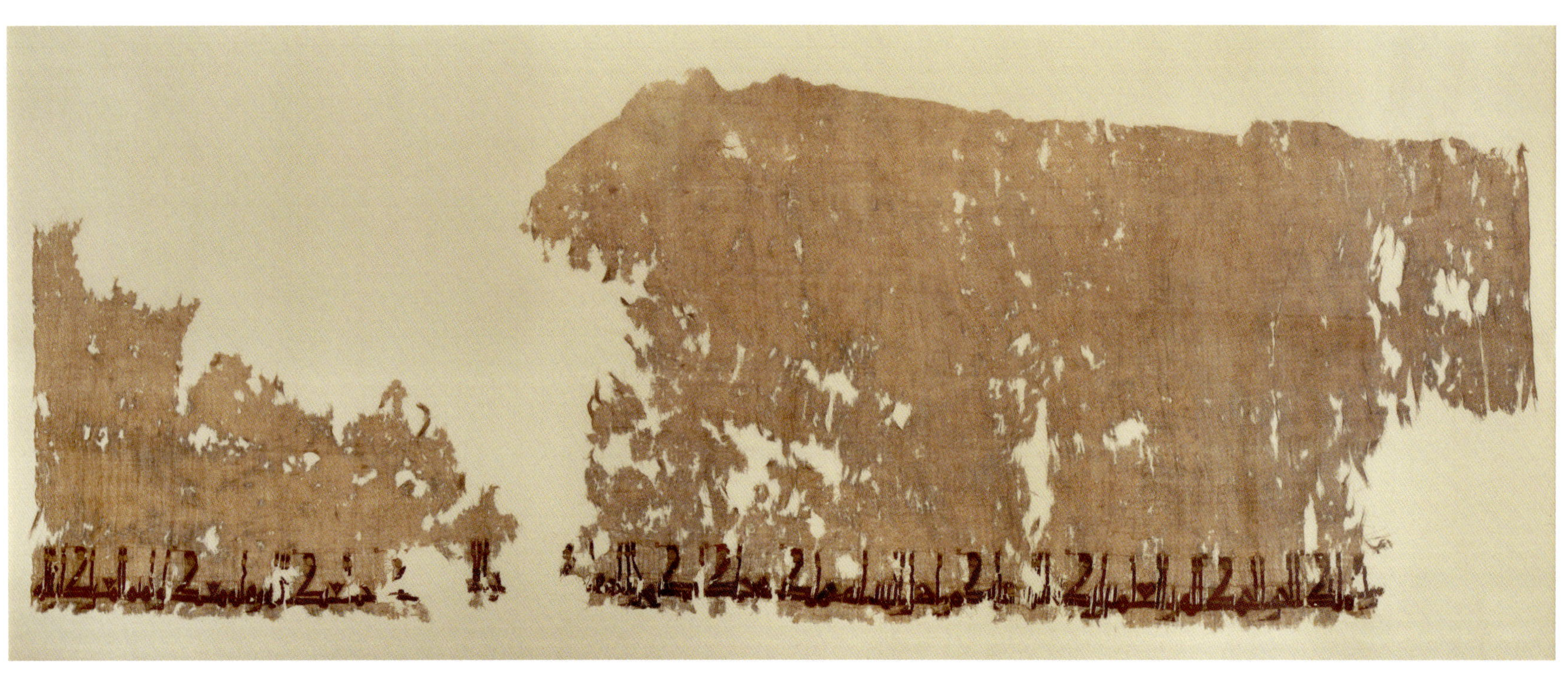

15

Tiraz textile naming the Fatimid caliph al-Muʿizz li-Din Allah

Egypt, 969–75

Dumbarton Oaks Research Library and Collection, Washington, D.C., BZ.1933.38

In addition to minting a new style of coinage in the name of the victorious caliph al-Muʿizz (r. 953–975), the Fatimids exercised another prerogative of Islamic rulership after conquering Egypt, namely tiraz inscriptions. In this textile, a pointed scriptural reference to the *ahl al-bayt*, or family of the Prophet, closely follows the evocation of God's holy names "the King" and "the Truth." Associating the two cemented the connection between the Fatimid claim of legitimacy and right rulership as justified in the Qur'an. The Fatimids took the position that they, descendants of the Prophet through his daughter Fatima, were always meant to lead within Islam, as God granted their family special blessings and foresight in the Qur'an.

In contrast to the revolutionary content of the inscription, the overall appearance of the textile defers to Abbasid precedent. The swan-neck termini of the letters, as well as the "floating" style of tapestry against a sheer ground weave, recall tiraz produced in the name of the Abbasid caliph al-Mutiʿ (r. 946–974) in the years before the Fatimid conquest of Egypt. It appears the same Egyptian workshops that had prepared textiles for the Abbasid administration and its governors continued under the new rulers. A practical need for tiraz to be recognizable in order to be accepted might explain this conservatism, although in creating currency, the Fatimids intentionally broke with precedent. Alternatively, the continuity may reflect the deep-rooted nature of weaving practices and the inability of the new arrivals to effect aesthetic changes.

Unfortunately, none of the extant tiraz in this style preserves a place of production.[1] While some tiraz produced under al-Mutiʿ do record workshop locations (see, for instance, cat. 14), they are stylistically quite distinct from the present example.[2] This tiraz, woven for al-Muʿizz, and similar examples from the reign of al-Mutiʿ nevertheless do bear resemblance to a textile woven for al-Muʿizz's son and successor, al-ʿAziz (r. 975–996), at Tinnis (cat. 16). The Tinnis group integrated the floating appearance of embroidered letters into the inherently plastic medium of tapestry. Tinnis may therefore be the site at which all the "floating" tapestry tiraz were produced, first for the Abbasids and then for the Fatimids, who took the town in battle in December 971. One might thus date this tiraz to just after that year.

— MLW

1 For other examples, see Metropolitan Museum of Art 31.106.45 (undated, but listing al-Mutiʿ, probably before 969) and Textile Museum 73.215 (dated 345/956) and 73.400 (350/961–62).

2 See also Textile Museum 73.445, which was woven for al-Mutiʿ at Misr (Cairo).

3 Thread count from Glidden and Thompson 1988, 126.

INSCRIPTION (ARABIC)

[بسم الله الرحمن الرحيم] الملك الحق الحمد لله رب العلمين بركة الله عليكم اهل البيت انه حميد مجيد نصر من الله و [بركة؟] [. . .] لعبد الله ووليه ابي تميم المعز لدين الله [. . .]

[In the name of God, the Merciful, the Compassionate,] the King, the Truth. Praise be to God the Lord of the Worlds. The blessing of God be upon ye, O people of the House! Verily, He is to be praised and glorified. Help from God and [blessing?] [. . .] to the servant of God and His close friend Abu Tamim al-Muʿizz li-Din Allah [. . .]

TECHNICAL DESCRIPTION

First fragment: 33.3 (warp) × 43.1 (weft) cm; second: 46.8 (warp) × 89 (weft) cm

Linen and silk: plain weave with in-woven tapestry weave

Plain weave: ecru linen, S, single, 24 warp × 19 weft/cm³; tapestry: 1 tapestry, slit, with non-horizontal weft, especially to outline inscription, and supplementary weft wrapping to fill and stabilize negative spaces (warp: same as plain weave; weft: red silk, thrown, single; and ecru linen, S, single)

Above and below the inscription, transition to tapestry marked by a band of yellow silk (nine sheds, single yarn) in plain weave slightly denser than surrounding ground fabric. Fragmentary selvedge on right and left. Reverse inaccessible.

PROVENANCE

Acquired from Tano Collection, Cairo, via Frances Morris, 1932.

SELECTED REFERENCES

Glidden and Thompson 1988, 126, Fig. 5

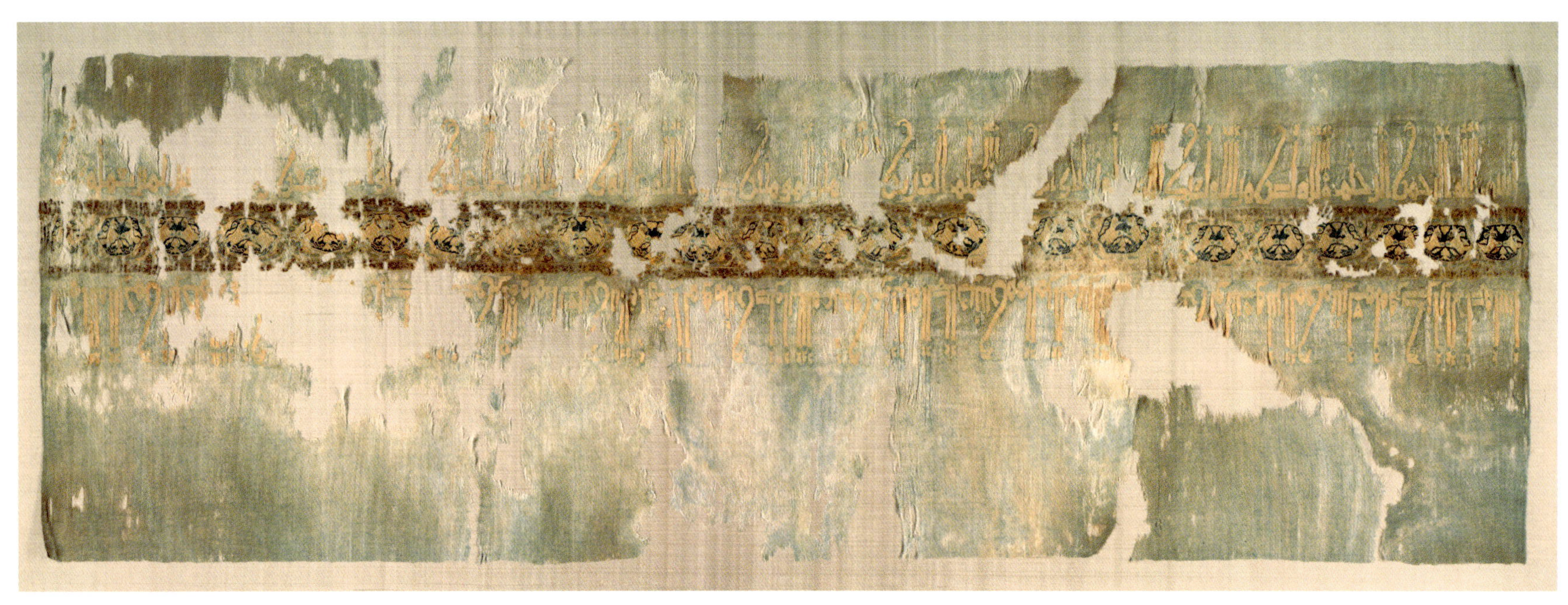

16

Tiraz textile naming the Fatimid caliph al-ʿAziz bi-Allah

Egypt, Tinnis, c. 977–91

Cleveland Museum of Art, Purchase from the J. H. Wade Fund, 1950.354

1 Mackie 2015, 98.

2 Ibid. For the many references made by Arab geographers to *sharb* and Tinnis, see Serjeant 1972, 93–100.

3 Serjeant 1972, 99; and al-Maqrīzī 1959, 507.

4 Examples include Textile Museum 73.400 and 73.215.

5 Walker 2017.

6 Serjeant 1972, 99; and al-Maqrīzī 1959, 507.

7 Thread counts by Dorothy G. Shepherd, unpublished manuscript, cat. 110.

8 Shepherd recorded (in ibid.) that in the "shafts and tails of letters, the linen wefts do not turn back and do not interlace with the warps but are left floating on the reverse; the warps thus freed are bound by silk tapestry wefts."

This five-foot-wide tiraz made in the name of Caliph al-ʿAziz (r. 975–996) exudes the luxury to which the Fatimid caliphate aspired in its rivalry with the Abbasids in Baghdad. Despite having faded from what would once have been a vibrant color palette, the piece draws the viewer in with its masterfully fluid use of tapestry.[1] (For details of the weaving, see pp. 27, 53, 145.) The open weave of the ground fabric conforms to that of a *sharb*, a particularly fine and sheer linen associated with Damietta and Tinnis.[2] According to Mamluk historian al-Maqrizi, "At Tinnis they wove linen *sharb* cloths such as were woven nowhere else in the world, and they used to make for the caliph a garment called *badana* into the composition of which the only thread introduced for the warp and woof was two ounces."[3] His description of a featherweight cloth could apply to this textile, whose ground weft is thrown infrequently in the tapestry-woven inscription, making the letters appear to float on its surface. A similar technique and style of epigraphy can already be seen in Egyptian tiraz of the Abbasid caliph al-Mutiʿ (r. 946–974), which may suggest that the Fatimids at first followed Abbasid aesthetic precedents. Nevertheless, this textile, with its classicizing inhabited vine scrolls and generous use of color and scale, exceeds the examples from the reign of al-Mutiʿ in sheer lavishness.[4]

The inscription is particularly interesting for mentioning its commissioner, Abu al-Faraj bin Yusuf, more commonly known by his patronymic, Yaʿqub ibn Killis. An advisor to al-Muʿizz (r. 953–975) and subsequently al-ʿAziz, Ibn Killis is known from historical sources as the first Fatimid official to receive the title of vizier, in recognition of his service and allegiance to the Fatimids for over a decade, even prior to the conquest of Egypt. Ibn Killis held the office from 367/977 until his death in 380/991. Originally born in Baghdad, he converted to Islam from Judaism in 356/967, while working in government service for the Ikhshidids in Egypt.[5] Ironically, given the luxury and artistic achievement of this textile, al-Maqrizi's later writings accuse Ibn Killis and his tax policy as damaging *sharb* production in Egypt beyond repair.[6]

— MLW

INSCRIPTION (ARABIC)

UPPER

نصر من الله لعبد الله ووليه نزار ابي المنصور الامام العزيز بالله امير المؤمنين صلوات
[sic] بسم الله الرحمن الرحيم لا اله الله عليه وعل ابائه الطاهرين [. . .]

In the name of God, the Merciful, the Compassionate. There is no god [*sic*: "but God" omitted]. Help from God to the servant and friend of God, Nizar Abu al-[Mansur], the imam al-ʿAziz [bi-Allah], Commander of the Believers, the blessings of God be upon him and on his pure forefathers [. . .]

LOWER

Repeats the same text as the upper line until the word "forefathers," then continues:

[. .] ما أمر الوزير ابو [الفرج يعقب] بن يوسف وزير المؤمنين بعمله في طراز الخاصة
بتنيس [. . .]

Of that which the vizier Abu [al-Faraj Yaʿqub] bin Yusuf, vizier of the Faithful, ordered to be made in the private tiraz in Tinnis [. . .]

TECHNICAL DESCRIPTION[7]

Overall: 49.5 (warp) × 151.1 (weft) cm

Linen and silk: plain weave with in-woven tapestry weave

Plain weave: variegated light-blue linen, S, composite, 30 warp × 15 weft/cm; tapestry: 1 tapestry, slit, with non-horizontal weft, including wedge-like inserts, and outlining weft (warp: same as plain weave; weft: polychrome silk, thrown, single; and light-blue linen, single and paired)

Fragmentary selvedge on right and left. Reverse inaccessible.[8]

PROVENANCE

Purchased from Paul Mallon, Paris.

SELECTED REFERENCES

Cleveland 1966, 213

Mackie 2015, 97–98, Fig. 312

17

Tiraz textile naming the Fatimid caliph al-Hakim bi-Amr Allah

Egypt, c. 1013–21

Cleveland Museum of Art, John L. Severance Fund, 1950.549

The Fatimids presented robes of honor (*khila'*) woven with gold thread only to the highest-ranking courtiers during annual investiture ceremonies.[1] Given their value, it is perhaps to be expected that very few caliphal tiraz textiles with gold inscriptions or decoration have survived. In the present piece, the Kufic inscription in the name of the Fatimid caliph al-Hakim (r. 996–1021) is set against a gold background, accompanied by bands of golden birds on a dark-blue background. The gold threads consist of a thinly hammered strip wound around a thread core (for details, see pp. 15, 55).

Apart from the use of gold thread, this textile is important for its reference in the inscription to 'Abd al-Rahim ibn Ilyas, a cousin of al-Hakim and the heir apparent to his throne. His name is mentioned in at least five other surviving tiraz inscriptions.[2] A great-grandson of Caliph al-Mahdi (r. 909–934), 'Abd al-Rahim ibn Ilyas was born in Cairo to a Christian mother. Al-Hakim broke with convention when he declared in 404/1013–14 that his cousin would succeed him, defying the direct line of succession. In the surviving inscriptions and on al-Hakim's coinage, 'Abd al-Rahim is given the title *wali 'ahd al-muslimin* (heir to the throne of the Muslims), underlining his status as next in line. He was also appointed governor of Syria and moved to Damascus to serve in that role.

As caliph, al-Hakim attempted to introduce separation of religious and temporal power and had many of the ruling elite murdered, actions that caused rupture with his sister, Sitt al-Mulk, who looked after his wife and younger son, Abu al-Hasan 'Ali. When al-Hakim mysteriously disappeared on 27 Shawwal 411/February 13, 1021, his sister swiftly took the reins of power and proclaimed Abu al-Hasan 'Ali as the new caliph al-Zahir. Several weeks later, 'Abd al-Rahim returned from Damascus, whereupon he was arrested, imprisoned, and most likely assassinated on the orders of Sitt al-Mulk.[3]

—JS

The upper and lower lines repeat the same inscription, with some variations. The text has been damaged badly but can be reconstructed to read:

بسم اللة لا إله إلّا اللَّه نصر من اللَّه و فتح قريب لعبد اللَّه و وليّه الـ[ـمنصور أبى علـ]ـىّ
الإ[ما]م [الحا]كم بأمر [اللَّه بن] الإما م [العزيز باللَّه] أمير المؤمنين و لولىّ عهد المسلمين و
خليفة أمير المؤمنين أبى القسم عبد الـ[ـرحيم][. . .]

In the name of God. There is no god but God. Help from God and proximate victory to the servant of God and his friend, al-[Mansur Abu 'Al]i, the i[ma]m al-[Ha]kim bi-Amr [Allah, son] of the imam [al-'Aziz bi-Allah], Commander of the Faithful, and to the heir apparent of the Muslims and successor of the Commander of the Faithful, Abu al-Qasim 'Abd al-Rahim [. . .]

TECHNICAL DESCRIPTION[4]

Overall: 23.5 (warp) × 62.3 (weft) cm
Linen, silk, and gold *filé*: plain weave with in-woven tapestry weave
Plain weave: ecru linen, S, single, 40 warp × 32 weft/cm; tapestry: 1, 2 tapestry, slit, with non-horizontal weft (warp: same as plain weave; weft: ecru linen [same as plain weave]; red and blue silk, thrown, single; ecru linen, S, single; and *filé* [gold foil twisted Z on yellow silk core, Z])
Transition marked by crossing of warps above and below each tapestry band to form groups of single and paired warp ends in irregular sequence; warp crossing followed by three to four sheds of red silk (single). Reverse inaccessible.

PROVENANCE

Purchased December 1950 from Émil Delmár. In 1933 and 1937, Delmár traveled to Cairo, visiting dealers E. A. Abemayor and Maurice Nahman.

SELECTED REFERENCES

Combe, Sauvaget, and Wiet 1931–37, 6:120–21, cat. 2214
Wadsworth 1951, cat. 56
Mackie 2015, 99, 215
O'Kane 2018a, 182–83

---

1 Mamluk historian al-Maqrizi describes in detail the insignia presented and lists gold tiraz as part of the robes bestowed on the vizier, chief qadi, head chamberlain, and comptroller of the *diwan al-majlis* (central bureau). For a discussion, see Bierman 1980, 79.

2 Combe, Sauvaget, and Wiet 1931–37, 6:118–19, 121–23, cats. 2212, 2216–17; Bouvier Collection, Geneva, I 26 (see Bouvier 1993, 203–4, no. 120); and Museum of Islamic Art, Cairo, 8264 (see Wiet 1930, 80; Combe, Sauvaget, and Wiet 1931–37, 6:119, cat. 2213; Wiet 1935a, 41, no. 155; Marzouk 1942, 107, 194, pl. 7 [detail]; Marzouk 1943, 165n6, Fig. 7; and Hasan 1948, 352).

3 Lev 1987.

4 Thread counts by Dorothy G. Shepherd, unpublished manuscript, cat. 112.

18

Tiraz textile naming the Fatimid caliph al-Musta'li bi-Allah

Egypt, c. 1094–1101

Cleveland Museum of Art, Gift of the Textile Arts Club to commemorate its 30th anniversary, 1965.313

1 Combe, Sauvaget, and Wiet 1931–37, 8:36–37, cat. 2864; and Cornu 1999a, 331–37.

2 Wiet 1936; Combe, Sauvaget, and Wiet 1931–37, 8:49–50, cat. 2882; and Delluc and Delluc 1983.

3 Thread count by Dorothy G. Shepherd, unpublished manuscript, cat. 125. For results of dye analysis, see Table 2 on p. 58.

This is a magnificent example of a caliphal tiraz inscription set within a complex and colorful arrangement of decorative bands comprising floral scrolls and interlaced ribbons inhabited by a variety of birds (see the detail on p. 54). This arrangement would once have run the width of a large shawl or scarf near the fringe, remnants of which have survived. In the upper- and lowermost bands, the birds are set within small lozenges, while in the two bands enclosing the central band with the inscription, they are perched within a floral scroll. The central band reprises in an original manner the tripartite composition familiar from countless late antique and Byzantine cuff bands (see, for example, cats. 21–22): an inhabited vine scroll in the middle is framed above and below with borders of reflected designs whose vertical elements point upward and downward.

The inscription, which is in the name of the Fatimid caliph al-Musta'li (r. 1094–1101), mentions his vizier Abu al-Qasim Shahanshah bin Badr al-Jamali al-Malik al-Afdal (in office 1094–1121), who brought al-Musta'li to power. The vizier's name is also inscribed on what is known as the Veil of St. Anne, made in Damietta in 489/1096–97 or 490/1097–98, not long after Abu al-Qasim Shahanshah took office (see p. 26).[1] Another inscription mentioning this vizier is that of the so-called Suaire de Cadouin.[2] However, while the latter inscriptions are perfectly legible, despite lacunae, and follow a standard caliphal protocol, the present inscription seems corrupted in parts and digresses from procedural norms. It mentions the *kunya* (given name) of Caliph al-Mustansir (r. 1036–1094) and omits the title *amir al-mu'minin* immediately following al-Musta'li's name. The text is a squarish style of Kufic. In fact, the style of the inscription, as well as details of the decoration, can be compared to those found on the Veil of St. Anne and the Suaire de Cadouin, and it is therefore possible that the present piece dates from the beginning of Abu al-Qasim Shahanshah's tenure. The use of a more traditional type of script may represent a sense of continuity of earlier models, as opposed to the cursive script that appears to have been used later in his vizierate.

—JS

INSCRIPTION (ARABIC)

Largely damaged, corrupted, and with mistakes, probably to be read as:

UPPER

[. . .] فتح قريب لعبد الله ووليه معدّ ابي تميم (. . .) الامام احمد [ابي] القسم المستعلي بالله
و ابنا[ـ]ـه [. . .]

[. . .] proximate victory to the servant of God and his friend Ma'add Abu Tamim (. . .), the imam Ahmad [Abu] al-Qasim al-Musta'li bi-Allah and his so[ns] [. . .]

LOWER

[. . .] امير المؤنين بن [ابي] [ا]لقاسم شاهنشاه (. . .) (. . .) اللمؤمنين [؟] المسلمين [؟] [. . .]

[. . .] Commander of the believers bin [a]l-Qasim Sha[han]shah (. . .) of the believers [?] (. . .) the Muslims [?] [. . .]

TECHNICAL DESCRIPTION[3]

Overall: 62.15 (warp) × 54.6 (weft) cm

Linen and silk: plain weave with in-woven tapestry weave

Plain weave: ecru linen, S, single, 24 warp × 20 weft/cm; tapestry: 1 tapestry, slit, with non-horizontal weft (warp: same as plain weave; weft: polychrome silk, thrown, single; and ecru linen, S, single and paired)

Transition to tapestry above and below the three scroll bands consists of two picks of silk (red or yellow) followed by a self-band of four to five yarns of linen. Finishing (or starting) end at bottom edge: band of off-white silk followed by wide section of plain weave ground, then narrow band of green silk, and finally warp fringe. Reverse inaccessible.

PROVENANCE

Purchased 1965 from Mrs. Paul Mallon, Paris.

SELECTED REFERENCES

Cleveland 1966, 213

Wardwell 1984, 18

Mackie 2015, 108–111, Fig. 3.25, 117, 215

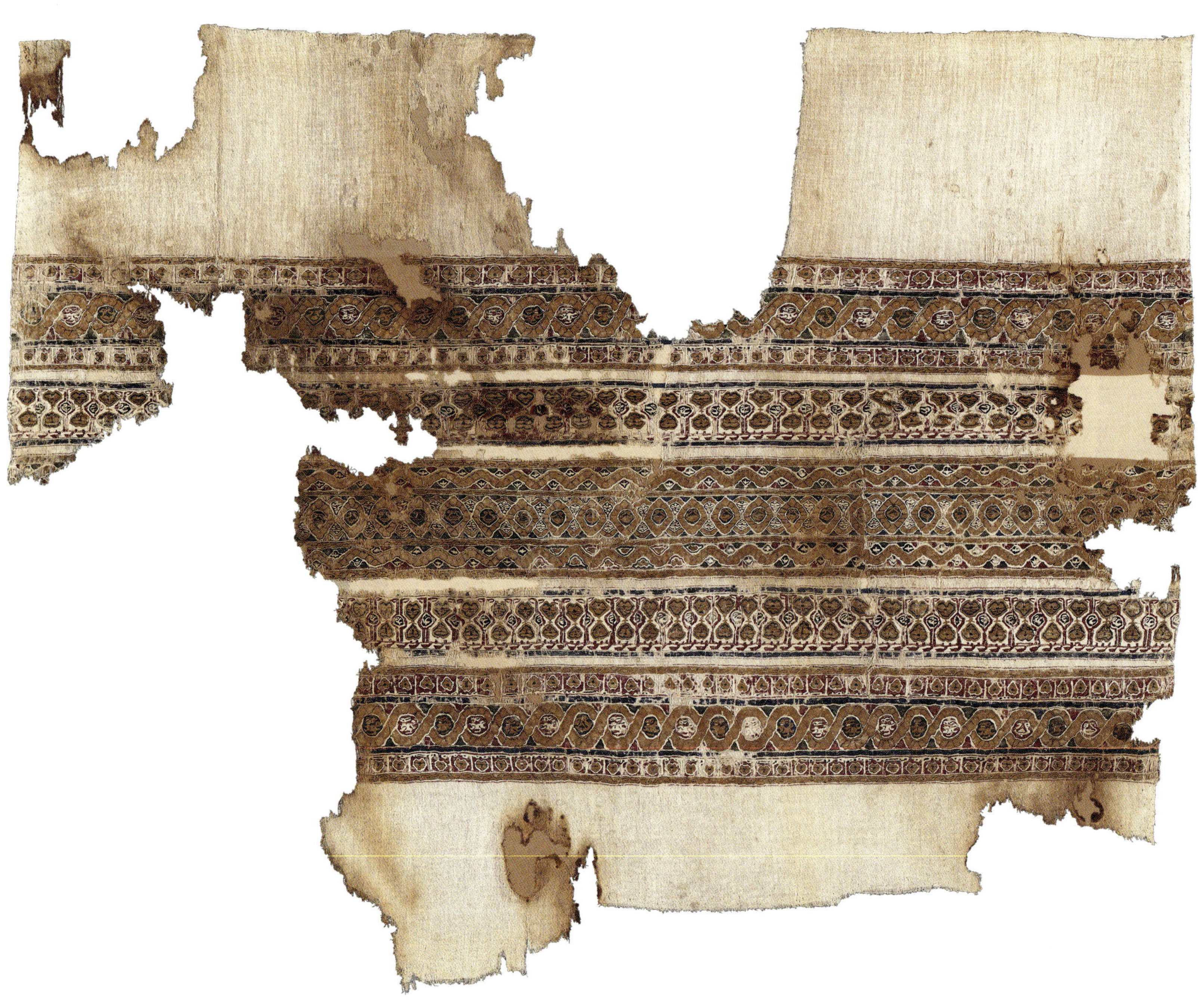

19

Tiraz textile with geometric and scrolling designs

Egypt, late 11th century

Museum of Fine Arts, Boston, Maria Antoinette Evans Fund, 32.33

The elegance and dense decoration with which this tapestry was executed employed relatively straightforward and established weaving techniques to masterful effect. Both the slit tapestry and the significant use of non-horizontal weft yarns for outlining and shaping are already attested in the Byzantine period. In addition, pre-Islamic compositional elements, such as stacked and mirrored decorative bands and inhabited vine scrolls (see the detail on p. 38), indicate a clear return to a tapestry aesthetic that predates the introduction of embroidery in the Abbasid era.

The shift away from protocollary formulae seen here, not to mention the general illegibility of the inscription, might indicate that the textile was produced for an owner who, while wealthy, was not part of the caliphal network. The allusive use of text may result from a newfound confidence among the Fatimid elite to emulate caliphal practice. Seemingly illegible evocations of God or benedictory phrases stand in contrast to the primarily legible inscriptions of the caliphs, particularly the Abbasids, whose protocollary conventions were aimed at communicating administrative procedure. This new, abstracted style of inscription was perhaps particularly well suited to the Fatimid conception of revelation, wherein only those initiated in the concealed ways (*al-batin*) had true access to divine knowledge. An exception to the intentionally obscure tapestry-woven texts is an embroidered inscription added to the upper left corner after weaving. Despite losses, it is possible to make out a phrase — "correct Ahmad bin 'Abd Allah" — perhaps a confirmation that the textile met the standards of a workshop supervisor. As such, the only clearly legible inscription on this textile served an administrative function, which may also explain the relative crudeness of the embroidery. One may speculate that the Arabic name 'Abd Allah appearing in conjunction with techniques more prevalent in the pre-Islamic era suggests that the piece was produced in a workshop with Coptic weavers overseen by a Muslim.

— MLW

INSCRIPTION (ARABIC)

TAPESTRY

Benedictory repeat-inscription in stylized Arabic letters

EMBROIDERY

سح [؟] احمد بن عبدالله [. . .]

Correct [as certified by] Ahmad bin 'Abd Allah [. . .]

TECHNICAL DESCRIPTION

73.6 (warp) × 93.3 (weft) cm

Linen and silk: plain weave with in-woven tapestry

Plain weave: ecru linen, S, single, 27 warp × 16 weft/cm; tapestry: 1 tapestry, slit, with non-horizontal weft (warp: same as plain weave; weft: polychrome silk, thrown, single; and ecru linen, S)

Transition to tapestry marked by one to four sheds of red silk (single), followed by a self-band of ecru linen (three to four yarns per shed). Fragmentary selvedge on right and left.

PROVENANCE

Purchased November 1931 with a group of "inscribed textiles" in Cairo by Joseph Lindon Smith for the Museum of Fine Arts, Boston; the purchase was approved by Denman Waldo Ross through cablegram.

SELECTED REFERENCES

Weinstein 2015, 37, cat. 11

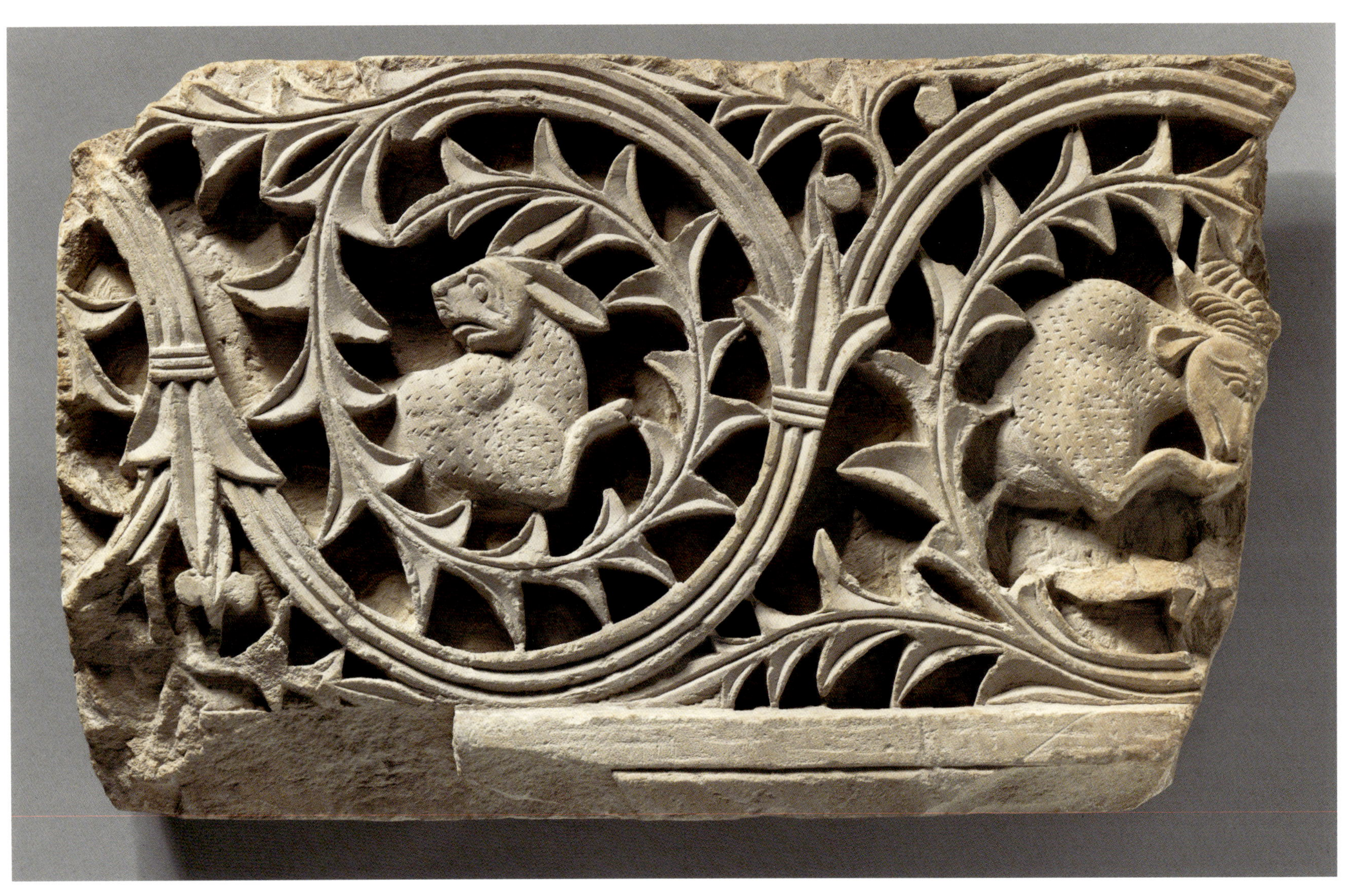

20

Section of an architectural frieze

Egypt, 5th century

34.7 × 57.5 cm

Carved limestone

Harvard Art Museums/Arthur M. Sackler Museum, Gift of the Hagop Kevorkian Foundation in memory of Hagop Kevorkian, 1975.41.53

1 For production of stone reliefs, see Thomas 2000, 22–28.

2 Ibid., 3–13.

3 Gonosová 1986.

4 Compare Egyptian Museum, Cairo, 47113, 7315, and 7305. See Monneret de Villard 1923, Figs. 82, 86, 87; Török 1970; and McKenzie 2008, 261–67.

Coiling vines not only enlivened textiles, they also scrolled across wall friezes, floor mosaics, and furniture, enveloping interior environments in vegetal pattern. This revetment from the Byzantine period in Egypt features an inhabited acanthus scroll. At center, a bounding rabbit looks back over its shoulder at another animal (now lost). Its neighbor, a goat or antelope, charges to the right, its energetic motion mirroring the unfolding of the running vine.

The soft limestone common in the Nile valley was favored by Egyptian artisans and patrons over costlier imported marble. This frieze's carving is particularly fine, with carefully rendered facial expressions and modeled musculature. Short chisel strikes create the texture of fur. Most contemporary limestone sculptures show evidence of stucco and painted polychromy, an effect that would have made such architectural elements appear even more similar to the colorful textiles whose iconography they shared.[1]

The original location of this frieze is unknown, since, like textiles, late antique architectural elements were often removed from their original contexts before entering the antiquities market.[2] This piece came to Harvard as part of a group of limestone fragments collected by antiquities dealer Hagop Kevorkian (1872–1962), with a tentative attribution to the site of Bawit.[3] However, this fragment bears greater similarities to objects excavated at a rock-cut cemetery in the city of Heracleopolis Magna (modern Ahnas) on the edge of the Fayyum.[4] Harvard's scrolling frieze would have been appropriate decoration for the tomb of a pagan or Christian.

—KMT

SELECTED REFERENCES

Unpublished

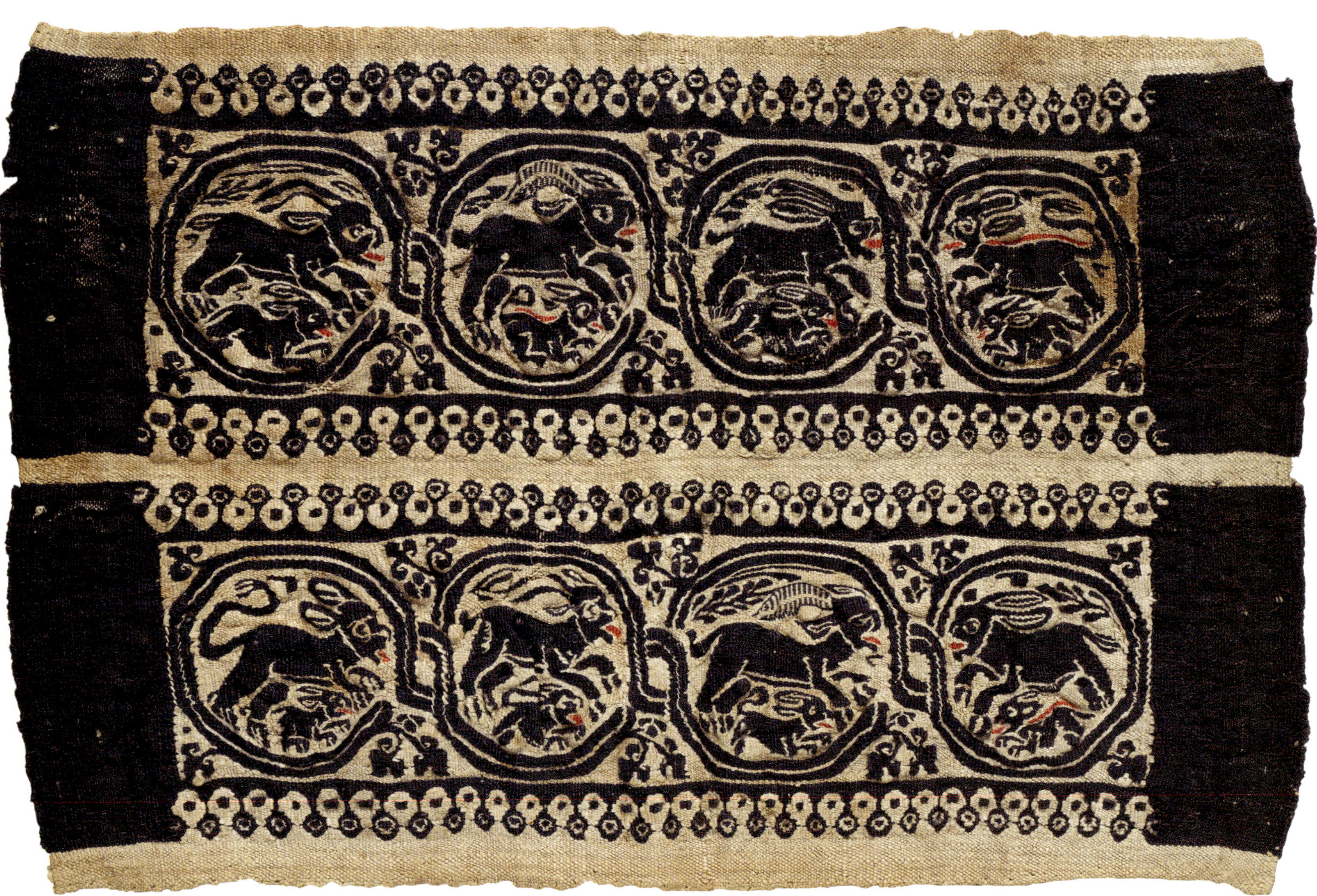

21

Cuff band with animals in interlocking scrolls

Egypt, late 4th–early 5th century[1]

Harvard Art Museums/Arthur M. Sackler Museum, Gift of Benjamin and Lilian Hertzberg, 2004.204

Representations of flora and fauna are pervasive on clothing and furnishings from early Byzantine Egypt, evoking the fertile marshlands created by the annual rising of the Nile, on which life in the region depended. On this textile, energetic animals run through vine scrolls, their panting tongues depicted with jolts of bright red yarn against the blue pattern (for a detail, see p. 52). The rightmost pairs in both scrolls face in the opposite direction of the rest, reversing the flow of movement. Exact repetition and symmetry were often deliberately disrupted like this in late antique art to energize compositions, an effect easily afforded by the freedom of weaving in tapestry.

Though the animals share essentially the same quadrupedal body, attributes such as horns, long ears, and tufted tails distinguish rabbits, goats, gazelles, and felines. The inhabited vine scroll, originating on Hellenistic diadems, was the most common symbol for expressing natural abundance in the late antique Mediterranean.[2] Grape leaves sprout from the medallions on this textile: an attribute of Dionysos, god of wine, revelry, and rebirth, the flourishing grapevine is a powerful symbol for the good life.[3] The vine and its connotations of vitality had wide appeal and spread eastward into Sasanian, Gandharan, and Chinese art.[4] Within Christianity, it was reinterpreted as symbolic of rebirth and salvation attained through Christ. This cuff band, woven during the period of Christianization in Egypt, could have adorned the wrist of a pagan or a Christian.[5] The vine scroll's continued prominence in Egyptian textiles after the Arab Muslim conquest demonstrates the enduring influence of Byzantine heritage and the fluid transfer of nature-derived iconographies across religious traditions.

— KMT

1   This textile most likely dates from about 377–430 and can be dated to roughly 346–528 with 95.4 percent probability, according to accelerated mass spectrometry radiocarbon analysis carried out at the University of Georgia Center for Applied Isotope Studies (sample number 42807) in 2019.

2   Dauphin 1987.

3   Maguire 1999.

4   Rowland 1956; and Ettinghausen 2007, 47–59.

5   Bowersock 1990, 41–53. On Egypt's conversion, see Bagnall 1982.

6   For results of dye analysis, see Table 2 on p. 58 and the photomicrograph on p. 59. Warp and weft fibers identified via microscopic analysis by Julie Wertz at the Harvard Art Museums in 2019.

TECHNICAL DESCRIPTION[6]

19.7 (warp) × 30.7 (weft) cm

Wool and linen: tapestry weave

Tapestry: 1 tapestry, slit and dovetail, with non-horizontal weft and supplementary weft wrapping (warp: ecru wool, S, single, 16/cm; weft: ecru linen, S, single, 30/cm; and blue and ecru wool, S, single)

On reverse, floats of weft between color areas. Selvedges on left and right.

PROVENANCE

Purchased by Benjamin Hertzberg, New York, from Edward R. Lubin, 3 East 75th Street, New York, in June 1987; possibly in the collection of Florence J. Gould, Villa el Patio, Cannes, France, until 1984.

SELECTED REFERENCES

Unpublished

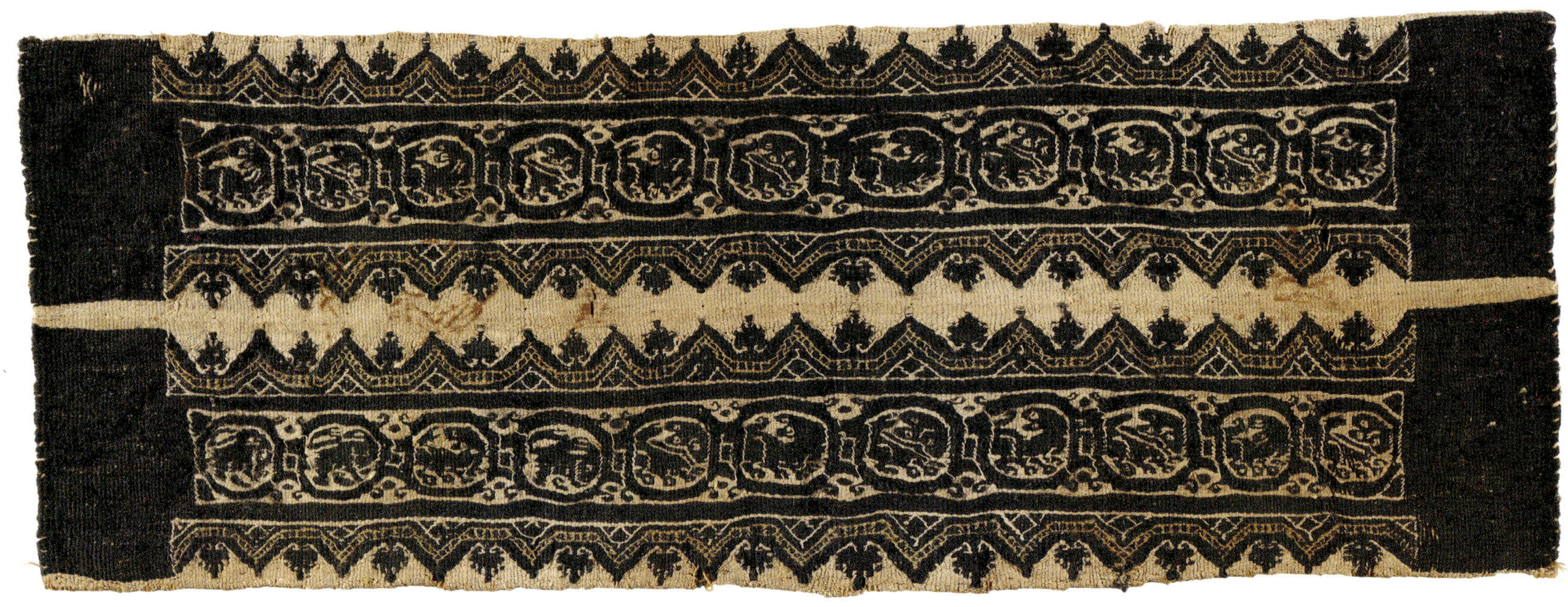

22

Cuff band with stylized animals in interlocking scrolls

Egypt, mid-6th to early 7th century[1]

Harvard Art Museums/Arthur M. Sackler Museum, Gift of Dr. Denman W. Ross, 1924.124

1 This textile most likely dates from about 534–608 and can be dated to approximately 435–608 with 95.4 percent probability, according to accelerated mass spectrometry radiocarbon analysis carried out at the University of Georgia Center for Applied Isotope Studies (sample number 42808) in 2019.

2 Museum of Fine Arts, Boston, 96.152a–b (single band and cuff band) and Harvard Art Museums 1924.117 (single band).

3 For the protective function of wool in the Roman world, see Gines Taylor 2018, 14–60.

4 For results of dye analysis, see Table 2 on p. 58.

Like the previous textile (cat. 21), this tapestry fragment once embellished the end of a tunic sleeve. Both pieces employ a standard composition for Byzantine cuff bands: two parallel vine scrolls bookended by solid blocks of color. Probably produced less than 150 years apart, the two textiles approach the persistently popular theme of the inhabited vine scroll very differently, demonstrating the stylistic range possible in late antiquity and the enduring preference for designs drawn from nature. The weaver of this later cuff band has miniaturized and abstracted the animals — possibly hares wearing neck ribbons and lions turning to look over their shoulders — transforming hunt or chase imagery into a smaller, more decorative device that suggests the standardization of drawloom patterns.

Three other fragments of the tunic to which this band belonged survive, giving a better picture of its original appearance: a companion cuff band and two single seven-unit bands (probably portions of the clavi that descended from the shoulders down the fronts and backs of Roman and Byzantine tunics). Now divided between the Museum of Fine Arts, Boston, and the Harvard Art Museums, these fragments were gifts from Denman Waldo Ross, who used them in his teaching program at the two museums (see the essay by Mary McWilliams in this volume).[2]

The weft in this tapestry consists of natural linen and dyed wool, as in the majority of contemporary tunics. However, the yellowish warp is wool — an uncommon feature outside of children's clothing, often made entirely of the material, which was considered apotropaic.[3] The wool warp makes the transition between the areas of tapestry and plain weave less pronounced, as the yarns do not need to be regrouped to accommodate the introduction of wool tapestry weft (see the essay by Julie Wertz et al.).

— KMT

TECHNICAL DESCRIPTION[4]

12.7 (warp) × 33.22 (weft) cm

Wool and linen: tapestry weave

Tapestry: 1 tapestry, slit, with non-horizontal weft and supplementary weft wrapping (warp: light-yellow wool, S, single, 11/cm; weft: ecru linen, Z and S, single, 65–70/cm; dark-purple wool, S, 65–70/cm; light-yellow wool, S and Z, single; supplementary weft wrapping)

On reverse, floats of weft yarns between color areas. Fragmentary selvedge on right.

SELECTED REFERENCES

Unpublished

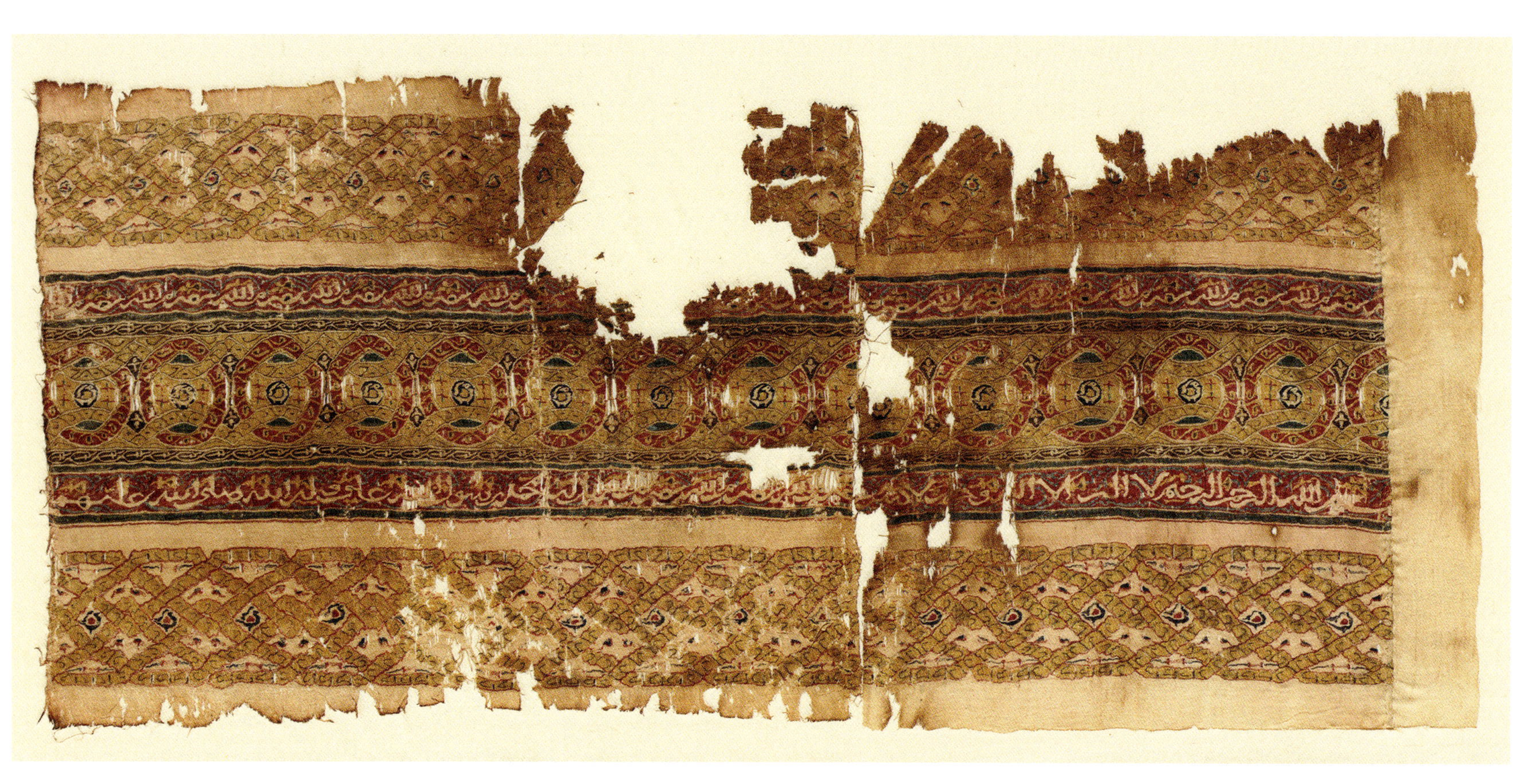

23

Tiraz textile with scrolls and interlace

Egypt, 12th century
Cleveland Museum of Art, J. H. Wade Fund, 1982.291

Toward the end of the Fatimid period (late 11th–early 12th century), textile decoration became increasingly focused on colorful, complicated interlaces, often arranged in multilayered tapestry-woven bands, as seen in the central band of this textile, where intersecting circles and half-circles are sandwiched by inscriptions in cursive script. An intricate braid borders the band above and below. In its use of complex interlace and rows of intersecting geometric forms, this tiraz exemplifies the resurgence of late antique decorative motifs in Fatimid textiles (see the detail on p. 90). Although separated by some seven centuries, it echoes the decorative program of the fifth- or sixth-century textile that follows (cat. 24), which similarly employs knot and braid patterns, as well as a band of intersecting geometric shapes — in this instance, half-circles and lozenges. Both textiles also invoke religious figures: Christian in the earlier piece, Muslim in the later.

The religious inscriptions in this tiraz include the repetition of the benedictory formula *nasr min Allah* (victory is from God), above, and the *shahada* (the Islamic proclamation of faith), with particular references to the Prophet Muhammad and his cousin and son-in-law ʿAli ibn Abi Talib, below. The latter reference places the inscription firmly in the sphere of Fatimid Ismaʿili religiosity. Interestingly, the inscription is executed in a cursive style, rather than the angular Kufic favored in the early years of the Fatimid caliphate. First used in public text in the eastern Islamic world during the early eleventh century, where it has been associated with the revival of Sunnism under the Seljuqs and Ghaznavids, cursive script appeared in Egypt by the early twelfth century, well before the Fatimid dynasty came to an end in 1171.[1] It is possible that in Egypt this was less a religious development than one reflecting changes in how the government was run. Beginning in the late eleventh century, when the authority of the Fatimid caliphate was in decline due to internal power struggles within the caliphal family and revolts by the Turkish and Berber military, power was increasingly exercised by viziers on behalf of the ruling caliph. While Kufic script was possibly viewed as more conservative, reflecting an older, more orthodox order, cursive script perhaps came to be symbolic of change and of the vizier's increased sway of expression. A number of textiles have survived from the early twelfth century with cursive script spelling out the name and inflated titles of Abu al-Qasim Shahanshah bin Badr al-Jamali al-Malik al-Afdal, son of the famous Armenian-born vizier Badr al-Jamali.[2] Abu al-Qasim held office from 487/1094 until his own assassination in 515/1121, serving under the Fatimid caliphs al-Mustansir (r. 1036–1094), al-Mustaʿli (r. 1094–1101), and al-Amir (r. 1101–1131). As kingmaker, Abu al-Qasim brought al-Mustaʿli to the throne when the latter was still a child. Following the reign of that caliph, cursive tiraz inscriptions became ever more common until the end of the Fatimid caliphate.[3]

—JS

INSCRIPTION (ARABIC)

UPPER
Repetition of the phrase:

نصر من الله

Victory is from God

LOWER

بسم الله الرحمن الرحيم لا اله الا الله وحده لا شريك له عز من الله نصر من الله نصر من
الله بركة محمد رسول الله علي ولي الله صلى الله عليهمـ[ا]

In the name of God, the Merciful, the Compassionate. There is no god but God alone. There is no one associated with Him. Glory is from God. Victory is from God. Victory is from God. Blessing. Muhammad is the apostle of God. ʿAli is the true friend of God, may God bless the[m].

TECHNICAL DESCRIPTION[4]

27 (warp) × 63.2 (weft) cm
Linen and silk: plain weave with in-woven tapestry weave
Plain weave: ecru linen, S, single, 35 warp × 24 weft/cm[5]; tapestry:
1, 2 tapestry, slit, with non-horizontal weft (warp: same as plain weave; weft: polychrome silk, thrown, single; and ecru linen, S, often paired)
Transition marked by warp-crossing above and below tapestry bands to form groups of single and paired warp ends; the exception is the section of ground fabric between the main inscription band and the lower interlace band, which maintains the rearranged position of the warp in plain weave. Fragmentary selvedge on left. Reverse inaccessible.

PROVENANCE

Purchase 1982 from Mrs. Paul Mallon, Paris.

SELECTED REFERENCES

Mackie 2015, 117–18, Fig. 3.36
O'Kane 2018b, 186

---

1   For a discussion on the transformation of public text from Kufic to cursive, see Tabbaa 1994.

2   Museum of Islamic Art, Cairo, 9762 (see Combe, Sauvaget, and Wiet 1931–37, 8:130, no. 2987; and Marzouk 1942, pl. 17); Biblioteca Apostolica Vaticana 6741 (see Cornu 1992, 228–30); Museum of Islamic Art, Cairo, 9350 (Marzouk 1942, pl. 16); and Textile Museum 73.680 (Kühnel and Bellinger 1952, 80–81, pl. 38).

3   Examples include an inscription from the reign of al-Amir in the Textile Museum (73.680; see Kühnel and Bellinger 1952, 80–81, pl. 38) and two from the reign of al-Hafiz (r. 1130–1149) in the Museum of Fine Arts, Boston (30.677; see Britton 1938, 67–68, no. 30.677, Fig. 83) and the Textile Museum (73.199; see Kühnel and Bellinger 1952, 81–82, pl. 38).

4   For results of dye analysis, see Table 2 on p. 58.

5   Thread counts by Dorothy G. Shepherd, Cleveland Museum of Art curatorial records.

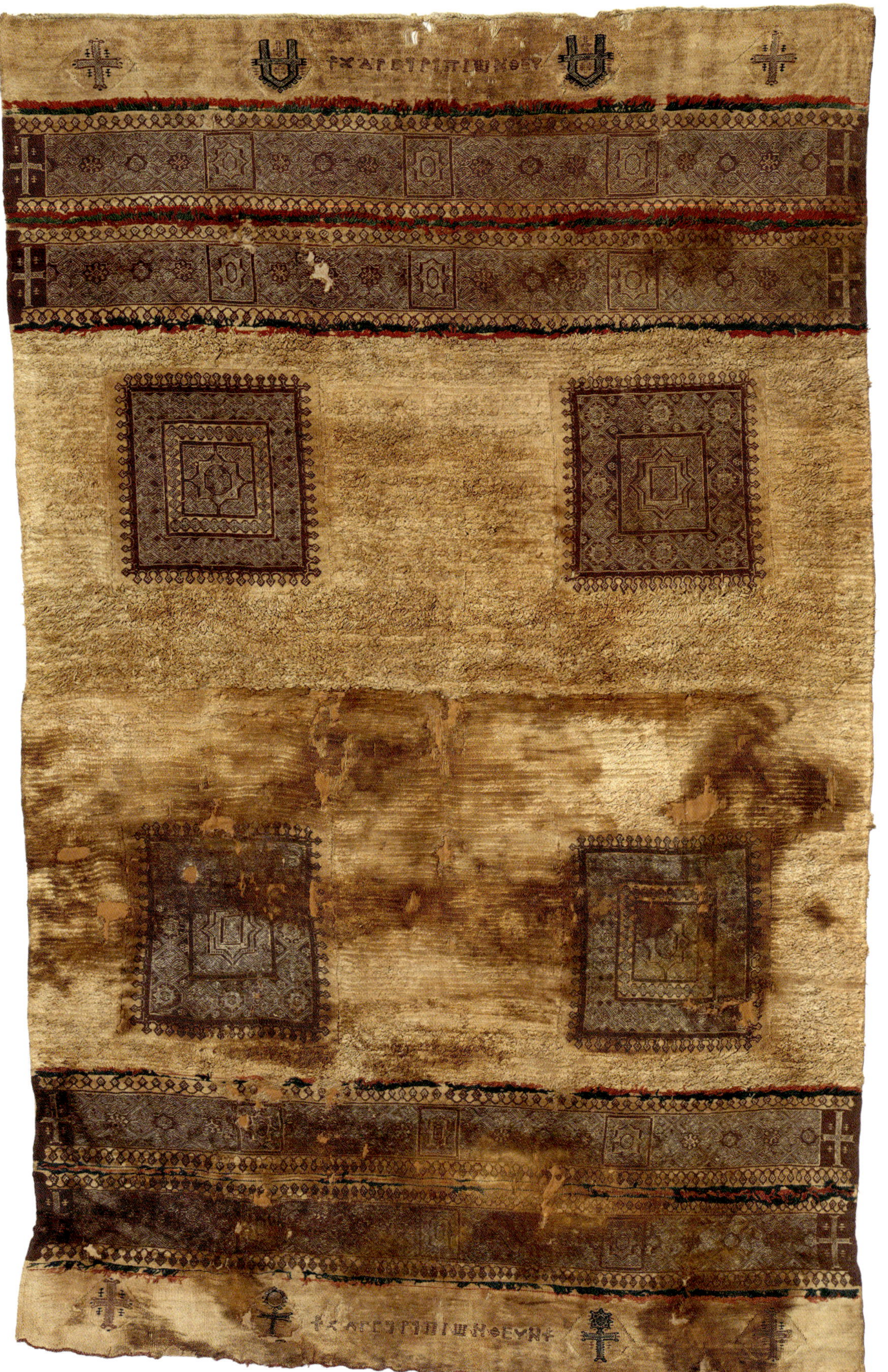

24

Large cover

Egypt, 5th–6th century[1]

Harvard Art Museums/Arthur M. Sackler Museum, Gift of the Hagop Kevorkian Foundation in memory of Hagop Kevorkian, 1975.41.28

The textual decoration on this large and relatively complete textile presents a comparison to the role of inscriptions on later Islamic tiraz. Its text — paired inscriptions and elaborated letterforms that served as Christian symbols — acts as a talisman, marshaling protective and magical signs to benefit the individual named in the inscriptions.

The inscriptions at either end are nearly identical (see details below, at left).[2] They start and finish with staurograms, a symbol of the crucified Christ,[3] and pair a Christian magical formula (ΧΜΓ)[4] with the name Sarapion Theun.[5] Protective inscriptions were widespread in the Byzantine world, but their survival on textiles is very rare.[6] Supplementary weft wrapping (see rightmost detail below and the detail on p. 146) renders intricate interlace that may have been considered apotropaic snares for evil forces.[7] Aniconic signs and letterforms complete the decorative — and protective — program. Purple crosses mark the textile's four corners (center detail, below). Two blue ankhs (cruces ansatae) stand at one end of the textile, and large blue alphas at the other.[8] Such quasi-architectural alphas appear on only a small set of related textiles featuring ankhs and interlace decoration.[9]

The original function of this textile is uncertain, though its fields of loop pile (see p. 145) create a plush and inviting surface. A modern seam runs across the middle where damage was presumably excised. The pattern of the stains and pile loss suggests that it became a funerary shroud.

— KMT

1. This textile can be dated to roughly 417–545 with 95.4 percent probability, according to accelerated mass spectrometry radiocarbon analysis carried out at the University of Arizona AMS Laboratory (sample number AA112489) in 2019.
2. One inscription is truncated.
3. Hurtado 2006, 207–26.
4. Nongbri 2011; and Llewelyn 1998, 156–68.
5. Clarysse and Paganini 2009. Theun was previously read as "Thekla"; see Brooklyn 1941, 83.
6. Van der Vliet 2006, 29–30.
7. Ball 2016, 54–65. For votive gifts of inscribed textiles, see ibid., 26; and Gaselee 1923, 78–79, no. 8.
8. Bowen 2014, 291–303.
9. They have been interpreted as church facades or sacred niches; see Du Bourguet 1953, 11–31; and Török 1993, 11.
10. For results of dye analysis, see Table 2 on p. 58 and the photomicrograph on p. 60.

INSCRIPTION (GREEK)

☧ ΧΜΓ ϹΑΡΑΠΙΩΝ ΘΕΥΝ ☧
☧ ΧΜΓ Sarapion Theun ☧

TECHNICAL DESCRIPTION[10]

221.5 (warp) × 148 (weft) cm
Linen and wool: tapestry weave and supplementary weft pile
Tapestry: allover 2 tapestry, slit and dovetail, with non-horizontal weft and supplementary weft wrapping (warp: ecru wool, S, paired, 10/cm; weft: ecru linen, S; and polychrome wool, 18/cm); pile: ecru linen, S, paired; green and red wool, S, paired
Upper edge created by plaiting of warp yarns; scalloped lower edge created by looping polychrome wool yarns in Z-direction onto warp yarns. Selvedge on left and right. Reverse inaccessible.

SELECTED REFERENCES

Brooklyn 1941, 47, 83, cat. 262 (not illustrated)

Figs. 1–4 Details

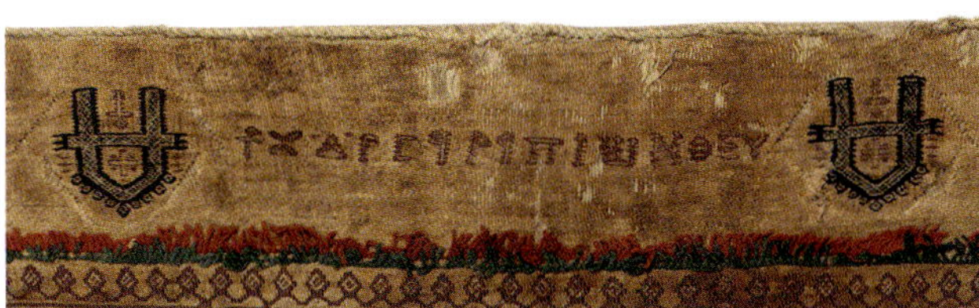

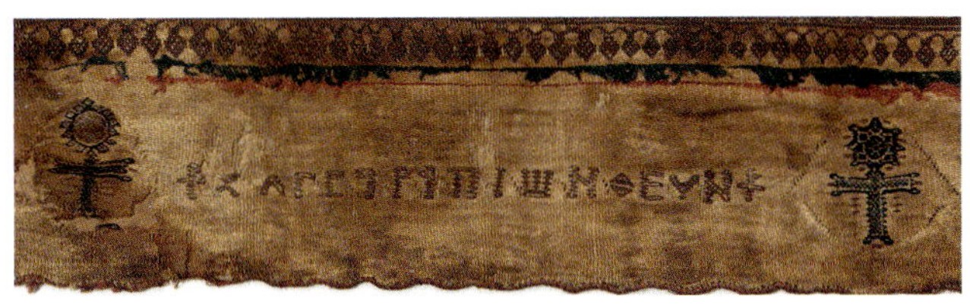

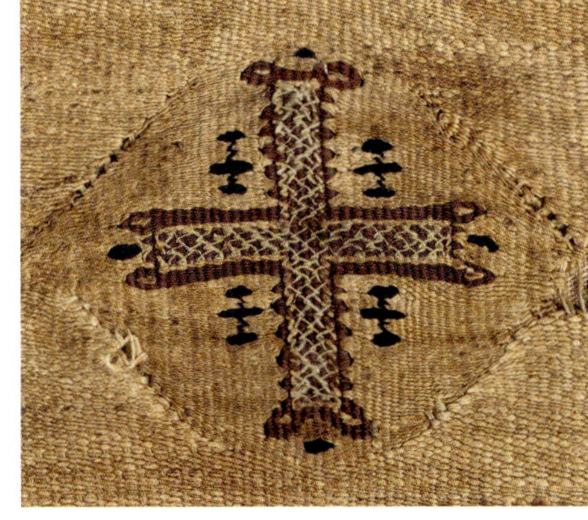

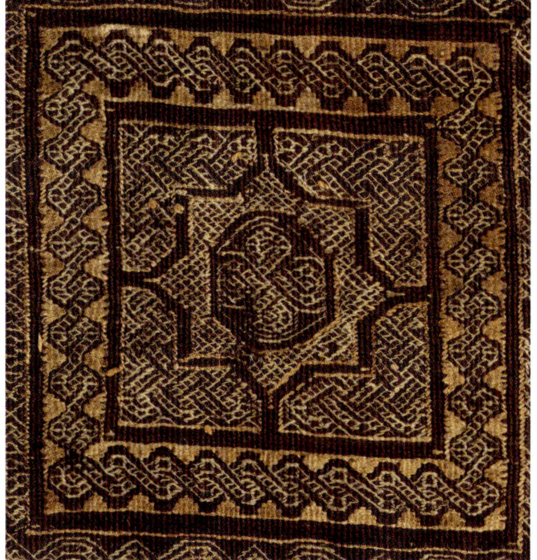

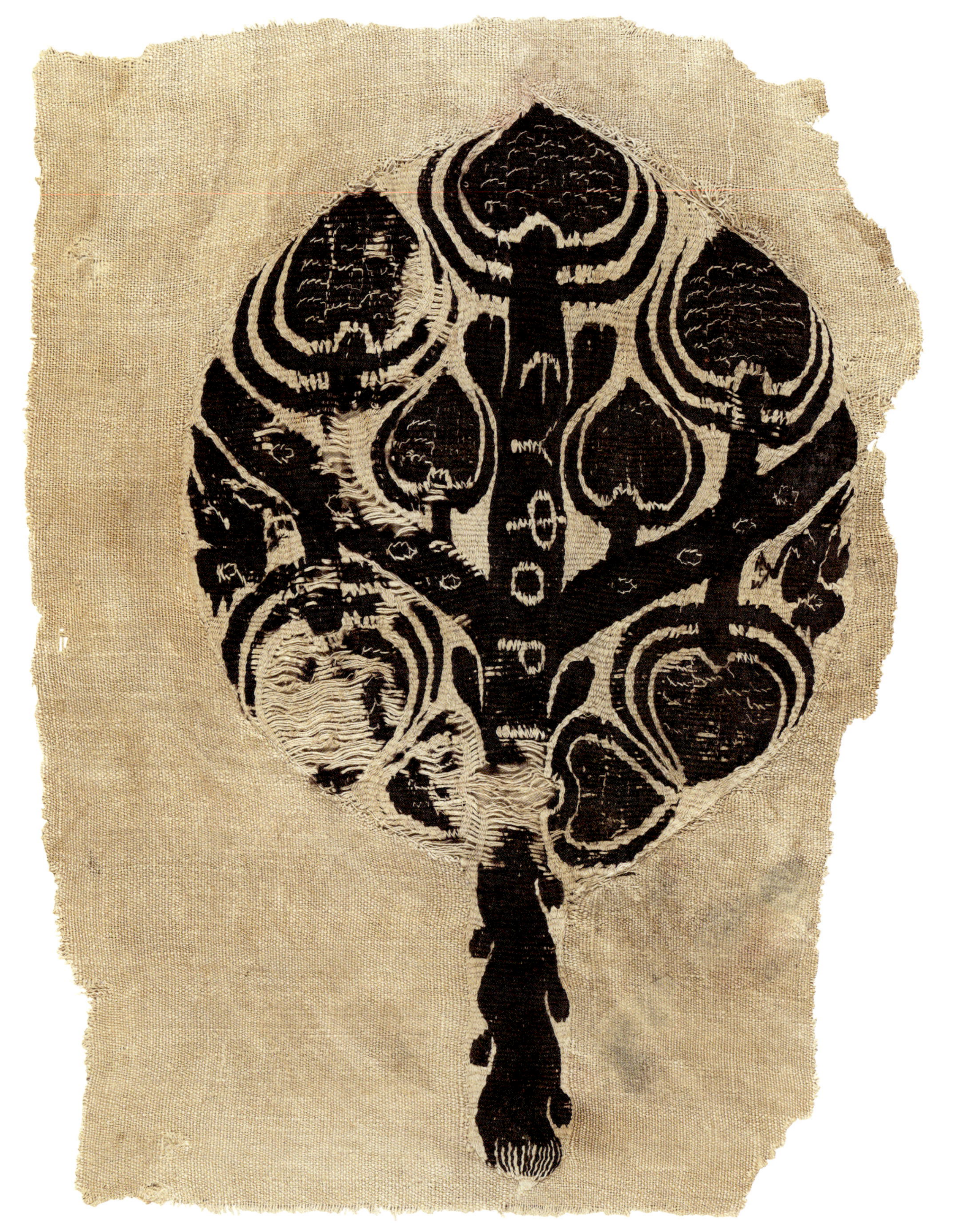

25

Textile with tree and Greek inscription

Egypt, 4th–5th century

Museum of Fine Arts, Boston, Denman Waldo Ross Collection, 23.177

1 Maguire 1990.
2 Katoen Natie Museum 437.
3 De Moor, Verhecken-Lammens, and Van Strydonck 2006, 223, Fig. 73.
4 Kondoleon 2016, 87–95.
5 De Jonghe and Tavernier 1983.
6 For results of dye analysis, see Table 2 on p. 58.

Although script on pre-Islamic Egyptian textiles primarily served to identify figures in pictorial compositions, texts also worked apotropaically to protect a user from harm or attract good fortune.[1] On this furnishing textile, a beneficent Greek inscription decorates a burst of foliage inhabited by a pair of symmetrical birds: image and text work together to conjure abundance and prosperity for the home it embellished. The word on the stem of the stylized plant can be read as Εὐφορί (Flourish!) if complete or Εὐφορία (Fertility) if missing the final alpha. A clue to its interpretation lies in a textile fragment of similar size and design in the Katoen Natie Museum, Antwerp.[2] Radiocarbon dated to 250–400, the Antwerp textile bears a purple branch with heart-shaped foliage and two small birds nestled inside.[3] The plant's stem is inscribed KATATPIB[E], the imperative form of κατατρίβω, meaning "to use up" — here probably "to make full use of your life" or "to enjoy it fully." This comparison suggests the verb of the Boston textile should also be understood in the imperative, either as a reminder to the viewer or a wish for the household.

The linen warp runs perpendicular to the orientation of the tapestry pattern, indicating that the fragment was cut from a wall hanging of significant size. Roman interior design had long sought to "bring the garden indoors" through spatial illusions in paint, tapestry, and mosaic.[4]

This fragment exhibits several distinctive late antique Egyptian weaving techniques. Supplementary weft wrapping creates fine details of the birds and vegetation. The tapestry section is woven into the plain linen ground instead of applied later (see the details on p. 52) — a common technique among Byzantine artisans, despite the complexity of weaving in an irregular shape such as this.[5]

— KMT

INSCRIPTION (GREEK)

ΕΥΦΟΡΙ

Flourish!

TECHNICAL DESCRIPTION[6]

27 (warp) × 36 (weft) cm

Linen and wool: plain weave with in-woven tapestry weave

Plain weave: ecru linen, S, single, 23 warp × 11 weft/cm; tapestry: 2, 3 tapestry, slit and dovetail, with non-horizontal weft and weft wrapping (warp: same as plain weave; weft: dark-purple wool, S, single; and ecru linen, S, single)

Transition to tapestry marked by warp crossing and grouping of warp yarns into two and three. On reverse, floats of tapestry weft between color areas; surplus warp yarns reserved in tapestry section.

SELECTED REFERENCES

Van der Vliet 2006, 29

Maguire 1990, 217, Fig. 8

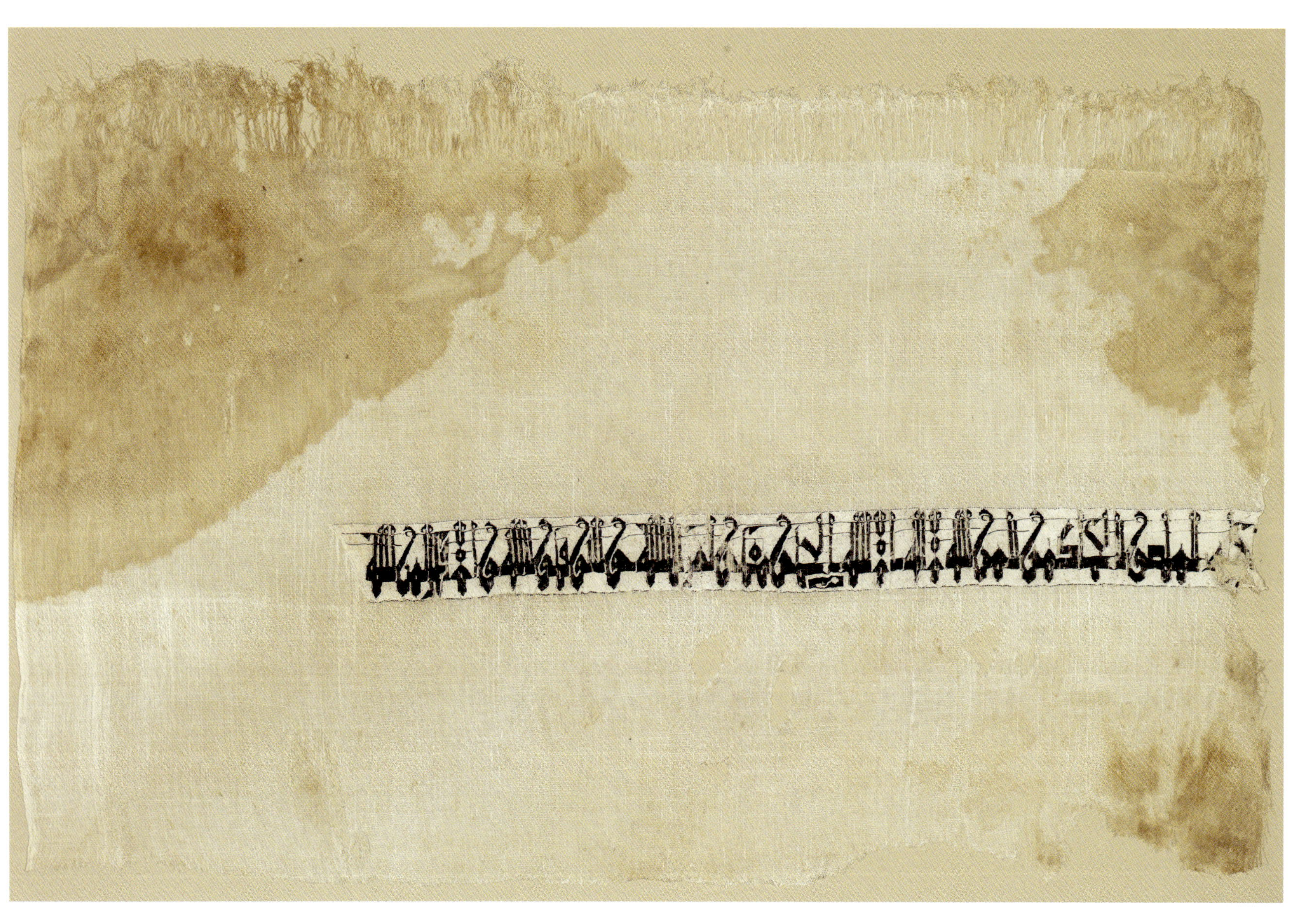

26

Tiraz textile naming the Fatimid caliph al-Hakim bi-Amr Allah

Egypt, c. 996–1021

Museum of Fine Arts, Boston, Helen and Alice Colburn Fund, 34.116

[1] For results of dye analysis, see Table 2 on p. 58.

The elaborately foliated and plaited Kufic inscription on this tiraz summons prosperity and good fortune for its user. In this, it is similar to the previous textile (cat. 25), though they are separated by some five hundred years, with telling differences in their means of visual communication. In the earlier work, a Greek exhortation to flourish is implanted within a large fruiting tree, allowing the pictorial representation of the theme to predominate over the single word of text. The later textile relies purely on epigraphic means to convey its message, embedding it within a religious matrix, with multiple references to God.

Egyptian tiraz textiles bearing large inscriptions in floriated Kufic were woven during the reign of al-Muti' (r. 946–974), the last Abbasid caliph before the Fatimid conquest of the country in 969. The new rulers quickly internalized the elaborate epigraphic style (cat. 15) and employed it for monumental public inscriptions in architecture, including the Mosque of al-Hakim, commissioned by the caliph named in this tiraz (r. 996–1021).

This tapestry relies on a system of self-bands similar to that found in an Abbasid tiraz in the exhibition (cat. 14), which regulate tension and carry linen and silk tapestry yarns to their respective zones of the design. But the weaving in al-Hakim's tiraz has become more intuitive, taking on a life of its own. Whereas in the former example the tapestry merges imperceptibly into the ground fabric, here the weavers have chosen to accentuate the difference between the open ground weave and dense tapestry band, doubling the linen weft throughout the tapestry section. This structural choice might also have secured the tapestry within the overall fabric.

— MLW

INSCRIPTION (ARABIC)

[. . .] المص‍[ـو]ر الحاكم بأمر الله لا اله الّا الله الخير معين ممن بالله والتوفيق بالله يالاقبال من الله

[. . .] al-Mans[u]r al-Hakim bi-Amr Allah. There is no god but God. The good is an aid. Fortune is in God. And success is in God. And prosperity comes from God.

TECHNICAL DESCRIPTION[1]

49 (warp) × 74 (weft) cm

Linen and silk: plain weave with in-woven tapestry weave

Plain weave: off-white linen, S, single, 19 warp × 11 weft/cm; tapestry: 1 tapestry, slit and dovetail, with non-horizontal weft and weft wrapping (warp: same as plain weave; weft: off-white linen, S, paired; and dark-brown silk, thrown, single)

Transition to tapestry marked by a self-band (paired weft: one linen, one silk). Additional self-bands (also paired: one silk, one linen) run between most letters, connecting slits and calibrating letters. Open-weave band and fringe preserved at upper edge. Fragmentary selvedge on left.

PROVENANCE

Purchased December 1933 with a group of "fine textiles cufic inscriptions" in Cairo by Joseph Lindon Smith for the Museum of Fine Arts, Boston; the purchase was approved by Edward Jackson Holmes and Gertrude Townsend through cablegram.

SELECTED REFERENCES

Britton 1938, 54, Fig. 41

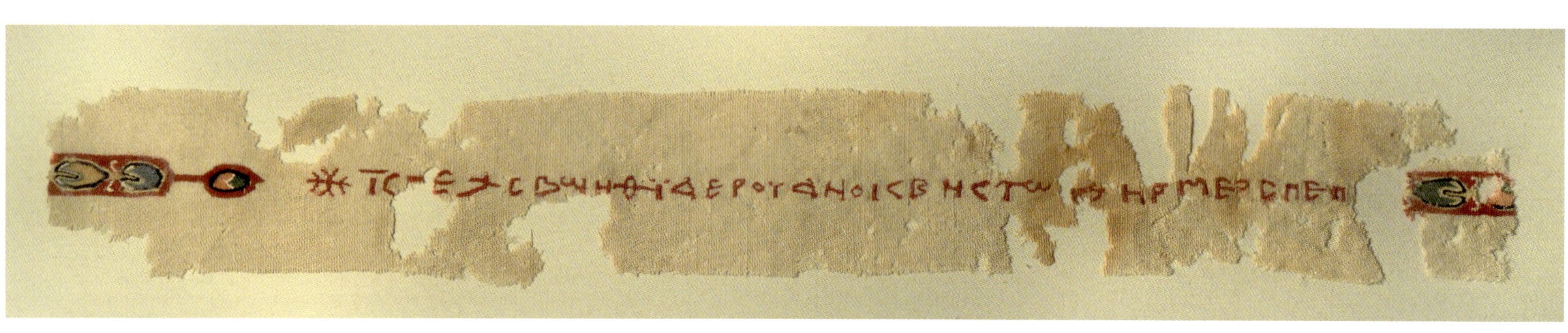

27

Fragment of a garment with Coptic inscription

Egypt, 8th century

Dumbarton Oaks Research Library and Collection, Washington, D.C., BZ.1953.2.3

The banded decoration and vivid red lettering on this textile fragment offer parallels to several Islamic tiraz in the exhibition. Yet the Coptic-language inscription, beginning with a cross and nomina sacra of Jesus Christ, is explicitly Christian, illustrating the energetic cultural interchange that took place in Egypt in the centuries after the Arab conquest. Like early tiraz that confer blessings or protection (see cats. 34–35), the woven letters convey a plea for divine help. Interesting is the continued emphasis on personal names in amuletic Christian inscriptions, in contrast to the tiraz that leave their recipients anonymous. In keeping with pre-Islamic magical traditions (see, for example, cat. 24), the parents and occupations of individuals are specified to ensure the requests would be correctly understood (see the essay by Elizabeth Dospěl Williams in this volume).

Several stylistic features of the late antique tapestry tradition are also apparent. The red band at left terminates in an arrow-shaped finial, a detail that appeared on the ends of Roman clavi.[1] A new incarnation of the ubiquitous vine motif appears here as well: the bands on either side of the lettering contain evenly spaced, organic shapes connected by a yellow stem sprouting pairs of curling tendrils. The stylized ensemble suggests a vine carrying flower buds, fruits, or lily pad–like leaves.

Red bands of tapestry ornament and Coptic script occur in several other contemporary textiles, suggesting a cohesive group of objects responding to the social and religious value of tiraz. A band that traverses an uninscribed textile from the collection of Denman Waldo Ross forms a close comparison.[2] A simplified version of this design appears on a textile in the Metropolitan Museum of Art, New York, with an almost illegible inscription beginning and ending with small crosses.[3] The phrases "use it in happiness" and "and rejoice" have been read, as well as the possible name Mishael.

— KMT

1. Paetz gen. Schieck 2012, 85–108.

2. Now in two fragments: Harvard Art Museums 1916.395 and Museum of Fine Arts, Boston, 96.344.

3. Metropolitan Museum of Art 90.5.877 (radiocarbon dated to 810–1010); see Evans and Ratliff 2012, 183–84, no. 124B. For other comparanda, see Williams and Dospěl 2019.

4. For results of dye analysis, see Table 2 on p. 58.

5. Deborah Thompson, introduction to unpublished manuscript, 2 and cat. 110.

INSCRIPTION (COPTIC)

+ ⲓ̅ⲥ̅ ⲡⲉⲭⲥ ⲃⲱⲏⲑⲓ̈ⲁ ⲉⲣⲟⲓ̈ ⲁⲛⲟⲕ ⲃⲓⲕⲧⲱ[ⲣ] ⲡ̣ϣⲏⲣⲙⲉⲟⲥ ⲡⲉⲡ[ⲣ(ⲉⲥⲃⲩⲧⲉⲣⲟⲥ)] [. . .]

+ Lord Jesus Christ, help me; I (am) the priest Viktor son of Meus [. . .]

TECHNICAL DESCRIPTION[4]

Overall: 7.5 (warp) × 58.3 (weft) cm

Wool: tapestry weave

Tapestry: allover 1 tapestry, slit, with slight use of non-horizontal weft and weft wrapping (warp: off-white wool, S, single, 11/cm; weft: polychrome wool, S, single, 27/cm)

Reverse inaccessible

PROVENANCE

Formerly in the collection of Mrs. William H. Crocker; gifted to Dumbarton Oaks by the children of Mrs. William H. Crocker; said to have been acquired in Egypt between 1900 and 1910 through or from Sir John Maxwell, then chief of staff of the British Army.[5]

SELECTED REFERENCES

Williams and Dospěl 2019

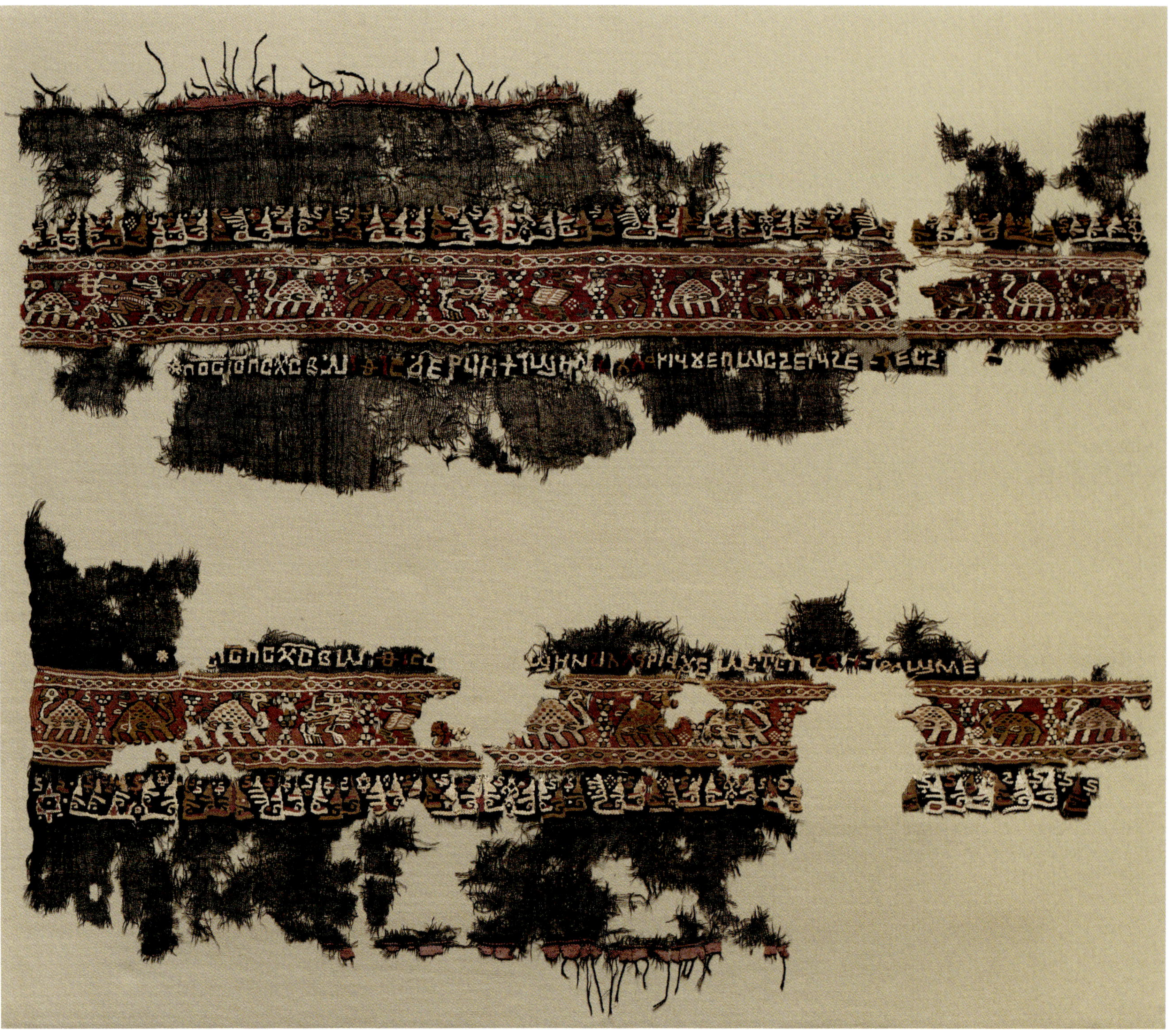

28

Decorated ends of a shawl

Egypt, probably Fayyum, late 8th–late 9th century[1]

Cleveland Museum of Art, Gift of the Textile Arts Club, 1956.330

The animals parading across what would have been the top and bottom of a woolen shawl have clear precedents in the iconography of Byzantine textiles, especially the creatures that may be rabbits and gazelles and the charging horseman at upper left. But these tapestry bands are embedded in a new format: woven with long lines of Coptic and Arabic script, the bilingual shawl belongs to a small group of textiles that signal the adoption of the tiraz style by Egypt's Christian population. The Coptic inscriptions invoke Jesus Christ through nomina sacra and begin with crosses (in contrast, rosettes surround the Arabic). The Coptic inscription requests divine help for a person whose name is difficult to discern. The phrase "the daughter of Hillaria" can be read, making this shawl one of the few examples that name a female owner.[2]

Even less legible than the Coptic inscription, the Arabic text may repeat the words *baraka min Allah* (blessing from God). The foliated letterforms mimic the colors and shapes of the animals inside the band, taking on an almost pictorial quality.[3] On a similar tapestry band in the Nationalmuseum, Stockholm, the gaps between Arabic letters are filled with numerous small crosses, showing the extent to which Arabic script was embraced by the Christian community.[4]

Camels, white and gold with spotted humps, are most numerous among the animals represented in the tapestry frieze (see the detail on p. 30). This is noteworthy, as the species is not seen on late antique textiles. Representations of camels — a non-native, domesticated species whose use increased throughout late antiquity — probably brought to mind cross-desert trade and perhaps served as a new way of picturing prosperity.[5]

Although quite different in character, this shawl fragment and a twelfth-century tiraz textile with scrolls and interlace (cat. 23) employ the same types of dyes (see the essay by Julie Wertz et al. in this volume). The varied effects and range of shades demonstrate the skill of the weavers and dyers.

— KMT

1 This textile can be dated to roughly 770–887 with 95.4 percent probability, according to accelerated mass spectrometry radiocarbon analysis carried out at the University of Georgia Center for Applied Isotope Studies (sample number 42811) in 2019.

2 Van der Vliet 2006, 40.

3 Mackie 2015, 89–91.

4 Lamm 1936, 52, 76, no. 58, pl. 15b.

5 An identical camel design with Arabic script appears on Metropolitan Museum of Art 53.124.4 and Museum of Islamic Art, Cairo, 9061. The camel usually appears with St. Menas in Byzantine art, but compare Coptic Museum, Cairo, 7964, a limestone frieze with a man and camel in a vine scroll. For the camel in late antiquity, see Bagnall 1985.

6 Fiber identification and thread count by Dorothy G. Shepherd, unpublished manuscript, cat. 90. For results of dye analysis, see Table 2 on p. 58.

INSCRIPTIONS

ARABIC (POSSIBLY)

بركة من الله

Blessing from God

COPTIC (POSSIBLY)

+ ⲠⲞⲤ ⲒⲤ ⲠⲤ ⲬⲤ ⲃⲱⲓⲑⲓ [. . .] Ⲧⲩⲏ ⲛⲅⲓⲗⲗⲁⲣⲓⲁ [. . .]

+ Lord Jesus Christ help [. . .] the daughter of Hillaria [. . .]

TECHNICAL DESCRIPTION[6]

Overall: 41.9 (warp) × 68.6 (weft) cm

Wool, linen, and silk: plain weave with in-woven tapestry weave

Plain weave: dark-blue wool, S, single, 12 warp × 12 weft/cm; tapestry: 1 and occasionally 2 tapestry, slit and dovetail, with non-horizontal weft, wedge-like inserts, and weft wrapping (warp: same as plain weave; weft: polychrome wool, S, single; red silk, thrown, single; and ecru linen, S, single)

Selvedge fragments on right and left. Braided warp fringe at top and bottom edges. Reverse inaccessible.

PROVENANCE

Purchased 1956 from Mrs. Paul Mallon, New York and Paris.

SELECTED REFERENCES

Mackie 2015, 89–91, Fig. 3.5

Wardwell 1984, 17, Fig. 9

Wadsworth 1951, cat. 57

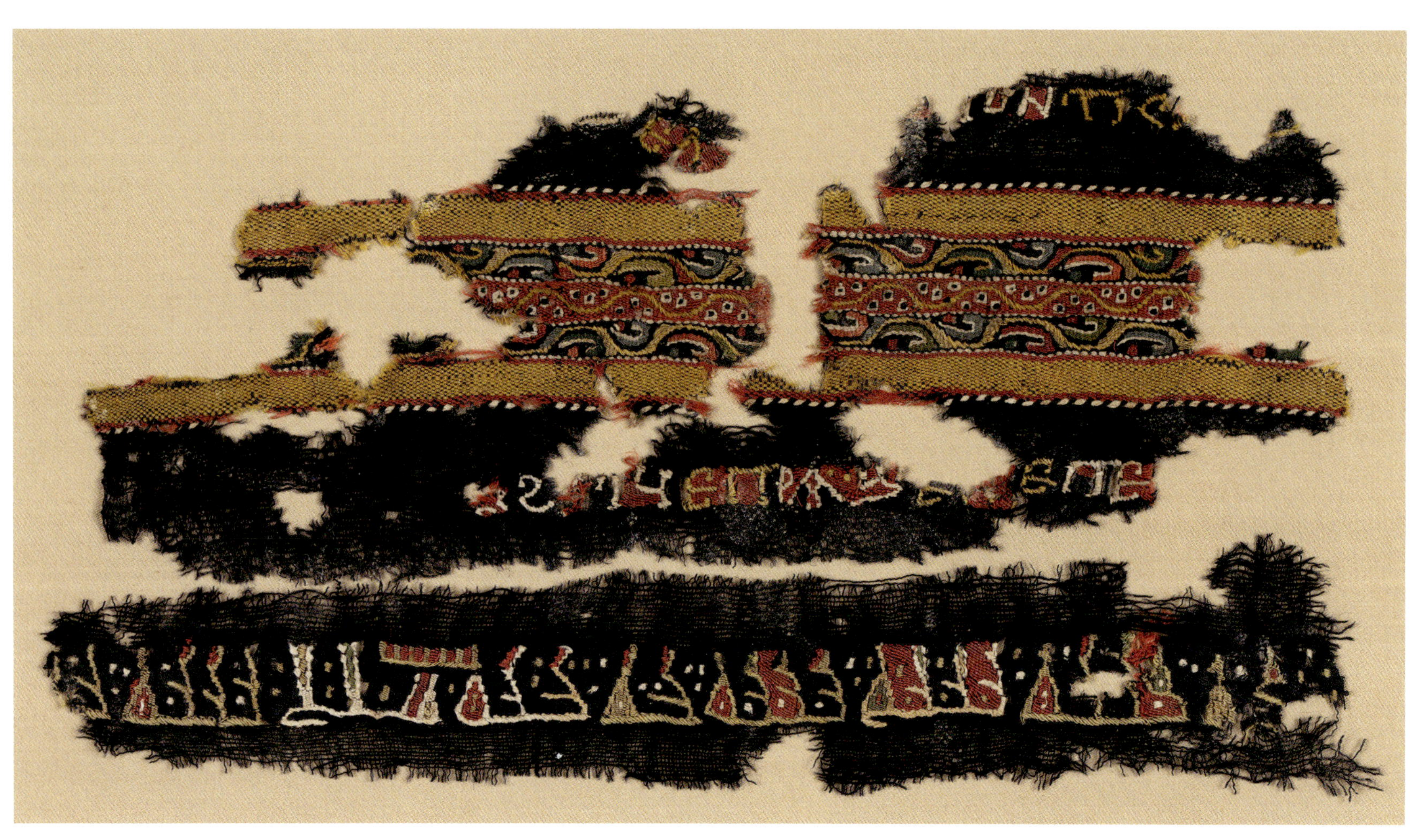

29

Decorative border of a shawl

Egypt, probably Fayyum, late 8th–9th century
Museum of Fine Arts, Boston, Denman Waldo Ross Collection, 11.1398

Vivid golds and reds illuminate the tapestry band and three lines of woven script against the dark-blue ground fabric of this textile, probably made in the Fayyum in Upper Egypt. The two partial lines of Coptic indicate that the textile did not originate within the Islamic system of administrative patronage. However, the piece certainly imitates many features of the tiraz owned by the ruling elite, showing the wide appeal of prestige forms across religious and cultural groups. The cross at the beginning of the lower line of Coptic tells us that this shawl was made for a Christian owner; the simple Arabic phrase invoking Allah communicates good wishes and recalls the appearance of high-status tiraz. The rare bilingual text illustrates the process of language conversion and cultural change occurring at this time, when Arabic was well on its way to becoming the colloquial language of the Christian population.

The Coptic inscription may belong to a specific formula found only on some Christian tiraz-style textiles and a group of ninth-century Coptic book colophons, all from the Fayyum. It expresses the hope that the recipient of the object will "use it" (ϩⲉⲧϥ) in "happiness" (ⲣⲁϣⲉ). Usually, the formula continues with a list of other positive states in which the garment will find its user, such as joy, righteousness, wisdom, and so on. On this textile, the rest of the inscription is lost after the beginning of the second noun. Evidence suggests that this formula was a standard choice for inscribing objects offered as gifts.[1]

The decoration in the tapestry band accompanying the text is made up of three stacked scrolling vines whose golden stems are created using the technique of weft wrapping (see the details on pp. 42, 147). The central vine runs across a red background; the empty hills and valleys of its path are each filled with three white dots with black centers. Curving blue, green, and red leaves highlighted with white or gold surround the upper and lower vines. Red and green dots interspersed around the leaves may represent fruits or additional foliage. This textile testifies to the survival of deep-rooted iconographic motifs drawn from the natural world and the continued importance of pictorial decoration in the Islamic era.

—KMT

1 Van der Vliet 2006, 38–40.
2 For results of dye analysis, see Table 2 on p. 58.

INSCRIPTIONS

COPTIC (POSSIBLY)
+ ϩ[ⲉ]ⲧϥ ⲉⲡⲣⲁϣⲉ [ϫ]ⲉ ⲡⲉ [. . .]
+ Use it in happiness [. . .]

ARABIC (POSSIBLY)

لا إله إلّا الله

There is no god but God

TECHNICAL DESCRIPTION[2]
Overall (three fragments): 14.5 (warp) × 28.5 (weft) cm
Wool and linen: plain weave with in-woven tapestry weave
Plain weave: dark-blue wool, S, single, 13 warp × 11 weft/cm; tapestry: 1 tapestry, slit, with non-horizontal weft and weft wrapping (warp: same as plain weave; weft: polychrome wool, S, single; and ecru linen, S, triple)
Transition to tapestry band (with vine pattern) marked by a linen weft yarn (quadruple) twined with a wool weft yarn (triple). On reverse, floats of tapestry weft between color areas.

SELECTED REFERENCES
Britton 1938, 42, Fig. 18

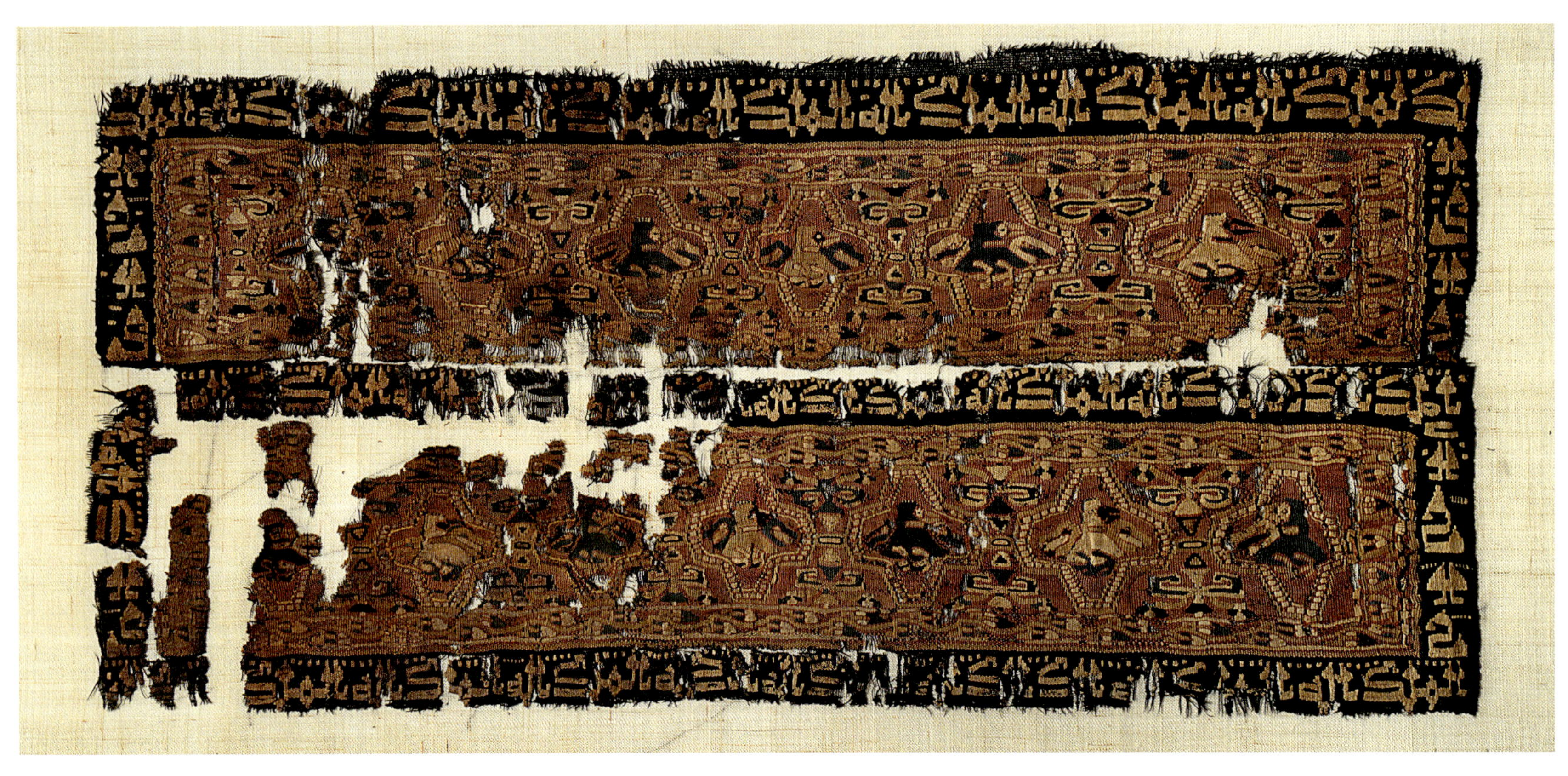

30

Decorative bands from a shawl

Egypt, probably Fayyum, 10th–early 11th century[1]

Dumbarton Oaks Research Library and Collection, Washington, D.C., BZ.1933.25

These two tapestry bands sewn together like a cuff band are actually the decorative ends of a shawl. A stretch of plain-woven fabric of blue-black wool would have separated the tapestry sections in accordance with the typical design of inscribed shawls produced in the Fayyum region (see the essays by Jochen Sokoly and Elizabeth Dospěl Williams in this volume). Bits of this plain weave survive around the edges of the tapestry; the openness of the weave and the silky texture of the finely spun wool hint at the diaphanous productions for which Fayyum workshops were renowned.[2]

Borders of tapestry-woven Arabic text once wrapped the four sides of each figural band, though the bottom edge of the upper band was lost in the creation of the modern pastiche. These inscriptions repeat the conventional phrase "dominion belongs to God" around all edges of the band. Text is treated here almost as a decorative frame for the more traditional pictorial subjects inside the design field. The Arabic words relay none of the factual information found in official tiraz inscriptions, such as a textile's place of manufacture or the names of rulers. Their role here is to replicate the fashionable appearance of tiraz and to act as additional adornment for the scenes of figural weaving.[3]

Schematic birds — very different in appearance from their Byzantine predecessors — fly with raised wings within repeating pearled, four-lobed shapes. These "medallions" are separated by reflected pairs of candelabra trees, a motif adopted into Byzantine and Islamic art from Sasanian textiles.[4] Although heavily influenced by eastern styles and imagery, this pattern of abstracted birds and foliate forms maintains the general sense of late antique Egyptian textile iconography, where vegetation, birds, and other animals stood as symbols of abundance and renewal. The primary pattern of birds is bound by interior borders of gold scrolling vines with teal and beige heart-shaped leaves, direct descendants of the vine rinceaux of earlier centuries.

— KMT

1   This textile can be dated to 901–1023 (most likely after 962) with 95.4 percent probability, according to accelerated mass spectrometry radiocarbon analysis carried out at the University of Georgia Center for Applied Isotope Studies (sample number 42810) in 2019.

2   For the admiration of Fayyum textiles, see Kühnel and Bellinger 1952, 84–85, 122.

3   Several other dark-blue fabrics with tapestry bands depicting animals surrounded on all sides by epigraphic borders survive, including Museum of Fine Arts, Boston, 38.40 and Metropolitan Museum of Art 31.19.16. For the role of text on Christian tiraz fabrics, see Van der Vliet 2006.

4   Thompson 1971, cat. 26.

5   So little of the ground weave is preserved that determining thread count is difficult. For results of dye analysis, see Table 2 on p. 58.

תְּהִלָּה יִתֵּן וְכֹל אוֹזֶכֹל הַשְׁמִיעַ לֹ֗ל מוֹשֵׁל בְּכֹל הַמְתִּיקוּ ק

כב ברקו הַלְלוּיָהּ הַלְלוּהוּ בְּקָדְשׁוֹ הַלְלוּהוּ בִּרְקִיעַ עֻזּוֹ
הַלְלוּהוּ בִגְבוּרֹתָיו הַלְלוּהוּ כְּרֹב גֻּדְלוֹ הַלְלוּהוּ בְּתֵקַע
שׁוֹפָר הַלְלוּהוּ בְּנֵבֶל וְכִנּוֹר הַלְלוּהוּ בְּתֹף וּמָחוֹל
הַלְלוּהוּ בְּמִנִּים וְעֻגָב הַלְלוּהוּ בְצִלְצְלֵי שָׁמַע הַלְלוּהוּ
בְצִלְצְלֵי תְרוּעָה כֹּל הַנְּשָׁמָה תְּהַלֵּל יָהּ הַלְלוּיָהּ

תַּחַת בְּנֵי יָנִין בְּנִיָּן שָׁחוּ. הֵבִי צְדָקָה חִיטָּה וַתְּהוּמֶס בק
תִּרְעַשׁ לְבוֹזוֹי תִּתְקַע בַּשׁוֹפָר בְּסַעֲרֹת תֵּרָנִימוּ אֲזֵילֵך ק
עַל יד נב וַיְיָ עֲלֵיהֶם יֵרָאֶה וְיָצָא כַבָּרָק חִצּוֹ
וַיְיָ אֱלֹהִים בַּשׁוֹפָר יִתְקָע וְהָלַךְ בְּסַעֲרוֹת תֵּימָן יְיָ
צְבָאוֹת יָגֵן עֲלֵיכֶם וְעָלֵיטוֹ וְעַל עַמּוֹ יִשְׂרָאֵל בְּרַחֲמִים
כֵּן תָּגֵן עֲלֵי עַמָּךְ בִּשְׁלוֹמָךְ

וְיִתְקַע   תְּקִיעָה   תְּרוּעָה   וּתְקִיעָה

וְנָעִיר לְרַאוּבַע אלמטו

וינבני אן נדכר לטבאעאת לרצ תגֹב פיה והמא זיארת עֹ
צנעה לטולטן וינצעה אלולב פאמא לטולטן פאנה ינב אן
נערח לטא עראשא פי מאורלנא תחת לסמא אמא עלי
מטח אופי סאחה לדאר ונצער חואבזא מן גנהאת חתי
לא יכון לה מרכל לא מן נהה ואחדה והדה לחואבז ינגה
אן תכון משרדהה בחבל חתי לא ימכן אן ישילהא אנכאן
פידכל מתהא פאן בקי מן אסאפל וסכתוד ובין לארץ אכל
מן תלאת קבצאת פאיו ואמא אכתר פלא ויכון נפס
לטולטו

31

Folio from a prayer book manuscript by Saʿadiah Gaon

Egypt, probably Cairo, 11th century

Ink on paper

25.4 × 18.5 cm

University of Pennsylvania, Library of the Herbert D. Katz Center for Advanced Judaic Studies, Cairo Genizah Collection, Halper 171

The leaf shown here is the lone survivor of an early copy of the first Jewish prayer book. The prayer book was compiled by Saʿadiah ben Joseph (882–942), usually known by his title Saʿadiah Gaon, the leading intellectual figure of late rabbinic Jewish culture in Babylonia. Although earlier sages had written legal treatises on the liturgy, Saʿadiah was the first to compose an actual prayer book or siddur (literally, ordering) intended for a wide audience that included prayers both for daily use and for the Sabbath, holidays, and fast days. Enormously popular, Saʿadiah's siddur circulated widely in the Arabic-speaking Jewish world until it was eclipsed by other prayer books in the twelfth century.

The codex from which this particular folio came was produced in the Near East sometime in the eleventh century, less than a hundred years after Saʿadiah's death. It was almost certainly a deluxe book. Written in black ink on paper, the layout of the page and its scribal flourishes, like the elegantly elongated necks of the lameds (the Hebrew equivalent of the English letter "l") in the top line and the centered title above the block at bottom, indicate the sophistication of scribal artistry in the period.

Perhaps the most striking feature of the page is its bilingualism. The top half of the page contains the conclusion of a *teki'ata*, a Hebrew liturgical poem intended to accompany the blowing of the ram's horn on Rosh Hashanah, the Jewish New Year; the lines of the poem itself are written in a large Oriental script, while the smaller condensed and indented blocks of text between the poem's stanzas are biblical verses to be recited as refrains. The text at the bottom of the page, also in the larger square Oriental script, relates laws about building a sukkah, the thatched hut traditionally built on the holiday of Sukkoth to commemorate the Israelites' wanderings in the desert. These laws are written in Judeo-Arabic — an Arabic dialect written in Hebrew letters — which was the common language of Jews living in the Arabic-speaking world in the period. Whether or not his readers knew enough Hebrew to understand the prayers, Saʿadiah clearly wanted them to understand how to build a sukkah. In bearing both languages on the same page, the leaf literally inscribes the hybrid culture in which the book was produced and used.

This fragment derives from the famed Cairo Genizah — a dedicated storage space for worn-out and no-longer-usable written texts in Hebrew — located in the Ben-Ezra Synagogue in al-Fustat (Old Cairo). It was bought in the early twentieth century by David Werner Amram, a professor of law at the University of Pennsylvania, from a book dealer in Jerusalem and was later acquired by Dropsie College in Philadelphia, America's first degree-granting institution for Jewish doctoral and post-doctoral studies. The Dropsie College Library is now part of the Library of the Herbert D. Katz Center for Advanced Judaic Studies at the University of Pennsylvania.

—DS

SELECTED REFERENCES

Stern 2007, 15, cat. 7

ⲟⲩⲟϩ ⲁϥϯⲉⲣϣⲓϣⲓ ⲛⲁϥ ⲉ
ⲣⲉϥⲓⲣⲓ ⲛⲟⲩϩⲁⲡ ϫⲉ ⲟⲩ
ⲡϣⲏⲣⲓ ⲙⲫⲣⲱⲙⲓ ⲡⲉ
ⲙⲡⲉⲣⲉⲣϣⲫⲏⲣⲓ ϧⲉⲛ ⲫⲁⲓ
ϫⲉ ⲥⲛⲏⲟⲩ ⲛϫⲉ ⲟⲩⲟⲩⲛⲟⲩ
ϩⲟⲧⲉ ⲟⲩⲟⲛ ⲛⲓⲃⲉⲛ ⲉⲧⲭⲏ
ϧⲉⲛ ⲛⲓⲙϩⲁⲩ ⲉⲩⲉⲥⲱⲧⲉⲙ
ⲉⲧⲉϥⲥⲙⲏ ⲟⲩⲟϩ ⲉⲩⲉⲓ ⲉⲃⲟⲗ
ⲛϫⲉ ⲛⲏ ⲉⲧⲓⲣⲓ ⲛⲛⲓⲡⲉⲑⲛⲁ
ⲛⲉⲩ ⲉⲩⲁⲛⲁⲥⲧⲁⲥⲓⲥ ⲛⲱⲛϧ
ⲟⲩⲟϩ ⲛⲏ ⲉⲧⲁⲩⲓⲣⲓ ⲛⲛⲓⲡⲉⲧ
ϩⲱⲟⲩ ⲉⲩⲁⲛⲁⲥⲧⲁⲥⲓⲥ ⲛⲧⲉ ⲭⲣⲓⲥⲓⲥ ⲙⲙⲟⲛ ϣϫⲟⲙ ⲙⲙⲟⲓ ⲁⲛⲟⲕ
ⲛⲟⲥ ⲉⲃⲟⲗ ϩⲓⲧⲟⲧ ⲙⲫⲣⲏϯ
ⲉϯⲥⲱⲧⲉⲙ ϯϯϩⲁⲡ ⲟⲩⲟϩ
ⲡⲁϩⲁⲡ ⲁⲛⲟⲕ ⲟⲩⲙⲏⲓ ⲡⲉ
ϫⲉ ⲛϯⲕⲱϯ ⲁⲛ ⲛⲥⲁ ⲡⲁⲟⲩⲱϣ

ⲁⲗⲗⲁ ⲫⲟⲩⲱϣ ⲙⲫⲏⲉⲧ
ⲧⲁⲩⲟⲓ
ⲉϣⲱⲡ ⲁⲛⲟⲕ ⲁⲓϣⲁⲛⲉⲣⲙⲉⲑⲣⲉⲛ
ϧⲁⲣⲟⲓ ⲧⲁⲙⲉⲧⲙⲉⲑⲣⲉⲟ
ⲛⲟⲩⲙⲏⲓ ⲁⲛ ⲧⲉ ⲕⲉⲟⲩⲁ ⲡⲉⲧⲉⲣ
ⲙⲉⲑⲣⲉ ϧⲁⲣⲟⲓ ⲟⲩⲟϩ ϯ
ⲉⲙⲓ ϫⲉ ⲧⲉϥⲙⲉⲧⲙⲉⲑⲣⲉⲟⲩ
ⲙⲏⲓ ⲧⲉ ⲑⲙⲉⲑⲣⲉ ⲉⲧⲉϥⲉⲣⲙⲉⲑⲣⲉ
ⲛⲑⲱⲧⲉⲛ ⲁⲣⲉⲧⲉⲛⲟⲩⲱⲣⲡ ϩⲁ ⲓⲱⲁⲛ
ⲛⲏⲥ ⲁϥⲉⲣⲙⲉⲑⲣⲉ ⲛⲧⲉ ⲧⲙⲏⲓ
ⲁⲙⲟⲓ ⲇⲉ ⲛⲁⲓϭⲓ ⲙⲉⲧⲙⲉⲑⲣⲉ ⲁⲛ
ⲛⲧⲉⲛ ⲣⲱⲙⲓ ⲁⲛ ⲁⲗⲗⲁ ⲛⲁⲓ
ϯϫⲱ ⲙⲙⲱⲟⲩ ϩⲓⲛⲁ ⲛⲑⲱ
ⲧⲉⲛ ⲛⲧⲉⲧⲉⲛⲛⲟϩⲉⲙ
ⲫⲏⲉⲧⲉⲙⲙⲁⲩ ⲛⲉ ⲛⲟⲩ
ⲡⲉⲛⲓ ϧⲏⲃⲥ ⲉⲑⲙⲟϩ ⲟⲩⲟϩ
ⲉⲧⲉⲣⲟⲩⲱⲓⲛⲓ

32

Twenty folios from a Coptic manuscript of the Gospel of John with glosses and translation in Arabic

Probably Egypt, 13th–14th century

Ink on paper

17.2 × 12.5 cm

Harvard Art Museums/Arthur M. Sackler Museum, Gift of Mr. and Mrs. Thorvald Ross, 1939.187

1   For an assessment of the paper, we are grateful to Penley Knipe, the Philip and Lynn Straus Senior Conservator of Works on Paper and Head of the Paper Lab in the Straus Center for Conservation and Technical Studies at the Harvard Art Museums.

This quire from a bilingual text of the Gospel of John preserves a portion of the Christian scripture in both Coptic and Arabic. The first folio of those extant begins in the middle of John 4:35, and the final folio ends with 7:5. The text on the spread illustrated here (folios 7v and 8r, 5:27–35) concerns the Day of Judgment, "when all who are in the sepulchres shall hear His voice, and shall come forth."

Since the folios read from left cover to right, it is clear that the Coptic text was the primary language and that the accompanying Arabic served as a translation. The Arabic phrasing is awkward in places, suggesting a utilitarian rather than an intellectual motivation for the bilingual text, and this is further borne out by the relatively modest materials and script.

The absence of illumination could also suggest that such codices were used more widely among worshippers, as opposed to serving a ritual purpose. The fragmentary manuscript thus reflects the transitional status of language usage within the Coptic Christian community. Throughout the medieval period, the Copts of Egypt were exposed to the Arabic used by the Islamic rulers and Muslim population; many adopted the Arabic language outright. Increasingly, then, worshippers would have struggled to understand the Coptic language used in the Christian rites and scriptures and would have needed bilingual texts such as this. On the basis of the paper and script, the work is estimated to date to the thirteenth or fourteenth century.[1] Although final dates vary for estimating when Arabic became the primary language of daily life and worship, the manuscript shows that Arabic-language bibles were already in use among Coptic Christians and may suggest the process of "Arabicization" was close to complete by this date. Furthermore, the gospel fragment underlines the complex of factors upon which identities were built in medieval Egypt. Language and religion were two such elements, but as the manuscript shows, they were neither dependent on each other nor unchanging. These bilingual folios, like the earlier bilingual textiles in the exhibition, reveal a longstanding, diverse community in which cultures influenced and adapted to one another.

— MLW

SELECTED REFERENCES

Unpublished

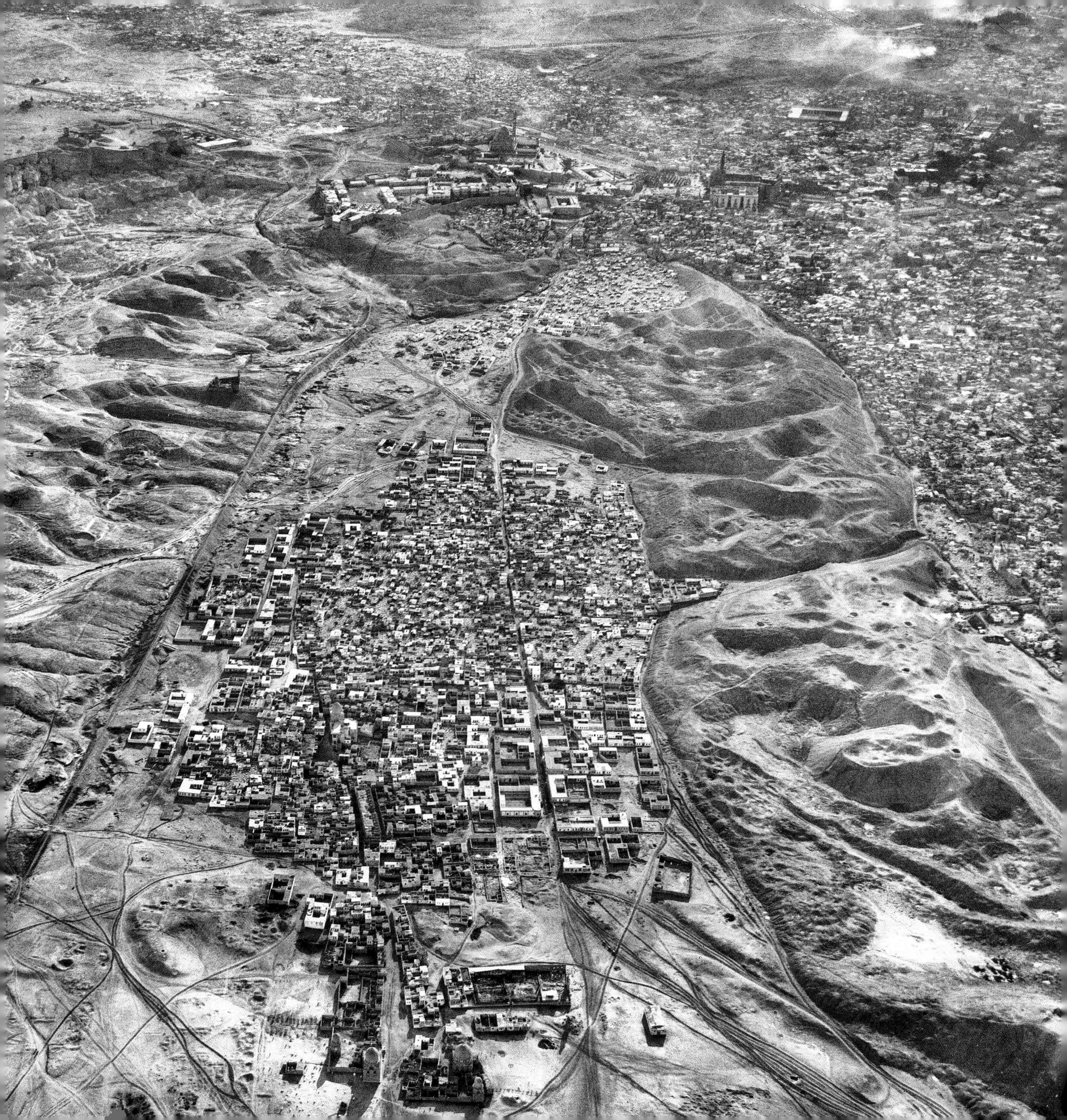

3 Blessings for the Afterlife: The Burial Context

Most surviving tiraz textiles were recovered from Cairo's vast urban cemeteries, known collectively as the Qarafa, where they were preserved by the region's dry climate. Although almost all lack reliable archaeological data, the patterns of stain and deterioration of these fragments reveal long centuries of close contact with the human body. This section considers the presence of inscribed textiles in a burial context, acting as a coda to the preceding discussions of the use and making of tiraz by the living.

Egyptian burial practices for both Muslim and Christian communities involved enfolding the deceased in multiple layers of fabric. Dressed in a tunic or robe, with head or feet sometimes resting on a cushion, the body was swathed in one or more shrouds, and the ensemble completed with an outer wrapping consisting of a reed mat. For Muslim burials, it seems, tiraz textiles served a purpose beyond the practical and material. The inscriptions, particularly those naming the caliph, the Prophet Muhammad, or the Imam ʿAli, were likely intended to bestow blessings on the deceased and to ease the transition into the afterlife.

Central to Islamic eschatology is the belief in a day of reckoning. As frequently expressed by Qurʾanic excerpts on tombstones, all souls shall be brought before God for judgment, and eternal justice meted out accordingly. The Prophet might intercede on behalf of those whose lives have been less than perfect. In a similar though less potent manner, the caliph, as leader of the Muslim community, was considered a source of blessing, and the mere presence of his name on one's burial fabrics might transmit religious favor. The exalted status of Fatimid caliphs, revered by Ismaʿili Muslims as imams and believed to have intercessory influence, surely intensified the amuletic value of their names. A mark of prestige during life, tiraz textiles carried the cherished power of caliphal associations to the grave—and perhaps beyond.

Aerial view of the Qarafa, taken in 1904 by Swiss balloonist and photographer Eduard Spelterini (1852–1931). In this south-facing view, the Northern Cemetery occupies the foreground, and the ʿAin al-Sira, from which many early Islamic tiraz and tombstones were excavated, lies in the far distance, beginning at upper right.

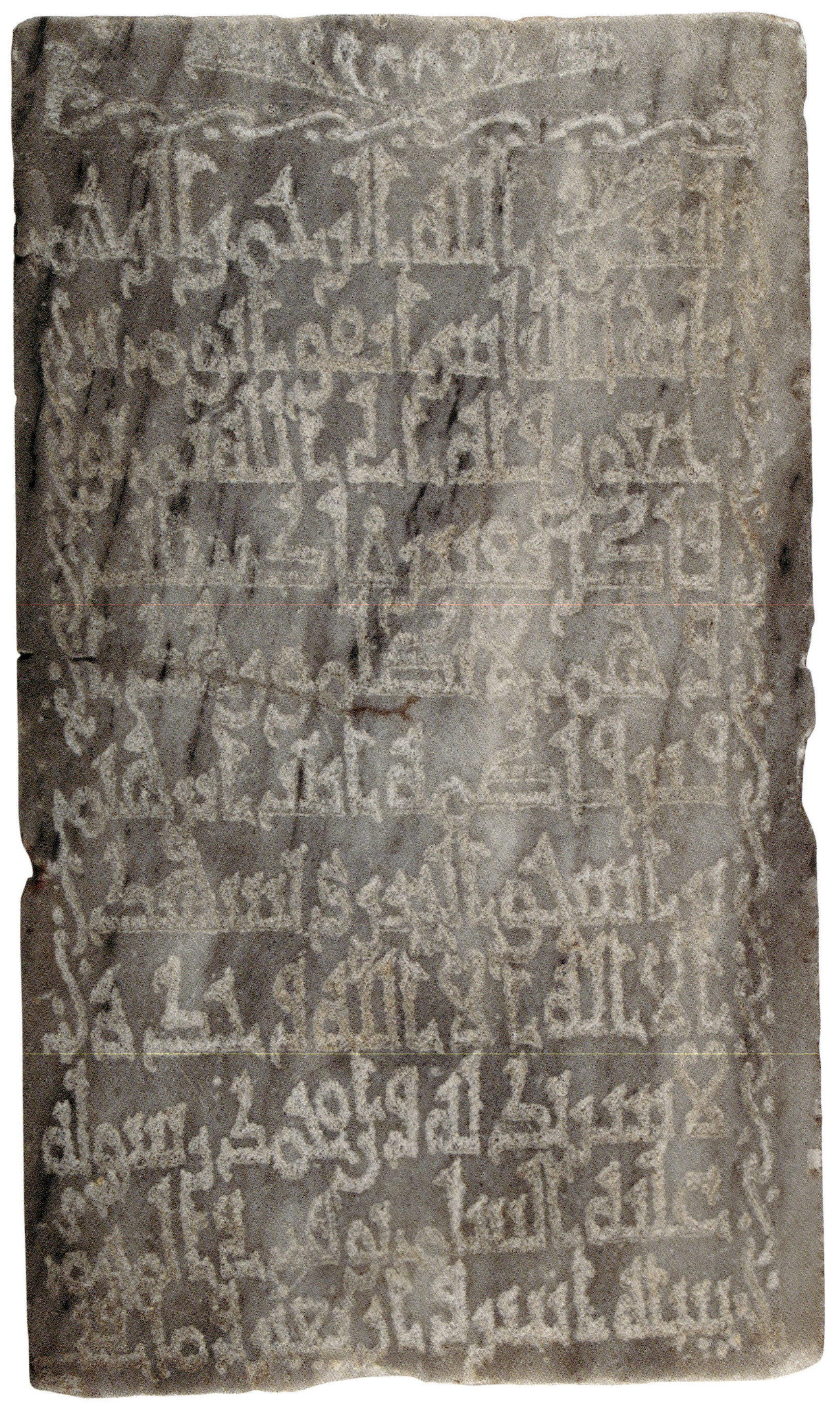

33

Tombstone of Fatima ibnat Ibrahim ibn Ishaq al-Hajjari

Egypt, dated Muharram 242/May–June 856

Incised marble

42.3 × 25.5 × 3.8 cm

Harvard Museum of the Ancient Near East, 1890.6.13

1   For discussion and an extensive bibliography, see Ragib 2001.

2   The phrase commonly referred to as *basmala* ("In the name of God, the Merciful, the Compassionate") opens all but one chapter of the Qur'an.

3   For the location of the ʿAin al-Sira, see Massignon 1958, pl. 1.

4   Marzouk 1959, 283n3. I am grateful to Jochen Sokoly for this reference.

With certain parallels to tiraz textiles, early Islamic tombstones from Egypt constitute a critical resource for studying Arabic calligraphy, decorative programs, social connections, and evolving demographics and religious values.[1] On this small tombstone, eleven lines of text are incised in simple Kufic script. Only one letter is ornamented: in the first line, the final *mim* on *bism* (in the name of) tips backward into a half-palmette. Three sides of the text block are framed by a chain of S-curves punctuated by dots. The top border terminates in split leaves and is crowned at the midpoint by two half-palmettes intersecting at a diagonal, a foliated echo of the classical *tabula ansata*. The frequent use of decorative borders on grave steles contrasts with the austerity of Abbasid and early Fatimid tiraz, where script stands alone.

Beginning with the obligatory *basmala*,[2] the texts used for both art forms are generally formulaic and repetitive. However, while the state-controlled inscriptions of tiraz textiles served a political elite, epitaphs reflected the preferences and personal circumstances of a wider socioeconomic base. Nearly half of the individuals named on Egyptian gravestones are female — a radical departure from tiraz and a notable anomaly within the broader medieval world. Here, a woman with the given name Fatima is identified by two generations of patrilineal genealogy, plus a family name — al-Hajjari — that links her to the Qahtan, an ancient Arab tribe. Fatima's Arab pedigree undoubtedly conferred prestige during life, and a Qahtan affiliation might have been considered an advantage on the Day of Judgment, for the tribe traced its ancestry to Hud, a pre-Islamic Arabian prophet for whom a chapter of the Qur'an is named. Belief in the Day of Judgment, an essential tenet of Islam, is usually expressed on these gravestones with conventional phraseology asserting the truth of death, paradise, hell, and resurrection. Fatima's epitaph offers an uncommon choice: a stern Qur'anic verse (2:281) that underlines the anxiety this event inspired.

For most of the nearly five thousand Egyptian tombstones from the early Islamic era that are preserved in Cairo's Museum of Islamic Art, the circumstances of recovery were only generally recorded. The provenance for many of those early steles, as well as Fatima's epitaph, is listed simply as ʿAin al-Sira, a cemetery in the southwestern part of Cairo's vast burial grounds collectively known as the Qarafa, or City of the Dead.[3] The ʿAin al-Sira also yielded many of the tiraz in the Museum of Islamic Art.[4]

— MMcW

INSCRIPTION (ARABIC)

بسم الله الرحمن الرحيم يا يها الناس اتقوا يوم تجعون فيه الى الله ثم توفى كل

نفس ما كسبت وهم لا يظلمون هذا قبرفاطمة ابنت اله الا الله وحده لا شرك

له وان محمد رسوله عليه السلم توفيت في المحرم سنة [*sic*] ابر هيم بن

اسحق الحجرى تشهد الا اثنين و اربعين و مائتان

In the name of God, the Merciful, the Compassionate. O, Ye people! Fear the day when ye shall be brought to Allah. Then shall every soul be paid what it earned and none shall be dealt with unjustly. This is the grave of Fatima ibnat Ibrahim ibn Ishaq al-Hajjari. She testifies that there is no god but God, the One, there is no partner with Him and that Muhammad is His messenger, upon him be peace. She died in the month of al-Muharram in the year two and forty and two hundred.

PROVENANCE

Purchased 1890 in Cairo by archaeologist Farley B. Goddard as an agent for the Harvard Semitic Museum (now the Harvard Museum of the Ancient Near East); reportedly from the ʿAin al-Sira cemetery of al-Fustat.

SELECTED REFERENCES

Unpublished

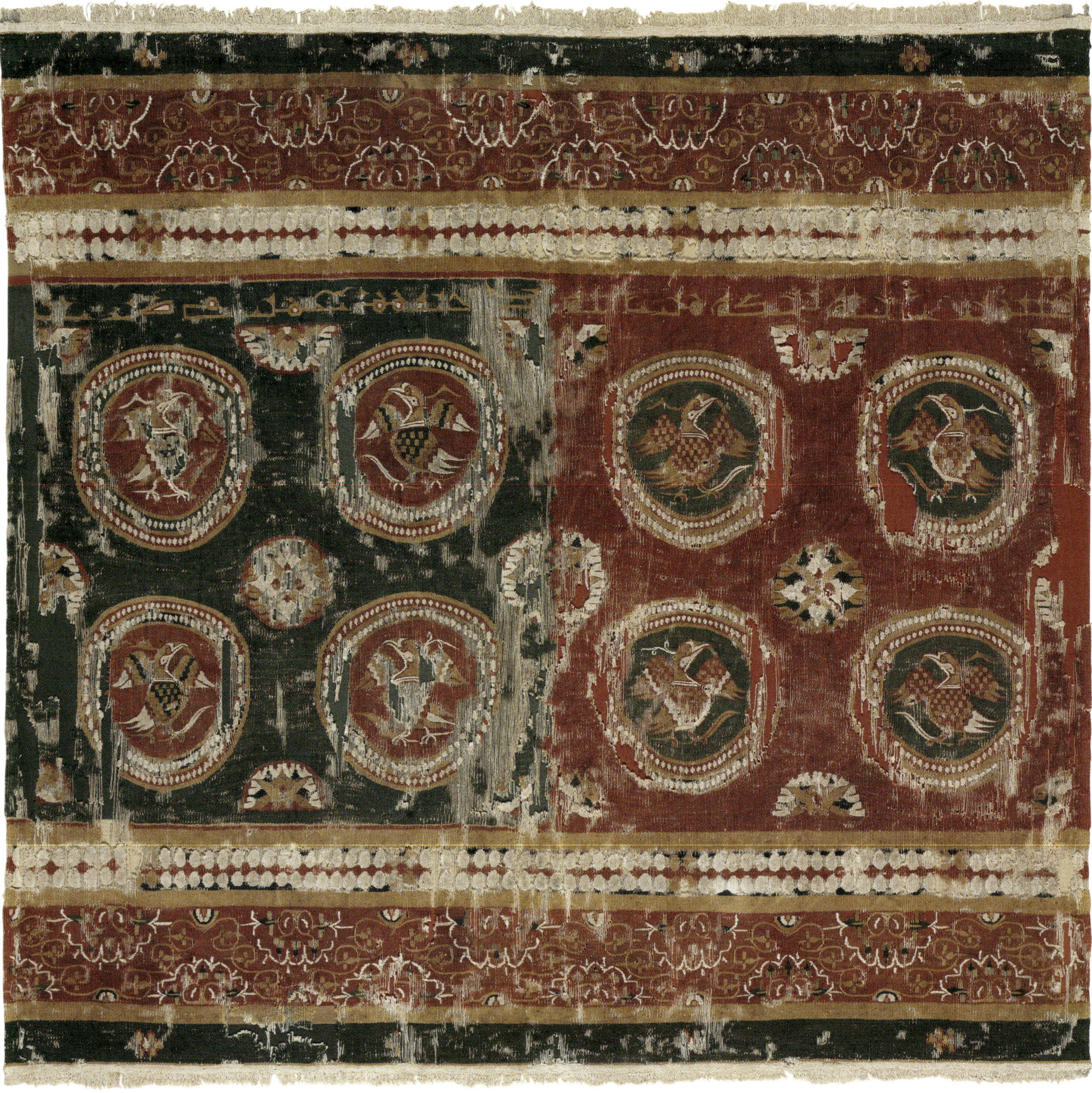

34

Cushion cover with tiraz inscription

Egypt, early 9th century
Cleveland Museum of Art, J. H. Wade Fund, 1959.48

1 Paetz gen. Schieck 2009,
esp. 122–31.
2 For comparison to the Marwan
group, including the well-
known "Marwan silk," see
Mackie 2015, 52–57.
3 Ibid., 57.
4 Thread count by Dorothy
G. Shepherd, unpublished
manuscript, cat. 88. For results
of dye analysis, see Table 2 on
p. 58.

The areas of red and teal that mirror each other in the design fields of
this spectacular tapestry would not have been visible simultaneously
during use: the textile originally served as the cover for a square
cushion, meaning the striking inversion could be observed only by
turning over the pillow. A vertical line of losses shows that the tapestry once folded in half over a soft filling.

Discovered in a tomb, the object illustrates that the late Roman
burial practice of supporting the head and feet of the deceased
with cushions continued into the early Islamic era.[1] Its square shape
embellished with four equally spaced design elements also preserves
the general appearance of pre-Islamic pillows, albeit translated
from primarily monochromatic designs of purple wool and undyed
linen into a new color palette. This cushion's interment enabled it to
remain remarkably intact, with all four original edges surviving.

Referring to an unnamed patron, the epigraphic style of the
Kufic inscription seen here, with its prominent hook-like letter
terminals, suggests a date in the early Abbasid period. The cushion's
decoration shares stylistic characteristics — red grounds, vine-scroll
borders, and roundels containing animals with checkered bodies —
with the so-called Marwan group of textiles associated with the last
Umayyad caliph, Marwan II (r. 744–750).[2] This group represents
some of the earliest extant tiraz textiles (see the essay by Jochen
Sokoly in this volume). Their fabrics exhibit technical features typical
of products made outside of Egypt and were possibly woven in Iran
or Iraq. The cushion cover, on the other hand, shows great continuity with the Byzantine weaving tradition and likely represents an
Egyptian reaction to the tiraz associated with Marwan II and other
elites. Its pearled roundels and geometric rosettes recall the patterns
of fine Sasanian-influenced drawloom-woven silks. These elements
are translated here into techniques and materials reflective of Egypt's
Mediterranean heritage: tapestry weave, S-spun linen, and a soft variety of wool (see the detail on p. 146). An origin in al-Bahnasa (ancient
Oxyrhynchus) has been suggested.[3]

— KMT

INSCRIPTION (ARABIC)

بسم الله بركة من الله لصاحبه مما عمل في طراز[. . .]

In the name of God. Blessing from God to its owner. What has been
made in the tiraz [. . .]

TECHNICAL DESCRIPTION[4]

80 (warp) × 83.2 (weft) cm
Wool and linen: tapestry weave
Tapestry: allover 1 tapestry, slit and dovetail, with non-horizontal
weft in all colors, and weft wrapping (warp: off-white linen, composite [S, plied Z], 10/cm; weft: polychrome wool, S, 50/cm; and ecru
linen, S, single)
Fragmentary selvedges on right and left. Warp fringe at top and bottom. Reverse inaccessible.

PROVENANCE

Purchased 1958 from Mrs. Paul Mallon, New York and Paris.

SELECTED REFERENCES

Shepherd 1960
Sourdel-Thomine and Spuler 1973, 241, Fig. 156
Cleveland 1978, 269
Paetz gen. Schieck 2009, 122–31
Mackie 2015, 57–59, Fig. 2.20
Williams 2019, Fig. 14

35

Burial shroud with tiraz inscription

Egypt, Misr, c. 800

The Textile Museum, Washington, D.C., Acquired by George Hewitt Myers in 1936, 73.447

1   An identical inscription can be found on a similar textile in the Museum of Islamic Art, Cairo (12769).

The simple Arabic inscription placed only at one end of this linen shroud — the earliest tiraz in the exhibition — names a private factory (*tiraz al-khassa*) at Misr (likely indicating Old Cairo, or Misr al-Fustat) as its place of production.[1] This city, which had served as the newly founded capital of Islamic rule in Egypt under the Umayyads, remained an important site of textile manufacture during Abbasid rule and into the Fatimid era. The style of the inscription (Fig. 1) is related to one of the earliest dated textiles from Egypt, the so-called turban of Samu'il ibn Murqus (see p. 22). The word "private" in the inscription signals that this textile was woven at a workshop that may have been controlled by the provincial admin-istration. Dark markings across the length of the unadorned fabric stand as indices of its final purpose as a burial shroud.

Produced only a century and a half after the Arab conquest of Egypt, the textile illustrates the use of characteristically Byzantine weaving techniques in the new institution of court tiraz. Traditional elements include the adherence to tapestry weaving over embroidery and the incorporation of wool tapestry bands into a plain-woven, undyed linen ground. Like the majority of late antique textiles that feature in-woven tapestry bands, the transition from plain weave to tapestry is accomplished in this shroud through the pairing and crossing of the linen warps to accommodate the greater thickness of the wool wefts introduced into areas of tapestry (see the detail on p. 147).

The new tiraz format is also balanced by a preference for a traditional decorative vocabulary: the design of the two tapestry bands can be seen as a transformation of the running vine motif that dominated late antique weavings, now rendered in a distinctly contemporary color palette of gold, red, teal, dark blue, and white. The interstices above and below the undulating gold "vines" (created with strongly non-horizontal wefts that emphasize its scrolling energy) contain clusters of three white dots joined by lines of red,

resembling relics of the berries, flowers, and leaves that surrounded the vine scrolls of earlier periods. The ogival centers of the vine loops each contain five layers of color radiating out from a central point, transmuting the ancient vine into a jeweled necklace.

— KMT

INSCRIPTION (ARABIC)

بسم الله بركة من الله مما عمل في طراز الخاصة بمص[ـر]

In the name of God. Blessing from God. From what has been made in the private factory at Mis[r].

TECHNICAL DESCRIPTION

234 (warp) × 66.5 (weft) cm

Linen and wool: plain weave with in-woven tapestry weave

Plain weave: off-white linen, S, single, 16–17 warp × 13–14 weft/cm; tapestry: 2 tapestry, slit, with non-horizontal weft (warp: same as plain weave, but paired or tripled; weft: polychrome wool, S, single; and off-white linen, S, paired)

Transition to tapestry marked by self-bands (two or three yarns), warp crossing, and grouping of warp yarns. Warp fringe preserved at both ends. Selvedges on right and left.

PROVENANCE

Purchased July 1936 from L. J. Moutafoff, Paris. In February 1931, Moutafoff shipped to George Hewitt Myers a parcel of 75 "Arabian textiles" purchased from Mr. J. O. Mardik of Egypt and said to have been found in the "*nécropoles d'Égypte* 1930–31." Myers acquired the majority of the textiles over the next decade.

SELECTED REFERENCES

Kühnel and Bellinger 1952, 83–84, pl. 43

Shepherd 1960, 10–11

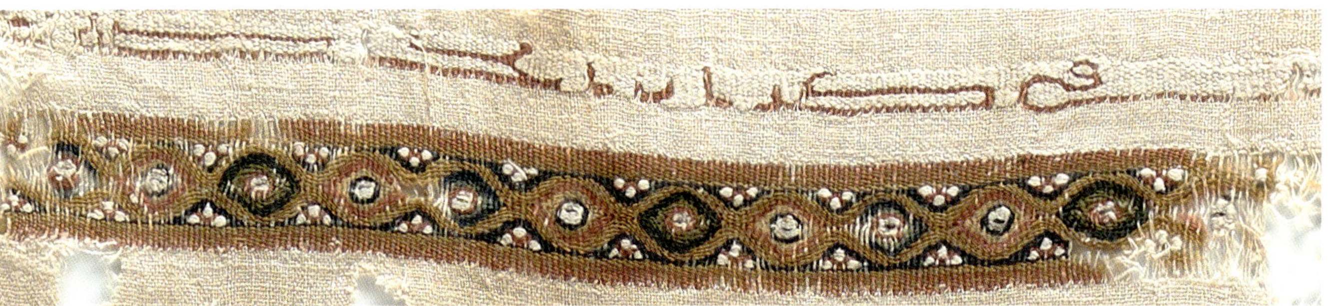

Fig. 1 Detail

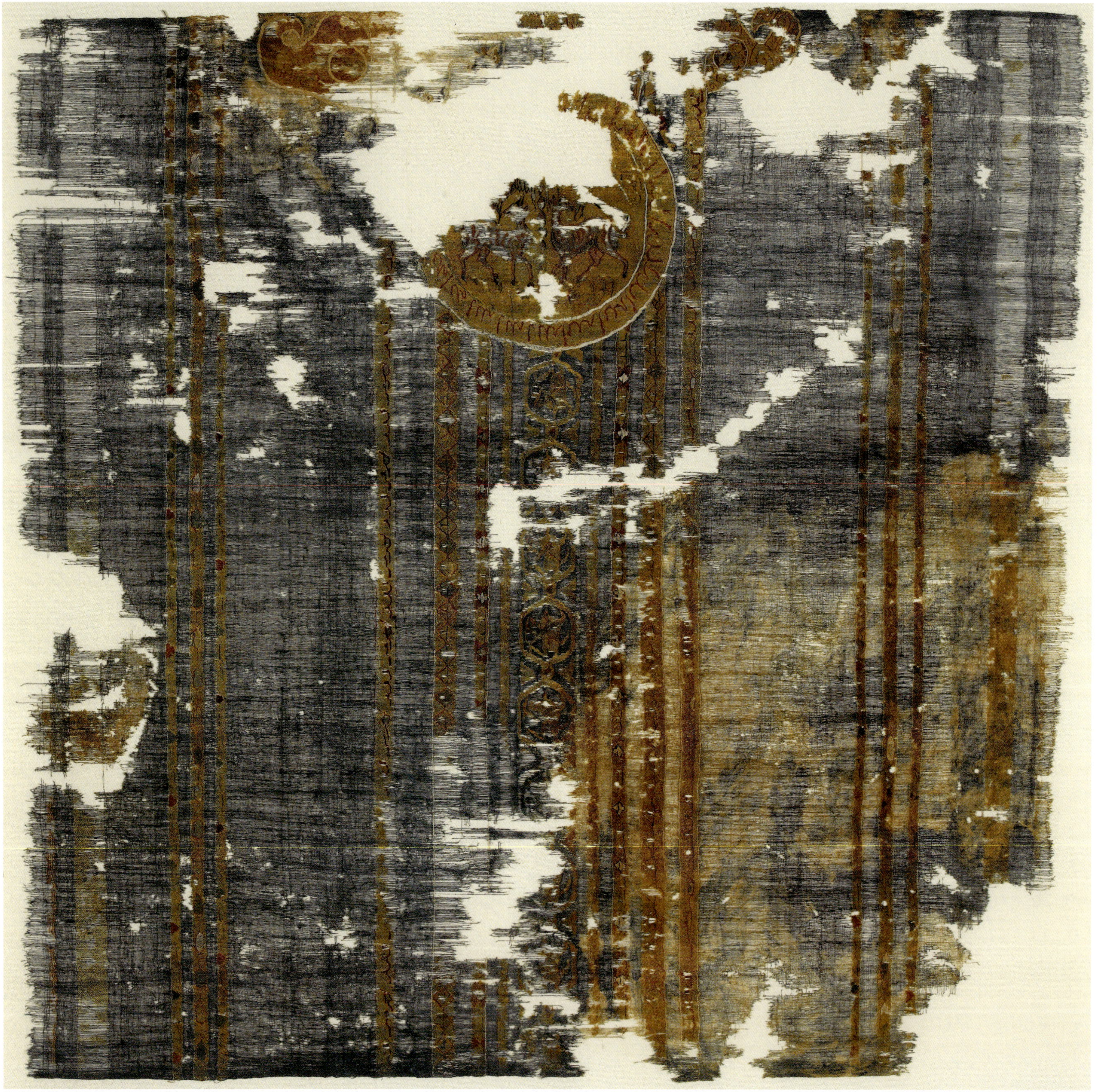

36

Fragment of a garment with pious inscriptions

Egypt, Damietta, c. 1094–1101

Metropolitan Museum of Art, New York, Rogers Fund, 32.96

This is a fragment of a once much larger — and surely spectacular — rectangular cloth. Comprised of a loosely woven linen ground fabric dyed in a dark shade of blue, it is decorated in silk tapestry with a sequence of bands that grow into a pair of curling wings on either side of the circular medallion above. The medallion encloses within it a pair of gazelles confronted against a leafy tree. The main band leading up to the medallion is formed by an interlocking column of hexagonal cartouches containing quadrupeds striding forward. Despite suffering a loss of silk threads in a number of places, the primarily golden-yellow color of the tapestry-woven decoration gives the impression of gold from a distance. The inscriptions and borders are accentuated in dark red. Textiles such as this were called *sharb*, referring to a sheer, lightweight linen cloth (see also cat. 16).

In terms of the arrangement of the decoration, this fragment is related to the famous Veil of Saint Anne, a Crusader reliquary that survives in a church in Apt, in southern France (see p. 26). The veil, too, features a large medallion bordered by a Kufic inscription and connected to a set of curled wings, albeit with a pair of addorsed sphinxes in place of gazelles.[1] The theme of paired sphinxes is carried on in two further medallions. The base fabric of the veil is also a sheer, loosely woven linen, albeit undyed. A full loom length and width survives. The main color of the decoration is yellow, with accents in red and blue. The veil is inscribed with the name of the Fatimid caliph al-Musta'li (r. 1094–1101) and mentions its order by his vizier, Abu al-Qasim Shahanshah bin Badr al-Jamali al-Malik al-Afdal, in the private tiraz at Damietta, an area of the Nile delta not far from the Mediterranean Sea, in the year 489/1096–97 or 490/1097–98. It has been suggested that a garment such as the Veil of Saint Anne, which shows no signs of stitching, was worn loosely over a long tunic or shirt, possibly with the central motif covering the back of the shoulder. Its ostentatiousness would have made it a perfect gift as a robe of honor to a chosen courtier of the caliphal household.

—JS

1 Cornu 1999a, 331–37.

INSCRIPTION (ARABIC)

The inscriptions are highly stylized. The letters in the medallion border may read الله (Allah); the text in the flanking bands can be read as نصر من الله (Victory from God).

TECHNICAL DESCRIPTION

72.9 (warp) × 72.4 (weft) cm

Linen and silk: plain weave with in-woven tapestry weave

Plain weave: variegated blue linen, S, single, 10–16 warp × 7–9 weft/cm; tapestry: 1, rarely 2 tapestry, slit, with non-horizontal weft (warp: same as plain weave; weft: polychrome silk, thrown, single, occasionally paired; and white linen, S, single and paired) Transition to tapestry sometimes marked by self-bands (two to three yarns) of white linen, S. Selvedges on right and left. Reverse inaccessible.

PROVENANCE

Purchased 1932 from E. A. Abemayor, Cairo.

SELECTED REFERENCES

Dimand 1933
Ettinghausen, Grabar, and Jenkins-Madina 2001, 209, Fig. 335
Carboni 2008, 5, Fig. 5

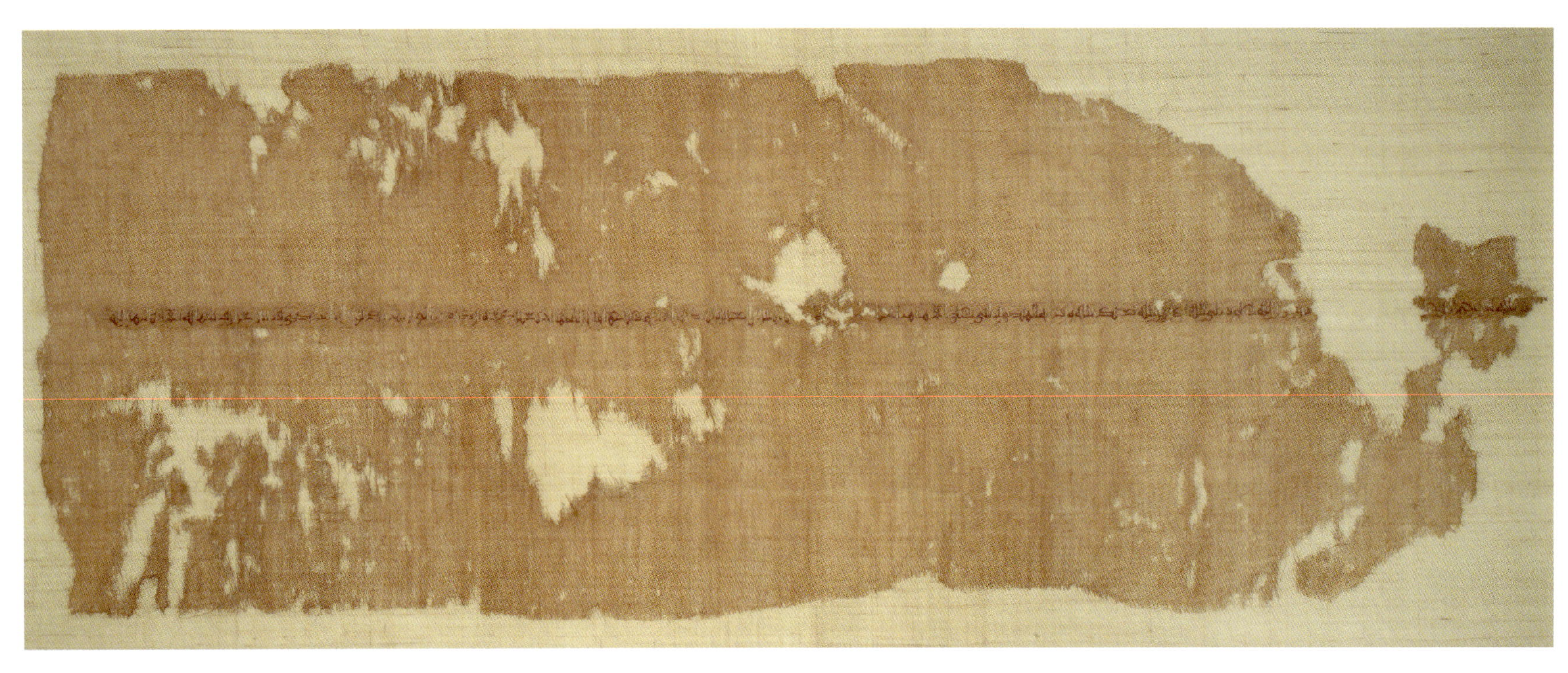

37

Tiraz textile naming the Fatimid caliph al-Hakim bi-Amr Allah

Egypt, 391/1000–1001

Dumbarton Oaks Research Library and Collection, Washington, D.C., BZ.1933.10

1   For a discussion of the date and the interchangeability of the spelling of numbers seven and nine in Arabic, see Glidden and Thompson 1988, 129n7.

This fragment is a very fine, loosely woven linen textile inscribed with a single line of dark-red silk tapestry-woven script containing invocations and blessings directed at the Fatimid caliph al-Hakim (r. 996–1021), his father al-ʿAziz (r. 975–996), and his ancestors. The inscription concludes with the year of manufacture, which reads 371/982 — more than a decade before al-Hakim's reign, and which therefore must surely have been intended as 391/1000–1001.[1] Given that the ground fabric is so sheer, almost translucent, the inscription was executed within a band of tightly packed linen weft threads in slit tapestry that keep the letters in place and also make the inscription stand out. The inscription must have been woven from right to left, as the red silk yarn carries over from one word to the next, forming horizontal bridges between the upper letter finials. It is possible that inscriptions such as this, with their carefully executed calligraphic style, were woven with the aid of cartoons designed by calligraphers. Cartoons were used by weavers in Egypt since antiquity, and it makes sense that weavers carrying out complicated inscriptions would have had such tools on hand.

The content of the inscription here clearly expresses Shiʿa religiosity, not only in alluding to the idea of the pure ancestry of the dynasty stemming from the Prophet's family, but also by invoking the eschatological dimension of Shiʿa belief whereby the imam can intercede on behalf of believers on the Day of Judgment. As a piece of clothing, this textile may once have been the end of a large shawl or turban cloth, given the fabric's light weight.

—JS

INSCRIPTION (ARABIC)

بسم الله الرحمن الرحيم [لا اله الّا الله محمـ]ـد رسول الله على ولى الله نصر من الله لعبد الله ووليه المنصور ابى على الامام الحاكم [بـ]ـامر [الله] امير المؤمنين بن العزيز بالله صلوت الله عليهما وعلى ابائهما اجمعين صلاة ترضيهم الى يوم الدين سنة احدى وسبعين (تسعين) وثلثمائة الاقبال من الله

In the Name of God, the Merciful, the Compassionate. [There is no god but God. Muhamma]d is the messenger of God. May help come from God to the servant of God and His close friend al-Mansur Abu ʿAli the imam al-Hakim [bi-] Amr [Allah], the Commander of the Faithful, son of al-ʿAziz bi-Allah. May the blessings of God be upon them both and upon all of their forefathers, a blessing that will satisfy them until the Day of Judgment. In the year one and seventy [for ninety] and three hundred. Prosperity comes from God.

TECHNICAL DESCRIPTION

28.7 (warp) × 79.6 (weft) cm
Linen and silk: plain weave with in-woven tapestry weave
Plain weave: ecru linen, S, single, 17–18 warp × 17–18 weft/cm; tapestry: 1 tapestry, slit, with non-horizontal weft (warp: same as plain weave; weft: ecru linen, S, paired, no ply; and red silk, thrown, single)
The linen and silk tapestry wefts occasionally float between color areas and across slits. Three weft yarns of red silk run width of tapestry band, calibrating the letter shafts. Transition to tapestry marked by a single weft yarn of red silk at top and bottom edge. Reverse inaccessible.

PROVENANCE

Reportedly found in Egypt. Acquired from Tano Collection, Cairo, via Frances Morris, 1932.

SELECTED REFERENCES

Combe, Sauvaget, and Wiet 1931–37, 4:40–41, no. 2084
Glidden and Thompson 1988, 128–29, Fig. 7

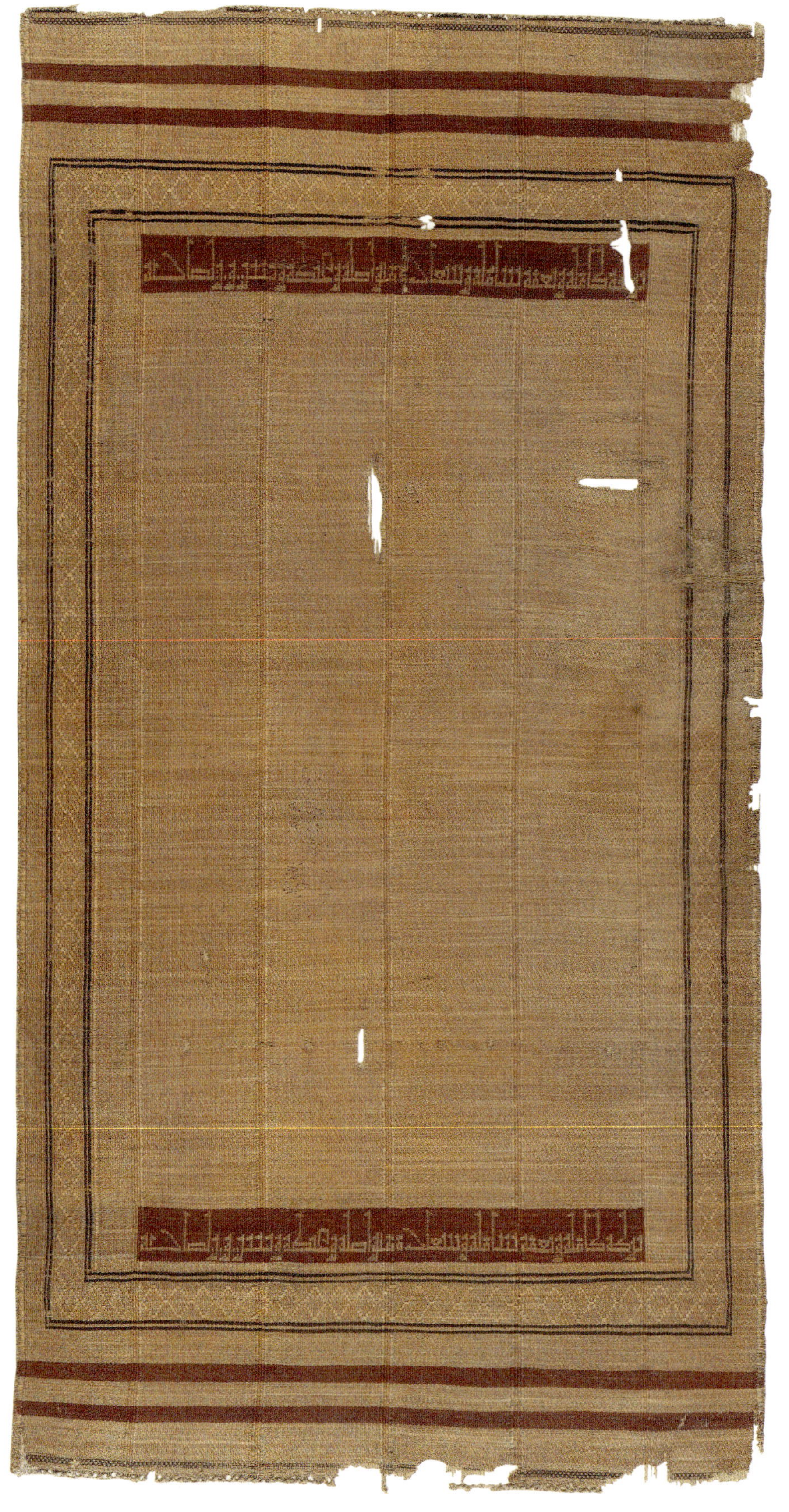

38

Reed mat with benedictory inscription

Probably present-day Israel, Tiberias, first half 10th century

Metropolitan Museum of Art, New York, Purchase, Joseph Pulitzer Bequest, 39.113

1   Evans and Ratliff 2012, 263–64, cat. 185.

2   Museum of Islamic Art, Berlin, I. 68/63.

3   Gildemeister 1885, 128.

4   This analysis appears in Ekhtiar et al. 2011, 50–51. The object is mounted and framed within a plexiglass shadow box. The reverse is inaccessible.

Mats such as this were once used in burials to envelop the deceased, as recent excavations in Cairo and the Fayyum have shown, where enshrouded bodies were laid onto one half of the mat and loosely covered with the other (see the images on pp. 28–29). During a person's lifetime, they may have served as prayer mats. Woven in straw or a type of dried grass on hemp warps, much like a textile, this mat follows an aesthetic established by tiraz in terms of the placement and style of the inscriptions. At either end, two lines of text in an elegant and refined monumental Kufic are contained in a red band. The texts confer blessings and good wishes for prosperity and happiness on the textile's owner. While several surviving fragments with similar inscriptions have been excavated in Egypt and dispersed across museum collections, this is one of two that have survived almost intact. The other is in the Benaki Museum in Athens.[1] Its inscription is similar to the one shown here in style and content, but it mentions its manufacture in a private workshop (*tiraz al-khassa*) in Tiberias. A mat fragment in the Museum of Islamic Art, Berlin, relates to the Benaki piece so closely in terms of construction and inscription — it, too, cites manufacture in a private workshop — that it may well have been produced in the same workshop in Tiberias.[2] A city founded by the Romans in the province of Palestine, Tiberias is mentioned by medieval Islamic geographer al-Idrisi as a location famed for the production of what he called *al-samaniyya* mats.[3]

— JS

INSCRIPTION (ARABIC)

بركة كاملة و نعمة شاملة و سعادة متواصلة و غبطة و سرور لصاحبه

Complete blessing and universal prosperity and continued happiness and joy to its owner

TECHNICAL DESCRIPTION[4]

161 (warp) × 86 (weft) cm

Hemp (warp) and straw (weft): weft-faced plain weave, brocaded

PROVENANCE

Purchased 1939 from Maurice Nahman, Cairo.

SELECTED REFERENCES

Ekhtiar et al. 2011, 50–51, cat. 28

Boehm and Holcomb 2016, 169, cat. 85, Fig. 85

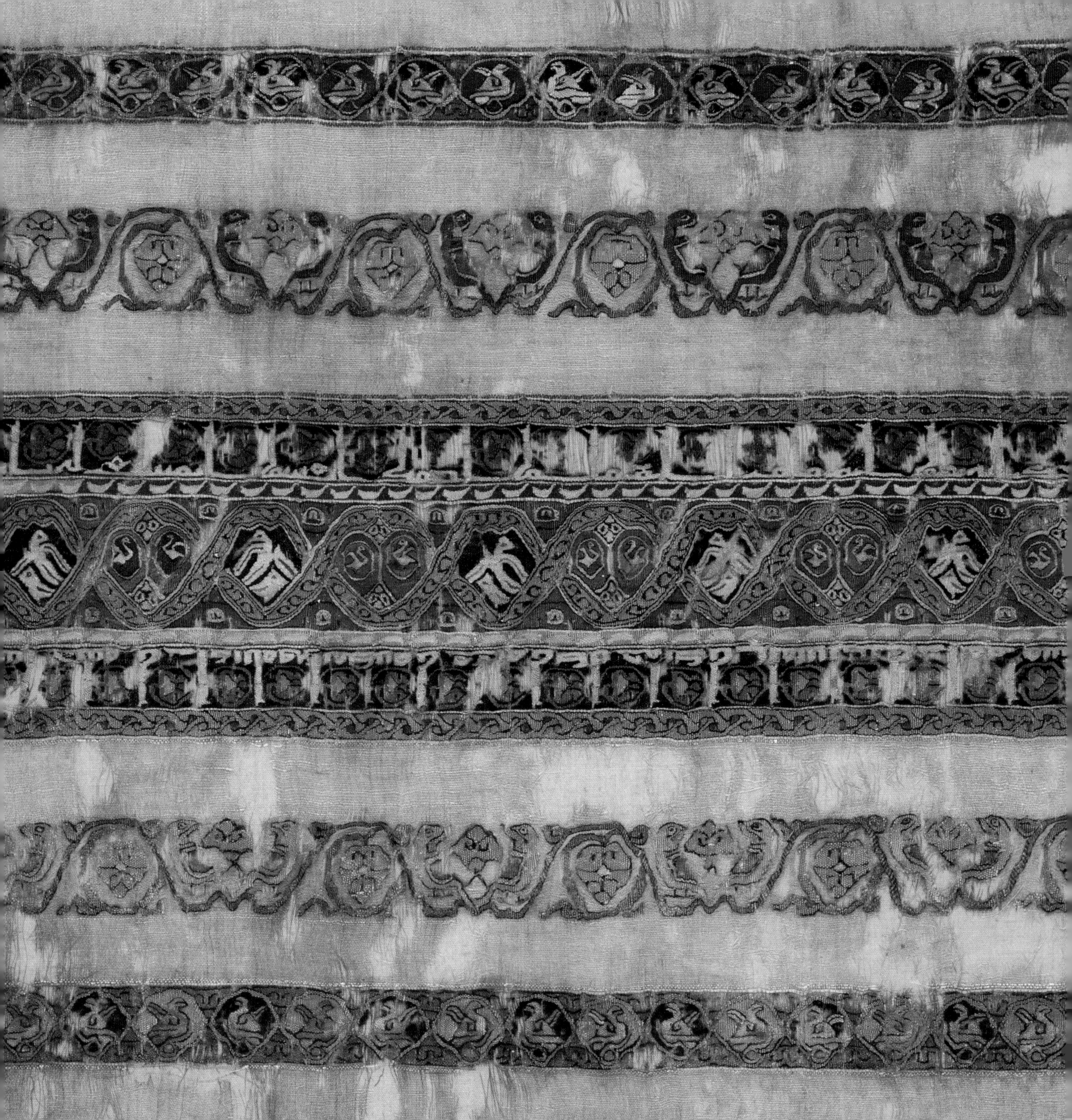

INSTITUTION	ACC. NO.	CAT. NO.	PAGE
Cleveland Museum of Art	1932.25	1	65
	1950.354	16	95
	1950.549	17	97
	1956.330	28	119
	1959.48	34	133
	1965.313	18	99
	1982.291	23	109
Dumbarton Oaks Research Library and Collection	BZ.1933.10	37	139
	BZ.1933.22	10	81
	BZ.1933.25	30	123
	BZ.1933.32	13	87
	BZ.1933.37	11	83
	BZ.1933.38	15	93
	BZ.1953.2.3	27	117
Harvard Art Museums	1924.124	22	107
	1939.187	32	127
	1951.31.4.2315	4	71
	1951.31.4.2316	5	71
	1960.193	8	77
	1975.41.28	24	111
	1975.41.53	20	103
	2002.50.84	7	75
	2004.204	21	105
Harvard Museum of the Ancient Near East	1890.6.13	33	131
Herbert D. Katz Center for Advanced Judaic Studies, University of Pennsylvania	Halper 171	31	125
Metropolitan Museum of Art	31.106.27	9	79
	32.96	36	137
	39.113	38	141
Museum of Fine Arts, Boston	11.1398	29	121
	23.177	25	113
	32.33	19	101
	34.115	12	85
	34.116	26	115
	34.118	14	89
The Textile Museum	73.17	2	67
	73.444	6	73
	73.447	35	135
	73.660	3	69

Detail of cat. 18.

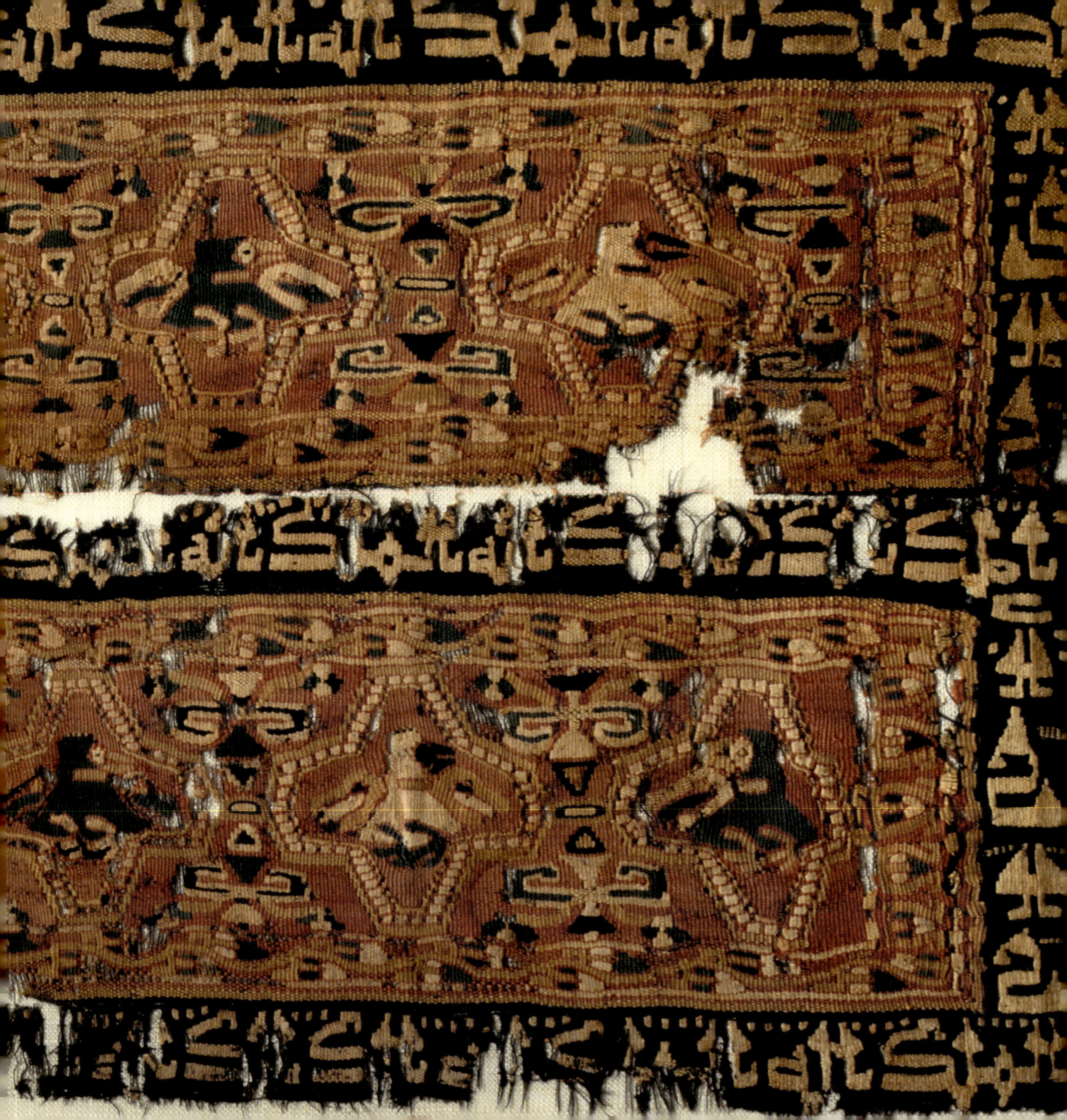

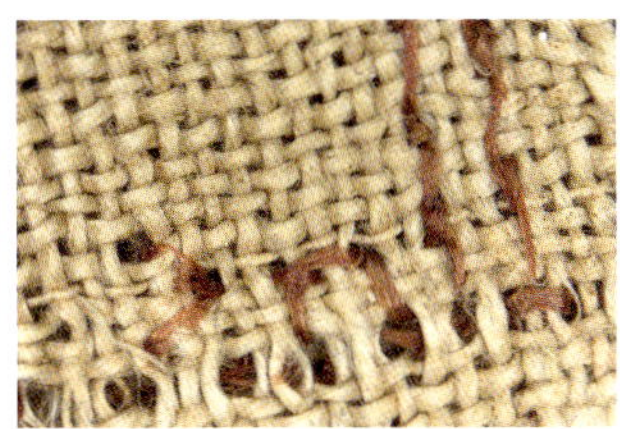

Fig. 1 Drawn weft (detail of cat. 6).

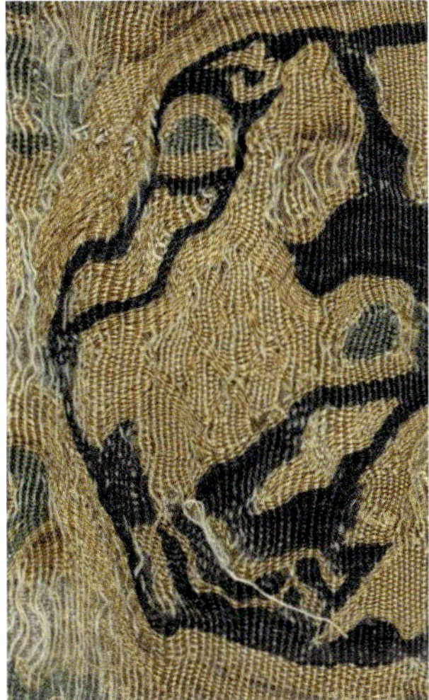

Fig. 2 Non-horizontal weft (detail of cat. 16).

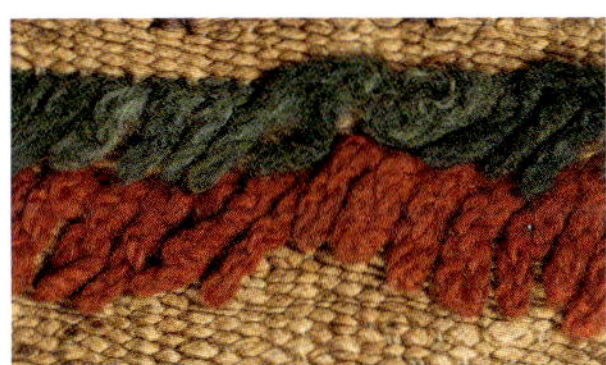

Fig. 3 Pile (detail of cat. 24).

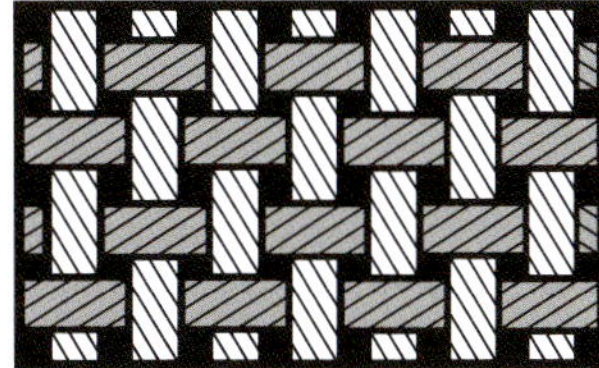

Fig. 4 Diagram of plain weave.

Opposite: Detail of cat. 30.

burnishing a post-weaving finishing technique that typically involves using a broad metal tool to flatten the fibers of the textile, creating a smooth, shining effect

cotton thread or yarn produced by processing the fiber of plants in the genus *Gossypium*

drawn weft a post-weaving technique that prepares a finished textile for embroidery; a single weft yarn is pulled from the textile, baring the warp yarns for one pick, to establish a straight line (Fig. 1)

embroidery a post-weaving technique used primarily to apply ornament to a finished textile with needle and thread

embroidery stitches

back
creates uniform lines with a minimum of punctures; accomplished by stitching half a step backward on the face, then a full step forward on the reverse

chain
a versatile stitch of interlocking loops able to create lines, curves, or filling; the needle exits and re-enters the same hole, creating a loop through which the needle passes upon exiting for the next stitch; used prevalently in Iranian/Iraqi embroidery

couching
a filling stitch in which a laid filament is secured by smaller stitches, allowing precious materials to be displayed without wastefully passing to the reverse; the laid filament, often metallic, is seen virtually uninterrupted

split
finished appearance similar to chain stitch, technique closer to backstitch; after making a simple running stitch, the needle loops slightly back on itself on the reverse to resurface between two filaments of the yarn, splitting the thread

stem
sometimes called "outline"; lines of variable width and shape are created by overlapping stitches in close proximity; the needle is inserted to the right and brought out to the left, slightly above and overlapping with the previous stitch

end an individual warp yarn; less commonly, an individual thread twisted with one or more threads to make a plied yarn

face the front side of a textile, or the side from which it is meant to be viewed

filament a long, fine, structurally continuous fiber

ikat a process wherein the warp, weft, or both are resist-dyed with predetermined patterns prior to weaving, or a fabric made with this technique (orig. Indonesia)

linen a thread or yarn produced by processing the fiber of the flax plant

loom a frame that holds the warp under tension to allow insertion of the weft; the primary equipment for weaving, looms vary in size and complexity

mulham in the medieval period, a half-silk fabric (the other half typically cotton); from the Arabic root *lhm*, "to join," which also gives us *lahmah*, "weft"

non-horizontal weft in tapestry, weft that does not stay within the "grid" of the weaving matrix, so that it bends to create contours or wedge-like inserts; also known as "eccentric weft" (Fig. 2)

pass the insertion of a weft yarn from selvedge to selvedge

pick the weft yarn (or yarns) used in a particular pass

pile supplementary yarns that extend out from a ground fabric (Fig. 3)

plain weave the simplest of fabric structures, wherein each weft yarn passes over then under exactly one warp end (Fig. 4)

ply to twist together two or more threads or ends to make a thicker yarn

resist-dyeing any of several techniques that block a fabric or yarn from receiving colors; e.g., tie-dyeing, wax resist

reverse the back of a textile, or the side not meant to be viewed

self-band two or more weft yarns carried in a single pass; in the textiles studied here, self-bands often appear to stabilize a plain weave before transition to tapestry

selvedge the finished sides of a textile, running in warp direction, created when the weft turns back around at the end of each pass

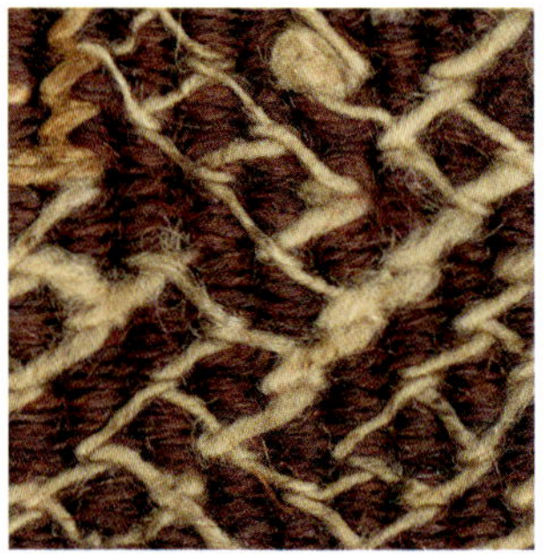

Fig. 5 Supplementary weft wrapping (detail of cat. 24).

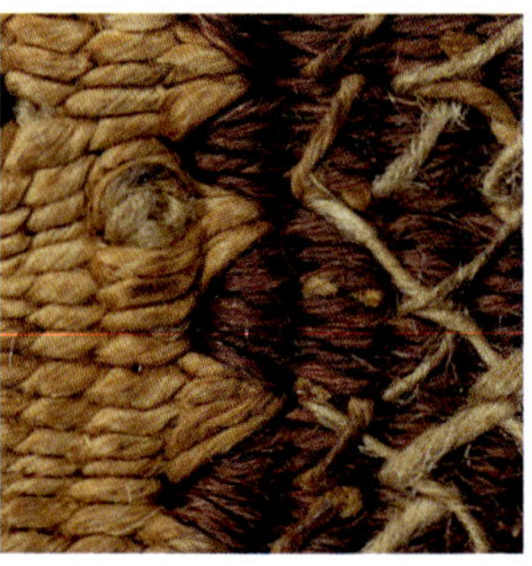

Fig. 6 Dovetail tapestry (detail of cat. 24).

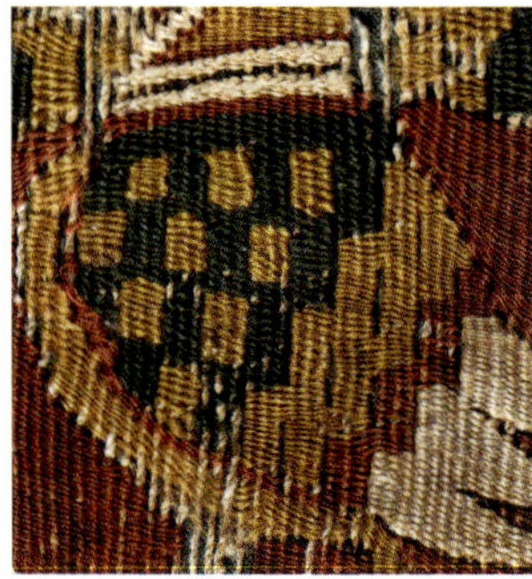

Fig. 7 Slit tapestry (detail of cat. 34).

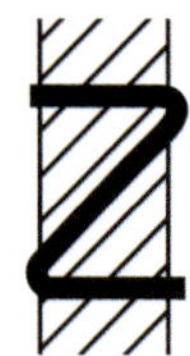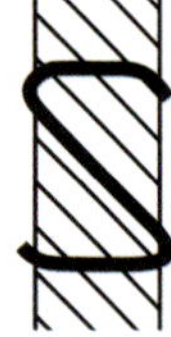

Fig. 8 Diagram of Z- and S-twist thread.

shed   the opening in the warp through which the weft is passed

silk   a thread or yarn produced by processing a continuous filament secreted by various insects, particularly the larvae of the caterpillar *Bombyx mori* (silkworm)

size/sizing   a post-weaving finishing technique in which a viscous or starchy substance is spread over a finished textile and left to dry, creating an even, shining finish

spin   to twist together various fibers (other than filaments) into a continuous thread

structure   the way in which warp, weft, and any supplementary yarns interact to create a textile

supplementary   describes an element usually employed for decorative purpose that, if removed, would remove nothing from the structure of the ground fabric

supplementary weft wrapping   a technique for creating fine linear design elements with a supplementary weft during the weaving of tapestry; employs a thin weft yarn of a contrasting color that wraps around a warp yarn, usually skipping several picks on the face of the fabric; in earlier literature, sometimes called "flying shuttle" (Fig. 5)

surplus warp   in a fabric with in-woven tapestry, the warp yarns of the plain-weave ground fabric that are dropped out of the tapestry section; sometimes these warps are cut off, sometimes they float across the tapestry section on the reverse (see detail of cat. 25 on p. 52)

tapestry   a type of weave generally characterized by two principles: weft yarns are closely packed to hide the warp and create the appearance of solid color, and rather than extended from selvedge to selvedge, weft yarns are independently carried back and forth within a pattern area; the binding is most commonly plain weave (as in the examples in this catalogue)

types of tapestry

allover
tapestry that extends from end to end and from selvedge to selvedge with no other ground weave

dovetail
tapestry weave in which the weft yarns are turned back around a common warp end where areas of different color meet; the weft yarns may move singly (sometimes called "toothed tapestry") or in groups of two or more (Fig. 6)

in-woven
tapestry segment that occurs in bands (extending from selvedge to selvedge) or inserts (not touching any textile edge) as opposed to covering the entire fabric

slit
tapestry weave in which the weft yarns are turned back around adjacent warp ends where areas of different color meet, leaving a vertical slit (Fig. 7)

tapestry 1, 2, 3
notation indicating the number of yarns grouped in the warp with which the tapestry weft interlaces: tapestry 1 = single yarn, tapestry 2 = two yarns, and so on

technique   the processes by which a textile is made

tension   the relative tightness or slack held in the warp during weaving

thread   a generic term (sometimes called yarn) denoting a strand, single or compound, used for warp, weft, or needlework and made from any fiber or filament through various processes such as reeling, spinning, twisting, or throwing

thrown   describes a silk thread or yarn produced by twisting together two or more filaments or groups of filaments

twist   the direction a thread is wound around its axis due to the processes of spinning, twisting, throwing, or plying; twist direction is conventionally indicated by the letters "S" or "Z," following the slant of the central bar of the letter (Fig. 8)

warp   the collection of longitudinal or vertical yarns within a textile stretched across the loom and into which the weft is interlaced

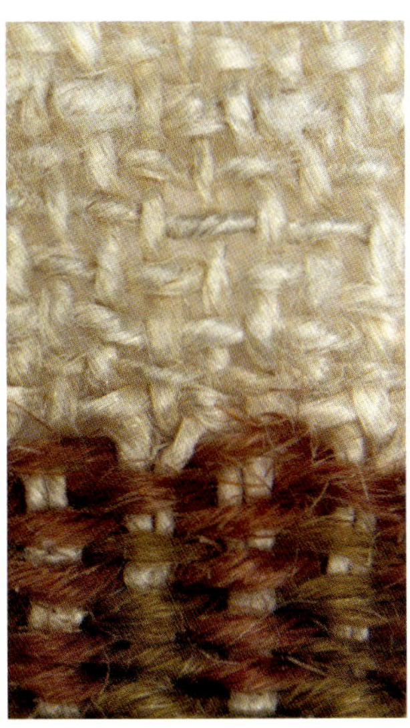

Fig. 9 Warp crossing and warp grouping from single to paired warp at point of transition from plain weave to tapestry 2 (detail of cat. 35).

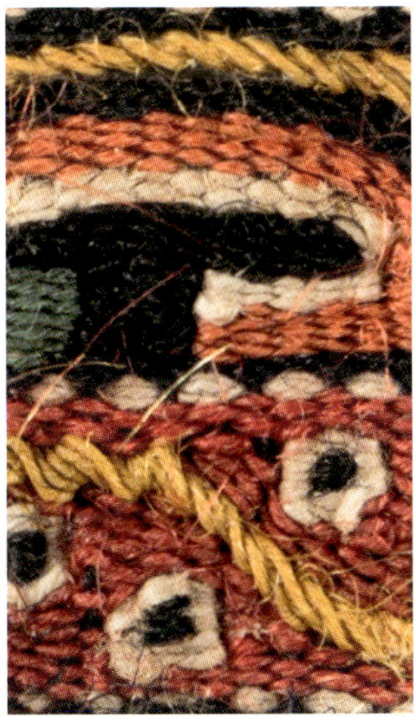

Fig. 10 Weft wrapping (detail of cat. 29).

warp crossing — when individual warp elements cross over (or under) adjacent warp elements and the transposed positions are retained by the interlacing of weft elements; in this study, warp crossing occurs at the point of transition between plain weave and tapestry, when single yarns of the plain weave are grouped (warp grouping) into pairs or triples for the tapestry weave (Fig. 9)

weft — the collection of transverse or horizontal yarns within a textile passed back and forth through sheds to interlace with the warp

weft wrapping — a decorative technique used in tapestry in which a weft yarn progresses forward across two or more warp ends, then backward, encircling at least one warp end, then forward again; the movement of the weft yarn can be freely non-horizontal; the wrapping weft may be the sole weft of the fabric or supplemental to the ground weave (Fig. 10)

wool — thread or yarn produced by processing the covering coat of domesticated sheep (and other animals)

yarn — a thread prepared for weaving or knitting

zone of transition — in a fabric with in-woven tapestry, the area where ground fabric switches to tapestry weave, sometimes requiring various strategies to maintain tension between the sections (see Fig. 9)

1   Textile terminology is varied and sometimes contradictory. This glossary is not intended to be comprehensive, but rather to define terms as used in this volume. Major sources for the definitions provided here are Kühnel and Bellinger 1952, Emery 1980, Burnham 1981, and Maguire 1999.

ʿAbbās Muḥammad Salīm 1997
ʿAbbās Muḥammad Salīm, Muḥammad. 1997. "The Function of Some Woven Fabrics in Riggisberg." In *Islamische Textilkunst des Mittelalters: Aktuelle Probleme*. Riggisberg, Switzerland: Abegg-Stiftung, 65–69.

Abdulfattah 2020
Abdulfattah, Iman R. 2020. "A Forgotten Man: Maurice Nahman, an Antiquarian-Tastemaker." In *Guardian of Ancient Egypt: Studies in Honor of Zahi Hawass*, vol. 1, ed. Janice Kamrin, Miroslav Bárta, Salima Ikram, Mark Lehner, and Mohamed Megahed. Prague: Faculty of Arts, Charles University.

Abulhimal 2011
Abulhimal, Mustafa. 2011. "The Medieval Egyptian Homeland and Inhabitants: The Intelligentsia Speak." *International Journal of the Humanities* 8 (12): 81–93.

Abu-Lughod 1971
Abu-Lughod, Janet. 1971. *Cairo: 1001 Years of the City Victorious*. Princeton, N.J.: Princeton University Press.

Abu Shama 1956–62
Abu Shama, Shihab al-Din. 1956–62. *Kitab al-Rawdatayn fi Akhbar al-Dawlatayn al-Nuriyya wa-l-Salahiyya*. 2 vols. Ed. Muḥammad H.M. Aḥmad and M. M. Ziyāda. Cairo: Matbaʿat Lajnat al-Taʾlif.

Ahmed et al. 2017
Ahmed, Harby E., Ibrahim F. Tahoun, Ibrahim Elkholy, Adel B. Shehata, and Yassin Ziddan. 2017. "Identification of Natural Dyes in Rare Coptic Textile Using HPLC-DAD and Mass Spectroscopy in Museum of Faculty of Arts, Alexandria University, Egypt." *Dyes and Pigments* 145: 486–92.

Allen 1997
Allen, Robert C. 1997. "Agriculture and the Origins of the State in Ancient Egypt." *Explorations in Economic History* 34 (2): 135–54.

AlSayyad 2011
AlSayyad, Nezar. 2011. *Cairo: Histories of a City*. Cambridge, Mass.: Belknap Press of Harvard University Press.

Altislamische 1947
"Altislamische Stoffe und indische Miniaturen im Berner Kunstmuseum." 1947. *Die Berner Woche*, September 11, 1947.

Antrim 2012
Antrim, Zayde. 2012. *Routes and Realms: The Power of Place in the Early Islamic World*. Oxford: Oxford University Press.

ʿAshur and ʿAshur 1999
ʿAshur, Ahmad, and Subhi al-Sayyid ʿAshur. 1999. *Al-Watan al-Umm: Dirarsa fi al-Thaqafa al-Qawmiyya al-Misriyya, Taʾsis Tarikhi*. Cairo: n.p.

Bacharach 1993
Bacharach, Jere L. 1993. "Muḥammad b. Ṭughdj al-Ikhshīd." In *The Encyclopaedia of Islam, Second Edition*, vol. 7, 411. Leiden, Netherlands: Brill.

Badamo 2019
Badamo, Heather. 2019. "Depicting Religious Combat in the Thirteenth-Century Program at the Monastery of St. Anthony at the Red Sea." *Gesta* 58 (2): 157–81.

Baer 1989
Baer, Eva. 1989. "Jeweled Ceramics from Medieval Islam: A Note on the Ambiguity of Islamic Ornament." *Muqarnas* 6 (1): 83–97.

Bagnall 1982
Bagnall, Roger. 1982. "Religious Conversion and Onomastic Change in Early Byzantine Egypt." *Bulletin of the American Society of Papyrologists* 19 (3/4): 105–24.

Bagnall 1985
Bagnall, Roger. 1985. "The Camel, the Wagon, and the Donkey in Later Roman Egypt." *Bulletin of the American Society of Papyrologists* 22 (1): 1–6.

Ball 2016
Ball, Jennifer. 2016. "Charms: Protective and Auspicious Motifs." In *Designing Identity: The Power of Textiles in Late Antiquity*, ed. Thelma K. Thomas. Princeton, N.J.: Princeton University Press.

Barnes and Ellis, n.d.
Barnes, Ruth, and Marianne Ellis. n.d. "The Newberry Collection of Islamic Embroideries: An Unpublished Catalogue of the Ashmolean's Collection of Islamic Embroideries from Egyptologist Percy Newberry." http://jameelcentre.ashmolean.org/collection/7/10222.

Behrens-Abouseif 2018
Behrens-Abouseif, Doris. 2018. "The Fatimid Dream of a New Capital: Dynastic Patronage and Its Imprint on the Architectural Setting." In

The World of the Fatimids, ed. Assadullah Souren Melikian-Chirvani. Toronto: Aga Khan Museum.

Bénazeth and Dal-Prà 1995
Bénazeth, Dominique, and Patricia Dal-Prà. 1995. "Renaissance d'une tapisserie antique." *La Revue du Louvre et des musées de France* 24 (4): 29–40.

Bianquis 1998
Bianquis, Thierry. 1998. "Autonomous Egypt from Ibn Ṭūlūn to Kāfūr, 868–969." In *Cambridge History of Egypt, Volume One: Islamic Egypt, 640–1517*, ed. Carl F. Petry. Cambridge: Cambridge University Press.

Bier 2001
Bier, Carol. 2001. *A Calligrapher's Art: Inscribed Cotton Ikat from Yemen*. Washington, D.C.: The Textile Museum.

Bier 2014
Bier, Carol. 2014. "Inscribed Cotton Ikat from Yemen in the Tenth Century CE." In *Ninth International Shibori Symposium*, ed. Waverly Liu, Irene Lu, Elizabeth Veale, and Diana Young. Hangzhou, China: 9ISS.

Bierman 1980
Bierman, Irene. 1980. "Art and Politics: The Impact of Fatimid Uses of Tirāz Fabrics." Ph.D. diss., University of Chicago.

Blair 1992
Blair, Sheila. 1992. *The Monumental Inscriptions from Early Islamic Iran and Transoxiana*. Leiden, Netherlands: Brill.

Bloom 1985
Bloom, Jonathan M. 1985. "The Origins of Fatimid Art." *Muqarnas* 3 (1): 20–38.

Boehm and Holcomb 2016
Boehm, Barbara D., and Melanie Holcomb. 2016. *Jerusalem 1000–1400: Every People under Heaven*. New York: Metropolitan Museum of Art.

Bora 2015
Bora, Fozia. 2015. "Did Salah al-Din Destroy the Fatimids' Books? An Historiographical Enquiry." *Journal of the Royal Asiatic Society of Great Britain & Ireland* 25 (1): 21–39.

Bosworth 1996
Bosworth, C. E. 1996. "Sikka, 1. Legal and Constitutional Aspects." In *The Encyclopaedia of Islam, New Edition*, vol. 9. Leiden, Netherlands: Brill.

Bouvier 1993
Tissus d'Egypte: Témoins du monde arabe VIIIe–XVe siècles, Collection Bouvier. 1993. Geneva: Museé d'Art et d'Histoire.

Bowen 2014
Bowen, Gillian E. 2014. "The Crux Ansata in Early Christian Iconography: The Evidence from Dakhleh and Kharga Oases." In *Le myrte et la rose: Mélanges offerts à Françoise Dunand par ses élèves, collègues et amis*, ed. Gaëlle Tallet and Christiane Zivie-Coche. Montpellier, France: Université de Paul Valéry.

Bowersock 1990
Bowersock, Glen W. 1990. *Hellenism in Late Antiquity*. Ann Arbor: University of Michigan Press.

Brett 2001
Brett, Michael. 2001. *The Rise of the Fatimids: The World of the Mediterranean and the Middle East in the Tenth Century C.E.* Leiden, Netherlands: Brill.

Brett 2005
Brett, Michael. 2005. "Population and Conversion to Islam in Egypt in the Mediaeval Period." In *Egypt and Syria in the Fatimid, Ayyubid and Mamluk Eras*, vol. 4, ed. U. Vermeulen and J. van Steenbergen. Leuven, Belgium: Peeters.

Brett 2019
Brett, Michael. 2019. *The Fatimids and Egypt*. London: Routledge.

Britton 1938
Britton, Nancy Pence. 1938. *A Study of Some Early Islamic Textiles in the Museum of Fine Arts Boston*. Boston: Museum of Fine Arts.

Bronk Ramsey 2009
Bronk Ramsey, Christopher. 2009. "Bayesian Analysis of Radiocarbon Dates." *Radiocarbon* 51 (1): 337–60.

Brooklyn 1941
Pagan and Christian Egypt: Egyptian Art from the First to the Tenth Century A.D. 1941. Brooklyn: Brooklyn Museum.

Brunello 1973
Brunello, Franco. 1973. *The Art of Dyeing in the History of Mankind*. Vicenza, Italy: Neri Pozza Editore.

Burnham 1981
Burnham, Dorothy K. 1981. *Warp & Weft: A Dictionary of Textile Terms*. New York: Charles Scribner's Sons.

Cabrera-Lafuente and Rosser-Owen 2020
Cabrera-Lafuente, Ana, and Mariam Rosser-Owen. 2020. "Following the Thread: Revisiting the Marwān Tirāz." In *The Textile Centre Akhmīm-Panopolis (Egypt) in Late Antiquity: Material Evidence for Continuity and Change in Society, Religion, Industry and Trade*, ed. Rafed El-Sayed and Cäcilia Fluck, 69–81. Studia Panopolitana Occasional Papers 4. Wiesbaden: Ludwig Reichert Verlag.

Carboni 2008
Carboni, Stefano. 2008. "The Arts of the Fatimid Period at the Metropolitan Museum of Art." *The Ismaili*.

Carder 2008
Carder, James. 2008. "The Blisses as Collectors." In *Dumbarton Oaks, The Collections*, ed. Gudrun Bühl. Washington, D.C.: Dumbarton Oaks Research Library and Collection.

Carder 2010
Carder, James N. 2010. *A Home for the Humanities: The Collecting and Patronage of Mildred and Robert Woods Bliss*. Cambridge, Mass.: Harvard University Press.

Clarysse and Paganini 2009
Clarysse, Willy, and Mario C.D. Paganini. 2009. "Theophoric Personal Names in Graeco-Roman Egypt: The Case of Sarapis." *Archiv für Papyrusforschung und verwandte Gebiete* 55 (1): 68–89.

Cleveland 1966
Handbook of the Cleveland Museum of Art. 1966. Cleveland: Cleveland Museum of Art.

Cleveland 1978
Handbook of the Cleveland Museum of Art. 1978. Cleveland: Cleveland Museum of Art.

Combe, Sauvaget, and Wiet 1931–37
Combe, Etienne, Jean Sauvaget, and Gaston Wiet, eds. 1931–37. *Repèrtoire chronologique d'épigraphie arabe*. Vols. 1–9. Cairo: Institut français d'archéologie orientale.

Cornu 1992
Cornu, Georgette. 1992. *Tissus islamiques de la collection Pfister*. Vatican City: Biblioteca Apostolica Vaticana.

Cornu 1999a
Cornu, Georgette. 1999. "Les tissus d'aparat fatimides, parmi les plus sompteux le 'voile de Sainte Anne' d'Apt." In *L'Égypte fatimide, son art et son histoire*, ed. Marianne Barrucand. Paris: Presses de l'Université de Paris-Sorbonne.

Cornu 1999b
Cornu, Georgette. 1999. "Le 'Suaire' de Cadouin. Un tiraz fatimide." *Archéologie islamique* 8/9: 29–36.

Crone 1991
Crone, P. 1991. "Mawlā, II, In Historical and Legal Usage." In *The Encyclopaedia of Islam, Second Edition*, vol. 6, 974–82. Leiden, Netherlands: Brill.

Daftary 1990
Daftary, Farhad. 1990. *The Isma'ilis: Their History and Doctrines*. 2nd ed. Cambridge: Cambridge University Press.

Daftary 2018
Daftary, Farhad. 2018. "The Iranian Da'is and Fatimid Egypt." In *The World of the Fatimids*, ed. Assadullah Souren Melikian-Chirvani. Toronto: Aga Khan Museum.

Dale 1993
Dale, Thomas. 1993. "The Power of the Anointed: The Life of David on Two Coptic Textiles in the Walters Art Gallery." *Journal of the Walters Art Gallery* 51: 23–42.

Daneshvari 2005
Daneshvari, Abbas. 2005. "Cup, Branch, Bird and Fish: An Iconographical Study of the Figure Holding a Cup and a Branch Flanked by a Bird and a Fish." In *The Iconography of Islamic Art: Studies in Honour of Robert Hillenbrand*, ed. Bernard O'Kane, 103–25. Edinburgh: Edinburgh University Press.

Darley-Doran 1996
Darley-Doran, R. E. 1996. "Sikka, 2. Coinage Practice." In *The Encyclopaedia of Islam, New Edition*, vol. 9. Leiden, Netherlands: Brill.

Dauphin 1987
Dauphin, Claudine. 1987. "The Development of the 'Inhabited Scroll' in Architectural Sculpture and Mosaic Art from Late Imperial Times to the Seventh Century A.D." *Levant* 19 (1): 183–212.

David-Weill 1957
David-Weill, Jean. 1957. "Emendanda." *Arabica* 4 (January): 73–76.

Day 1952
Day, F. E. 1952. "The Tiraz Silk of Marwan." In *Archaeologica Orientalia in Memoriam Ernst Herzfeld*, ed. George C. Miles, 39–61. Locust Valley, N.Y.: J. J. Augustin Publisher.

Décobert 1992
Décobert, Christian. 1992. "Sur l'arabisation et l'islamisation de l'Egypte médiévale." In *Itinéraires d'Égypte. Mélanges offerts au Père Maurice Martin, SJ*, ed. Christian Décobert. Cairo: IFAO.

De Jonghe and Tavernier 1983
De Jonghe, Daniël, and Marcel Tavernier. 1983. "Le Phénomène du croisage des fils de chaîne dans les tapisseries coptes." *CIETA Bulletin* 57/58: 174–86.

Delluc and Delluc 1983
Delluc, Brigitte, and Gilles Delluc. 1983. "Le suaire de Cadouin: Une toile brodée." *Bulletin de la Société Historique et Archéologique du Périgord* 110: 3–19.

De Moor et al. 2008
De Moor, Antoine, Chris Verhecken-Lammens, André Verhecken, and Hugo Maerten. 2008. *3500 Years of Textile Art: The Collection in HeadquARTers*. Tielt, Belgium: Lannoo.

De Moor, Verhecken-Lammens, and Van Strydonck 2006
De Moor, Antoine, Chris Verhecken-Lammens, and Mark Van Strydonck. 2006. "Relevance and Irrelevance of Radiocarbon Dating of Inscribed Textiles." In *Textile Messages*, ed. Cäcilia Fluck and Gisela Helmecke. Leiden, Netherlands: Brill.

Dimand 1927
Dimand, Maurice S. 1927. "Egypto-Arabic Textiles: Recent Accessions." *Bulletin of the Metropolitan Museum of Art* 12: 275–79.

Dimand 1930
Dimand, Maurice S. 1930. "Special Exhibition of Coptic and Egypto-Arabic Textiles." *Bulletin of the Metropolitan Museum of Art* 25: 126–31.

Dimand 1933
Dimand, Maurice S. 1933. "A Recent Accession of Egypto-Arabic Textiles." *Bulletin of the Metropolitan Museum of Art* 28 (2) (February): 37.

Du Bourguet 1953
Du Bourguet, Pierre. 1953. "La fabrication des tissues coptes aurait-elle survécu à la conquête arabe?" *Bulletin de la Société Archéologique d'Alexandrie* 40: 1–31.

Durand 2006
Durand, Maximilien. 2006. "Vers une pseudo-épigraphie textile en langue copte: Diogène, Panopé, Thétis." In *Textile Messages: Inscribed Fabrics from Roman to Abbasid Egypt*, ed. Cäcilia Fluck and Gisela Helmecke. Leiden, Netherlands: Brill.

Durand and Rettig 2002
Durand, Maximilen, and Simon Rettig. 2002. "Un atelier sous controle califal identifié dans le Fayoum: Le ṭirāz privé de Ṭuṭūn." In *Egypte, la trame de l'histoire: Textiles pharaoniques, coptes et islamiques*, ed. Maximilien Durand and Florence Saragoza. Paris: Somogy.

Ehrenkreutz 1972
Ehrenkreutz, Andrew. 1972. *Saladin*. Albany: State University of New York Press.

Ehrenkreutz 1997
Ehrenkreutz, A. S. 1997. "Kāfūr, Abu'l Misk." In *The Encyclopaedia of Islam, Second Edition*, vol. 4, 418–19. Leiden, Netherlands: Brill.

Ekhtiar et al. 2011
Ekhtiar, Maryam, Priscilla Soucek, Sheila R. Canby, and Navina Najat Haidar, eds. 2011. *Masterpieces from the Department of Islamic Art in The Metropolitan Museum of Art*. New Haven, Conn.: Yale University Press.

Elbendari 2002
Elbendari, Amina. 2002. "The Worst of Times: Crisis Management and *Al-Shidda Al-ʿUzma*." In *Money, Land and Trade: An Economic History of the Muslim Mediterranean*, ed. Nelly Hanna. London: I. B. Tauris.

Elisséeff 1967
Elisséeff, Nikita. 1967. *Nur ad-Din, un grand prince musulman de Syrie au temps des Croisades (511–569/1118–1174)*. 3 vols. Damascus: Institut français de Damas.

Emery 1980
Emery, Irene. 1980. *The Primary Structures of Fabrics*. Washington, D.C.: The Textile Museum.

Ettinghausen 1939
Ettinghausen, Richard. 1939. "Arabic Inscriptions on Medieval Textiles from the Near East in the Dumbarton Oaks Collection." Unpublished manuscript.

Ettinghausen 1962
Ettinghausen, Richard. 1962. *Arab Painting*. Cleveland: Albert Skira and the World Publishing Company.

Ettinghausen 2007
Ettinghausen, Richard. 2007. "Dionysiac Motifs." In *Late Antique and Medieval Art of the Mediterranean World*, ed. Eva R. Hoffman. Malden, Mass.: Blackwell Publishing.

Ettinghausen, Grabar, and Jenkins-Madina 2001
Ettinghausen, Richard, Oleg Grabar, and Marilyn Jenkins-Madina. 2001. *Islamic Art and Architecture, 650–1250*. New Haven, Conn.: Yale University Press.

Evans and Ratliff 2012
Evans, Helen C., and Brandie Ratliff, eds. 2012. *Byzantium and Islam: Age of Transition, 7th–9th century*. New York: Metropolitan Museum of Art.

Fluck and Helmecke 2006
Fluck, Cäcilia, and Gisela Helmecke, eds. 2006. *Textile Messages: Inscribed Fabrics from Roman to Abbasid Egypt*. Leiden, Netherlands: Brill.

Frank 2011
Frank, Marie. 2011. *Denman Ross and American Design Theory*. Hanover, N.H.: University Press of New England, 2011.

Galliker and Bogensberger, forthcoming
Galliker, Julia, and Ines Bogensberger. Forthcoming. "Ambition, Adventure and Opportunity: The Inscribed Textile Collection at the Kelsey Museum of Archaeology." In *Explorers, First Collectors and Traders of Textiles from Egypt of the 1st Millennium AD: Proceedings of the 11th Meeting of the Study Group "Textiles from the Nile Valley," Antwerp, 26–27 October 2019*, ed. A. De Moor, C. Fluck, and P. Linscheid. Tielt, Belgium: Lannoo.

Gaselee 1923
Gaselee, Stephen. 1923. "Lettered Egyptian Textiles in the Victoria and Albert Museum." *Archaeologia: Tracts Relating to Antiquity Published by the Society of Antiquaries of London*, 2nd ser. 73: 73–84.

Gayraud 2002
Gayraud, Roland-Pierre. 2002. "La nécropole fatimide du Caire." In *Égypte, la trame de l'histoire: Textiles pharaoniques, coptes et islamiques*, ed. Maximilien Durand and Florence Saragoza. Paris: Somogy.

Gayraud, Björnesjö, and Speiser 1994
Gayraud, Roland-Pierre, Sophia Björnesjö, and Philipp Speiser. 1994. "Istabl 'Antar (Fostat) 1992. Rapport de fouilles." *Annales Islamologiques* 28: 1–27.

Gayraud et al. 1995
Gayraud, Roland-Pierre, Sophia Björnesjö, Paolo Gallo, Jean-Michel Mouton, and François Paris. 1995. "Istabl 'Antar (Fostat) 1992. Rapport de fouilles." *Annales Islamologiques* 29: 1–24.

Gildemeister 1885
Gildemeister, J. 1885. "Beiträge zur Palästinakunde aus arabischen Quellen V." *Zeitschrift des Deutschen Palästina-Vereins* 8: 117–45.

Gines Taylor 2018
Gines Taylor, Catherine. 2018. *Late Antique Images of the Virgin Annunciate Spinning: Allotting the Scarlet and the Purple*. Leiden, Netherlands: Brill.

Glidden and Thompson 1988
Glidden, Harold W., and Deborah Thompson. 1988. "Tirāz Fabrics in the Byzantine Collection, Dumbarton Oaks. Part One: Tirāz from Egypt." *Bulletin of the Asia Institute* 2: 119–39.

Glidden and Thompson 1989
Glidden, Harold W., and Deborah Thompson. 1989. "Tirāz in the Byzantine Collection, Dumbarton Oaks. Parts Two and Three: Tirāz from the Yemen, Iraq, Iran, and an Unknown Place." *Bulletin of the Asia Institute* 3: 89–105.

Godlewski 2002
Godlewski, Włodzimierz. 2002. "Les textiles issus des fouilles récentes de Naqlun." In *Égypte, la trame de l'histoire: Textiles pharaoniques, coptes et islamiques*, ed. Maximilien Durand and Florence Saragoza. Paris: Somogy.

Godlewski 2004
Godlewski, Włodzimierz. 2004. "Naqlun (Nekloni): Season 2003." *Polish Archaeology in the Mediterranean* 15: 141–51.

Godlewski 2005
Godlewski, Włodzimierz. 2005. "The Medieval Coptic Cemetery at Naqlun." In *Christianity and Monasticism in the Fayoum Oasis*, ed. Gawdat Gabra. Cairo: American University in Cairo Press.

Godlewski 2011
Godlewski, Włodzimierz. 2011. "In the Shade of the Nekloni Monastery (Deir Malak Gubrail, Fayum)." *Polish Archaeology in the Mediterranean* 20: 467–82.

Godlewski 2014
Godlewski, Włodzimierz. 2014. "Naqlun (Nekloni). Excavations in 2010–2011." *Polish Archaeology in the Mediterranean* 23 (1): 173–91.

Goitein 1969
Goitein, S. D. 1969. "Cairo: An Islamic City in the Light of the Geniza Documents." In *Middle Eastern Cities*, ed. Ira Lapidus. Berkeley: University of California Press.

Goitein 1983
Goitein, S. D. 1983. *A Mediterranean Society: The Jewish Communities of the Arab World as Portrayed in the Documents of the Cairo Geniza.* Vol. 4, *Daily Life*. Berkeley: University of California Press.

Gonosová 1986
Gonosová, Anna. 1986. "A Note on Coptic Sculpture." *Journal of the Walters Art Gallery* 44: 10–15.

Grohmann 1924
Grohmann, Adolf. 1924. *Corpus Papyrorum Raineri, Archiducis Austriae III, Series Arabica*. Vol. 1, part 3, *Protokolle*. Vienna: Burgverlag Ferdinand Zöllner.

Grohmann 1934
Grohmann, Adolf. 1934. "Ṭirāz." In *The Encyclopaedia of Islam*. Leiden, Netherlands: Brill.

Grohmann 1971
Grohmann, Adolf. 1971. *Arabische Paläographie, II. Teil*. Vienna: H. Bohlaus Nachf.

Gulmini et al. 2017
Gulmini, Monica, A. Idone, P. Davit, M. Moi, M. Carrillo, C. Ricci, F. Dal Bello, et al. 2017. "The 'Coptic' Textiles of the 'Museo Egizio' in Torino (Italy): A Focus on Dyes through a Multi-Technique Approach." *Archaeological and Anthropological Sciences* 9 (4): 485–97.

Haarmann 1980
Haarmann, Ulrich. 1980. "Regional Sentiment in Medieval Islamic Egypt." *Bulletin of the School of Oriental and African Studies* 43 (1): 55–66.

Haas 1997
Haas, Christopher. 1997. *Alexandria in Late Antiquity: Topography and Social Conflict*. Baltimore: Johns Hopkins University Press.

Halevi 2007
Halevi, Leor. 2007. *Muhammad's Grave: Death Rites and the Making of Islamic Society*. New York: Columbia University Press.

Halm 1997
Halm, Heinz. 1997. *The Fatimids and Their Tradition of Learning*. London: I. B. Tauris.

Hamdan 1980–84
Hamdan, Jamal. 1980–84. *Shakhsiyyat Misr, Dirasa fi-'Abqariyyat al-Makan*. 4 vols. Cairo: 'Alam al-Kutub.

Hanna 1994
Hanna, Milad. 1994. *The Seven Pillars of the Egyptian Identity*. Cairo: General Egyptian Book Organization.

Hasan 1948
Hasan, Zāki Muḥammad. 1948. *Funūn al-islām*. Cairo: Dār al-Fikr al-'Arabi.

Heidemann 1998
Heidemann, Stephan. 1998. "The Merger of Two Currency Zones in Early Islam: The Byzantine and Sasanian Impact on the Circulation in Former Byzantine Syria and Northern Mesopotamia." *Iran: Journal of the British Institute of Persian Studies* 36: 95–112.

Helmecke 2004
Helmecke, Gisela. 2004. "Textiles with Arabic Inscriptions Excavated in Naqlun 1999–2003." *Polish Archaeology in the Mediterranean* 16: 195–202.

Hofmann-de Keijzer, Van Bommel, and De Keijzer 2007
Hofmann-de Keijzer, Regina, Maarten R. van Bommel, and Matthijs de Keijzer. 2007. "Coptic Textiles: Dyes, Dyeing Techniques and Dyestuff Analysis of Two Textile Fragments of the MAK Vienna." In *Methods of Dating Ancient Textiles of the 1st Millennium AD from Egypt and Neighbouring Countries*, ed. A. De Moor and C. Fluck. Tielt, Belgium: Lannoo.

Hurtado 2006
Hurtado, Larry W. 2006. "The Staurogram in Early Christian Manuscripts: The Earliest Visual Reference to the Crucified Jesus?" In *New Testament Manuscripts: Their Text and Their World*, ed. Thomas J. Kraus and Tobias Nicklas. Leiden, Netherlands: Brill.

Ibn ʿAbd al-Zahir 1996
Ibn ʿAbd al-Zahir, Muhiyy al-Din. 1996. *Al-Rawda al-Bahiyya fi Khitat al-Qahira al-Muʿizziyya*. Ed. Aymna Fuʾad Sayyid. Cairo: al-Dar al-ʿArabiyya lil-Kitab.

Ibn al-Dawadari 1961
Ibn al-Dawadari, Abu Bakr ibn ʿAbdallah. 1961. *Kanz al-Durar wa-Jamiʿ al-Ghurar*. Vol. 6, *Al-Durra al-Mudiyya fi Akhbar al-Dawla al-Fatimiyya*. Ed. Salah al-Din al-Munajjid. Cairo: German Archaeological Institute.

Ibn Ḥawqal 2001
Ibn Ḥawqal, Muḥammad. 2001. *La configuration de la terre: Kitab surat al-ard*. Paris: Maisonneuve et Larose.

Ibn-Shaddad 1964
Ibn-Shaddad, Bahaʾ al-Din. 1964. *Al-Nawadir al-Sultaniyya wa-l-Mahasin al-Yusufiyya*, ed. Jamal al-Din al-Shayyal. Cairo: Dar al-Kutub.

Ibrahim and Ibrahim 2003
Ibrahim, Fouad N., with Barbara Ibrahim. 2003. *Egypt: An Economic Geography*. London: I. B. Tauris.

Jaubert 1836–40
Jaubert, P. Amédée, trans. and ed. 1836–40. *Géographie d'Édrisi traduite de l'arabe en français d'après deux manuscrits de la Bibliothèque du roi et accompagnée de notes*. 2 vols. Paris: L'imprimerie royale.

Kahle 1935
Kahle, Paul. 1935. "Die Schätze der Fatimiden." *Zeitschrift der Deutschen Morgenländischen Gesellschaft* 89 (n.s. 14) (3/4): 329–62.

Kendrick 1924
Kendrick, A. F. 1924. *Catalogue of Muhammadan Textiles of the Medieval Period*. London: Published under the authority of the Board of Education.

Kennedy 1993
Kennedy, H. 1993. "Al-Mutawakkil ʿAlāʾllāh." In *The Encyclopaedia of Islam, New Edition*. Leiden, Netherlands: Brill.

Kennedy 2004
Kennedy, Hugh. 2004. *The Prophet and the Age of the Caliphates: The Islamic Near East from the 6th to the 11th Century*. 2nd ed. London: Longman.

al-Khamis 1990
al-Khamis, Ulrike. 1990. "The Iconography of Early Islamic Lusterware from Mesopotamia: New Considerations." *Muqarnas* 7: 109–18.

Khan 1992
Khan, Geoffrey. 1992. *Arabic Papyri: Selected Material from the Khalili Collection*. Oxford: Azimuth Press, 1992.

al-Kindī, Guest, and al-ʿAsqalānī 1912
al-Kindī, Muḥammad ibn Yūsuf, Rhuvon Guest, and Aḥmad ibn ʿAlī Ibn Ḥajar al-ʿAsqalānī. 1912. *The Governors and Judges of Egypt; or, Kitāb el ʾumarāʾ (el wulāh) wa Kitāb el qudāh of el Kindī*. Leiden, Netherlands: Brill.

Klein 2011
Klein, Holger. 2011. "The Elusive Mr. Whittemore: The Early Years, 1971–1916." In *The Kariye Camii Reconsidered*, ed. Holger Klein, Robert Ousterhout, and Brigitte Pitarakis. English ed. Istanbul: İstanbul Araştırmaları Enstitüsü.

Kondoleon 2016
Kondoleon, Christine. 2016. "Late Antique Textiles at the Museum of Fine Arts, Boston: Expanded Vistas." In *Designing Identity: The Power of Textiles in Late Antiquity*, ed. Thelma Thomas. Princeton, N.J.: Princeton University Press.

Kühnel 1927
Kühnel, Ernst. 1927. *Islamische Stoffe aus Ägyptischen Gräbern in der Islamischen Kunstabteilung und in der Stoffsammlung des Schlossmuseums*. Berlin: Verlag Ernst Wasmuth.

Kühnel and Bellinger 1952
Kühnel, Ernst, and Louisa Bellinger. 1952. *The Textile Museum Catalogue of Dated Tiraz Fabrics: Umayyad, Abbasid, Fatimid*. Washington, D.C.: National Publishing Company.

Labrusse and Podzemskaia 2000
Labrusse, Rémi, and Nadia Podzemskaia. 2000. "Naissance d'une vocation: Aux sources de la carrière byzantine de Thomas Whittemore." *Dumbarton Oaks Papers* 54: 43–69.

Lamm 1936
Lamm, Carl Johan. 1936. "Some Woollen Tapestry Weavings from Egypt in Swedish Museums." *Le Monde Oriental* 30: 43–77.

Lamm 1937
Lamm, Carl Johan. 1937. *Cotton in Mediaeval Textiles in the Near East.* Paris: Librairie orientaliste P. Geuthner.

Leiser 1985
Leiser, Gary. 1985. "The *Madrasa* and the Islamization of the Middle East: The Case of Egypt." *Journal of the American Research Center in Egypt* 22: 29–47.

Lermer and Shalem 2010
Lermer, Andrea, and Avinoam Shalem, eds. 2010. *After 100 Years: The 1910 Exhibition "Meisterwerke muhammedanischer Kunst" Reconsidered.* Leiden, Netherlands: Brill.

Lev 1987
Lev, Yaacov. 1987. "The Fātimid Princess Sitt al-Mulk." *Journal of Semitic Studies* 32 (2) (Autumn): 319–28.

Lev 1991
Lev, Yaacov. 1991. *State and Society in Fatimid Egypt.* Leiden, Netherlands: Brill.

Lev 1999
Lev, Yaacov. 1999. *Saladin in Egypt.* Leiden, Netherlands: Brill.

Llewelyn 1998
Llewelyn, Stephen R. 1998. "The Christian Symbol XMΓ, an Acrostic or an Isopsephism?" In *New Documents Illustrating Early Christianity*, vol. 8. Grand Rapids, Mich.: Eerdmans.

Luijendijk 2011
Luijendijk, AnneMarie. 2011. "'Jesus Says: "There Is Nothing Buried That Will Not Be Raised."' A Late-Antique Shroud with Gospel of Thomas Logion 5 in Context." *Zeitschrift für Antikes Christentum* 15 (3): 389–410.

Lyster 2002
Lyster, William. 2002. "Reflections of the Temporal World: Secular Elements in Theodore's Program." In *Monastic Visions: Wall Paintings in the Monastery of St. Antony at the Red Sea*, ed. Elizabeth S. Bolman. New Haven, Conn.: Yale University Press.

Mackie 1996
Mackie, Louise W. 1996. "Increase the Prestige: Islamic Textiles." *Arts of Asia* 26 (1) (January–February): 82–93.

Mackie 2015
Mackie, Louise W. 2015. *Symbols of Power: Luxury Textiles from Islamic Lands, 7th–21st Century.* Cleveland: Cleveland Museum of Art.

Madelung 1965
Madelung, Wilferd. 1965. *Der Imam al-Qāsim ibn Ibrahim und die Glaubenslehre der Zaiditen.* Berlin: de Gruyter.

Madelung 2002
Madelung, Wilferd. 2002. "Zaydiyya." In *The Encyclopaedia of Islam, Second Edition*, vol. 11, ed. P. Bearman, Th. Bianquis, C. E. Bosworth, E. van Donzel, and W. P. Heinrichs, 477–81. Leiden, Netherlands: Brill.

Maguire 1990
Maguire, Henry. 1990. "Garments Pleasing to God: The Significance of Domestic Textile Designs in the Early Byzantine Period." *Dumbarton Oaks Papers* 44: 215–24.

Maguire 1999
Maguire, Eunice Dauterman. 1999. *Weavings from Roman, Byzantine, and Islamic Egypt: The Rich Life and the Dance.* Urbana: University of Illinois Press, 1999.

Major 2010
Major, Ben. 2010. "'The Socialite Archaeologist': Thomas Whittemore (1871–1950) and the Roles of Patronage, Politics, and Personal Connections in Cultural Heritage Preservation." Honors thesis, Rutgers University.

al-Maqrizi 1853
al-Maqrizi, Taqiyy al-Din. 1853. *al-Mawa'iz wa'l-i'tibar bi-dhikr al-khiṭaṭ wal-athar.* 2 vols. Cairo: Bulaq.

al-Maqrīzī 1959
al-Maqrīzī, Aḥmad ibn ʿAlī. 1959. *Kitāb al-Khiṭaṭ al-Maqrīzīyah: al-Musammāh bi-al-Mawāʿiz wa-al-i'tibār bi dhikr al-khiṭaṭ wa-al-Āthār, yakhtaṣṣu dhālika bi-akhbār iqlīm Miṣr wa-al-Nīl wa-dhikr al-Qāhirah wa-mā yataʿallaqu bi-hā wa-bi-iqlīmihā.* Vol. 1. al-Shiyyāḥ, Lebanon: Maktabat Iḥyā' ʿUlūm al-Dīn.

Martin 1912
Martin, F. R. 1912. *The Miniature Painting and Painters of Persia, India and Turkey, from the 8th to the 18th century*. Vol. 2. London: B. Quaritch.

Marzouk 1942
Marzouk, Muḥammad 'Abdu'l Azīz. 1942. *Al-zakhrafa al-mansūja fī al-aqmisha al-fāṭimīyya*. Cairo: Dār al-Kutub al-Misrīyya.

Marzouk 1943
Marzouk, Muhammad 'Abdu'l Azīz. 1943. "The Evolution of Inscriptions on Fatimid Textiles." *Ars Islamica* 10: 164–66.

Marzouk 1954
Marzouk, Muhammad 'Abdu'l Azīz. 1954. "The Turban of Samuel Ibn Musa, the Earliest Dated Islamic Textile." *Bulletin of the Faculty of Arts Cairo University* 16 (December): 143–51.

Marzouk 1959
Marzouk, Muhammad 'Abdu'l Azīz. 1959. "Five Tiraz Fabrics in the Völkerkunde-Museum of Basel." In *Aus der Welt der Islamischent Kunst: Festschrift für Ernst Kühnel*, ed. Richard Ettinghausen. Berlin: Mann Verlag GmbH.

Mason 2004
Mason, Robert B. 2004. *Shine Like the Sun: Lustre-Painted and Associated Pottery from the Medieval Middle East*. Costa Mesa, Calif.: Mazda Publishers.

Massignon 1958
Massignon, Louis. 1958. "La cité des morts au Caire (Qarâfa — Darb al-Aḥmar)." *Bulletin de l'Institut français d'archéologie orientale* 57: 25–81.

McKenzie 2008
McKenzie, Judith. 2008. *The Architecture of Alexandria and Egypt, c. 300 B.C. to A.D. 700*. New Haven, Conn.: Yale University Press.

McWilliams 2013
McWilliams, Mary, ed. 2013. *In Harmony: The Norma Jean Calderwood Collection of Islamic Art*. Cambridge, Mass.: Harvard Art Museums.

Meisterwerke 1912
Meisterwerke Muhammedanischer Kunst auf der Austellung München 1910. 1912. 3 vols. Munich: F. Bruckmann.

Meyer and Brysac 2015
Meyer, Karl E., and Shareen Blair Brysac. 2015. *The China Collectors: America's Century-Long Hunt for Asian Art Treasures*. New York: Palgrave MacMillan, 2015.

Migeon 1907
Migeon, Gaston. 1907. *Manuel d'art musulman: Les arts plastiques et industriels*. Paris: A. Picard et fils.

Monneret de Villard 1923
Monneret de Villard, Ugo. 1923. *La scultura ad Ahnâs: Note sull'origine dell'arte copta*. Milan: Tipografia della Reale accad. nazionale dei Lincei in Roma.

Mordini 1957
Mordini, Antonio. 1957. "Un tissu musulman du Moyen Âge provenant du couvent de Dabra Dāmmò." *Annales d'Éthiopie* 2: 75–79.

al-Muqqadasi 1906
al-Muqqadasi, Shams al-Din. 1906. *Ahsan al-Taqasim fi-Ma'rifat al-Aqalim*. Ed. M. J. de Goeje. Leiden, Netherlands: Brill.

Myers 1931
Myers, George Hewitt. 1931. "The Washington Textile Museum." *American Magazine of Art* 22 (5): 335–45.

Nauerth 2006
Nauerth, Claudia. 2006. "David oder Achill?" In *Textile Messages: Inscribed Fabrics from Roman to Abbasid Egypt*, ed. Cäcilia Fluck and Gisela Helmecke. Leiden, Netherlands: Brill.

Nelson 2004
Nelson, Robert S. 2004. *Hagia Sophia, 1850–1950*. Chicago: University of Chicago Press.

Nelson 2005
Nelson, Robert S. 2005. "Private Passions Made Public: The Beginnings of the Bliss Collection." In *Sacred Art, Secular Context*, by Asen Kirin. Athens: Georgia Museum of Art.

Nongbri 2011
Nongbri, Brent. 2011. "The Lord's Prayer and XMΓ: Two Christian Papyrus Amulets." *Harvard Theological Review* 104 (1): 59–68.

O'Kane 2018a
O'Kane, Bernard. 2018. "The Egyptian Art of the Tiraz in Fatimid Times." In *The World of the Fatimids*, ed. Assadullah Souren

Melikian-Chirvani. Toronto: Aga Khan Museum in association with the Institute of Ismaili Studies and Hirmer.

O'Kane 2018b
O'Kane, Bernard. 2018. "Monumental Calligraphy in Fatimid Egypt: Epigraphy in Stone, Stucco, and Wood." In *The World of the Fatimids*, ed. Assadullah Souren Melikian-Chirvani. Toronto: Aga Khan Museum.

O'Sullivan 2006
O'Sullivan, Shaun. 2006. "Coptic Conversion and the Islamization of Egypt." *Mamluk Studies Review* 10 (2): 65–79.

Paetz gen. Schieck 2009
Paetz gen. Schieck, Annette. 2009. "Late Roman Cushions and the Principles of Their Decoration." In *Clothing the House: Furnishing Textiles of the 1st Millennium AD from Egypt and Neighboring Countries: Proceedings of the 5th Conference of the Research Group "Textiles from the Nile Valley," Antwerp, 6–7 October 2007*, ed. Antoine de Moor and Cäcilia Fluck, 115–31. Tielt: Lannoo.

Paetz gen. Schieck 2012
Paetz gen. Schieck, Annette. 2012. "A Late Roman Painting of an Egyptian Officer and the Layers of Its Perception: On the Relation between Images and Textile Finds." In *Wearing the Cloak: Dressing the Soldier in Roman Times*, ed. Marie-Louise Nosch. Oxford: Oxbow.

Pancaroğlu 2013
Pancaroğlu, Oya. 2013. "Feasts of Nishapur: Cultural Resonances of Tenth-Century Ceramic Production in Khurasan." In *In Harmony: The Norma Jean Calderwood Collection of Islamic Art*, ed. Mary McWilliams, 25–36. Cambridge, Mass.: Harvard Art Museums.

Pfister 1936a
Pfister, Rudolf. 1936. "Matériaux pour servir au classement des Textiles Égyptiens postérieurs à la Conquête Arabe." *Revue des arts asiatiques* 10 (1): 1–16.

Pfister 1936b
Pfister, Rudolf. 1936. "Matériaux pour servir au classement des Textiles Égyptiens postérieurs à la Conquête Arabe (suite)." *Revue des arts asiatiques* 10 (2): 73–85.

Pfister 1945–46
Pfister, R. 1945–46. "Toiles à inscriptions Abbasides et Fatimides." *Bulletin d'Études Orientales* 11: 47–90.

Pintaudi 1993
Pintaudi, Rosario. 1993. "Documenti per una storia della papirologia in Italia." *Analecta Papyrologica* 5: 155–81.

Rabbat 1996
Rabbat, Nasser. 1996. "Al-Azhar Mosque: An Architectural Chronicle of Cairo's History." *Muqarnas* 13: 45–67.

Ragib 2001
Ragib, Yusuf. 2001. "Les pierres de souvenir: Stèles du Caire de la conquête arabe à la chute des Fatimides." *Annales islamologiques* 35: 321–83.

Rāġib 2009
Rāġib, Youseff. 2009. "Un papyrus arabe de l'an 22 de l'hégire." In *Histoire, archéologies et littératures du monde musulman*, ed. Ghislaine Alleaume, Sylvie Denoix, and Michel Tuchscherer, 363–72. Cairo: Institut français d'archéologie orientale.

Rapoport 2004
Rapoport, Yossef. 2004. "Invisible Peasants, Marauding Nomads: Taxation, Tribalism, and Rebellion in Mamluk Egypt." *Mamluk Studies Review* 8 (2): 1–22.

Raymond 2000
Raymond, André. 2000. *Cairo*. Cambridge, Mass.: Harvard University Press.

Reimer et al. 2013
Reimer, Paula J., Edouard Bard, Alex Bayliss, J. Warren Beck, Paul G. Blackwell, Christopher Bronk Ramsey, Caitlin E. Buck, et al. 2013. "IntCal13 and Marine13 Radiocarbon Age Calibration Curves 0–50,000 Years cal BP." *Radiocarbon* 55 (4): 1869–87.

Romberg 1985
Romberg, Helen. 1985. "The Fatimid Treasury." M.Phil. thesis, University of Oxford, Trinity.

Ross 1907
Ross, Denman W. 1907. *A Theory of Pure Design*. Boston: Houghton, Mifflin and Co.

Rowland 1956
Rowland, Benjamin, Jr. 1956. "The Vine-Scroll in Gandhāra." *Artibus Asiae* 19 (3/4): 353–61.

Roxburgh 2000
Roxburgh, David J. 2000. "Au Bonheur des Amateurs: Collecting and Exhibiting Islamic Art, ca. 1880–1910." *Ars Orientalis* 30: 9–38.

Rózsavölgyi 2010
Rózsavölgyi, Andrea. 2010. "Delmár Emil műgyűjtő művészettörténeti kapcsolatai." In *Ars Perennis*, ed. Anna Tüskés. Budapest: CentrArt.

Rózsavölgyi 2013
Rózsavölgyi, Andrea. 2013. "20 Years in Emigration: Emil Delmár and the Disintegration of His Collection." In *Hungary in Context: Studies on Art and Architecture*, ed. Anna Tüskés et al. Budapest: CentrArt.

Saba 2012
Saba, Matthew D. 2012. "Abbasid Lusterware and the Aesthetics of 'Ajab." *Muqarnas* 29: 187–212.

Sanders 1994
Sanders, Paula. 1994. *Ritual, Politics, and the City in Fatimid Cairo*. Albany: State University of New York Press.

Sanders 2001
Sanders, Paula. 2001. "Robes of Honor in Fatimid Egypt." In *Robes and Honor: The Medieval World of Investiture*, ed. Steward Gordon. New York: Palgrave.

Serjeant 1972
Serjeant, R. B. 1972. *Islamic Textiles: Material for a History up to the Mongol Conquest*. Beirut: Librairie du Liban.

Shepherd 1960
Shepherd, Dorothy G. 1960. "An Early Ṭirāz from Egypt." *Bulletin of the Cleveland Museum of Art* 47 (1): 7–14.

Shibayama, Wypyski, and Gagliardi-Mangilli 2015
Shibayama, Nobuko, Mark Wypyski, and Elisa Gagliardi-Mangilli. 2015. "Analysis of Natural Dyes and Metal Threads Used in 16th–18th Century Persian/Safavid and Indian/Mughal Velvets by HPLC-PDA and SEM-EDS to Investigate the System to Differentiate Velvets of These Two Cultures." *Heritage Science* 3 (1): 1–20.

Sijepestein 2007
Sijepestein, Petra. 2007. "The Arab Conquest of Egypt and the Beginning of Muslim Rule." In *Egypt in the Byzantine World, 300–700*, ed. Roger S. Bagnal, 437–59. Cambridge: Cambridge University Press.

Simpson 1980
Simpson, Marianna Shreve. 1980. *Arab and Persian Painting in the Fogg Art Museum*. Cambridge, Mass.: Fogg Art Museum, Harvard University.

Smith 1962
Smith, Corinna Lindon. 1962. *Interesting People: Eighty Years with the Great and the Near-Great*. Norman: University of Oklahoma Press.

Sokoly 2002
Sokoly, Jochen. 2002. "Ṭirāz Textiles from Egypt: Production, Administration and Uses of Ṭirāz Textiles from Egypt under the 'Umayyad, 'Abbāsid and Fāṭimid Dynasties." D.Phil. diss., University of Oxford.

Sokoly 2006
Sokoly, Jochen. 2006. "Textiles." In *Medieval Islamic Civilization: An Encyclopedia*, vol. 2, ed. Josef W. Meri, 801–5. New York: Routledge.

Sokoly 2017
Sokoly, Jochen. 2017. "Textiles and Identity." In *The Companion to Islamic Art and Architecture*, ed. Finbarr Barry Flood and Gülru Necipoğlu. Hoboken, N.J.: Wiley-Blackwell.

Sourdel-Thomine and Spuler 1973
Sourdel-Thomine, Janine, and Bertold Spuler. 1973. *Die Kunst der Islam: Propyläen Kunstgeschichte*. Vol. 4. Berlin: Propyläen-Verlag.

Stern 1972
Stern, Samuel. 1972. "Cairo as the Centre of the Isma'ili Movement." In *Colloque International sur l'Histoire du Caire*, ed. André Raymond et al. Cairo: Ministry of Culture.

Stern 1983
Stern, Samuel. 1983. *Studies in Early Isma'ilism*. Leiden, Netherlands: Brill.

Stern 2007
Stern, David. 2007. *Chosen: Philadelphia's Great Hebraica*. Philadelphia: Rosenbach Museum & Library.

Stillman 1995
Stillman, Yedida. 1995. "Costume as Cultural Statement: The Esthetics, Economics, and Politics of Islamic Dress." In *The Jews of Medieval Islam: Community, Society, and Identity*, ed. Daniel H. Frank. Leiden, Netherlands: Brill.

Stillman 2003
Stillman, Yedida. 2003. *Arab Dress: A Short History from the Dawn of Islam to Modern Times*. 2nd ed. Leiden, Netherlands: Brill.

Stillman and Sanders 2000
Stillman, Yedida Kalfon, and Paula Sanders. 2000. "Ṭirāz." In *The Encyclopaedia of Islam, Second Edition*, vol. 10, 534–38. Leiden, Netherlands: Brill.

al-Ṭabarī 1987
al-Ṭabarī, Abū Jaʿfar Muḥammad b. Jarīr. 1987. *The Commentary on the Qurʾān*. Ed. Wilferd Madelung and Alan Jones, trans. J. Cooper. London: Oxford University Press.

Tabbaa 1993
Tabbaa, Yasser. 1993. "Survivals and Archaisms in the Architecture of Northern Syria, ca. 1080–ca. 1150." *Muqarnas* 10: 29–41.

Tabbaa 1994
Tabbaa, Yasser. 1994. "The Transformation of Arabic Writing: Part 2, the Public Text." *Ars Orientalis* 24: 119–47.

Thomas 1998
Thomas, Thelma K. 1998. "Christians in the Islamic East." In *The Glory of Byzantium: Art and Culture of the Middle Byzantine Era, A.D. 843–1261*, ed. Helen C. Evans and William D. Wixom. New York: Metropolitan Museum of Art.

Thomas 2000
Thomas, Thelma K. 2002. *Late Antique Egyptian Funerary Sculpture: Images for This World and for the Next*. Princeton, N.J.: Princeton University Press.

Thomas 2012
Thomas, Thelma K. 2012. "Silks of the Akhmim Group." In *Byzantium and Islam: Age of Transition*, ed. Helen C. Evans and Brandie Ratliff. New York: Metropolitan Museum of Art.

Thompson 1971
Thompson, Deborah. 1971. *Coptic Textiles in the Brooklyn Museum*. New York: Brooklyn Museum.

Thompson 1976
Thompson, Deborah. 1976. "Catalogue of Textiles in the Dumbarton Oaks Collection." Unpublished manuscript.

Török 1970
Török, László. 1970. "On the Chronology of the Ahnas Sculpture." *Acta archaeologica Academiae Scientiarum Hungaricae* 22 (1): 163–82.

Török 1993
Török, László. 1993. *Coptic Antiquities*. Vol. 2. Budapest: L'Erma di Bretschneider.

Touwaide 1992–93
Touwaide, Alain. 1992–93. *Farmacopea Araba Medievale*. Milan: Antea Edizioni.

Upton 1931
Upton, Joseph M. 1931. "Dated Egypto-Arabic Textiles in the Metropolitan Museum of Art." *Metropolitan Museum Studies* 3 (2) (June): 158–73.

Van der Vliet 2006
Van der Vliet, Jacques. 2006. "'In a Robe of Gold': Status, Magic and Politics on Inscribed Christian Textiles from Egypt." In *Textile Messages: Inscribed Fabrics from Roman to Abbasid Egypt*, ed. Cäcilia Fluck and Gisela Helmecke, 23–67. Leiden, Netherlands: Brill.

Van Strydonck and Bénazeth 2014
Van Strydonck, Mark, and Dominique Bénazeth. 2014. "Four Coptic Textiles from the Louvre Collection 14C Redated after 55 Years." *Radiocarbon* 56 (1): 1–5.

Van Strydonck, De Moor, and Bénazeth 2004
Van Strydonck, Mark, Antoine De Moor, and Dominique Bénazeth. 2004. "14C Dating Compared to Art Historical Dating of Roman and Coptic Textiles from Egypt." *Radiocarbon* 46 (1): 231–44.

Verhecken 2007
Verhecken, André. 2007. "Relation between Age and Dyes of 1st Millennium AD Textiles Found in Egypt." In *Methods of Dating Ancient Textiles of the 1st Millennium AD from Egypt and Neighbouring Countries*, ed. Antoine De Moor. Tielt, Belgium: Lannoo.

Vernoit 2000
Vernoit, Stephen. 2000. *Discovering Islamic Art: Scholars, Collectors and Collections, 1850–1950*. New York: I. B. Tauris.

Von Karabacek 1909
Von Karabacek, Joseph. 1909. *Zur Orientalischen Altertumskunde, II, Die arabischen Papyrusprotokolle*. Vienna: Hölder.

Wadsworth 1951
Two Thousand Years of Tapestry Weaving: A Loan Exhibition. Wadsworth Atheneum, Hartford, Dec. 7, 1951 to Jan. 27, 1952. The Baltimore Museum of Art, Feb. 27, 1952 to Mar. 25, 1952. 1951. Hartford, Conn.: Wadsworth Atheneum.

Walker 1997
Walker, Paul E. 1997. "Fatimid Institutions of Learning." *Journal of the American Research Center in Egypt* 34: 179–200.

Walker 2017
Walker, Paul E. 2017. "Ibn Killis." In *The Encyclopaedia of Islam, Third Edition*, ed. Kate Fleet, Gudrun Krämer, Denis Matringe, John Nawas, and Everett Rowson. Brill Online. http://dx.doi.org/10.1163/1573-3912_ei3_COM_30871.

Wardwell 1984
Wardwell, Anne E. 1984. *Material Matters: Fifty Years of Gifts from the Textile Arts Club, 1934–1984.* Cleveland: Cleveland Museum of Art.

Watson 2004
Watson, Oliver. 2014. *Ceramics from Islamic Lands: The al-Sabah Collection.* New York: Thames & Hudson.

Weinstein 2015
Weinstein, Laura. 2015. *Ink, Silk & Gold: Islamic Art from the Museum of Fine Arts, Boston.* 1st ed. Boston: MFA Publications.

Wheatley 2000
Wheatley, Paul. 2000. *The Places Where Men Pray Together: Cities in Islamic Lands, Seventh through the Tenth Centuries.* Chicago: University of Chicago Press.

Wiet 1930
Wiet, Gaston. 1930. *Album du Museé Arabe du Caire.* Cairo: Imprimerie de l'Institut français d'archeologie orientale.

Wiet 1935a
Wiet, Gaston. 1935. *Exposition des tapisseries et tissus du Musée Arabe du Caire (du VIIe au XVIIe siècle): Période musulmane.* Paris: Musée des Gobelins.

Wiet 1935b
Wiet, Gaston. 1935. "Les tissus et tapisseries de l'Egypte musulmane." *Revue de l'Art Ancien et Moderne* 68: 3–14, 61–68.

Wiet 1935c
Wiet, Gaston. 1935. "Tissus et tapisseries du Musée Arabe du Caire." *Syria* 16: 278–90.

Wiet 1936
Wiet, Gaston. 1936. "Un nouveau tissu fatimide." *Orientalia* 5: 385–88.

Wiet and Halm 2012
Wiet, G., and H. Halm. 2012. "Shaṭā." In *The Encyclopaedia of Islam, Second Edition*, ed. P. Bearman, Th. Bianquis, C. E. Bosworth, E. van Donzel, and W. P. Heinrichs. Brill Online. http://dx.doi.org/10.1163/1573-3912_islam_SIM_6862.

Wilkinson 1973
Wilkinson, Charles K. 1973. *Nishapur: Pottery of the Early Islamic Period.* New York: Metropolitan Museum of Art.

Williams 2014
Williams, Elizabeth Dospěl. 2014. "'Into the hands of a well-known antiquary of Cairo': The Asssiut Treasure and the Making of an Archaeological Hoard." *West 86th: A Journal of Decorative Arts, Design History, and Material Culture* 21 (2): 251–72.

Williams 2019
Williams, Elizabeth Dospěl. 2019. "A Taste for Textiles: Designing Umayyad and 'Abbāsid Interiors." In *Catalogue of the Textiles in the Dumbarton Oaks Byzantine Collection*, ed. Gudrun Bühl and Elizabeth Dospěl Williams. Online catalogue. https://www.doaks.org/resources/textiles/essays/williams.

Williams and Dospěl 2019
Williams, Elizabeth Dospěl, and Marek Dospěl. 2019. "Fragment with Coptic Inscription." In *Catalogue of the Textiles in the Dumbarton Oaks Byzantine Collection*, ed. Gudrun Bühl and Elizabeth Dospěl Williams. Online catalogue. https://www.doaks.org/resources/textiles.

Winnik, forthcoming
Winnik, Arielle. Forthcoming. "Tiraz Textiles with Coptic Inscriptions for the Living and the Dead." In *Medieval Eurabia: Religious Crosspollinations in Architecture, Art and Material Culture during the High and Late Middle Ages*, ed. Sami DeGiosa and Nikolaos Vryzidis. Cairo: American University in Cairo Press.

Wouters 1993
Wouters, Jan. 1993. "Dye Analysis of Coptic Textiles." In *Coptic Textiles from Flemish Private Collections*, ed. Antoine De Moor. Zottegem, Belgium: Provinciaal Archaeologisch Museum van Zuid-Oost-Vlaanderen.

al-Yāqūt 1906

al-Yāqūt. 1906. *Kitāb Muʿjam al-Buldān*. Vol. 1. Ed. Muḥammad Amīn Khānajī. Cairo: ʿalā nafqat Aḥmad Nājī al-Jamālī [wa-ghayrih].

Zambaur 1927

Zambaur, E. de. 1927. *Manuel de Généalogie et de Chronologie pour l'Histoire de l'Islam*. Hanover: Librairie Orientaliste Heinz Lafaire.

Zetterstéen and Bosworth 1997

Zetterstéen, K. V., and C. E. Bosworth. 1997. "al-Muḵtadir bi-llāh, Abu ʾl-Faḏl Ḏjaʿfar." In *The Encyclopaedia of Islam, Second Edition*, vol. 7, 541–42. Leiden, Netherlands: Brill.

Washington, D.C.; cat. 31: University of Pennsylvania, Kislak Center
for Special Collections; cat. 32: © President and Fellows of Harvard
College; full-page image facing Section 3 introduction: Swiss National
Library/Wikimedia Commons, photo by Eduard Spelterini; cat. 33: ©
President and Fellows of Harvard College; cat. 34: Cleveland Museum
of Art; cat. 35: The Textile Museum, Washington, D.C.; cat. 36: The
Metropolitan Museum of Art, New York; cat. 37: © Dumbarton Oaks,
Byzantine Collection, Washington, D.C.; cat. 38: The Metropolitan
Museum of Art, New York

Glossary of Textile Terms
Fig. 1: The Textile Museum, Washington, D.C.; Fig. 2: Cleveland
Museum of Art; Figs. 3–6: © President and Fellows of Harvard
College; Fig. 7: Cleveland Museum of Art; Fig. 8: © President and
Fellows of Harvard College; Fig. 9: The Textile Museum, Washington,
D.C.; Fig. 10: © 2021 Museum of Fine Arts, Boston

This book accompanies the exhibition *Social Fabrics: Inscribed Textiles from Medieval Egyptian Tombs*, on view at the Harvard Art Museums, Cambridge, Massachusetts, from January 22 through May 8, 2022.

Published by
Harvard Art Museums
32 Quincy Street
Cambridge, MA 02138-3847
harvardartmuseums.org

Distributed by
Yale University Press
302 Temple Street
PO Box 209040
New Haven, CT 06520-9040
yalebooks.com/art

Managing Editor: Micah Buis
Editors: Sarah Kuschner, Cheryl Pappas
Design Manager: Zak Jensen
Designers: Becky Hunt, Angela Lorenzo, Adam Sherkanowski

Typeset in Adobe Text Pro and Gill Sans Nova by Matt Mayerchak
Printed on Condat matt Périgord
Printed in Belgium by Graphius
ISBN: 978-0-300-26009-0
Library of Congress Control Number: 2021931434

Cover image: Detail of cat. 34.

Image opposite title page: Detail of cat. 16.